Born Under a Bad Sky

Notes from the Dark Side of the Earth

Jeffrey St. Clair

Born Under a Bad Sky

Notes from the Dark Side of the Earth

Jeffrey St. Clair

CounterPunch
PETROLIA

AK
PRESS

First published by
CounterPunch and AK Press 2008
© *CounterPunch* 2008
All rights reserved.
CounterPunch
PO Box 228, Petrolia, California, 95558

AK Press
674-A 23rd St., Oakland, California 94612-1163

ISBN 978-1-904859703

A catalog record for this book is available from the Library of Congress.
Library of Congress Control Number: 2007928473

Typeset in *Minion Pro*, designed by Robert Slimbach for Adobe Systems Inc.; and
Univers LT, designed by Adrian Frutiger for Linotype GmbH.

Printed and bound in Canada.

Cover Photography by Robin Silver.

Design and typography by Tiffany Wardle.

For Kimberly

"Whispering into you,
through us,
the grace."

—Gary Snyder

Table of Contents

Part Three: Politicians and Other Strangers

Part Four: The Beautiful and the Dammed

The Once and Future Environmental Movement

Hamm: Nature has forgotten us.
Clov: There's no more nature.
Hamm: No more nature! You exaggerate.
Clov: In the vicinity.
Hamm: But we breathe, we change. We lose our hair, our teeth!
Our bloom! We lose our ideals!
Clov: Then she hasn't forgotten us.

—From *Endgame*
Samuel Beckett

Can't Buy a Thrill: The Once and Future Environmental Movement

"The Dark Ages. They haven't ended yet."—Kurt Vonnegut, Jr.

A KIND OF POLITICAL NARCOLEPSY HAS SETTLED OVER THE AMERICAN environmental movement. Call it eco-ennui. You may know the feeling: restlessness, lack of direction, evaporating budgets, diminished expectations, a simmering discontent. The affliction appears acute, possibly systemic.

Unfortunately, the antidote isn't as simple as merely filing a new lawsuit in the morning or skipping that PowerPoint presentation to join a road blockade for the day. No, something much deeper may be called for: a rebellion of the heart. Just like in the good old days, not that long ago.

What is it, precisely, that's going on? Was the environmental movement bewitched by eight years of Bruce Babbitt and Al Gore? Did it suffer an allergic reaction to the New Order of Things? Are we simply adrift in a brief lacuna in the evolution of the conservation movement, one of those Gouldian (Stephen Jay) pauses before a new creative eruption?

Perhaps, the movement, such as it was, experienced an institutional uneasiness with the rules of engagement during the long cold war in Clintontime. A war (War? Did someone say war?) where hostilities, such as they were, remained buried beneath graceful gestures at meaningful discourse—where the raw passions for rare places are, at the insistence of lawyers and lobbyists, politically sublimated or suppressed altogether.

Environmentalism has never thrived on an adherence to etiquette or quiet entreaties. Yet, that became the organizational posture during Clintontime and it has continued through the rougher years of Bush and Cheney. Direct confrontation of governmental authority and corporate villainy was once our operational *metier*. No longer. Non-aggression pacts have been signed, an unofficial *détente* declared. Was it sealed in the spring of 1993 on the lawn of Blair House, perhaps, while the cherry blossoms were in bloom? Did the late Jay Hair, CEO of the National Wildlife Federation, forge a deal in the fall of that year to greenlight the logging of the last ancient forests in the Pacific Northwest? Cold wars, naturally, engender such paranoid perambulations.

More than a decade later, this much is clear: the vigor of the environmental movement has been dissipated, drained by the enforced congeniality displayed in our disputes with Clinton and Bush, the Democrats in congress, and the grim, green-suited legions of the Forest Service and the Bureau of Land Management. Despite the rampages of the Bush administration, the big green groups can't even rouse themselves into much more than the most reflexive kind of hysteria, fundraising letters printed in bold type.

Like so many vacant-eyed victims of Stockholm Syndrome, most professional environmentalists find themselves conscripts to the conference room and the consensus table, situations about as satisfying as computerized chess or phone sex.

Accusations of elitism, hurled at us like political cream pies, from the property rights jihadis, hit their targets more often than not these days. Once highly regarded (and deeply reviled) as fierce advocates of the "public interest," environmentalists now are largely dismissed in the living rooms of America as merely another "special interest" group (weaker than most), peddling its meager influence on the Hill, angling for access to the anterooms (never the control room) of power, or, at least, a line item in the federal budget.

What's worse, our best efforts these days hardly seem to even raise a hackle on the hierophants of industry. After okaying the logging of ancient forests, signing off on anti-wilderness legislation in Oregon, Idaho, and Montana, pampering the whims of Bruce Babbitt (and Dick Cheney), endorsing NAFTA and GATT, the failure to stand up for high level whistleblowers like former BLM head Jim Baca, the mainstream environmental groups don't scare anyone anymore. Except maybe their own members. Yes, they may scare them a great deal, indeed.

Something Happened

The surest sign of decadence in a social/political movement is its engagement in the suppression of internal dissent: such decadence now erodes the moral core of the environmental movement. Stray beyond the margins of permitted discourse, publicly critique the prevailing "strategy," strike out in an unauthorized new direction and the overlords of the environmental movement crack down. They enfilade the insurgents with legalistic maledictions, gag orders, and accusations of sedition.

Witness the Sierra Club's threats to sue renegade chapters that publicly opposed anti-wilderness bills proposed by the Club's political favorites in Montana. Or its attacks on anti-war protesters in the Club's ranks in Utah. Or NRDC's attempt to squelch the filing of endangered species petitions, for on-the-run critters such as the Queen Charlotte's goshawk. Or the Sierra Club Legal Defense Fund's arm-twisting of its own clients in the spotted owl cases. Or the Environmental Defense Fund's betrayal of at-risk communities across America when it endorsed Dow Chemical's proposed "revamping" of the Superfund Act. (Col. Fred Krupp, EDF's CEO, was once overheard telling Carol Browner, Clinton's head of the EPA, "You are our general. We are your troops. We await your orders.") Or the sado-masochistic pleasure that NRDC (yes, them again) displayed while boasting about "breaking the back of the environmental opposition to NAFTA."

You don't have to be versed in the works of Hannah Arendt or Michel Foucault (although *Madness and Civilization* ought to be required reading for all activists and other "eccentrics") to understand the dynamics of power and repression at work here. Activists are now aliens on the political landscape; their relationship to the lawyers, lobbyists, economists, marketing agents, PR flacks, and CEOs that manage the environmental movement parallels that of welfare mothers to the welfare bureaucrats: abusive indifference.

Something happened. Somewhere along the line, the environmental movement disconnected from the people, rejected its political roots, pulled the plug on its vibrant and militant tradition. It packed its bags, starched its shirts, and jetted to DC, where it became what it once despised: a risk-aversive, depersonalized, hyper-analytical, humorless, access-driven, intolerant, centralized, technocratic, deal-making, passionless, direct-mailing, lawyer-laden monolith to mediocrity.

The environmental movement didn't so much go awry as it simply flatlined, cruise-controlled right into an entropic cooldown—the ultimate thermodynamic fate of all closed systems. The Group of Ten (aka: Gang Green) now manifests all the intensity of an insurance cartel; their executives and administrative underlings are much more likely to own dog-eared copies of Donald Trump's *The Art of the Deal* or Kissinger's *Diplomacy,* than Donald Worster's *Rivers of Empire*, Bill Kittredge's *Hole in the Sky*, or Doug Peacock's *Grizzly Years*. Forget the eyes, a person's bookshelf is the real window to their soul.

National environmental policies are now engineered by an Axis of Acronyms: EDF, NRDC, WWF: groups without voting memberships and little responsibility to the wider environmental movement. They are the undisputed mandarins of techno-talk and lobbyist logic, who gave us the ecological oxymorons of our time: "pollution credits," "re-created wetlands," "sustainable development."

In their relativistic milieu, everything can be traded off or dealt away. For them, the tag-end remains of the native ecosystems on our public lands are endlessly divisible and every loss can be recast as a hard-won victory in the advertising copy of their fund-raising propaganda. Settle and move on, is their unapologetic mantra. And don't expect them to stick around to live with the consequences of their deals and trade-offs.

Into this political vacuum rough beasts have already been loosed and others are bound to follow. The decline of a militant environmental movement has been countered by the rise of a militant anti-environmental movement, unrestrained, and all too often encouraged by the agents of federal and state governments. The new anti-environmental movement, a strange hybrid of Aryan Nationists, gun-fetishists, and the loonier incarnations of the Wise-Use crowd, have used arson, muggings, and deaths to intimidate local environmental activists across the West.

The ranks of this malicious mélange continue to expand up and down the spine of the Rockies and across the Great Basin. Like deranged Deadheads on tour, these neo-militians follow roving weapons bazaars across the rural backwaters of the American West, from Libby, Montana to Tonopah, Nevada.

At these moveable conclaves of righteousness, the blonde, blue-eyed penitents can purchase enough firepower to call forth the Second Coming—a state goal of some attendees. Here's the Defense Dividend we've all been waiting for, where the Pentagon largesse of the Cold War is offered for sale on the homefront at discount prices: tanks, armor-piercing bullets, APCs, night-vision gunsights, Humvees. It's all there for the bidding.

Living embodiments of the quaint cultural traditions of the West, memorialized at places like Wounded Knee and Sand Creek, these characters are preparing to defend what's theirs and what they think ought to be theirs. By force if necessary—perhaps preferably.

What do they want? Simply unfettered rights to grazing, mining, and logging on public lands, the federal lands themselves revested to the states or private corporations and—to quote one Arly Gruder, a rancher from somewhere near Salmon, Idaho, America's most inhospitable town—"To run all the damn feds, Jews, Spics, and homo-enviros the hell out of here." Run them back across the 100th Meridian, no doubt. But how far? Back to Brooklyn? Back to Juarez? Back to Buchenwald?

Listen to Hugh McKeen, a rancher and former commissioner in Catron County, New Mexico, who told reporter Tony Davis that his neighbors and friends are arming themselves, preparing for a new range war, against greens and their sidekicks, the illegal immigrants: "The people have fought for this land in the past. There have been killings over water. It runs in the genes. You have very independent people here. They want to be left alone. But the government oppresses them. And the environmentalists come in here and want to oppress their life." Apparently, the West is theirs to waste by virtue of the Doctrine of Manifest Genetics.

The absence of a forceful opposition from progressive greens and the appearance/reality of collaboration with the federal government by Beltway groups, only strengthens the cause of the extreme right. As the left migrates toward the center, the right repels further to the right—and the government follows suit. This a recipe for a future in which things, to crib from Thomas Pynchon, will not be quite so amusing.

Toward a Resolute Clarity of Place

Still, there's no reason to begin strumming a threnody just yet. Beneath the six-figure salaries, limo-driven executives, and glossy magazines clotted with ads for SUVs there's a flickering pulse to the grassroots environmental movement—in the hinterlands and barrios, in the secret gardens of the Bronx, and amid the toxic detritus of New Orleans. Foucault and Tom Paine sang the same refrain: the more pervasive the repression, the more profound the rebellion to come. Well, the rebellion has started.

In the southwest, a small outfit called Living Rivers is campaigning to decommission Glen Canyon Dam and restore the Colorado River. In Montana, the Alliance for the Wild Rockies remains the grizzly bear's most unflinching ally and advocate. In the Pacific Northwest, the Western Land Exchange Project is nearly alone in challenging the disposal of public lands to private concerns, and the Center for Environmental Equity is chasing the big gold mining companies out of Oregon. In the Midwest, Heartwood is defending the incredibly diverse hardwood forests of the Ohio Valley and waging an intense campaign against the proliferation of noxious and inhumane confined-animal feeding operations or CAFOs. In the heart of cancer alley, the Louisiana Environmental Action Network (AKA LEAN) is taking on chemical and oil companies, as well as the toxic sludge left behind by Katrina. In South Dakota, the Lakota Student Alliance is waging a courageous battle to have the Black Hills and other sacred lands returned to the Sioux Nation. Deep in Appalachia, Save Our Cumberland Mountains is fighting the most destructive form of mining ever devised by man or satan: mountain top removal.

Like snowpeaks sprouting from a far horizon, these scattered pockets of resistance can help us triangulate our way back home, entrench with a resolute clarity of place. And that move, as Terry Tempest Williams suggests in her shimmering book, *The Unspoken Hunger*, may be the most radical act of all.

Environmentalism was once a people's cause, unaligned with any political party and independent from the demands of the shadowy syndicate of mega-foundations (Pew, Rockefeller, Ford) that now hold the mortgage on the movement—those high priests of what Foucault called "condescending philanthropy." Environmentalism was once driven by a desire for social justice and an unremitting passion for the wild. We need to tap back into those populist currents. Let the vision attract the money and don't allow it to be refracted through the ideological prism of neoliberal foundations.

The power of the environmental movement derives from its essential and shared imagery, its sensual tangibilities. Simply put: the destruction of the wild sparks militancy in the heart. At least it does for me. Wild places communicate their own passion and power, sensations that are the antithesis of political abstractions.

It's all about the singular sense of openness on the Snake River plains. The way light plays across ancient petroglyphs on the canyon walls of Navajo sandstone outside Moab. The smell of sagebrush in the high desert on the north slope of the Ruby Mountains. A cool rush of wind unleashed by distant storms hammering the Gallatin Range. The bluegray fogbanks that sleeve up the North Santiam River canyon on an August morning in Oregon. The crisp shock of being busted out of a raft by a rapid on the Selway River. The carcass of a grizzly-cleaned salmon annealed by the Alaskan sun to a granite boulder along the MacNeil River. The surrealistic explosion of October color from dense forest of oaks, poplars, and maples on Nebo Ridge in southern Indiana. The cry of a lone coyote trembling across the sepia sky in the predawn badlands of South Dakota. These are the threatened images that haunt my nights, the green fires that burn in my soul. You have your own. Nearly everyone does. Everyone with a heartbeat.

The power of the people can still overwhelm the influence of big money. Look at Chiapas. Listen to Mandela and Evo Morales. Anything is possible. Find your place, take a stand. People will join you.

PART ONE

Enter the Dragon

Summer grasses:
All that remain of great soldiers'
Imperial dreams.

—From "Narrow Road to the Interior"
Bashō

Hogwash: Fecal Factories
in the Heartland

GREW UP SOUTH OF INDIANAPOLIS ON THE GLACIER-SMOOTHED PLAINS OF central Indiana. My grandparents owned a small farm, whittled down over the years to about forty acres of bottomland, in some of the most productive agricultural land in America. Like many of their neighbors they mostly grew field corn (and later soybeans), raised a few cows, and bred a few horses.

Even then, farming for them was a hobby, an avocation, a link to a way of life that was slipping away. My grandfather, who was born on that farm in 1906, graduated from Purdue University and became a master electrician, helping to design RCA's first color TV. My grandmother, the only child of an unwed mother, came to the US at the age of thirteen from the industrial city of Sheffield, England. When she married my grandfather she'd never seen a cow. A few days after the honeymoon she was milking one. She ran the local drugstore for nearly fifty years. In their so-called spare time, they farmed.

My parent's house was in a sterile and treeless subdivision about five miles away, but I largely grew up on that farm: feeding the cattle and horses; baling hay; bushhogging pastures; weeding the garden; gleaning corn from the harvested field; fishing for catfish in the creek that divided the fields and pastures from the small copse of woods; learning to identify the songs of birds, a lifelong passion.

Even so, the farm, which had been in my mother's family since 1845, was in an unalterable state of decay by the time I arrived on the scene in 1959. The great red barn, with its multiple levels, vast hayloft, and secret rooms, was in disrepair; the grain silos were empty and rusting ruins; the great beech trees that stalked the pasture hollowed out and died off, one by one, winter by winter.

In the late-1960s, after a doomed battle, the local power company condemned a swath of land right through the heart of the cornfield for a high-voltage transmission corridor. A fifth of the field was lost to the giant towers and the songs of redwing blackbirds and meadowlarks were drowned out by the bristling electric hum of the powerlines.

After that the neighbors began selling out. The local dairy went first, replaced by a retirement complex, an indoor tennis center and a sprawling Baptist temple and school. Then came a gas station, a golf course, and a McDonald's. Then two large subdivisions of upscale houses and a manmade lake, where the water was dyed Sunday-cartoon blue.

When my grandfather died from pancreatic cancer (most likely inflicted by the pesticides that had been forced upon him by the ag companies) in the early 1970s, he and a hog farmer by the name of Boatenright were the last holdouts in that patch of blacksoiled land along Buck Creek.

Boatenright's place was about a mile down the road. You couldn't miss it. He was a hog farmer and the noxious smell permeated the valley. On hot, humid days, the sweat stench of the hogs was nauseating, even at a distance. In August, I'd work in the fields with a bandana wrapped around my face to ease the stench.

How strange that I've come to miss that wretched smell.

That hog farm along Buck Creek was typical for its time. It was a small operation with about twenty-five pigs. Old man Boatenright also ran some cows and made money by fixing tractors, bush hogs, and combines.

Not any more. There are more hogs than ever in Indiana, but fewer hog farmers and farms. The number of hog farms has dropped from 64,500 in 1980 to 10,500 in 2000, though the number of hogs has increased by about 5 million.

Hog production is a factory operation these days, largely controlled by two major conglomerations: Tyson Foods and Smithfield Farms. Hogs are raised in stifling feed-lots of concrete, corrugated iron, and wire, which house 15,000 to 20,000 animals in a single building. They are the concentration camps of American agriculture, the filthy abattoirs of our hidden system of meat production.

Pig factories are the foulest outposts in American agriculture. A single hog excretes nearly three gallons of waste per day, or 2.5 times the average human's daily total. A 6,000-sow hog factory will generate approximately fifty tons of raw manure a day. An operation the size of Premium Standard Farms in northern Missouri, with more than 2 million pigs and sows in 1995, will generate five times as much sewage as the entire city of Indianapolis. But hog farms aren't required to treat the waste. Generally, the stream of fecal waste is simply sluiced into giant holding lagoons, where it can spill into creeks or leach into ground water. Increasingly, hog operations are disposing of their manure by spraying it on fields as fertilizer, with vile consequences for the environment and the general ambience of the neighborhood.

Over the past quarter century, Indiana hog farms were responsible for 201 animal waste spills, wiping out more than 750,000 fish. These hog-growing factories contribute more excrement spills than any other industry.

It's not just creeks and rivers that are getting flooded with pig shit. A recent study by the EPA found that more than 13 percent of the domestic drinking-water wells in the Midwest contain unsafe levels of nitrates, attributable to manure from hog feedlots. Another study found that groundwater beneath fields which have been sprayed with hog manure contained five times as much nitrates as is considered safe for humans. Such nitrate-leaden water has been linked to spontaneous abortions and "blue baby" syndrome.

A typical hog operation these days is Pohlmann Farms in Montgomery County, Indiana. This giant facility once confined 35,000 hogs. The owner, Klaus Pohlmann, is a German, whose father, Anton, ran the biggest egg factory in Europe, until numerous convictions for animal cruelty and environmental violations led to his being banned from ever again operating an animal enterprise in Germany.

Like father, like son. Pohlmann the pig factory owner has racked up an impressive rapsheet in Indiana. In 2002, Pohlmann was cited for dumping 50,000 gallons of hog excrement into the creek, killing more than 3,000 fish. He was fined $230,000 for the fish kill. But that was far from the first incident. From 1979 to 2003, Pohlmann has been cited nine times for hog manure spills into Little Sugar Creek. The state Department of Natural Resources estimates that his operation alone has killed more than 70,000 fish.

Pohlmann was arrested for drunk driving a couple of years ago, while he was careening his way to meet with state officials who were investigating yet another spill. It was his sixth arrest for drunk driving. Faced with mounting fines and possible jail time, Pohlmann offered his farm for sale. It was bought by National Pork Producers, Inc., an Iowa-based conglomerate with its own history of environmental crimes. And the beat goes on.

My grandfather's farm is now a shopping mall. The black soil, milled to such fine fertility by the Wisconsin glaciations, now buried under a black sea of asphalt. The old Boatenright pig farm is now a Quick Lube, specializing in servicing SUVs.

America is being ground apart from the inside, by heartless bankers, insatiable conglomerates, a president who lies by remote control.

We are a hollow nation, a poisonous shell of our former selves.

BLOOMINGTON, INDIANA.

Crude Alliance: The Bi-Partisan Politics of Oil

SHORTLY AFTER JOHN KERRY SEWED UP THE DELEGATES NEEDED TO SEIZE the Democratic nomination for president in the spring of 2004, he huddled for two hours with James Hoffa, Jr., the boss of the Teamsters union. The topic was oil. The Teamsters wanted more of it at cheaper prices. They had suspicions about Kerry. After all, the senator had already won the backing of the Sierra Club, who touted him as the most environmentally enlightened member of the US senate.

Hoffa emerged from the meeting sporting a shark-like grin. Hoffa and the Teamsters had long pushed for opening up the Arctic National Wildlife Refuge (ANWR) to drilling and for the construction of a natural gas pipeline to cut across some of the wildest land in North America from the tundra of Alaska to Chicago. "Kerry says, look, I am against drilling in ANWR, but I am going to put that pipeline in, and we're going to drill like never before," Hoffa reported. "They are going to drill all over, according to him. And he says, we're going to be drilling all over the United States."

Kerry didn't stop to comment. He slipped out the door and into a waiting SUV. Don't worry, the candidate later assured worried greens, it wasn't Kerry's gas-guzzling, hydro-carbon belching behemoth. It belonged to his...family. (Apparently, this meant he couldn't take out a loan on the vehicle for his campaign.) Still, the senator's not a total hypocrite on this count. After all, Kerry voted against ratification of the Kyoto Protocol on Global Warming.

The Bush administration has been aptly pegged as a petroarchy. It isn't so much under the sway of Big Oil as it is infested top-to-bottom with oil operatives, starting with the president and vice president. Eight cabinet members and the National Security Advisor came directly from executive jobs in the oil industry, as did thirty-two other Bush-appointed officials in the Office of Management and Budget, Pentagon, State Department, and the departments of Energy, Agriculture, and—most crucially in terms of opening up what remains of the American wilderness to the drillers—Interior.

The point man in the Bush administration's oil raid on the public estate was Steven Griles, Gale Norton's top lieutenant at the Interior Department, an intimate of the super-lobbyist Jack Abramoff and now a convicted felon. As Deputy Secretary of Interior, Griles was the man who held the keys to the nation's oil and mineral reserves. Since he landed this plum position, he used those keys to unlock nearly every legal barrier to exploitation, opening the public lands to a carnival of corporate plunder.

He became the toast of Texas. But by the end of 2005, Griles fled from reporters and congressional investigators after accounts of his ongoing sleazy relationships with his former associates in big oil oozed out into the open. He hid from the press, but he couldn't escape federal prosecutors.

From the time he took his oath of office, Griles was a congressional investigation waiting to happen. The former coal industry flack was one of Bush's most outrageous appointments, a booster of the very energy cartel he was meant to regulate. His track record could not be given even the slightest green gloss. A veteran of the Reagan administration, Griles schemed closely with disgraced Interior Secretary James Watt to open the public lands of the West to unfettered access by oil and mining companies, many of whom funded Watt's strange outpost of divinely-inspired environmental exploitation, the Mountain States Legal Center.

As Deputy Director of Surface Mining, Griles gutted strip-mining regulations and was a relentless booster of the oil-shale scheme, one of the most outlandish giveaways and environmental blunders of the last century. He also pushed to overturn the popular moratorium on off-shore oil drilling on the Pacific Coast, a move of such extreme zealotry in the service of big oil that it even caught Reagan off guard.

After leaving public office, Griles quickly cashed in on his iniquitous tenure in government by launching a DC lobbying firm called J. Stephen Griles and Associates. He soon drummed up a list of clients including Arch Coal; the American Gas Association; National Mining Association; Occidental Petroleum; Pittston Coal; and more than forty other gas, mining, and energy concerns, big and small, foreign and domestic.

Then Griles was tapped as Gale Norton's chief deputy at Interior. After contentious senate hearings that exposed his various and lucrative entanglements with the oil and gas industry, Griles was finally confirmed to office on July 7, 2001. He later signed two separate statements agreeing to recuse himself from direct involvement in any Interior Department matters that might involve his former clients. He then flouted both of those agreements, as disclosed by his own calendar of meetings, liberated through a Freedom of Information Act filing made by Friends of the Earth.

As the calendar and meeting notes reveal, Griles used the cover of the 9/11 attacks and the war on Iraq to advance his looting of the public domain for the benefit of his former clients and business cronies. He has pushed for rollbacks in environmental standards for air and water, advocated increased oil and gas drilling on public lands, tried to exempt the oil industry from royalty payments, and drilled new loopholes in regulations governing strip-mining.

Griles wasted no time compiling a wish list from his pals. Within days of assuming office, he convened a series of parleys between his former clients and Interior Department officials to chart a game-plan for accelerating mining, oil leasing, and coal-methane extraction from public lands. Between August of 2001 and January 2004,

Griles met at least seven times with former clients; fifteen times with companies represented by his former client the National Mining Association; on at least sixteen occasions he arranged meetings between himself, former clients, and other administration officials to discuss rollback of air pollution standards for power plants, oil refineries, and industrial boilers; and on twelve occasions, he arranged similar meetings between regulators and former clients regarding coal mining.

But it now turned out that not only was Griles shilling for his former clients, he was also pushing policies to plump up his own pocketbook. Griles was an ownership partner in a DC lobbying firm called National Environmental Strategies (NES), a polluter's lobby founded in 1990 by Marc Himmelstein and Haley Barbour. Barbour soon left the firm to become head of the Republican National Committee. Griles moved in.

When he was nominated as deputy secretary of Interior, Griles was forced to sell his interest in the firm for $1.1 million, and he fixed up a deal with Himmelstein, a friend and Republican powerbroker. Instead of paying Griles off in a lump sum, Himmelstein was scheduled to pay the Bush official $284,000 each year over four years. Griles claimed he arranged this kind of payment plan in order to not leave NES "strapped for cash."

But in effect Griles remained financially tied to the health of Himmelstein's firm. And, in fact, Himmelstein admitted that from 2002 to 2004 he and Griles had gotten together several times over beers and dinner.

As these pungent episodes from Grile's tenure at Interior reveal, the Bush administration's fatal flaw has always been its inclination to over-reach, such as when the Interior Department, at the prodding of politically tone-deaf Dick Cheney, unveiled a plan to offer oil leases off the coast of Florida. The president's own brother, Jeb, shot the plan down. A similar blunder occurred in California, where new off-shore leasing had been banned since the oil spills of the 1970s. The Bush administration floated a plan for new leases off the coast of Northern California, Oregon and Washington. They backed down after the scheme proved too much for even Arnold Schwarzenegger. Still these should be viewed as probing raids, testing the tenacity of the opposition, while the real opportunities for plunder were being pursued in more hospitable terrain, where the door had already been opened by the Clinton administration.

* * *

But Jimmy Hoffa was on to something. Despite what you hear from the Sierra Club, Kerry and his Democratic cohorts never aligned themselves in opposition to the interests of the oil cartels. Far from it. In Clintontime, oil industry lobbyists flowed through the White House as easily as crude through the Alaskan pipeline, leaving behind campaign loot and wish lists. Several oil execs even enjoyed sleepovers in the Lincoln bedroom. Hazel O'Leary, Clinton's first Energy Secretary, traveled the world with oil execs in tow, brokering deals from India to China. Meanwhile, Ms. O'Leary, a former utility executive from Minnesota, compiled an enemies list of environmentalists and reporters who raised unsettling questions about her intimate ties to big oil.

In the summer of 1994, while Clinton vacationed in the Tetons, just down the trout stream from Dick Cheney's ranch, eight top oil executives dropped in for a visit. This confab in Jackson Hole became Clinton's version of the Cheney energy task force. The oil moguls pressed Clinton for a number of concessions: 1. Increased drilling on the Outer Continental Shelf, especially in the Gulf of Mexico; 2. A break on royalty payments; 3. Expedited leasing for coal-bed methane the Rocky Mountain Front; 4. Opening the National Petroleum Reserve-Alaska to drilling; 5. Removal of the ban on export of Alaskan crude oil to overseas refineries.

At 24 million acres in size, the National Petroleum Reserve-Alaska stood as the largest undeveloped tract of land in North America. Located on the Arctic plain just west of Prudhoe Bay, it is almost indistinguishable ecologically from the hallowed grounds of Arctic National Wildlife Refuge, which abuts its eastern edge. It's the same ecology, only much, much bigger. The oil industry had craved entry into the Reserve since the 1920s, when it was set aside for entry only in the case of a national emergency. Clinton and his Interior Secretary Bruce Babbitt gave them what Nixon, Ford, Reagan, and Bush had unable or unwilling to deliver.

But there's more. For twenty-five years, the oil companies operating on the North Slope had been required to refine the crude oil in the United States. Indeed, the opening of the North Slope to oil drilling, and the construction of the leaky 820-mile long Trans-Alaska Pipeline to transport the crude from Prudhoe Bay to Valdez, was sanctioned by the US Congress only because the oil was intended to buttress America's energy independence. Exports of raw crude were explicitly banned. At the time Senator Walter Mondale warned that the oil companies would eventually have the ban overturned, saying they had always intended it to be the "Trans-Alaska-Japan pipeline." Mondale correctly foresaw that the oil companies would export large shipments of the Alaskan crude to Asia in order to keep winter heating fuel prices high in the Midwestern states. In the summer of 2004, nearly three decades after this prediction, the oil companies had the jackpot in their grasp.

The winning strategy to lift the export ban was hatched by Tommy Boggs, the Kingpin of American lobbyists, whose firm, Patton, Boggs, represents a thick portfolio of oil companies, including Exxon, Mobil, Shell, and Ashland. In this instance, Boggs was the advance man for Alyeska, owned by the Alaskan oil consortium. Alyeska operates the Trans-Alaska pipeline and supervises oil extraction on the North Slope. Alyeska is owned by the consortium of companies doing business in northern Alaska. In an August 1995 memo to a prospective client, Boggs, a golfing pal of Bill Clinton, boasted of his bi-partisan expertise in moving the measure through Congress: "We have a very good working relationship with the Alaska delegation, having led the private-sector effort to get exports of Alaskan North Slope oil approved by the 104th Congress and signed by President Clinton." Boggs' normal price tag at that time was a robust $550 per hour, which translated into $22,000 for a forty-hour week.

Students of the political economy of the Clinton White House are correct in assuming that the billions handed over by Clinton to the Alaskan oil cartel were predicated on a substantial river of slush coming the other way.

After all, ARCO—the prime beneficiary of the new Alaskan oil bonanza—is one of the preeminent sponsors of the American political system. The oil giant maintains a hefty federal political action committee. In the 1996 election cycle, the ARCO PAC handed out more than $357,000. But this was only the beginning. Over the same period, ARCO pumped $1.25 million of soft money into the tanks of the Republican and Democratic national committees. The company contributed at least another $500,000 in state elections, where corporations can often give directly to candidates.

At the time, Robert Healy was ARCO's vice-president for governmental affairs. On October 25, 1995, Healy attended a White House coffee "klatsch" with Vice President Al Gore and Marvin Rosen, finance chairman of the Democratic National Committee. A few days before the session, Healy himself contributed $1,000 to the Clinton/Gore re-election campaign. But from July through December of 1995, largely under Healy's direction, ARCO poured $125,000 into the coffers of the DNC.

The man who did much of ARCO's political dirty work in Washington, DC was Charles T. Manatt, former chairman of the Democratic Party. Manatt runs a high-octane lobbying shop called Manatt, Phelps, Rothenberg, and Evans, formerly the lair of Mickey Kantor, longtime legal fixer for the Democrats. The lobbyist attended a White House session with Clinton on May 26, 1995. In 1995 and 1996, Manatt alone doled out $117,150 in hard and soft money. Members of Manatt's family threw in $7,000, his law firm kicked in $22,500, and the firm's PAC another $81,109.

Inside the Clinton cabinet, Manatt's former partner, Kantor became the most strident agitator for lifting the export ban on Alaskan oil, promoting it as a vital element in the administration's Asian trade policy. Kantor resigned his position as Secretary of Commerce and resumed his law practice with the Manatt, Phelps firm.

ARCO's former CEO, Lodwrick Cook, is a personal friend of Bill Clinton. In 1994, Cook celebrated his birthday at the White House. The President himself presented the oil executive with a towering cake. Cook traveled with Commerce Secretary Ron Brown on a trade junket to China in August 1994. During that trip, Cook and Brown negotiated ARCO's investment in the huge Zhenhai refinery outside Shanghai. The refinery is now ready to process Alaskan crude, which suggests that at least two years before Clinton's executive order on oil exports in the spring of 1996, ARCO had inside knowledge of what was to come.

In one of the ripest hypocrisies of the Clinton age, the green establishment largely went along with Babbitt's plan to open the petroleum reserve, under the deluded impression that to do so meant they would be able to keep the oil companies out of ANWR.

But by swallowing Babbitt's plan to open the petroleum reserve to oil drilling the Beltway greens undercut nearly every ecological and cultural argument for keeping the drillers out of ANWR.

Like ANWR, the petroleum reserve is home to a caribou herd. But the Western Arctic caribou herd that migrates across the reserve is almost twice as large as the herd that travels across ANWR. Similarly, the petroleum reserve is home to a roster of declining species, including polar bears, Arctic wolves and foxes, and musk ox.

Unlike ANWR, the petroleum reserve contains one of the great rivers of the Arctic, the Colville River, the largest on the North Slope. It starts high in the Brooks Range and curves for 300 miles through the heart of the reserve to a broad delta on the Arctic Ocean near the Inupiat village of Nuiqsut.

The Colville River canyon and the nearby lakes and marshes are one of the world's most important migratory bird staging areas. Over 20 percent of the entire population of Pacific black brant molt each year at Teshekpuk Lake. The bluffs along the Colville River are recognized as the most prolific raptor breeding grounds in the Arctic, providing critical habitat for the peregrine falcon and rough-legged hawk.

In early 2003, the Bush administration moved to expand the drilling in the NPR-A, originally approved by Babbitt and Clinton. Under the Bush plan, 9 million acres would be opened to drilling almost immediately and another 3 million acres, near the Inupiat village of Wainwright, would be opened later in the decade. The plan, tailored to meet the needs of ConocoPhillips, called for thousands of wells, hundreds of miles of road, dozens of waste dumps, and a network of pipelines to transport the oil to Prudhoe Bay and the Trans-Alaska pipeline.

But oil and gas may not be the only prize. The Bureau of Land Management, which never misses an opportunity to pursue maximum development of public lands, estimates that the petroleum reserve may harbor approximately 40 percent of all coal remaining in the US (400 billion to 4 trillion US tons).

Coming soon: strip mines in the Arctic.

* * *

When Hoffa vowed that Kerry and the Democrats were going to drill everywhere except ANWR like never before, he wasn't only talking about the NPR-A. He was also referring to plans to sink oil wells into the Kenai Peninsula and off of Kodiak Island and near the Chugach forest. There are also more than 670 lease applications piled up in the Clinton years for new offshore oil development in Alaska, from the Gulf of Alaska, to the Copper River Delta (perhaps the greatest remaining salmon fishery in the world), to Cook Inlet (flanked by the Katmai National Park and the Kenai Peninsula) to Bristol Bay, to the Chukchi Sea up by Point Hope, to the Beaufort Sea. In other words, under both Kerry and Bush's energy plans, the entire coast of Alaska was now in play.

And not only Alaska.

The biggest oil rush in recent American history is taking place not on the North Slope, where reserves are ebbing out, but on the Great Plains, at the foot of the Rocky Mountains, in Montana and Wyoming. Here are huge deposits of coal methane clustered in Power River Basin in Montana and Wyoming. These reserves are worth billions of dollars and long craved by the natural gas industry. This looms as the largest energy development project in the country and has been assailed by environmentalists and native groups as an environmental nightmare.

The project, which calls for the development of more than 80,000 coal-methane wells, is so fraught with danger that even the Bush administration's own EPA issued a report sharply criticizing the environmental consequences of the scheme. Among the findings: the 80,000 coal-methane wells will discharge nearly 20,000 gallons of salty water each day onto the ground surface, fouling the land, creeks, and aquatic life. Over its lifespan, the project will deplete the underground aquifer of more than 4 trillion gallons of water, that will take hundreds of years to replenish. Full-scale production will also require 17,000 miles of new roads, 20,000 miles of pipelines and turn nearly 200,000 acres of rangeland into an industrial zone.

This rare rebuke from the normally supine EPA roused Steven Griles into furious action. On April 12, 2002, Griles sent a scathing memo under his Department of Interior letterhead chastising the EPA for dragging its feet on the project. He chided the agency for being uncooperative with industry. It turned out that Griles had formerly represented the very companies that he was now accusing the EPA of failing to accord proper respect. As a lobbyist, Griles' clients included the Coal Bed Methane Ad Hoc Committee, Devon Energy, Restone, and Western Gas Resources, all companies seeking to gain access to the Powder Basin gas fields. His old firm, NES, also hosted an industry-sponsored tour of Powder Basin for EPA and Interior Department officials. NES also represented Griles' former client Devon Energy, which stood to make a killing if the deal was approved.

Griles' meddling in this matter came to the attention of the Department's lawyers. On May 8, 2004, they forced Griles to sign an agreement disqualifying himself from any further involvement in the coal-methane issue. He later said he did so "for all the world to know that I'm not even going to be talking to anybody about it again."

Griles was rightfully vilified for his role in the Powder River Basin scandal, which prompted investigations by the Justice Department, Congress, and the Inspector General's Office at the Interior Department. But none of this started under Bush. Not Alaska, not the Gulf of Mexico, not the Powder River Basin.

In July of 2000, David Hayes, Undersecretary of Interior for Energy, testified before Congress in July of 2000 on the Clinton legacy for oil leasing on public lands and off-shore sites. "The Clinton Administration is supportive of the US domestic oil and gas industry," Hayes told the Senate Committee on Energy and Natural Resources. "We have supported efforts to increase oil and natural gas recovery in the deep waters of the Gulf of Mexico; we have conducted a number of extremely successful, environmentally sound off-shore oil and gas lease sales; and we have opened a portion of the National Petroleum Reserve-Alaska (NPR-A) to environmentally responsible oil and gas development, where an estimated 10 trillion cubic feet (tcf) of recoverable natural gas resources lie in the northeast section of the reserve."

Hayes boasted that while domestic oil production had declined on private lands since 1989, the Clinton administration responded by boosting oil production on public lands. Under Clinton, oil production from public lands increased by more than 13 percent of the 1992 figures under Bush the first, who was widely decried by liberals as being owned by big oil. Here are the numbers cited by Hayes for BLM oil leasing under Clinton—he called the figures impressive, which they are, although sobering might have been a more precise description:

* Leasing in the Gulf of Mexico increased almost ten-fold between 1992 and 1997.

- From 1993 to 1999, 6,538 new leases were issued covering approximately 35 million acres of the Outer Continental Shelf.
- Lease Sale 175 in the Central Gulf of Mexico, held on March 15, 2000, offered 4,203 blocks (22.29 million acres) for lease. The Interior Department received 469 bids on 344 blocks. There were 334 leases awarded.
- More than 40 million acres of Federal OCS are currently under lease. Approximately 94 percent of the existing OCS leases (7,900) are in the Gulf, and about 1,500 of these leases are producing.

* Issued over 28,000 leases and approved over 15,000 permits to drill.

- In 1999, the BLM held a lease sale offering 425 tracts on 3.9 million acres in the National Petroleum Reserve-Alaska.

* Implemented legislation changing the competitive lease term from five years to ten years, allowing lessees greater flexibility in exploration without endangering the lease.

* Oversaw a 60 percent increase in the production of natural gas on Federal onshore lands over the past seven years—from 1.3 trillion cubic feet in 1992 to 2.0 trillion cubic feet in 1999.

Here's Hayes speaking reverently about those Powder River Basin coal bed methane leases, which liberals and greens have tried to lay solely at the feet of Bush and Griles: "Estimates of recoverable gas reserves on public lands from this basin alone are as high as 9 trillion cubic feet. If maximum operating capacity of the current pipelines in the Powder River Basin is achieved, production could be as much as 1 billion cubic feet per day. That will produce enough fuel to heat nearly 50,000 homes in the United States for twenty years. Industry is producing the gas and submitting applications for permits to drill at an unprecedented rate and, presently, there are more than 4,000 coal-bed methane wells in the basin. Upon completion of further environmental analysis, we expect to nearly double that amount."

The only real difference between the Clinton plan for the Powder River Basin and the Bush scheme is that the Bush administration, prodded by Steve Griles, moved to accelerate the leasing planned by Clinton, Babbitt and Hayes and truncate the environmental reviews. Under both administrations, the end result was a foregone conclusion.

So, the three biggest oil and gas bonanzas attributed to the rapacity of the Bush regime—the Alaska petroleum reserve, the Gulf of Mexico, and the Powder River—were all initiated by the Clinton administration.

One more note on David Hayes. Before joining the Clinton team, Hayes served as the chairman of the Environmental Law Institute, a DC green group. But this was only a part-time position. His day job was as a lawyer/lobbyist at the big DC firm of Latham and Watkins, which represents a plump roster of corporations seeking to plunder the very lands, as deputy secretary of Interior, he would be charged with protecting. After leaving the Clinton administration, Hayes navigated a soft-landing back to his old spot at Latham and Watkins. How is this any different from the lucrative migrations of the hated Steven Griles, who traveled from the Reagan administration to an oil lobbyshop to the Bush II administration? The revolving door is bi-partisan.

＊ ＊ ＊

When it comes to oil policy Bush relied on Griles, while the Democrats often turned to Ralph Cavanagh, the top energy strategist at the Natural Resources Defense Council

(NRDC), the neo-liberal environmental group headed by John Adams. In Clintontime, Adams and his group made a notorious splash when they publicly betrayed their fellow environmentalists by endorsing NAFTA, the trade pact with Mexico hotly opposed by a tender coalition labor and greens. NRDC's endorsement shattered the coalition and secured passage of the bill through congress, a prize that had been denied the first Bush administration. Adams felt no regrets. He later gloated about "breaking the back of the environmental opposition to NAFTA."

Ralph Cavanagh is exceptionally close to John Kerry and his wife, Teresa Heinz. In fact, Heinz's foundation bestowed on Cavanagh its annual eco-genius award and a $250,000 check for his pioneering work in energy policy. But just what did this work entail?

Well, while his boss John Adams pushed free trade, Ralph Cavanagh hawked the deregulation of the energy business in the name of environmental efficiency, an old ploy discredited in the progressive era. Cavanagh played the role of Betty Crocker in bestowing green seals of approval for enviro-conscience and selfless devotion to the public weal by corporations like, well, Enron.

These green seals of approval were part of the neoliberal pitch, that fuddy-duddy regulation should yield to modern, "market-oriented solutions" to environmental problems, which essentially means bribing corporations in the hope they'll stop their polluting malpractices. Indeed, NRDC and EDF were always the prime salesfolk of neoliberal remedies for environmental problems. In fact, NRDC was socked into the Enron lobby machine so deep you couldn't see the soles of its feet. Here's what happened:

In 1997, high-flying Enron found itself in a pitched battle in Oregon, where it planned to acquire Portland General Electric (PGE), Oregon's largest public utility. Warning that Enron's motives were of a highly predatory nature, the staff of the state's Public Utility Commission (PUC) opposed the merger. They warned that an Enron takeover would mean less ability to protect the environment, increased insecurity for PGE's workers and, in all likelihood, soaring prices. Other critics argued that Enron's actual plan was to cannibalize PGE, in particular its hydropower, which Enron would sell into California's energy market.

But at the very moment when such protests threatened to balk Enron of its prize, Ralph Cavanagh rode into town. Cavanagh lost no time whipping the refractory Oregon greens into line. In concert with Enron, the NRDC man put together a memo of understanding, pledging that the company would lend financial support to some of these groups' pet projects.

But Cavanagh still had some arduous politicking ahead. An OK for the merger had to come from the PUC, whose staff was adamantly opposed. So, on Valentine's Day, 1997, Cavanagh showed up at a hearing in Salem, Oregon, to plead Enron's case.

Addressing the three PUC commissioners, Cavanagh averred that this was "the first time I've ever spoken in support of a utility merger." If so, it was the quickest transition from virginity to seasoned service in the history of intellectual prostitution. Cavanagh flaunted the delights of an Enron embrace: "What we've put before you with this company is, we believe, a robust assortment of public benefits for the citizens of Oregon which would not emerge, Mr. Chairman, without the merger."

With a warble in his throat, Cavanagh moved into rhetorical high gear: "Can you trust Enron? On stewardship issues and public benefit issues I've dealt with this company for a decade, often in the most contentious circumstances, and the answer is, yes."

Cavanagh won the day for the Houston-based energy giant. The PUC approved the merger, and it wasn't long before the darkest suspicions of Enron's plans were vindicated. The company raised rates, tried to soak the ratepayers with the cost of its failed Trojan nuclear reactor and moved to put some of PGE's most valuable assets on the block. Enron's motive had indeed been to get access to the hydropower of the Northwest, the cheapest in the country, and sell it into the California market, the priciest and—in part because of Cavanagh's campaigning for deregulation—a ripe energy prize awaiting exploitation.

Then, after two years, the company Cavanagh had hailed as being "engaged and motivated" put PGE up on the auction block. Pending sale of PGE, Enron had been using it as collateral for loans approved by a federal bankruptcy judge. In the meantime, Enron continued to bilk the citizens of Oregon. Enron ordered PGE to raise rates in Portland purportedly to cover taxes owed by Enron that were unrelated to PGE business. The rates went up by $35 million. Enron executives pocketed the millions. The taxes were never paid.

Though notorious as George W. Bush's prime financial backer, Enron was a bipartisan purveyor of patronage: to its right, conservative Texas Senator Phil Gramm; to its left, liberal Texas Democrat Sheila Jackson-Lee (who had Enron's CEO Ken Lay as her finance chairman in a Democratic primary fight preluding her first successful Congressional bid; her Democratic opponent was Craig Washington, an anti-NAFTA maverick Democrat the Houston establishment didn't care for).

In the late 1990s, Cavanagh, backed by money from the Energy Foundation, marshaled environmental support for the disastrous scheme to deregulate California's electric utilities, a prize long sought by the state's two biggest power companies, Pacific Gas and Electric and Southern California Edison.

It so happens that the CEO of Southern California Edison was a lawyer named John Bryson, who, in the early 1970s, started a little environmental outfit with another lawyer, John Adams. That group was NRDC. According to Sharon Beder, Cavanagh considers himself a protégé of the utility mogul.

In support of the deregulation scheme, Cavanagh argued that regulation of the utilities was *passé*. He promised that after deregulation the competitive forces unleashed by the free market would keep a lid on prices, discourage new nuclear plants, and provide an incentive for conservation and renewable energy sources. Enough people bought this line to allow the deregulation bill to slide through the General Assembly.

Few of Cavanagh's promises materialized. Instead, rates and power company profits soared and, released from the scrutiny of regulators, corporate solicitude for the reliability of the power grid wilted and California was hit with a series of blackouts in the summers of 2000 and 2001.

Circling the carnage were Cavanagh's old pals from Enron, now free to prey on the newly deregulated California energy market. Remember Cavanagh's pledge "You can trust Enron." Thanks to a lawsuit brought by Judicial Watch, we have tapes of Enron executives plotting to prolong the misery of California residents and maximize their own profits.

One of the big concerns raised by consumer advocates and environmentalists about deregulation was the issue of reliability. Would private companies, driven solely by the profit motive, have an incentive to maintain powerlines and powerplants, to keep them in working order? Yes, said Cavanagh. It turned out quite differently. The companies actually had an incentive to turn the plants off at the precise moment demand was at a peak. In one of the tape-recorded conversations, two Enron executives are heard plotting to raise prices by shutting down a steamer at a power plant.

> "I was wondering, um, the demand out there is, er... there's not much, ah, demand for power at all and we're running kind of fat," one executive complains. "Um, if you took down the steamer, how long would it take to get it back up?"

> "Oh, it's not something you want to just be turning on and off every hour. Let's put it that way," another Enron employee replies.

> "If we shut it down, could you bring it back up in three—three or four hours, something like that?" the executive asks.

> "Oh, yeah," the other says.

> "Well, why don't you just go ahead and shut her down, then, if that's OK," the executive says.

On another occasion, two energy traders are joking about how Enron manipulated the prices for electricity in California.

> "They're taking all that fucking money back?" says one energy trader to an Enron executive. "All the money you guys stole from those poor grandmothers of California?"

"Yeah, Grandma Millie, man," the Enron executive replies. "But she's the one who couldn't figure out how to fucking vote on the butterfly ballot."

"Now she wants her money back for all the power you've charged right up, jammed right up her ass for $250 a megawatt hour," the other trader chuckled.

The Enron traders loved the blackouts, because that meant they could cash in on the sky-rocketing prices helpless consumers were forced to pay. "Just cut 'em off," one Enron executive said. "They're so fucked. They should just bring back fucking horses and carriages, fucking lamps, fucking kerosene lamps."

When wildfires threatened to incinerate powerlines and an electric transfer station, the Enron traders could be heard singing, "Burn, baby, burn."

One Enron employee is heard speaking reverently about one of the most gifted Enron energy traders preying on the California energy crisis.

"He just fucks California," says one Enron employee. "He steals money from California to the tune of about a million."

"Will you rephrase that?" asks a second employee.

"OK, he, um, he arbitrages the California market to the tune of a million bucks or two a day," replies the first. All under the watch of Enron's top executives Jeffrey Skilling and Ken Lay.

Through all of this, John Kerry remained curiously mute. Perhaps because his wife, and chief financial underwriter, Teresa Heinz was pals not only with Cavanagh, but Ken Lay as well.

Teresa Heinz's interest in environmental issues has been mostly expressed through her Heinz Foundation, whose board until very recently was adorned by that hero of free-market enviros, Ken Lay of Enron.

The Heinz Foundation put Ken Lay in charge of their global-warming initiative. When Enron went belly up, the Foundation stuck by their man: "Whatever troubles he had at Enron, Ken Lay had a good reputation in the environmental community for being a business man who was environmentally sensitive. When someone does wrong in one part of their life, it doesn't mean they can't do good in another part of their life."

It's the kind of sublime indifference to the messy realities of politics and life that inspired Democrats and environmentalists to rally behind Kerry, under the vacant banner, "Anybody But Bush." They got what they deserved.

* * *

On Memorial Day weekend 2004, the price of premium gas breached $3 a gallon. Yet there were no calls for price caps from the Democrats and no demand for a criminal investigation into price gouging by the oil cartel. Instead, all they could muster was a limp plea that the strategic petroleum reserves be tapped, an impotent measure unlikely to depress prices by more than two or three cents a gallon for a couple of weeks. But we all know where that oil comes from: drilling on public lands and on the outer continental shelf.

On the eve of the 2004 elections, Kerry raced off to a pow-wow with the American Gas Association, where he reiterated his message to Hoffa that he was ready to: "Drill everywhere, like never before." Shortly afterwards, the trade association issued a smirking press release affirming that Kerry was on board for increased drilling, especially for natural gas. So was his party.

Back in 1970s, Richard Nixon promoted an energy policy that was far more enlightened than anything offered up by the Republicans or Democrats these days. And Ken Lay, then a junior staffer at the Federal Energy Commission, had a hand in developing the Nixon plan. Yes, those truly were the good old days.

Rockin' the Pipeline:
Earthquakes and Alaska's Oil

I T WAS THE BIGGEST QUAKE TO HIT NORTH AMERICA THIS CENTURY, A 7.9 JOLT centered beneath the tundra about eighty miles south of Fairbanks that tickled seismographs all the way to New Orleans.

The trembler, on November 4, 2002, opened zigzag fissures in the earth, mangled roads, crushed a few remote cabins, triggered landslides, and cracked concrete from Fairbanks to Anchorage.

The Denali Fault appears to be awakening from a relatively long slumber. The fault, which curves through the Canadian Yukon through the Alaska Range past Mt. McKinley in Denali National Park, is the longest in the US where plates move horizontally, with land to the north slipping east and land to the south sliding west. It's a violent mix.

Two weeks before the big shake, a 6.7 quake rocked an area just south of the epicenter of the latest quake. "They're a very interesting pair of earthquakes," said Roger Hansen, a seismologist at the Earthquake Information Center in Fairbanks. "One began and unzipped in one direction, and the second just unzipped the fault in the other." For more than a month, hundreds of aftershocks continued to pulse across Alaska, some as powerful as 5.7.

Still, for all the rumbling, only one person was injured, a seventy-six-year-old woman from Mentasa Lake who broke her arm when she fell down the stairs of her home.

But the Denali quake did shake the foundations of the TransAlaska Pipeline. The pipeline, which carries about a billion barrels of oil a day, was shut down hours after the quake and remained closed for days.

In its 800-mile trek from the belching ruin of Prudhoe Bay to the tanker ship terminals of Valdez, the pipeline crosses eighty rivers and streams, three mountain ranges, and it dips under coves, ponds, and marshes. The oil courses through the line at 140 degrees. A rupture would spill steaming crude oil onto some of the most ecologically frail lands in the world, and by comparison, make the Exxon Valdez spill seem like an oil stain on a driveway.

The pipeline is managed by the Alyeska Corporation, a consortium of the oil companies that exploit the reserves of the North Slope: BP, Conoco-Phillips, Exxon Mobil,

Williams, Unocal and Amerada Hess. For the past twenty-five years, Alyeska's flacks have maintained that the pipeline is invulnerable to natural disasters.

But hours after the quake throttled the Alaskan interior, reports came that several of the H-shaped brackets that hold the forty-eight-inch pipeline off the ground had buckled and broken. Engineers have identified ten severely damaged supports, including two consecutive ones near the point where the pipeline crosses the Denali Fault.

The foulest fantasies of Dick Cheney and his cohorts to extract the rest of the North Slope's reserves may well rest on those frail and battered supports. Oil production at Prudhoe Bay is declining. Thus the oil companies are anxious to extend their domain west into the National Petroleum Reserve, east into Arctic National Wildlife Refuge and north into the Beaufort Sea. All of that oil would have to be sluiced down the pipeline to Valdez.

One of the biggest questions concerns the valves in the underground sections of the pipeline, long considered the most likely point for a catastrophic breach during a quake. Alyeska says it sent "sniffer probes" down tubes to check the valves. But most engineers say those probes are of limited value.

There was enormous pressure from the oil companies to get the pipeline back in operation. Quickly. It's estimated that more than $25 million worth of crude flows through the pipeline every day.

With this much at stake, no one could count on Alyeska to tell the truth about the damage to the pipeline. This is a company with a history of lies, known to abuse employees who have tried to tell the truth about problems with the pipeline in the past.

Richard Acord was a safety inspector on the pipeline. Back in 1991, he witnessed what has become a fairly typical occurrence. At Milepost 113.6, the pipeline dips below ground for one of twenty-five animal crossings, allowing caribou and other migrating animals to cross the pipeline corridor. A giant drilling rig, weighing more than 60,000 pounds, tried to cross over the buried line on wooden planks, slid off and sunk in the mud directly above the pipeline. The truck's oil line broke, spilling diesel fuel onto the tundra. Acord tried to issue a stop-work order to ensure that the pipeline itself had not been damaged in the accident and to develop a plan to extract the rig without further damage to fouled tundra. The drilling crew's supervisor chastised Acord and told him that he would either play ball or "they would find someone who would."

"We had oil running down the tundra," Acord stated in a deposition about the event. "We had a rig stuck across the pipeline, indeterminate material in the ground. All of those constitute a bad situation." After going public, Acord was fired.

Acord was not alone. In 1994, four other safety inspectors settled a whistleblower lawsuit with Alyeska, claiming, among other things, that the pipeline company blacklisted them from other jobs in the oil industry after they raised complaints about worker safety and environmental practices.

Take the case of Charles Hammel. Back in the late 1980s, pipeline workers and inspectors began feeding Hammel information about problems with the pipeline and with Alyeska's reckless cost-cutting and mismanagement. Hammel, an independent oil broker, took these concerns to congress and Alyeska was forced to spend millions of dollars to repair corrosion along the line.

The company, and the oil corporations behind it, didn't like this one bit, so they went after Hammel with a vengeance. In 1990, they hired the Wackenhut Corporation to dig up dirt on Hammel. They rummaged through his trash, ran credit reports on him, set up a fake enviro group to trick him into giving them information, and even hired a prostitute to try to seduce him. Hammel sued the company for invasion of privacy and won a $5 million settlement.

But that didn't stop Alyeska. When whistleblowers raised concerns to management or went public, they were fired. After one inspector got subpoenaed to testify before congress, his manager told him that he'd "break his fucking arm" if he said anything to damage the company.

When auditors from the BLM and other outfits began to look at Alyeska's books, the company's managers were caught "file stuffing"—adding post-dated documents to make the thin records look more robust. When one employee refused to go along, his manager threatened to fire him on the spot. In fact, Alyeska was so brazen in its intimidation tactics that it even spied on California Congressman George Miller, then chairman of the House Interior Committee.

Alyeska has plenty to cover up. A series of audits since 1990 have disclosed thousands of code violations. The company's maps don't accurately depict the location of the pipeline. In one instance, Alyeska's maps showed the pipeline being more than a mile away from its real location.

The fact is, the pipeline already leaks and has since nearly the beginning. The leaks are getting worse and more frequent as the pipeline ages. Between 1979 and 1993, the pipeline averaged about two shutdown incidents a year. Since then, the rate has increased to more than eight per year. In 2001, a twenty-one-inch shift in a section of pipeline at Atigun Pass went undetected by Alyeska for several months. This is oil spillage as normalcy.

As the problems get worse, Alyeska becomes more and more stingy, cutting costs at every turn. Since 1998, the company has cut manned stations along the pipeline from eleven down to four. That lack of oversight led to oil spraying undetected from the pipeline for more than thirty-six hours after a couple of drunks shot holes into it—also showing terrorists how easy it could be to turn the Alaskan tundra into a frozen facsimile of the Kuwaiti oil fields following Saddam's retreat.

None of this fazed the Bush administration, which moved swiftly to reauthorize the pipeline for thirty more years of service.

"You can't help but think about your physical safety when you are costing somebody $500 million," said one Alyeska whistleblower. "The theory is that they will use the equipment until the line is destroyed. When you step back and look at the big picture, God, it stinks."

Of course, one more twitch from the uneasy depths of Denali could bring it all crashing down.

FAIRBANKS.

The Worst Day of Ted Stevens' Life

BEFORE GEORGE BUSH BOARDED HIS HELICOPTER FOR EVACUATION INTO the Maryland hill country for Christmas at Camp David, the president-in-Lycra made the inexplicable observation that "it's been a great year for Americans." He probably wasn't speaking for the families of the 735 US troops who had been killed in Iraq in 2005, although increasingly, the military death-toll there is claiming the lives of recent Mexican immigrants, who Bush may not consider fully "American." Also Bush likely wasn't talking about the 300,000 people still displaced by Hurricane Katrina, perhaps because the First Mother has assured him that those who were dropped off in Texas have never had it so good. And he certainly wasn't referring to Senator Ted Stevens of Alaska, once the most powerful man on the Hill, who whined in a threnody worthy of a passage from Aeschylus, that the close of this year's congressional session had been the worst day of his life.

What tragedy could have cast such a gloomy pall across the mighty man from Anchorage, who, as chairman of the Senate appropriations committee, commands the flow of trillions of dollars from the federal treasury? The final days of congress are usually a joyous time for Stevens. This is the season when he gets to play Santa, by implanting billions of dollars of pork-barrel projects into the final budget bills of the states of senators who have shown him the proper obeisance over the previous year, and by stripping out cherished projects from those few who dared defy him.

But this year, it was Stevens who was rudely jolted by a last second reversal of fortune, when his brethren and sistren in the senate blocked his stealthy maneuver to open the Arctic National Wildlife Refuge to oil exploration.

Surely, the Porcupine caribou herd raised their heads at Stevens' long-distance howl and snorted in celebration at the news that their calving grounds on the Arctic plain had been spared for yet another year from intrusion by oil derricks and pipelines and that their nemesis for the last thirty years had received a rare rebuke.

Stevens' agony must be all the more acute because he was so tantalizingly close to achieving what he has said is his last major objective as a senator. Indeed, earlier this year, after the senator had slipped the ANWR drilling measure into the budget reconciliation bill in an effort to evade the senate filibusters that had frustrated his efforts in the past, Stevens told his hometown paper, the *Anchorage Daily News*, that his work in the senate was done and he could now retire a contented man.

Stevens wasn't counting on the Republican-controlled House of Representatives throwing a monkeywrench into his devious plans. But that's exactly what happened this fall when twenty-five Republicans, staring at polar-bear friendly poll numbers and not wanting to risk aligning themselves with the oil company executives who had gloated about making record profits in the wake of Katrina, demanded that the ANWR provision be stripped from the budget bill. The defeat of ANWR in what Stevens contemptuously calls the "other body" may also reflect the collapse of House discipline now that Tom DeLay has been forced to stand aside as leader following his indictment in Texas.

While the Sierra Club feted itself over a rare environmental victory in the GOP-ruled House, Stevens went back to his laboratory and brewed up another recipe from his book of legislative alchemy. The senator covertly affixed the ANWR measure to the Defense Appropriation Bill, hoping that Democrats and anti-drilling Republicans wouldn't have the guts to launch a last minute filibuster that might be seen as denying weapons, body armor, food, and Humvees to the troops in Iraq. The senate also linked Katrina relief money to the ANWR measure. "There'll be no Katrina money without ANWR drilling," Stevens brayed. But Stevens' gambit failed, when he fell four votes shy of overcoming a filibuster.

It is a sweet irony that, within a matter of months, both houses had approved opening ANWR to drilling, and then they both rejected it. In a mournful editorial, the *Wall Street Journal* called the turn of events "surreal." And for once they were right.

Of course, next spring, with the regularity of migrating warblers, the ANWR drilling forces will press their case once more, with Ted Stevens leading the charge. But the window of vulnerability is closing for ANWR. Stevens is in his twilight. He seems a frail and diminished figure these days, ranting in the well of the Senate, a Republican version of Bobby Byrd, who also once ruled the appropriations game and steered federal wealth to the carved hills of West Virginia.

Stevens must feel that the oil cartel has let him down, first by the orgy of profiteering in the wake of the hurricanes, then with the brazen performance of the oil executives during the congressional show hearings into their record profits, where the CEOs refused to even feign the slightest blush of contrition.

The final blow, though, was the distinct lack of vigor shown by oil industry lobbyists in the battle for ANWR. For Stevens this must seem like a kind of heresy. He is a crusader now, for whom the conquest of ANWR has assumed a religious fervor. Stevens wants to drill a well through the heart not only of ANWR, but the idea of ANWR, the paganistic precedent of a swath of public land in his state that is off-limits to industrial exploitation.

"It's an empty, ugly place," Stevens snarled. "It's almost treasonous that environmentalists are sacrificing our national security for such a place." The mad senator raged that he planned to visit the states of each senator who voted against him to inform the citizens of his or her treachery.

But for the oil companies it's always been about maximizing profits and there's mounting evidence that without generous federal subsidies or a major spike in global oil prices, there might not be enough oil lurking under the permafrost of ANWR to justify the legislative fight and the years of protracted litigation.

No one really knows how much oil lies under ANWR. There's only been a single test hole drilled in the area, and that was on native lands and the results have been kept a closely guarded secret for years. The geology of ANWR is suggestive of an oil field holding between 5 billion and 10 billion barrels. But if the price of oil stays below $100 a barrel, fully 30 percent of that total won't be economically recoverable. That leaves somewhere between 3.5 billion and 7 billion barrels—a big find, but not huge. At peak production, ANWR oil, sluiced down the Alaska pipeline, might satiate about 5 percent of US oil demand. But only for about three years. Then production would begin a steady decline until the reserves are exhausted in twenty years or so. Add to this prospectus, the expense and risk of transporting the crude from the Arctic to US refineries in southern California, assuming the crude isn't shipped across the Pacific to refineries in China and South Korea.

From the oil cartel's vantage, there are easier pickings to be had in the Alaskan National Petroleum Reserve just west of Prudhoe Bay, in the Canadian Yukon or in the Gulf of Mexico. If Stevens can deliver them ANWR gift-wrapped with production subsidies as his senatorial swan song, so much the better. If not, there's no reason to sweat it. As Exxon and its brethren proved this year, oil shortages—real or engineered—yield eye-popping profits with little costs. And when the price gets high enough, every last drop of crude will once again be within their clutches.

As for the environmental movement, ANWR has functioned as their own private cash reserve since the 1980s when James Watt put a bull's eye on that austere stretch of Arctic coastline. There's been no more lucrative fundraiser for the Sierra Club than the annual threat of oil wells being drilled in the home of the polar bear and musk oxen. To the political cynic, it might appear that the environmental movement profits from having ANWR under perpetual threat.

But with Stevens weakened and the oil industry distracted, it's time for the green cabal in Washington to push hard for permanent protection of America's Serengeti by demanding that the entire wildlife refuge to be designated a federal wilderness area forever immune from attack by the oil and gas companies, a stratagem they inexplicably chose not to pursue during Clintontime.

A successful wilderness campaign might mean a diminished flow of revenues in the future. But these green groups are supposed to be non-profits, aren't they?

Cancerous Air:
Born Under a Bad Sky

THIS IS WHAT IT HAS COME TO: THE AIR IN LA IS SO TOXIC THAT A CHILD born in the city of angels will inhale more cancer-causing pollutants in the first two weeks of life than the EPA (not known for understating risks) considers safe for a lifetime.

This risk never goes away. It comes with the first breaths a child takes. Being born in urban California now means that life expectancy is reduced, chances of getting cancer are elevated. All this before you've inflicted any damage on yourself through smoking, drinking booze, eating fast food, or watching CNN.

The situation is spelled out in a report released by the National Environmental Trust titled "Toxic Beginnings." The report pins much of the blame for this situation on so-called TACs, or Toxic Air Contaminants. These are poisons spewed into the atmosphere from cars, trucks, heavy equipment, and factories. Studies by the EPA and other agencies link TAC-exposure to cancer, birth defects, and other illnesses, such as asthma.

The National Environmental Trust report examined air quality and exposure to TACs in California's five most populous basins: Los Angeles, the San Joaquin Valley, the Sacramento Valley, the San Francisco Bay Area, and San Diego.

In Los Angeles the air is so clotted with ten cancer-causing chemicals that residents there face a cancer risk 1,005 times the level considered "safe" by the EPA. And the most vulnerable to those risks are children, especially poor and working-class children.

Prior to the National Environmental Trust report, the unique risks faced by children have rarely been deemed worthy of calculation. The EPA and the California Air Resources Board, for example, issue an annual report on air emissions and their consequences on human health. However, those risks are based solely on calculations made about the amount of carcinogens inhaled over the lifetime of an average adult.

But recent medical literature shows that children are much more susceptible to these toxins than adults, and that exposure to toxic air early in life is much more dangerous than breathing the same foul air for more extended periods as an adult.

This has to do with the physiology of children. They inhale more air than adults relative to their body weight. Thus, they are exposed to higher concentrations of cancer-causing chemicals.

The National Environmental Trust report took the data on TACs compiled by the Air Review Board and recalculated it to show the risks to children. It's not a pretty picture. The EPA (rather arbitrarily) sets a "one million standard" risk of getting cancer as its acceptable lifetime exposure risk. Children born and raised in these smog-laden California basins will far exceed these levels very early in life.

For example, in San Francisco the average infant will exceed the EPA's lifetime exposure to toxic air pollutants in 19 days. In LA, it takes only twelve days. By the time the average LA-born girl reaches her eighteenth birthday, she will have breathed enough toxic air to place her 344 times over what the EPA considers an acceptable lifetime exposure to these contaminants.

"The potential risk that a child rapidly accumulates in California for simply breathing will not go away when the child is older, even if the air is cleaner when the child reaches adulthood," the report warns. "Remarkably, if the carcinogens in California air were cleaned up to EPA's level immediately, a child born in California would still exceed the lifetime acceptable cancer risk by age four and an adult moving to California would exceed it in seven years."

Generally, these risks accumulate steadily leading to cancers in adulthood. But there's also evidence that exposure to toxic air is behind the mounting level of childhood cancers. "There has been a steady moderate increase in childhood cancers (ages 0–twenty) since the 1970s, which has not been explained by improved diagnostics" cautions a recent report by the California Office of Environmental Health Hazard Assessment. "Leukemias, lymphomas, and brain tumors are the most common childhood cancers."

The biggest culprit by far is particulate matter and chemicals belched out by diesel engines from trucks, cars, and "other mobile sources," such as farm and construction equipment.

Sue Martinez works at the Children's Hospital in Oakland and is a witness to the daily toll. "Diesel is the worst of the air pollutants, which our medical staff already sees through asthma cases," Martinez told me. "In West Oakland, diesel trucks line up at the Oakland ports from Saturday night through Sunday with their engines idling. By the time the ports open for business on Monday, our Emergency Department has begun receiving asthma emergencies. Asthma is the number one cause of emergency department admissions at our hospital."

But there are other sources as well, including dichlorobenzene (largely from pesticides), benzene (from oils and industrial greases), methylene chloride (from paint and paint removers), and formaldehyde (from adhesives and cleaning products).

The situation is so bad that even adults who have moved to California are not immune. In fact, the report reveals that, within a year, an adult breathing the air in one of California's major cities will exceed the lifetime exposure risk by more than a multiple of fifteen. Even if the diesel emissions were brought under control, exposure to current levels of these chemicals would cause a child to exceed the EPA's acceptable cancer risk by age four.

At a time when Bush was railing at Saddam Hussein for gassing his own people, his administration was coddling the coterie of oil and chemical companies turning the LA basin into a cancerous sink and poisoning infants and children across urban America. And instead of strengthening the Clean Act Air to deal with this homegrown problem, Bush and his cronies from Big Oil want to rip out the few teeth that remain in the law, a move that will make cancer a birthmark of being born in California.

OAKLAND.

Sweating It Out: Nike's Bad Air

THE PLACE IS IN HONDURAS, A SO-CALLED FREE-TRADE ZONE OR *MAQUI-ladora*—little more than a ragged swath hacked out of the rainforest and ringed by a tall fence, tipped with razor-sharp wire. Inside a clump of factories produce cut-rate apparel for American companies. Armed guards, many of them veterans of the Honduran Defense Forces (accused by human right groups of assassinations, drug-running, and torture of political prisoners), patrol the borders.

Most of the workers here are young and upwards of 80 percent are female. The average age of the Honduran sweatshop laborer is about fifteen, though some may be as young as ten. Workdays may stretch to fourteen hours, six days a week, in oppressive heat. Laborers are allowed only two tightly monitored breaks for water and bathroom use. And many days the work doesn't end at the factory. To meet production quotas, some workers lug their sewing home, where the entire family toils away late into the night.

Questions of health benefits, worker compensation, pensions and overtime pay simply have no relevance here. The issues facing workers inside these squalid factories are much more basic. It's about day-to-day survival, enduring the wrath of abusive managers, working through illness, injury, and depression. And it's about growing old very fast.

"It's hard and painful work," says Wendy Diaz, a sixteen-year-old Honduran girl who worked at the Global Fashions factory, making pants for sale at Wal-Mart under the "Kathie Lee Gifford" line. "I started work there at thirteen. The managers were cruel. They would yell at us all the time. They would lock the bathrooms all day long. When we got tired or talked to each other, they would beat us to keep us on schedule." Diaz's family couldn't afford to let her stay in school past the fifth grade. So she worked sixty-five hours a week, every week of the year.

This dire situation is hardly confined to Latin American countries or the garment industry. "Sweatshops are absolutely not limited to apparel," says Charles Kernaghan of the National Labor Committee in New York City. "Sporting goods, electronics, shoes, sneakers, agricultural products, coffee, bananas—you name it—it's made under some pretty rough conditions—in factories in Malaysia, the Philippines, Indonesia."

In Pakistan, children are often sold into servitude to factory owners where they are chained to looms for fifteen-hour days, making rugs and carpets for export to the United States; in Africa and Indonesia, male children, some only twelve years old, are sent into hazardous mines owned by American and Canadian firms to extract gold and silver that will be forged into rings and trinkets; in Colombia, children are forced into dangerous jobs making bricks or out into the coffee plantations to pick beans for Starbucks; in India, kids toil near blazing furnaces making glass bangles; in Siberia, American and Japanese timber companies are paying timber workers (one of the most dangerous professions) less than $1 an hour to log off the last wild forests in western Russia, home of the Siberian tiger. The Associated Press reported that there may be more than 200 million children working in overseas sweatshops producing goods for American consumers. This geography of shame is global, the dark underside of the new international economy.

In 1996, public concerns about overseas sweatshops prompted congressional hearings, lofty promises by apparel companies to more closely monitor their contractors and a presidential task force on the issue. In April 1997, following leafleting by the US/Guatemala Labor Education Campaign, Starbucks Coffee finally took action towards a pilot project that will implement a more humane code of conduct by coffee growers toward workers in Guatemala.

But so far there's no sign of a wide-spread shift toward restraints on child labor, better pay or safer working conditions. One reason for this is that new international trade pacts, such as GATT and NAFTA, make it difficult to enact sanctions against countries that permit labor abuses. And another reason is the obvious one: these cheap labor pools are enormously profitable for American corporations.

The consequences of the new global trade reach far beyond the wretched conditions inside the factories themselves. Environmental degradation is a hidden externality of the shift in industrial production from developed countries to Latin America and Southeast Asia. The new plants consume enormous amounts of energy in areas where power supplies have been primitive in the past. To meet the increased demand, Indonesia and Mexico have begun constructing huge coal-fired power plants, posing a grave threat to air quality in places like Jakarta and Mexico City. Similarly, China is in the midst of building dozens of new coal-fired plants that will emit thousands of tons of greenhouse gases each year, a dangerous contribution to global warming trends. But China also has more monumental ambitions: the Three Gorges hydroelectric dam. The 800-foot tall dam is the largest construction project since the building of the pyramids. It will impound nearly 400 miles of the Yangtze River, destroy the habitat of more than two dozen rare and endangered species, and force the dislocation of nearly 3 million people, all in order to power an estimated 2,500 new factories in China's southern provinces.

The attraction of Latin American and Southeast Asia for US companies, such as Sears, Gitano, and Eddie Bauer, is easy to understand: no pesky environmental standards to put up with, no worker safety codes, minuscule corporate taxes, and astoundingly cheap labor costs. In Haiti, for example, workers making the lucrative, movie-related clothing lines for Disney make no more than 28 cents an hour, or around $40 per month. Even in this impoverished country, that's not enough to live on without making sacrifices. Some costs, such as rent (which can consume half of the monthly pay), cannot be reduced. So usually it comes down to eating less. As Bob Herbert, a columnist with the *New York Times*, observes, these companies "thrive on the empty stomachs and other hardships of young women overseas."

Though largely unremarked on by the mainstream press and the American public, this situation has been building for more than a decade. During the mid-1970s, the US enjoyed a $3 billion trade surplus. Since 1976, however, America has suffered from a spiraling trade deficit, reaching $170 billion a year in 1987. US corporations that have shifted manufacturing operations overseas account for nearly 60 percent of this figure. The US Commerce Department reports that nearly 60 percent of the apparel sold in the United States in 1996 was imported, nearly twice the level of 1980. Most of these garments are made in sweatshops throughout the Third World, utilizing child labor.

Despite airy promises of tough standards on working conditions and environmental protection, international trade agreements passed in the early 1990s, such as NAFTA and GATT, have merely exacerbated the problem, according to Sarah Anderson, a researcher at the Institute for Policy Studies in Washington, DC. US companies, such as General Electric, Louisiana-Pacific, and Alcoa, have flocked to the Mexico to take advantage of the country's meager environmental provisions. The toxic legacy of this migration is already showing up. Alcoa, which has been hit with some of the largest criminal fines for hazardous waste violations in US history, opened a plant in Ciudad Acuña in 1993. Within a year, a series of poisonous gas leaks sent 226 workers to the hospital. When workers at GE's Ciudad Juárez plant talked to reporters about the deadly chemicals used at the factory, they were fired.

The figures on jobs lost in the US due to NAFTA are also sobering. Anderson points to a study from the University of Maryland that estimates that in 1994 alone more than 150,000 US jobs were lost as a result of Mexican imports—90,000 of those jobs in the apparel industry. The US Department of Labor estimates that America may lose another 759,000 manufacturing jobs by the year 2010.

"We find ourselves in a wage race with the rest of the world," says Charles Kernaghan. "It's a race to the bottom of the pay scale." The real wages of American workers have declined about 8 percent since 1989. Forced to compete with overseas sweatshops, American garment workers have watched their pay decline by more than 12 percent. But this trend shows up most starkly in the pay of American farm-workers, which has fallen by more than 20 percent in the last two decades. In the broccoli fields of California's Parajo Valley, workers are paid only $2.50 per box of broccoli picked, down from $3.70 in 1986. Meanwhile, truckloads of low-cost (and pesticide-laden) Mexican broccoli, strawberries, and other fruits and vegetables stream across the border every day.

This disaster for workers and the environment has been a bonanza for hundreds of multinational corporations. Take Nike, ostensibly an Oregon-based company that now controls 35 percent of the athletic shoe and apparel market. It began making shoes in Japan in 1967, where production costs were a quarter of that in the United States and Europe.

Rising labor costs prompted its production factories to move to South Korea in 1972. Donald Katz writes in *Just Do It*, a best-selling book about Nike, that the shoe plants were run by a combination "of terror and browbeating." After Korean workers won labor rights in the mid-1980s, Nike picked up its bags and moved once again, this time to Indonesia and China. In the mid-1990s Nike began to shift operations to an even more pliant labor market: Vietnam.

In Vietnam, Nike employs more than 25,000 workers who produce nearly a million pairs of shoes each year. The conditions are grim. Thuyen Nguyen of Vietnam Labor Watch, a New York-based group, says that Nike workers are subject to intense verbal, physical, and sexual abuse. In one factory outside Ho Chi Minh City, nearly sixty female workers were forced to run laps around the factory as punishment for not wearing the proper shoes. A dozen of the women fainted in the oppressive heat and had to be hospitalized. In another instance, twelve female workers were viciously beaten on the head with a shoe by plant supervisors. As discipline for talking on the factory floor, workers have had their mouths sealed with duct tape. "Nike is clearly not controlling its contractors," Thuyen said. "And the company has known that for a long time."

There's a simple reason companies like Nike have continued to turn a blind eye to these abuses: skyrocketing corporate profits. In Vietnam, it costs Nike only $1.50 to manufacture a pair of basketball shoes that can be sold for $150 in the US. The production costs are low largely because the average pay of a Nike worker in Vietnam is only $42 a month or about $500 a year. Compare this tiny sum to the $20 million a year Nike lavished on Michael Jordan to pitch its basketball shoes, shorts, and hats. Jordan's salary amounts to nearly twice the annual payroll of the entire workforce of Nike contractors in Vietnam. The disparity with Nike CEO Phil Knight's annual take is even more grotesque. Knight, who owns 100 million shares of Nike stock, pulls in roughly $80 million in dividend payments each fiscal quarter. At that pace, a Vietnamese worker would need to toil for nearly 4,000 years to equal Knight's annual income.

None of this seemed to penetrate too deeply into the popular consciousness until the National Labor Committee revealed, in 1996, that talk-show hostess Kathie Lee Gifford's Wal-Mart clothing line was manufactured by child laborers in Honduran work camps. Initially, Gifford denied the reports. Confronted with incontrovertible evidence, Gifford disclaimed any knowledge of the work camps. When it was later shown that some of her blouses had been assembled under sweatshop conditions at the Seo Fashions factory in New York City, Kathie Lee sent her husband, Frank, to hand out envelopes stuffed with $300 to underpaid laborers who had been making her clothing line. Wal-Mart later said it would reimburse the Giffords.

Shortly after Kathy Lee's embarrassing news, appalled American consumers began asking serious questions about the conditions under which consumer goods were being made. With the attention of the press and the public finally aroused, President Clinton convened a special task force to develop global labor standards for the apparel industry. The presidential panel included companies such as Nike, Reebok, Patagonia, and Liz Claiborne; two labor unions (Union of Needletrades, Industrial, and Textile Employees—UNITE—and the Retail, Wholesale, and Department Store Union); and the Robert F. Kennedy Memorial Center for Human Rights.

The presidential panel agreed to establish a voluntary code of conduct on working conditions for overseas apparel factories used by American companies and provides for the monitoring of those factories to ensure compliance. Companies that meet standards established by the task force win the right to put a "No Sweat" label in their clothing, thereby assuring consumers that their merchandise is not made with sweatshop labor.

"The problem is that the labor and human rights groups ended up making most of the sacrifices," says Ellen Braune of the National Labor Committee. "But these are only proposed rules, there's still a chance to improve them with enough public pressure." First, companies agreed to establish a maximum sixty-hour work week, unless employees volunteer for more. But many workers, who aren't making even subsistence wages, will feel compelled to work as much time as they can physically endure. Others will often "volunteer" to do anything management wants because they'll be fired if they don't.

The panel rejected calls from human rights groups to adopt a "living wage policy" which would require contractors to pay at least subsistence wages. Instead, the agreement also calls for companies to voluntarily pay their workers the prevailing minimum wage. In many Asian countries the prevailing wage is as little as 20 cents per hour, which does not come close to subsistence levels. In Indonesia, for example, the minimum wage is $2.36 a day, while it takes $4 a day just to meet basic needs. And corporations can even get an exemption from that pathetic standard. Nike has already violated minimum wage standards in Indonesia, and Disney has done the same in Haiti.

Labor organizations lobbied fiercely for independent monitoring of the overseas factories by church and human rights groups, but business furiously fought off that proposal. In the end the crucial task of monitoring the agreement was left to US accounting firms paid by the apparel makers, such as Arthur Andersen, Peat Marwicks, and Coopers & Lybrand. American companies will be able to get away with paying overseas workers 20 cents per hour and be rewarded with the coveted "No Sweat" seal of approval as well. This outcome illustrates a huge drawback in the current trend toward labeling products as worker-and-environment friendly.

The reason companies like Nike pay people like Michael Jordan $20 million is that their profits depend more on the image of the company than the quality of their products. That's why direct pressure on the corporations such as Nike, The Gap, and Disney may be the most effective consumer strategy of all. Disney, for example, could not long withstand a campaign that tells people that Mickey Mouse t-shirts are made by Haitian kids in oppressive sweatshops where they aren't paid enough to eat. "If Americans knew what was going on down here, the yelling, the hitting, the abuse," says Wendy Diaz, "I'm sure that they would help stop the maltreatment."

BEAVERTON, OREGON.

Arkansas Bloodsuckers

THE YEAR BILL CLINTON BECAME GOVERNOR OF ARKANSAS, THAT STATE'S prison board awarded a fat contract to a Little Rock company called Health Management Associates, or HMA. The company was paid $3 million a year to run medical services for the state's prison system, which had been blasted in a ruling by the US Supreme Court as an "evil place run by some evil men."

HMA not only made money from providing medical care to prisoners, but it also started a profitable side venture: blood mining. The company paid prisoners $7 per pint of their blood. HMA then sold the blood on the international plasma market for $50 a pint, splitting the proceeds 50/50 with the Arkansas Department of Corrections. Since Arkansas is one of the few states that does not pay prisoners for their labor, inmates were frequent donors at the so-called "blood clinic." Hundreds of prisoners sold as much as two pints a week to HMA. The blood was then sold to pharmaceutical companies, such as Bayer and Baxter International; blood banks, such as the Red Cross; and so-called blood fractionizers, who transformed the blood into medicines for hemophiliacs.

HMA's contract with the Arkansas Department of Corrections and its entry into the blood market coincided with the rise of AIDS in the United States. Regardless, HMA did not screen the torrents of prison blood, even after the Food and Drug Administration issued special alerts about the higher incidents of AIDS and hepatitis in prison populations. When American drug companies and blood fractionizers stopped buying blood taken from prisoners in the early 1980s, HMA turned to the international blood market, selling to companies in Italy, France, Spain, and Japan. But the prime buyer of HMA's tainted blood, largely drawn from Cummings Unit prisoners in Grady, Arkansas, was a notorious Canadian firm called Continental Pharma Cryosan Ltd. Cryosan had a shady reputation in the medical industry. It had been nabbed importing blood taken from Russian cadavers and relabeling it as though it was from Swedish volunteers. The company also marketed blood taken from Haitian slums.

Cryosan passed the Arkansas prison blood on to the Canadian Red Cross and to European and Asian companies. The blood was recalled in 1983 after the FDA discovered contamination, but less than one-sixth of the blood was recovered. In Canada alone, more than 7,000 people have died from contaminated blood transfusions, many of them hemophiliacs. More than 4,000 of them died of AIDS. Another 40,000 people in Canada have contracted various forms of hepatitis.

Dr. Francis "Bud" Henderson started HMA in the 1970s. As the company began to expand, he brought in a Little Rock banker named Leonard Dunn to run the firm. Dunn was a political ally and friend of the Clintons. He was appointed by Clinton to sit on the Arkansas Industrial Development Commission and served as finance chair of Clinton's 1990 gubernatorial campaign. Later that same year, Dunn purchased the Madison Guaranty Savings and Loan (later to achieve great notoriety in the Whitewater Scandal) from Clinton's business partner, James MacDougal. Dunn later served as chief of staff to Arkansas' Lt. Governor, Winthrop Rockefeller.

Dunn's ties to Clinton served HMA well after the company came under scrutiny for both abusive treatment of prison patients and shoddy management of the blood center. In 1983, the Food and Drug Administration stripped HMA of its license to sell blood after it found that the company had failed to exclude donors that had tested positive for Hepatitis B, often a precursor of HIV.

A state police report, compiled as part of an investigation into the company's operations at the Cummings Unit, noted that the FDA pulled the company's license to sell blood "for falsifying records and shipping hot blood." The report goes on to say that "the suspension was for collecting and shipping plasma which had been collected from donors with a history of positive tests for [Hepatitis B]...the violations were directly related to using inmate labor in the record and donor reject list."

Dunn, and the Arkansas Department of Corrections, convinced the FDA that the fault lay with a prison guard who was taking kickbacks from prisoners in order to let them get back into the blood trade. The license was quickly restored and tainted blood once more began to flow.

That didn't end the investigations. HMA's contract was up for renewal by the prison board. When investigators began probing the company's practices, Dunn repeatedly boasted of his ties to Bill Clinton. "Mr. Dunn spoke openly and freely and explained to these investigators that he was the financial portion of the corporation as well as its political arm," investigator Sam Probasco stated in his report. "Dunn advised that he was close to Gov. Clinton as well as the majority of state politicians presently in office."

The allegations against the company involved numerous health and safety violations, failure to test for diseases such as Hepatitis and syphilis, bad record keeping, falsification of records, and drawing blood from multiple patients with the same needle. Several former prisoners at Cummings are now charging that they contracted hepatitis and AIDS from the blood program.

Another incident involved a botched operation in which an HMA doctor unnecessarily amputated a prisoner's leg at the hip. According to Michael Galster, a prosthetics specialist who worked at the Cummings Unit at the time, HMA hired Vince Foster, then with the Rose Law firm, to help squash the investigation. Galster says that Foster approached him asking that he build the prisoner an artificial leg, with the hope that it would prevent the prisoner from moving forward with a legal claim against the company.

"The purpose of his being there was to convince me to take this, smooth it over, and everybody would be happy," said Galster. "I refused him. He said, 'I understand your predicament. But this could make it difficult for you to get a future state contract.'"

Although Galster refused to go along, Foster seems to have accomplished his task. The state's internal investigation of HMA cleared the company of any wrongdoing.

But an independent review by the Institute for Law and Policy Planning, a California firm, concluded that HMA's work in the prisons was extremely deficient. The report cited more than forty contract violations and was replete with instances of negligence—in the care of patients and handling of the blood center. Much of the blame for the problem landed on another Clinton pal, Art Lockhart, who was the head of the Arkansas Department of Corrections.

When the independent review came out, pressure mounted for Clinton to fire Lockhart. Clinton swiftly nixed the idea, telling reporters that he didn't believe the allegations were serious enough for him to "ask Mr. Lockhart to resign."

The Arkansas State police launched a half-hearted investigation into allegations that HMA was awarded a renewal of its contract after they bribed members of the state prison board. The investigation soon focused an attorney named Richard Mays, a close friend of Bill and Hillary Clinton. Mays was given at least $25,000 by HMA to act as an "ombudsman" for the company, a position that featured no job description and no apparent responsibilities.

Mays, who served as a vice-president for finance at the DNC, has been at the heart of several Clinton scandals. In 1996, he was credited with securing Little Rock restauranteur Charlie Trie's $100,000 contribution to the Democratic Party's coffers. He also appears in the Whitewater probe, where he tried to stave off the federal prosecution of David Hale. Mays and his wife were frequent guests the White House, including an overnight stay in the Lincoln bedroom. Dunn claims that Mays was recommended to him by Clinton, as well as prison board chairman and Clinton intimate, Woodson Walker.

In 1986, HMA's contract was revoked. But that didn't stop the Arkansas Department of Corrections' prison blood program. A new company, Pine Bluff Biologicals, took over the blood center and expanded it to include two other prison units. The new company's safety record turned out to be about as dismal as HMA's. Screening for AIDs was particularly lax. Pine Bluffs' president Jimmy Lord dismissed such concerns and suggested that AIDs was not a problem in Arkansas. "If anyone got caught in a homosexual act," Lords said, "we took them off the roster."

By the late 1980s, Arkansas was the only prison in the United States still running a blood program. In 1991, a reporter for the *Arkansas Times* asked John Byus, medical director of the Arkansas Corrections Department, how much longer they planned to continue the operation, and was told, "We plan to stick with it till the last day, to the last drop we're able to sell."

The blood trade program stayed in operation until Bill Clinton moved to Washington. It was finally shut down in 1993 by his successor, Jim "Guy" Tucker.

LITTLE ROCK.

What a Miner's Life is Worth

THE ONLY THING MORE PREDICTABLE THAN THE DEATHS OF THOSE TWELVE miners in the Sago coal mine on January 2, 2006 was the Bush administration's rush to exploit a tragedy that they helped foster.

Since 2001, Big Coal has benefited as Washington regulators have turn a blind eye to their rampages across Appalachia. The cost of such official laxity is borne by decapitated mountains, buried and polluted streams, and hundreds of miners injured and killed by an industry that has been liberated from even the most basic regulations governing worker safety and environmental protection.

The Sago miners didn't even have the minimal protections afforded by membership in a union. In the economics of coal country these days people are so desperate for a job that they will sign up for the most dangerous kind of work while asking few questions about the risks or the precautions taken by the companies. And that's exactly the way Big Coal wants it.

Since Bush arrived in Washington, more than 230 coal miners have perished in 206 mine accidents. Hundreds of others have been injured. Thousands suffer from chronic ailments and lung diseases caused by hazardous working conditions.

The Sago mine was a death trap. In 2005 alone, the Mine Safety and Health Administration slapped the mine with 208 citations for violations, ranging from the accumulation of flammable coal dust to ceiling collapses.

The accident rate at Sago was abysmal. In 2004, Sago had an accident rate of 15.90 accidents per 200,000 man-hours worked. This rate is nearly three times more than the national average of 5.66. The next year was even worse. In 2005, Sago's accident rate spiked to 17.04, with at least fourteen miners injured.

But these citations and accidents came without regulatory sanction. Most of them resulted only in negligible fines. In total, the mine was hit with just $24,000 worth of penalties. It's much cheaper to pay the fine than to fix the problems, even when the conditions are lethal. For example, in 2001 Jim Walters Resources paid only $3,000 in fines for an accident that led to the deaths of thirteen miners in Alabama. That's $230.76 per dead miner. The company earned more than $100 million that year. Other companies have paid less than $200 in fines for fatalities linked to safety violations.

And these token fines often go unpaid by the mining companies. A review of the Mine Safety and Health Administration's records since 2000 reveals that the agency has hit the mining industry with $9.1 million in fines following fatal incidents. But the companies have paid less than 30 percent of that puny amount.

All a company has to do is appeal its fine, and it will likely be reduced. More than $5.2 million in fines have been reduced to $2.5 million following appeals. Another $2.2 million is unpaid pending appeal. The agency lists more than $1.1 million in fines as being delinquent, but most of those mines remain in operation.

Under the Bush administration, Big Coal has essentially been handed the responsibility for regulating its own behavior, with few questions asked. Even in the aftermath of the Sago disaster there were no serious calls for congressional hearings or criminal sanctions against the mine bosses and their corporate chieftains. The biggest outrage was reserved for the false report, which stated that the twelve miners had miraculously survived their ordeal in the poisonous pit, where carbon monoxide levels had reached 1,300 parts per million, more than three times the maximum safety level.

Naturally, the Democrats offer the miners almost no relief. In the 2004 presidential campaign, when the election hinged on results from the coal belt, John Kerry wrote off the mining country of southeast Ohio and West Virginia, counties burdened by the highest unemployment in country, and lost by landslide margins to Bush.

If you're going to tie black ribbon on the gates of the White House, you might as well wrap one around a tree outside one of the Kerry-Heinz mansions, as well. Neither party gave a damn about the lives of those men.

The Cancer Agents of the FBI:
The Great Green Scare

WITH NOTHING MUCH BETTER TO DO AND AN UNLIMITED BUDGET TO burn, the FBI is turning its mighty inquisitorial arsenal on environmental groups across the country. Even now the feds are scouring green outfits from Moscow, Idaho to Cancer Alley Parish, Louisiana, looking to round up bands of eco-terrorists, the Osama Bin Ladens of the American outback.

Back in Reagantime the rightwingers smeared environmentalists as watermelons: green on the outside, red on the inside. In those halcyon days, economist John Baden, major domo of a rightwing think tank called FREE and the Svengali of the Sagebrush Rebels, made a small fortune hawking watermelon ties, woven of the finest petro-polyester, to his retinue of oil execs, federal judges, and range lords. Now that cap-C Communism has faded into the oblivion of high-school history text books, the corporate world's PR flacks have had to concoct a new spine-tingling metaphor to evoke the threat environmentalism poses to their bottom line: eco-terrorism.

Apparently, it's just a short step from al Qaeda to PETA. The money you save from not buying fur may be going to finance terrorist raids to liberate condemned mink from their isolation cages on rodent death row in Corvallis, Oregon.

The feds haven't had much luck finding Bin Laden. And our mean-spirited Clouseaus didn't stop any of Osama's kamikazes, even though their own agents shouted out repeated internal alarums. And when the whistle-blowing agents went public, the FBI brass cracked down on them, gagged some and gave others—such as the courageous Sibel Edmunds—the boot.

Several of the feds' biggest terrorism arrests have blown up in their faces. In Portland, Oregon, the FBI seized attorney Brandon Mayfield, trumpeting to the press that the mild-mannered immigration lawyer was a long-distance mastermind behind the Madrid train bombings, a Fu Manchu in Birkenstocks. The feds said the technicians in their crime lab had detected Mayfield's fingerprints on a bag found near the bomb site that was linked to the terrorists. After several harrowing weeks, he was released by a disgusted federal judge, over the FBI's virulent objections, after Spanish investigators revealed that the fatal fingerprint bore not the faintest resemblance to Mayfield's and, in fact, belonged to an Algerian. Yet another crushing blow to the FBI crime lab.

And after four years, the FBI's snark hunt for the anthrax killer has also come up empty.

So perhaps tree huggers shouldn't sweat these menacing invigilations from the big heat.

Then again perhaps they *should* worry.

What the FBI is truly proficient at is destroying the lives of innocent people, such as Brandon Mayfield, Judi Bari, and Wen Ho Lee. That's when they don't simply kill you outright, as they did to Fred Hampton; the blameless men, women, and kids in that house of flames in Waco; and Randy Weaver's wife, Vicki, as she held an infant in her arms on the front porch of their cabin at Ruby Ridge.

Armed with the bulging array of new police and surveillance powers handed to the agency in the wake of 9/11, the FBI is now free to prowl unfettered by even the thinnest strands of constitutional due process through the lives, email, and bank accounts of activists trying stop chemical plants from flushing toxins into their water or logging companies from slaughtering 800-year-old trees on lands that are purportedly part of the public estate.

In other words, the FBI is acting as a federally-funded paramilitary force for the cancer industry and Extinction, Incorporated, as the Pinkerton Agency and National Guard once did for Anaconda Copper and Standard Oil.

Apparently, no one has told Robert Mueller that the corpse of Edward Abbey has been moldering in the Arizona desert for fifteen years, his place taken by touchy-feely greens funded by organic body product companies, like Julia Butterfly, who would rather talk to trees than drive spikes into them for their own good.

This kind of glaring nuance won't deter an agency that persists in peddling the discredited slur that Judi Bari bombed herself.

Over on FoxNews, blinking eco-terrorist alerts replaced Tom Ridge's color-coded threat level as the latest alarmist metronome to distract viewer attention from the plight of Karl Rove, the convictions of corporate tycoons, and the bloodbath in Iraq.

Earlier this summer, FoxNews devoted extensive coverage to congressional testimony by John Lewis, the FBI's Deputy Director for Counterterrorism. Deftly sidestepping border vigilantes, anti-abortion zealots, and white supremacists, Lewis pointed to environmentalists as the great looming internal threat to the security of the nation. Lewis breathlessly claimed that the FBI had documented more than 1,200 acts of eco-terrorism over the last fifteen years, inflicting $110 million in property damage—or about the same amount that timber companies steal from the national forests each year. Oddly, executives at the Weyerhaeuser Company—a repeat offender—haven't done any time in Pelican Bay lately.

Most of these hotly reported stories fizzled out, with the purported acts of eco-terrorism turning to be insurance scams, disputes between neighbors or angry employees venting their rage with a match and a gallon of gasoline.

In December of 2004, more than a dozen homes in a Maryland subdivision near a wildlife reserve were torched. Before the embers from the smoldering houses had cooled, the FBI publicly fingered eco-terrorists for the arson. But it soon emerged that the fires in the largely middle-class black neighborhood had been committed by a drunken gang of white power pyromaniacs, called "The Family."

Meanwhile, the Rev. Pat Robertson broadcasts assassination proclamations on national television. Praise the lord and pay the hit man. Operation Rescue's Randal Terry publicly threatened federal judges during the national trauma over Terri Schiavo. One of David Horowitz's featured writers on *Frontpage* called for "Chomsky, Howard Zinn, Michael Parenti, Michael Moore, Ward Churchill, and [Justin] Raimondos to be found shot full of holes." A beer-gutted ultra-Patriot in Chicago openly pleaded online for the execution of Stan Goff, Alexander Cockburn, and your humble scribe.

None of these would-be terrorists are currently deemed a public menace by the FBI. Rev. Robertson's notoriously corrupt Operation Blessing is even sanctioned to receive FEMA money.

Over the past quarter of a century, only abortion providers and Muslim clerics have been on the receiving end of more death threats than environmental organizers. It comes with the territory. But these virulent acts of harassment—messages often driven home with dead Spotted Owls, bullet casings, and rocks through the front window— rarely rouse the interest of the FBI or even local cops. Apparently, the agency doesn't consider the violent suppression of political speech a terrorist act.

The environmental movement hasn't issued any fatwahs lately. Indeed, the greens haven't had many successes at all since Clinton and Gore drained the spinal fluid out of the big greens back in the mid-90s. With a few feisty exceptions in Montana, Oregon, and Louisiana, the movement is a paper tiger these days. Paper tigers are easily bullied into turning on their own, snitching out radical voices in order to protect their own sinecure, which may be the point.

The lack of a body count from green sleeper cells hasn't stopped the FBI from amassing bulging files on dozens of environmental organizers and environmental groups. This is an agency that harbored files on Sinatra, Liberace, and Louis Armstrong. Satchmo, though, certainly posed a greater threat to the nation's ruling elite than has ever been evinced by the National Audubon Society. In these tremulous times, it's the environmental activist who doesn't have an FBI file who should bear the greatest scrutiny—there's your potential infiltrator. So perhaps the FBI had done the environmental movement a service. The next time you're thinking about giving a green group a contribution, ask to see their FBI file. If it's thinner than 100 pages, donate to another group.

The feds display a particular obsession with Greenpeace. A recent lawsuit filed by the ACLU forced the FBI to reveal that it had accumulated more than 2,400 pages of information on Greenpeace. While they may be the Bush administration's most visible environmental critic, this isn't your grandfather's Greenpeace. Today's Greenpeace has largely abandoned the flashy direct actions of yore for glossy direct mailings and run-of-the-mill lobbying efforts. Think National Wildlife Federation with tongue-piercings.

And let us never forget that while Greenpeace has never been charged with any terrorist act, it has been the victim of a lethal terrorist bombing. In 1985, two French secret agents detonated three limpet mines on the hull of the Rainbow Warrior while it was docked in Auckland Harbor. The explosions killed Fernando Pereira, a Portuguese photographer.

Even the feds can't cite a single death resulting from an alleged act of eco-terrorism. But that doesn't matter. After the horrors of New Orleans, it should be clear to all that it's the protection of property, not people, that really gets the feds going.

Destruction of property in the name of a political cause is now deemed an act of terrorism that can carry with it prison terms equivalent to first-degree murder and allows the FBI to deploy the extra-constitutional powers granted by the PATRIOT Act and other anti-terrorism laws.

Take the strange ordeal of Tre Arrow, who faces a life sentence on federal charges of burning a cement truck and logging equipment in the ancient forests of Oregon. Today, Mr. Arrow, who denies the allegations against him, is being held in Canada, where he is fighting extradition. Those machines torched in the Oregon forests were valued at less than $500,000 combined. Yet Arrow, still in his twenties, is looking at seventy years hard time in federal prison. Compare that to the Nero of Tyco, Dennis Kozlowski, convicted, along with his partner in crime Mark Swartz, of stealing $600 million from his company. Kozlowski will be eligible for parole in seven years. Enron's Meyer Lansky (AKA Andrew Fastow), the numbers man responsible for engineering an accounting scheme that resulted in the largest bankruptcy in US history, got ten years in Club Fed—and he almost certainly won't serve all of that. They never do.

Under several state laws, and a bill introduced in the US congress by Rep. Richard Pombo, you don't even have to destroy property to be considered an eco-terrorist. All you have to do is block access to an animal research facility. Chain yourself to the door of entry into a Dachau of the chimp world and you might find yourself staring down a twenty-year prison term with all of your personal and organizational assets seized, as if you were a Colombian drug kingpin. Here the barbaric RICO statutes are being cast out as the agency's prosecutorial driftnet.

The crackdown on greens is happening at a time when legally sanctioned avenues of dissent against polluters and pillagers of nature are being foreclosed daily, as congress and the Bush administration curtail abilities to appeal and litigate federal rulings threatening the environment. It's even getting tougher and tougher to find out what is actually going on. With 9/11 as the inevitable rationale, the Bush administration shuttered the Toxic Release Inventory, which disclosed the kinds and amounts of pollutants spewed into the water and air by chemical plants, and squeezed the Freedom of Information Act in the name of national security (read: corporate wet dream). What was once a fundamental right of remonstrance against governmental and corporate outrages is now considered an act of sedition.

So this FBI witch-hunt is already well underway and will soon be coming to a community group near you. The lives of part-time activists, mothers, nurses, students, will be turned upside down. They will be harassed, bullied, and encouraged to inform on their colleagues. Organizations will be infiltrated and wrecked from the inside. False stories will be planted in the press. Environmental funders will be scared off. Foundations will be audited, hauled before hostile congressional committees, and threatened with revocation of their tax status. It's a creepy new twist in an old narrative.

Being an FBI agent means never having to say you're sorry. Just ask Richard Jewel, the man they wrongly fingered for the Olympic Park bombings.

EUGENE, OREGON.

The Scourging of Willie Fontenot: A Cancer Alley Story

FOR THE PAST THIRTY YEARS, THE PEOPLE LIVING AMID THE CHEMICAL plants and oil refineries along the Mississippi River, in the blighted area of Louisiana known as Cancer Alley, have had one steadfast ally in the halls of a state government that has set the high bar for official corruption. That ally: Willie Fontenot.

Since 1978, Fontenot has served as the community liaison officer for the Louisiana Attorney General's Office, where he helped small towns, many of them black, poor, and traditionally powerless, to organize themselves to confront global oil and chemical giants that are using their backyards as dumping grounds for toxic waste.

Fontenot was appointed by former Louisiana Attorney General, Billy Guste, Jr., a rare reform-minded state official, who was bothered by mounting reports of soaring cancers rates in black communities in the Delta region. "My job title was community liaison officer," says Fontenot. "When I started, it was part of the citizen access unit. Attorney General Guste said, 'The citizens need some help dealing with environmental problems, how to file a complaint, how to figure out what their problems are, how to work with public officials and the news media.'"

Over a span of nearly three decades, Fontenot assisted in the creation and organization of more than 400 community and environmental groups in Louisiana and across the deep south, a region scarred by the nearly unfettered rampages of the petro-chemical cartel. Fontenot earned a reputation as one of the nation's most effective voices for environmental justice.

Fontenot spent much of his time working in desolate small towns in the Mississippi Delta region, snaking the eighty river miles from Baton Rogue to New Orleans, where more than fifty-three chemical plants and oil refineries cluster along the river bank in grim groves of poison-belching stacks.

Welcome to Cancer Alley.

Louisiana leads the nation in cancer deaths, and cancer mortality among blacks in these Delta towns far outpaces that of whites in the state. The state ranks fourth in heart disease, and the Cancer Alley parishes score the highest rate of heart disease in the state. Both heart disease and strokes have been linked to air pollution. Louisiana is also at or near the top of the list in birth defects, respiratory diseases and learning disabilities. Only Texas, a state five times its size, generates more hazardous waste and toxic chemicals.

Down here in the Chemical Corridor, America's homegrown weapons of mass destruction—in the form of dioxin, mercury, and chlorine—are going off day after day, sprinkling poison into the lungs of the living and the bloodstreams of the unborn.

Down here in Cancer Alley, the weapons inspectors—environmentalists, lawyers, scientists, ministers—are regularly bullied, threatened, and run out of town.

Down here, both parties do the bidding of the oil and chemical industry—witness Democratic Senator Mary Landrieu's recent vote to open ANWR to drilling.

Down here, it's the rare brave bureaucrat who comes along with the courage to stand up and help people fight the corruption corroding Louisiana's political system from the inside out. Yet, that's what Willie Fontenot has done his entire career.

"A lot of people here think Willie's a hero," says Adam Babich, director of the Tulane Environmental Law Clinic in New Orleans. Babich knows a hero when he sees one. His own outfit has done much vital work in Cancer Alley, work that so unnerved the state's chemical industry that, in 1998, they got Louisiana's then governor, Mike Foster, to threaten the university with revocation of its tax-exempt status unless it pulled the plug on the law clinic. The university held firm, although the state Supreme Court, under pressure from the oil lobby and governor, soon moved to restrict the clinic's ability to represent poor communities in litigation against the big polluters.

But the people of Louisiana's most ravaged communities can no longer turn to Willie Fontenot for help in battling their abusers. On April 5, 2005, he was abruptly dismissed from his post without warning by the state's new Attorney General, Charles Foti, a darling of the oil industry. Fontenot said he was hauled into the AG's office and told he had a choice: retire immediately or be fired and risk losing his pension and health insurance. Fontenot retired.

The ouster of Fontenot was a long-sought goal of the oil and chemical junta that controls Louisiana politics and has turned the Mississippi Delta into one of the most toxic and cancer-stricken areas in North America. These companies are used to having complete control of all branches of government in Louisiana. After all, they had bought and paid for judges, governors, senators, and Attorneys General. But Fontenot, in his unique position within the AG's Office, had been a stubborn thorn in their side for many years, and with his help, small, impoverished communities with high unemployment and illiteracy rates had begun to stand up for themselves. Their struggle had briefly become a national story, until the Clinton administration suckered the press into believing that it had dealt sternly with the problem of environmental racism.

Then the oil industry scented blood, when they discovered that Fontenot was serving as a kind of tour guide to Cancer Alley for a group of master's students in environmental science from Antioch College in New Hampshire. Using the banner of

Homeland Security as a pretext, Fontenot, the students, and their two professors were detained by off-duty sheriffs—working as security guards for ExxonMobil—for taking photographs of the company's chemical plant, one of the most toxic in the nation. That sham arrest was then used as the basis to force Fontenot from his position.

Here's how this bizarre story played out.

Antioch College's Graduate School of Environmental Studies offers a field program called "Environmental Justice in the Mississippi Delta," which focuses on environmental racism in Cancer Alley. From March 14–25, thirteen master's students and two professors were slated to tour the Delta region to interview community leaders, environmentalists, residents, and industry executives.

On their second day out in the field, the group went to a small town called Norco, which has borne the brunt of toxic emissions from a giant chemical plant owned by Shell Oil. Several of the students took photographs of the sprawling facility standing on public property along the road outside the plant's grounds. The group was soon confronted by a corporate security guard, who briefly detained them. The guard lectured Steve Chase, the director of Antioch's Environmental Advocacy and Organizing Program, telling him that photographing chemical plants and oil refineries is a violation of federal law. He warned Chase that if his group continued taking such photographs they could expect a raid from the FBI.

The next day Willie Fontenot accompanied the group to a neighborhood in East Baton Rogue near the big ExxonMobil chemical plant, one of the nation's most poisonous. The emissions from the ExxonMobil facility are so foul and hazardous that the company was forced to buy out the properties of the entire neighborhood.

"We had just met with Baton Rogue mayor Kip Holden and went out to drive around and look at the industry in the area," said Abigail Abrash Walton, the other Antioch professor leading the trip. "We came to a house directly across from facility and Willie Fontenot let us know that the woman who lived there had decided not to relocate. So we pulled the van over on a side street and the students got out and took photos."

Once again, they were confronted by security forces. This time it only took two minutes for the guards to come, and this time the company cops were wearing official uniforms from the county sheriff's office and the Baton Rogue police department. It turned out that the pair were off-duty cops, moonlighting as security guards for ExxonMobil.

The guards detained the group and ordered Fontenot to collect driver's licenses from the students and the two professors. Fontenot refused, saying that he wasn't the leader of the group and that, while the police had a right to question them, they had no right to arrest them.

"I've researched this extensively over the years, because I often give tours for aca-demics and journalists" said Fontenot. "It's perfectly legal to stand on public property and photograph facilities."

Needless to say, this bit of constitutionally-based impertinence didn't sit well with the company goons.

One of the guards told Fontenot that he had seen three students trespass onto an ExxonMobil parking lot to take photos. This proved to be a lie. The entire stop had been videotaped by one of the students. The tape showed clearly that none of the students had strayed off public property.

When Abigail Walton asked whether a report on the incident was going to be written up and where it would be filed, she said one of the rent-a-cops "blew his top." The guard refused to answer her question, but began ranting at the group as if they were a band of eco-terrorists. He threatened to turn them over to the "Homeland Security" people who would detain them well into the night.

A public relations officer for ExxonMobil later said that the Maritime Transportation Security Act required the company to file a "suspicious activity report" with the Department of Homeland Security's National Response Center, which is then turned over for investigation by the US Coast Guard. But an official with the Coast Guard brushed this off, saying that it is not illegal to photograph industrial plants from public property.

After about an hour of cell phone calls and harassment, the corporate cops finally released the group.

The ordeal was over for the students from Antioch, but it was just beginning for Willie Fontenot. Shortly after the arrest, one of Exxon's cops called the Attorney General's office and griped about Fontenot being uncooperative with their secu-rity operation. Later that day, the sheriff's office lodged a formal complaint with the Attorney General about Fontenot.

The next day Fontenot was read the riot act at the Attorney General's office. After a short meeting, Fontenot was placed on administrative leave. A week later he was told to either resign or be terminated.

For the past thirteen years, Fontenot, sixty-two, has battled a degenerating eye disease. In fact, he is legally blind. In the past year, he has also suffered a mild stroke and is just finishing a course of radiation therapy for prostate cancer. The threat of being fired and possibly losing his health care was too high a risk for him to take. Fontenot opted for retirement.

When news of Fontenot's ouster leaked to the local press, the Attorney General's office began a smear campaign against their former community liaison. Attorney General Foti's press secretary, Kris Wartelle, suggested to some in the media that Fontenot was given the boot because he had not told his superiors of his plan to accompany the Antioch group. She also darkly suggested that Fontenot might be secretly in the employ of either Antioch or some fiendish environmental organization.

Neither slur holds up. Fontenot had joined similar outings hundreds of times. As was his usual habit, he prepared a detailed memo about the Antioch tour a month before the students arrived. On the morning he went to Baton Rogue, he told the office secretary precisely where he was going and with whom. Far from being in the employ of an environmental group, Fontenot paid his expenses out of his own pocket.

As for the students of Antioch, their harrowing experience was just a tiny taste of what environmentalists and community activists deal with every day down in the Delta.

"This incident showed our students a vivid example of how law enforcement and corporations can sometimes overstep their legitimate security duties in the guise of 'homeland security,'" says Abigail Walton. "We got a first-hand glimpse of the type of over-the-top repression that community members and their supporters told us they experience on the frontlines of trying to defend their communities' health and homes in Louisiana."

BATON ROGUE.

Pools of Fire: The Looming Nuclear Nightmare in the Woods of North Carolina

LOOKING FOR WEAPONS OF MASS DESTRUCTION? TRY THE BACKWOODS OF North Carolina. The site is easy to find. You don't need infrared telemetry, informants, or a global positioning satellite. Just follow the railroad tracks deep into the heart of the triangle area to the gleaming cooling tower of the Shearon Harris nuclear plant, which rises like a concrete beacon out of the forest.

It may not look like much—a run-of-the-mill nuke—but inside the confines of the steel fence that rings the plant, resides one of the most lethal patches of ground in North America. Shearon Harris is not just a nuclear power-generating station, but a repository for highly radioactive spent fuel rods from two other nuclear plants owned by Progress Energy.

Those railroad tracks? They're for hauling nuclear waste. The spent fuel rods are carted by rail from the Brunswick and Robinson nuclear reactors to Shearon Harris, where they are stored in four densely packed pools, filled with circulating cold water to keep the waste from heating up. The pools are interconnected and enclosed within one building. That building is attached to the reactor itself. Together, they form the largest radioactive waste storage pools in the country.

All this makes Shearon Harris a very inviting target for would-be terrorists. In fact, the Department of Homeland Security has fingered Shearon Harris as one of the most vulnerable terrorist targets in the nation.

Potential atomic terrorists don't have to steal plutonium, take a crash course in physics, or concoct a bomb to manufacture a radiological nightmare scenario in the heart of the Carolinas. All they have to do is penetrate the security fence of a lightly guarded commercial reactor and find a way to ignite the pools of high-level radioactive waste. The easiest method is to disrupt the circulation of the water system that keeps the pools cool.

The resulting fire would be virtually unquenchable. Moreover, because the water system that feeds the waste pools is also connected to the Shearon Harris reactor, a pool fire could also trigger a nuclear meltdown. And so it goes.

An uncontrolled pool fire and meltdown at Shearon Harris would put more than two million residents of this rapidly growing section of North Carolina in extreme peril. A recent study by the Brookhaven Labs, not known to overstate nuclear risks, estimates that a pool fire could cause 140,000 cancers, contaminate thousands of square miles of land, and cause over $500 billion in off-site property damage.

An October 2000 report from the Sandia Labs in Albuquerque painted a grim picture of the consequences from a pool fire. The report, which was kept under wraps for two years by the NRC, found that a waste pool fire could spread radioactive debris over a 500-mile radius, including Cesium-137, a carcinogen linked to birth defects and genetic damage.

When details from this report leaked out to the press, Mike Easley, the governor of North Carolina, responded by ordering that iodine pills be distributed to neighbors of the plant. It was a touching gesture. But iodine is no defense against the ravages of Cesium-137.

Despite vows of beefed up security by the nuclear industry, it's not that difficult to break into most commercial nuclear plants and security at Shearon Harris is notoriously lax. In 1999, NRC records show that two Progress energy employees gained access to the reactor and the waste pools without security clearance. The energy company has hired numerous employees with questionable security backgrounds, including three guards who failed psychological exams and one with a criminal record.

The whole plant could go up without the intervention of terrorists. Basic mismanagement and design flaws in the plant could well do the trick. In fact, the NRC has estimated that there's a 1:100 chance of a pool fire happening under the rosiest scenario. And the dossier on the Shearon Harris plant is far from rosy.

In 1999, the nuclear plant experienced four emergency shutdowns, or SCRAMS. The problems led plant managers to tell the *Charlotte News and Observer* that they were "very disappointed," engaged in "soul searching," and unsure whether the string of malfunctions were "coincidental or a sign of deeper problems."

A few months later, in April 2000, the plant's safety monitoring system, designed to provide early warning of a serious emergency, failed. It wasn't the first time. Indeed, the emergency warning system at Shearon Harris has failed fifteen times since the plant opened in 1987.

Between January and July of 2002, Harris plant managers were forced to manually shut down the reactors four times. Then in August of that year, the plant automatically shut itself down when the outside power grid weakened.

Documents uncovered from the Nuclear Regulatory Commission reveal other problems at Shearon Harris. Inspectors have found "rubber and other foreign material" clogging the cooling lines in the plant's heat removal system. There are also internal memos from the plant reporting that many of its evacuation sirens within the ten-mile emergency zone surrounding the plant are inoperable during severe weather.

In 2002 the NRC put the plant on notice about nine unresolved safety issues detected during a fire prevention inspection by NRC investigators. The plant was hit with a "Security Level III Notice of Violation." When the NRC returned to the plant a few months later for a reinspection, it determined that the corrective actions were "not acceptable."

"Progress Energy is far above the industry average in three important areas: emergency reactor shutdowns, required inspections, and the fact that it has interconnected Harris reactor's cooling system to four high-level waste pools: the largest in the nation," says Jim Warren, executive director of North Carolina WARN.

The problems continue with a chilling regularity. In the spring of 2003 there were four emergency shut downs of the plant, including three SCRAMs over a four-day period in the middle of May. One of the incidents occurred when the reactor core failed to cool down during a refueling operation while the reactor dome was off of the plant—a potentially catastrophic series of events.

Between 1999 and 2003, there were twelve major problems requiring the shutdown of the plant. According to the NRC, the national average for commercial reactors is one shutdown per eighteen months.

The situation at Shearon Harris is made more dire by virtue of the fact that the reactor is directly tied into the cooling system for the spent fuel pools. A breakdown (or sabotage) in either system could lead to serious consequences in the other.

Congressman David Price, the North Carolina Democrat, sent the Nuclear Regulatory Commission a study of the situation by scientists at MIT and Princeton. The report pinpointed the waste pools as the biggest risk at the plant. "Spent fuel recently discharged from a reactor could heat up relatively rapidly and catch fire," wrote Bob Alvarez, a former advisor to the Department of Energy and co-author of the report. "The fire could well spread to older fuel. The long-term land contamination consequences of such an event could be significantly worse than Chernobyl."

The study recommended that the spent fuel pools be replaced with low density, open frame racks and that the older waste assemblages be placed in hardened, aboveground storage units. The change could be done relatively cheaply, costing the energy giant about $5 million a year—less than the $6.6 million annual bonus for Progress CEO Warren Cavanaugh.

But Progress scoffed at the idea and recruited the help of NRC Commissioner Edward McGaffigan to smear the MIT/Princeton report. In an internal memo, McGaffigan instructed NRC staffers to produce "a hard-hitting critique that sort of undermines the study deeply."

McGaffigan is a veteran cold-warrior and a nuclear zealot, who has worked for both Democrats and Republicans. A veteran of the National Security Council in the Reagan administration, McGaffigan took a special interest in promoting nuclear plants to US client states. He left the White House to serve as the chief policy aide on energy and defense issues for Senator Jeff Bingaman, the Democrat from New Mexico. In 1996,

President Clinton appointed him to the Nuclear Regulatory Commission, where he became a tireless proponent of nuclear power on the ludicrous grounds that it will slow the onslaught of global warming. McGaffigan has also consistently dismissed the risks associated with the transport and storage of nuclear waste. Just prior to leaving office, Clinton reappointed him to another full term in 2000.

McGaffigan's meddling outraged many anti-nuke activists. "There's a huge credibility in the federal regulatory agencies," said Lewis Pitts, an environmental attorney in North Carolina. "After 9/11, the nuclear industry faked a report to convince the public that an airplane hitting a nuke plant is nothing to worry about and now the NRC has directed the production of a bogus study to deny decades of science on the perils of pool fires."

If the worst happens, the blame will reside in Washington, which has permitted the Shearon Harris facility to become a nuclear time bomb. The atomic clock is ticking.

WILMINGTON, NORTH CAROLINA.

Bad Days at Indian Point

THESE ARE DESPERATE DAYS FOR ENTERGY, THE BIG ARKANSAS-BASED power conglomerate that owns the frail Indian Point nuclear plant, located on the east bank of the Hudson River outside Buchanan, New York—just twenty-two miles from Manhattan.

First, a scathing report issued in 2005 by a nuclear engineer fingered Indian Point as one of the five worst nuclear plants in the United States, and predicted that its emergency cooling system "is virtually certain to fail."

This disclosure was hotly followed by the release of a study conducted by the Los Alamos National Laboratory for the Nuclear Regulatory Commission that ominously concluded that the chances of a reactor meltdown increased by a factor of nearly 100 at Indian Point, because the plant's drainage pits (also known as containment sumps) are "almost certain" to be blocked with debris during an accident.

"The NRC has known about the containment sump problem at Indian Point since September 1996," said David Lochbaum, a nuclear safety engineer with the Union of Concerned Scientists. "The NRC cannot take more than a decade to fix a safety problem that places millions of Americans at undue risk."

Entergy and the NRC both downplayed the meltdown scenario and defended the leisurely pace of the planned repairs. Entergy says that there's no rush to fix the problems with the emergency system because a breakdown isn't likely in the first place.

But that's flirting with almost certain disaster. Entergy and the NRC are staking the lives of millions on odds of a single water pipe not breaking under pressure. The problem is that these very kinds of pipes have corroded and been breached at other nuclear plants, which featured similar pressurized water design. At the Davis-Bessie plant near Toledo, Ohio, a vessel head on one of the cooling water pipes had been nearly corroded away by acid and was dangerously close to rupturing.

The cooling water in these pipes is kept at a pressure of 2,200 pounds per square inch. If a pipe breaks, the 500-degree water would blow off as steam, tearing off plant insulation and coatings. The escaped water will pour into the plant's basement, where sump pumps are meant to draw the water back into the reactor core. But the Los Alamos tests showed that the cooling water would collect debris along the way that will clog up the mesh screens on the pipes leading back into the reactor. If this happens, the cooling of the reactor fuel would stop, the radioactive core would start to melt, and the plant will belch a radioactive plume that will threaten millions downwind.

All this would happen very fast. The Indian Point 2 reactor would exhaust all of its cooling water in less than twenty-three minutes, while the number 3 reactor would consume all of its water in only fourteen minutes. Try getting a nuclear plumber that quickly.

Yes, it sounds trite, but that's essentially what Entergy proposes as its quick fix to the meltdown scenario. Jim Steets, Entergy's spokesman on Indian Point matters, told the *New York Times* that the company was training its workers to scour the plant for flaking paint and potential debris, and that if an accident occurred, they would pump the water into the core more slowly, a plan that would buy plant managers and executives a few more minutes to flee the scene.

Where people would go and how they would get there in the event of a nuclear meltdown or other radioactive release at Indian Point is unclear. In September 2002, New York Governor George Pataki commissioned a report on Indian Point's evacuation plan. He picked James Lee Witt, the former Rose Law Firm attorney who served as head of FEMA during the Clinton administration, to oversee the investigation. At the time, Pataki said that he would support closure of the plant if Witt's report revealed that communities near the plant could not be safely evacuated.

Witt submitted his report on January 10, 2003. While somewhat timid and cautious, Witt concluded that Entergy's off-site evacuation plans for Indian Point were woefully inadequate.

Witt wrote: "It is our conclusion that the current radiological response system and capabilities are not adequate to overcome their combined weight and protect the people from an unacceptable dose of radiation in the event of a release from Indian Point, especially if the release is faster or larger than the design basis release."

In the end, Witt concluded that it was not possible to fix the evacuation plan, given the problems at the plant, the density of the nearby communities and looming security threats.

This scenario was followed by news that a review of the company's security record revealed that Entergy, in cahoots with the Nuclear Regulatory Commission, faked a test designed to determine whether the plant is vulnerable to a terrorist attack.

The NRC assured members of Congress that Entergy had developed a "strong defensive strategy and capability" for the plant and passed a so-called "force-on-force" test—a mock assault—with flying colors.

It turns out that the NRC gave Entergy officials months of advance warning about the test and then, as the Indian Point team cribbed for the exam, dumbed down the assault to ensure that they would pass.

Most assessments by the CIA and other intelligence agencies suggest that a raid on a nuclear plant would require a squad-sized force of between twelve and fourteen attack-ers, assaulting the plant by night, armed with explosives, machine guns with armor-penetrating bullets, and rocket-propelled grenades.

This isn't the attack that was repelled by the Entergy security team. Instead, Entergy's men battled off a squad of four mock terrorists, armed only with hunting rifles, who assaulted the plant in broad daylight. Moreover, the attacking squad weren't former Delta Force operatives trained in terrorist tactics, but security officers from a nearby nuclear plant, who assault the plant from only one point after crossing open fields in plain view of Indian Point's security guards.

Just to make sure that there were no surprises, the Entergy security team, which consisted largely of guards hired only for the test, was warned that a mock attack would take place sometime within the next hour. Even under these rigged conditions, Entergy barely passed the security test.

Environmentalists and anti-nuke activists living near the plant hoped this would be the final straw for the aging reactor. They marshaled their evidence of safety violations, inept evacuation plans, and lax security and headed off to offices of the most powerful Democrat in America, Hillary Clinton.

But Hillary remained as reserved as Pataki on Indian Point, issuing robotic requests for more studies, but refusing to call for the plant's closure. Not that her words mean much. The senator pledged to filibuster the nomination of Utah governor Mike Leavitt for director of the EPA. She ended up voting to confirm his nomination.

Of course, Hillary's ties to Entergy are almost primal. The Little Rock-based Entergy Corporation, which once employed John Huang, the infamous conduit to the Lippo Group, was one of Bill Clinton's main political sponsors, shoveling more than $100,000 into his campaign's bank accounts from 1992 to 1996.

The more plaintive the cries for Indian Point's closure, the more money Entergy spreads around to politicians with reputation for flexibility in these matters. Already this year, Entergy's New York Political Action Committee—ENPAC New York—has doled out more than $25,000 to New York politicians alone. Everyone got into the act from Pataki and Clinton to Democratic congressman Eliot Engel to lowlier foot-soldiers for the nuclear plant, including two state assemblymen; commissioners from Westchester and Orange counties; Bronx Borough president Adolfo Carrion; and state comptroller Alan Hevesi, whose election campaign was endorsed by the Sierra Club.

Political money isn't the only tool in Entergy's bag of tricks. In late October, community activists in the Bronx reported that emissaries from Entergy were canvassing black and Hispanic neighborhoods in New York City and Westchester County with an ominous warning: If Indian Point closes, air quality in urban areas will deteriorate and more blacks and Hispanics will develop respiratory illnesses. The Entergy reps told people that new coal-fired power plants would be built in their neighborhoods and urged them to sign a petition.

"In recent years, nearly all proposals for new power plants in New York state have been in or adjacent to areas with high concentrations of people of African descent and Latinos," a memo handed out at the door warns. There is, naturally, much truth to this claim, and Entergy is in a unique position to know, since throughout the Southeast the company has targeted its power plants in black neighborhoods, where it has heralded them as bringing economic engines for impoverished communities.

The canvassers also carried cell phones as they ambled from door to door. They hit the speed dial number of a local legislator, handed the phone to the resident and then prompted them on how to express their concerns about the possible closure of Indian Point.

The petition drive, which discreetly by-passed the thirteen predominately white districts in Westchester County, was run by a group calling itself by the lofty-sounding name: "The Campaign for Affordable Energy, Environmental & Economic Justice."

The group was supposedly based in Manhattan. In fact, it was created and wholly funded by Entergy.

NYACK, NEW YORK.

Downwinders Be Damned

J UST AS THE BUSH ADMINISTRATION CONTEMPLATED ORDERING UP A NEW generation of nuclear weapons (which may, in turn, spark a new round of nuclear testing in the high deserts of Nevada), the Center for Disease Control (CDC), a federal outpost in Atlanta charged with supervising the nation's physical well-being, pulled the plug on a long-term study into the dire health consequences from nuclear testing in the 1950s and 1960s on people living in the American southwest.

The study, started in 1997, was designed to track the thyroid conditions of 4,000 former students who lived in southwestern Utah and eastern Nevada in 1965, at the height of nuclear weapons testing at the Nevada Test Site. The lead rescarcher, Dr. Joseph L. Lyons, a professor at the University of Utah, was informed via a curtly worded letter that funding for the study had been inexplicably yanked.

The letter terminating the research in midstream was written by Michael A. McGeehin, director of the CDC's Division of Environmental Hazards and Health Effects. McGeehin claimed the study was killed because of financial considerations. "The CDC does not have the resources to extend funding for this study beyond the current budget period," McGeehin wrote. "We recommend that you take measures to close out this study by the end of the current budget period, which will occur on August 31, 2005."

The Utah Thyroid Disease Study was scarcely a financial burden on the federal purse. In seven years, the investigation into thyroid cancers linked to radioactive fallout cost the federal treasury only $8,049,988, roughly the amount the Pentagon spends every two hours in Iraq. From 1990 to 1995, the federal government spent more than $90 million in legal fees to fight off claims from downwinders and workers at nuclear weapons plants over the health consequences of bomb-making and testing.

Lyons believes, with good reason, that the study was axed for political reasons. "The only interpretation I can put on it is that the Bush administration doesn't want to know the health effects of fallout on American citizens," Lyons told the *Deseret News*.

The scientist also said it was an extremely rare occurrence for the CDC to pull funding in the middle of a major study. "I've never known it to happen before," said Lyons, who has been researching the links between cancer and fallout since 1977.

Located sixty-five miles northwest of Las Vegas, the Nevada Test Site, established in 1951, sprawls over 1,500 square miles of desert basin and range country. Between 1951 and 1992, the Pentagon and Department of Energy conducted at least 925 nuclear blasts at the site. More than 100 of the explosions were above ground, open-air tests that cast a radioactive pall over much of the American West. Even the underground tests vented plumes of radiation.

A 1997 study by the National Cancer Institute reported that the fallout from the blasts deposited large amounts of radioactive iodine across the lower-forty-eight states. The report concluded that the contamination was so severe that it may cause as many as 70,000 cases of thyroid cancer alone. By way of comparison, that's 65,000 more casualties than Saddam Hussein is alleged to have caused in his 1988 poison gas attack on the Kurdish village of Halabja.

It was Lyons' groundbreaking study in 1979 for the *New England Journal of Medicine* that proved that radioactive fallout from the open-air nuclear tests in Nevada led to increased incidents of cancer in communities downwind of the blasts. A subsequent study demonstrated that those same downwind communities faced an increased likelihood of leukemia deaths. These two reports prompted Congress to finally enact a fallout compensation measure for downwinders.

In 1993, Lyons and his colleagues began studying the thyroid conditions of former school children who lived downwind of the blasts. That research, published in the *Journal of the American Medical Association*, found that the schoolchildren exposed to the highest levels of radiation were 3.4 times more likely to suffer from thyroid tumors than would normally be expected.

Until 1970, these same students were monitored by federal researchers, who, unsurprisingly, claimed not to have found any link between exposure to fallout and thyroid tumors. But Lyons and his colleagues began examining those students as adults and found that fifty-eight of the former downwinders had nodules on their thyroids. Of those, eight were malignant tumors and eleven were benign tumors.

This initial study buttressed the theory held by Lyons and many other scientists that there is a lifetime risk to fallout exposure and that thyroid problems, in particular, develop very slowly across a span of decades. These results prompted Lyons to apply for funding from the CDC for a larger study that would examine the thyroid conditions of all 4,000 former schoolchildren in southwestern Utah and eastern Nevada—those who were originally identified in 1965 as being exposed to the most extreme levels of fallout from the blasts. The incidence of thyroid problems in those students was to be compared to a control group in Safford, Arizona.

One of the first problems Lyons ran into was the realization that the radioactive fallout extended farther than he anticipated, meaning that most of the population of Safford had also been exposed to radiation, though in much smaller doses. Fallout has gone global. When it comes to thermonuclear weapons, we all live downwind.

By the end of 2003, the researchers had tracked down more than 90 percent of the former students, most of whom agreed to be examined for the study. "We've already reported that there's an excess of tumors of the thyroid gland," Lyons said, "and we've got pretty strong indications that there are other disease problems that ought to be looked at."

Originally, Lyons planned to have the study completed within five years, but he encountered continual meddling and roadblocks from the CDC that consumed both time and much of the grant money. "The federal government put all kinds of bureaucratic hurdles in our path that were not part of the original agreement," Lyons contends.

The agreement called for Lyons research to be overseen by the University of Utah. Then the CDC said that the study needed to be scrutinized by an institutional review board at the CDC, a requirement that delayed the research by two years. Next the CDC informed Lyons that he had to submit the plans for his study to a panel at the National Academy of Sciences, an inquisition that lasted another two years. Then the CDC called for yet another review of Lyons' methodology by a three-person panel at the Department of Energy.

When Lyons and his colleagues finally got out into the field and began to get results, the CDC pulled the plug. "Essentially, they said, 'Tough luck, we don't want your study,'" said Lyons. "I've been working on this now since 1977. I'm about to retire and I'd really like to finish up this thyroid study and get some definitive answers."

Those answers might prove to be unsettling for the Bush administration as it pursues a new generation of nuclear weapons and grooms the killing grounds of the Nevada Test Site for another go-round of nuclear blasts.

People are getting sick and dying in the American Southwest and the Bush administration doesn't want them to learn why.

Downwinders be damned.

SALT LAKE CITY.

Nuclear Saviors? Kyoto, Gore, and the Atom Lobby

STRIDING INTO KYOTO CLAIMING TO BE A MIGHTY WARRIOR IN THE BATTLE against global warming was a familiar beast: the nuclear power industry. Some of the industry's biggest lobbyists, men such as James Curtis (a former deputy secretary of energy during the Reagan years), prowled the streets and sushi bars of this ancient city (itself running on juice from an aging nuke) angling for some positive words in the treaty for their troubled enterprise. The big reactor makers, GE, CBS, and Combustion Engineering, were there too, dissing the oil and coal lobby, downplaying the long-term viability of natural gas and generally treating the eco-summit as if it were an international trade show.

On the eve of the Climate Change summit, I was slipped a copy of the nuclear industry's Kyoto briefing book prepared by the Nuclear Energy Institute, a $100 million a year trade organization. The book was written by researchers at Bechtel, the giant construction firm that built dozens of nuclear plants across the globe. The document touts the latest "advanced light water nuclear reactor" as the most ecologically benign engineering feat since the solar panel, and argues that the only realistic way to reduce greenhouse gas emissions to 1990 levels in the next ten years is to bring at least an additional fifty reactors on-line. "Nuclear energy has been the largest single contributor to reduced air pollution in the world over the past twenty years," the NEI's Kyoto global warming book boasted. "And it promises to play an even greater role in the future, especially in developing countries, like India and China, which need to increase their electricity supplies to accommodate their expanding populations and economies."

The NEI book tactfully avoided the unsavory subject of radioactive waste, but did go to some lengths to argue on behalf of China's vigilance in the battle against nuclear proliferation. China, the NEI suggested, would never secretly export nuclear technology because it "has expressed strong concern over the possibility of nuclear-armed neighbors." More significantly, the NEI warned that China "plans to standardize its nuclear generating technology, selecting one or two standardized reactor designs for future construction. If US reactor manufacturers are barred from competing, China will not have the option of selecting the safest technology in the world, and the market will be permanently closed to US suppliers."

With China and other Asian countries planning to build more than seventy nuclear plants by 2025, the financial stakes are staggering. American companies, such as GE,

Westinghouse, and Bechtel, crave those multi-billion dollar contracts. "In theory these could all be US plants," boasted Ian Butterfield, CBS' vice-president for international affairs. With a little help from the US government.

The NEI's Kyoto packet includes a long list of endorsements ranging from Tom Clancy and Pope John Paul II to Hazel O'Leary and green guru James Lovelock, inventor of the Gaia Hypothesis, who is quoted as saying, "Nuclear power has an important contribution to make." Also proudly displayed for the Kyoto conferees was a statement by Al Gore's good friend, Rep. Bob Clement, Democrat from Tennessee, who pronounced, "With the implementation of the Clean Air Act and the administration's increased concern about global climate change and acid rain, renewed attention has been focused on nuclear energy's significant environmental benefits. Environmental awareness coupled with increased basic needs for electricity are becoming critical in certain regions of the country. Nuclear energy, along with a strong conservation program and energy efficiency programs, is a smart choice."

Sadly for the credibility of the atom lobby, some of the more eye-grabbing numbers in the NEI's report simply didn't check out. For example, the nuclear industry claims that the world's 447 nuclear plants reduce CO_2 emissions by 30 percent. But the true villain behind global warming is carbon. Existing nuclear plants save only about 5 percent of total carbon emissions, hardly much of a bargain given the costs and risks associated with nuclear power. Moreover, the nuclear lobby likes to compare its record to coal-fired plants, rather than renewables such as solar, wind, and geothermal. Even when compared to costs of coal-fired plants, nuclear power fails the test if investments are made to increase the efficient use of the existing energy supply. One recent study by the Rocky Mountain Institute found that "even under the most optimistic cost projections for future nuclear electricity, efficiency is found to be 2.5 to ten times more cost effective for CO_2-abatement. Thus, to the extent that investments in nuclear power divert funds away from efficiency, the pursuit of a nuclear response to global warming would effectively exacerbate the problem."

The activities of the Nuclear Energy Institute do not meet with universal approbation in the nuclear industry. The dues are onerous—the Tennessee Valley Authority is reputed to fork up no less than $10 million a year—while the results are in some cases at least, risible. Some years ago, for example, the watchdogs of the industry noted that *The Simpsons*, the enormously popular cartoon series, was depicting nuclear power in an unfavorable light. Bart Simpson's father Homer works at a local nuclear plant where the reactors are held together with chewing gum, and a river fed by waste-water from the plant is rife with three-eyed trout and other mutations. The NEI sprang into action, sponsoring intensive briefings and tours of reassuringly shiny nuclear facilities for the Simpson's creative team—all without any discernible effect on Homer Simpson, who continues to absent-mindedly drop radioactive fuel rods into his pocket at work and then toss them out of the car on the way home.

In many ways, the NEI's global warming initiative is largely a replay of their attempt to profit off of acid rain legislation in the late 1980s, a campaign that miserably failed to attract much sympathy from legislators, and only seemed to anger the public. But in Clintontime the NEI encountered a somewhat warmer reception in the White House and on the Hill. Indeed, in the weeks before the Kyoto conclave, the nuclear industry scored a series of amazing triumphs not seen since the waning days of the Reagan administration.

One reason for its renewed success may be that the NEI began putting its money into more profitable investments than its campaign to greenwash *The Simpsons*, namely into the coffers of the DNC and RNC. In the four years before Kyoto, the NEI and its members doled out $13 million in political contributions to key senate and house members, including John Dingell ($122,700), Tom Delay ($106,500), Dick Gephardt ($104,000), Thomas Bliley ($100,000), and David Bonior ($80,075).

Another reason for its success is that the nuclear lobby has enjoyed a long and profitable relationship with both Clinton and Gore. Al Gore, who wrote of the potential green virtues of nuclear power in his book *Earth in the Balance*, earned his stripes as a congressman protecting the interests of two of the nuclear industry's most problematic enterprises, the TVA and the Oak Ridge Labs. And, of course, Bill Clinton backed the Entergy Corporation's outrageous plan to soak Arkansas ratepayers with the cost overruns on the company's Grand Gulf reactor which provided power to electricity consumers in Louisiana.

First came the deal to begin selling nuclear reactors to China, announced during Jiang Zemin's 1997 Washington visit, even though Zemin brazenly vowed at the time not to abide by the so-called "full scope safeguards" spelled out in the International Atomic Energy Act. The move was apparently made over the objections of Clinton's National Security Advisor Sandy Berger, who cited repeated exports by China of "dual use" technologies to Iran, Pakistan, and Iraq. The CIA also weighed in against the deal, pointing out in a report to the president that "China was the single most import supplier of equipment and technology for weapons of mass destruction" worldwide. In a press conference on the deal, Mike McCurry said these nuclear reactors will be "a lot better for the planet than a bunch of dirty coal-fired plants" and will be "a great opportunity for American vendors"—that is, Westinghouse.

A day later Clinton signed an agreement to begin selling nuclear technology to Brazil and Argentina for the first time since 1978, when Jimmy Carter canceled a previous deal after repeated violations of safety guidelines and nonproliferation agreements.

In a letter to congress, Clinton vouched for the South American countries, saying they had made "a definitive break with earlier ambivalent nuclear policies." Deputy National Security Advisor Jim Steinberg justified the nuclear pact with Brazil and Argentina as "a partnership in developing clean and reliable energy supplies for the future." Steinberg noted that both countries had opposed binding limits on greenhouse emissions and that new nuclear plants would be one way "to take advantage of the fact that today we have technologies available for energy use that were not available at the time that the United States and other developed countries were going through their periods of development."

On the eve of the Kyoto meetings, the nuclear industry secured another startling windfall, this time a promise of nearly $400 million in research and development subsidies. The key man here was one of Al Gore's intellectual Svengalis, John P. Holdren. While a professor at Berkeley, Holdren portrayed himself as a mighty foe of nuclear weapons. His popularity among Berkeley students soared after he gave ecological backing to Carl Sagan's scary scenarios about nuclear winter. Now Holdren is ensconced at Harvard's Kennedy School of Government, where he presides as the John and Teresa Heinz professor of environmental policy. Yes, that Teresa Heinz, she of the $2 billion fortune, wife of John Kerry, and head of a $200 million foundation which gives money for "practical solutions to global environmental problems." She is also a long-time board member of the nuke-happy Environmental Defense Fund.

Holdren was tapped by Gore and Clinton's science advisor Jack Gibbons to head a task force on energy and climate policy as part of the Presidential Commission on Science and Technology. Holdren's panel was well stocked with allies of the nuclear lobby, headlined by Bechtel's Lawrence Papay, as well as William Fulkerson, former associate director of the Oak Ridge National Lab and a senior fellow at the Gore-endowed Joint Institute for Energy and Environment at the University of Tennessee. Masquerading as an academic was Charles Vest, a former president of MIT and a driving force behind the American Nuclear Society's Eagle Alliance.

Another prominent spot went to the person who must hold the all-time record for appointments to presidential commissions involving environmental matters, Virginia Weldon, chief flack for Monsanto. Weldon rarely misses an opportunity to praise irradiation as a cure for all of the dangers lurking in the US food supply.

Environmentalists were given two slots. One went to Daniel Lashof, a scientist at the Natural Resources Defense Council. The other was reserved for one of Lashof's biggest funders, Hal Harvey, executive director of the Energy Foundation. In 1996, both Lashof and Harvey supported the disastrous bail out of the California nuclear industry.

With this roster of advisers, it's not surprising that the Gore-Holdren report largely parroted the line advanced by the Nuclear Energy Institute, calling for increased research and development subsidies for fusion and fission, export of US nuclear technology, and the creation of a new Nuclear Energy Research Initiative to underwrite "new reactor designs with higher-efficiency, lower-cost, and improved safety to compete in the global market."

Holdren's panel recommended that federal spending for research and development on commercial nuclear reactors be tripled from $40 million to $120 million, a bigger percentage increase than is recommended for either renewables or energy efficiency. The money is essentially a direct subsidy to help nuclear companies and utilities deal with the industries two biggest problems: radioactive waste disposal and aging reactors. "The interest is not so much in building new nukes in the US, but in finding a way to keep the old reactors up and running so that they can be relicensed," says Auke Piersma of the Critical Mass Energy Project. "It's a shame that people like Holdren use global warming as way to justify this handout."

"Nuclear energy currently generates about 17 percent of the world's electricity," Holdren writes. "If this electricity were generated instead by coal, world carbon dioxide emissions from fossil fuel consumption would be almost 10 percent larger than they currently are. Given the desirability of stabilizing and reducing greenhouse gas emissions, it is important to establish fission energy as a widely viable and expandable option. World leadership in nuclear energy technologies and the underlying science is also vital to the United States from the perspective of national security, international influence, and global stability."

Incredibly, Holdren and his gang also recommended spending $280 million on fusion research, a proven waste of money in terms of energy production. Under even the most optimistic scenarios, fusion reactors will be able to generate electricity for about 50 cents per kilowatt hour, ten times more than the cost of natural gas turbines. But a boost in fusion research can go a long way toward solving a problem that has vexed the nuclear industry and the defense lobby: How to keep testing nuclear weapons technology under the restrictions of the Comprehensive Test Ban Treaty. The answer: funnel fusion energy research money to places like the Lawrence Livermore Labs and its mammoth National Ignition Facility.

The Department of Energy didn't sit by idly either. Ever on the lookout for any opportunity to advance the cause of nuclear power was Dr. Terry Lash, the Energy Department's director of nuclear operations under Clinton and Gore. Lash is the man who almost single-handedly keeps Hanford's Fast Flux Breeder Reactor humming along on "hot standby" until it can once again be fired up to make tritium for H-bombs and, in some distant future, be put to the more humanitarian use of making medical isotopes. To fund the Fast Flux project, Lash diverted $40 million a year from the strapped cleanup budget for Hanford, which the Department of Energy itself calls the most toxic site in North America.

Lash also promoted nuclear power's global mission, fervently lobbying inside the DOE for nuclear trade pacts with China, India, Argentina, and Brazil. "Lash was a shrewd and incredibly calculating operator," a senior DOE staffer told me. "He'd employ any argument for the cause of nuclear power. He pressed for sales of reactors to Brazil and China, saying that it was vital to combat the greenhouse effect."

Lash also played a key role in stuffing the annual clean air budgets with lavish hand-outs to the nuclear industry. Sources say Lash originally pushed for a $50 million "clean air" subsidy to utilities laden with nuclear plants, but the figure was eventually scaled back to $30 million by deficit hawks at the Office of Management and Budget.

Longtime anti-nuke activists remember Lash from his days as a senior scientist for the Natural Resources Defense Council in the 1970s, when the group touted itself as a fierce foe of nuclear power and raised millions off the Three Mile Island disaster. During his tenure there, Lash co-wrote a book for NRDC on nuclear waste. Lash's co-author was none other than John Bryson, a co-founder of the group. Bryson went on to become the CEO of Edison International (formerly Southern California Edison), which operates the San Onofre nuclear plant. In 1997, Bryson was fresh off an amazing victory, where he and his pals convinced the California legislature to stick ratepayers and taxpayers with $26 billion in "stranded costs" to make his company's nuke's "more competitive in the deregulated electricity market."

One last goal remained for the nuclear lobby: to split the environmental community on nuclear power. There was every reason for optimism. Nuclear energy had divided the greens in the past, most spectacularly in 1969 when David Brower publicly attacked fellow Sierra Club leaders who helped Pacific Gas & Electric pick the Nipomo Dunes as the site for the company's Diablo Canyon reactor. This principled stance led to Brower's ouster as the Club's executive director. In 1990, scientists from the EDF and NRDC signed a statement saying that nuclear power had an essential role to play in curbing air pollution.

As Al Gore packed his day pack for his whirlwind trip to Kyoto, a full-page ad appeared in the *Wall Street Journal* that must have warmed the hearts of the men at the NEI. Under the headline, "A Business Climate Challenge: America Needs to Get Serious About Climate Change," sixty corporate executives, led by Nike, Mitsubishi, CalEnergy, Pacific Energy, Mitchell Energy, and Ted Turner endorsed the need for a strong climate change treaty. The ad was also signed by Enron and Bechtel, two companies with interests in nuclear power. The companies had been rounded up by three environmental groups: World Wildlife Fund, Ozone Action, and NRDC. "The idea for this really came from the Clinton administration," Brandon MacGillis told me. "They said if we wanted to see a good treaty we needed to show that property owners and Republican business leaders cared about global warming."

Using a grant from the Ford Foundation, money from Ozone Action and contributions from Nike and Mitchell Energy, the groups began asking corporate leaders to sign onto the ad. "We asked everyone we could think of," MacGillis says, and admits that the environmental reputation of the companies wasn't a factor. "Sure some wanted onto the ad purely for economic or PR reasons," MacGillis confessed. "But other companies really think they can make a difference. Nike, for example, believes that by improving air quality in its factories it can increase productivity." (This is a staggering admission. Up till then, Nike has rigorously claimed it has no control over the operations of its Asian factories.)

As all of this was going on, a coalition of environmental groups, spearheaded by Critical Mass Energy Project, Greenpeace, and Friends of the Earth, drafted a letter to Clinton and Gore on the subject of nuclear power. The letter harshly denounced the Holdren report, DOE's budget for nuclear power, and all "proposals to use nuclear power to reduce greenhouse emissions." More than forty groups signed the letter. One major group refused: NRDC.

WASHINGTON, DC.

Glow River Glow: Leaks and Plumbers at Hanford

THE OUTBACK OF THE HANFORD NUCLEAR RESERVATION IN EASTERN Washington State is called the T-Farm. It's a rolling expanse of high desert sloping toward the last untamed reaches of the Columbia River. The "T" stands for tanks—huge single-hulled containers buried some fifty feet beneath basalt volcanic rock and sand holding, the lethal detritus of Hanford's fifty-year run as the nation's H-bomb factory.

Those tanks had an expected lifespan of thirty-five years; the radioactive gumbo inside them has a half-life of 250,000 years. Dozens of those tanks have now started to corrode and leak, releasing the most toxic material on earth—plutonium and uranium-contaminated sludge and liquid—on an inexorable path toward the Columbia River, the world's most productive salmon fishery and the source of irrigation water for the farms and orchards of the Inland Empire, centered on Spokane in eastern Washington.

Internal documents from the Department of Energy and various private contractors working at Hanford reveal that at least one million gallons of radioactive sludge have already leaked out of at least sixty-seven different tanks. Those tanks and others continue to leak and, according to these sources, the leaks are getting much larger.

One internal report shows the results from a borehole drilled into the ground between two of Hanford's largest tanks. Using gamma spectrometry, geologists detected a fifty-fold increase in contamination between 1996 and 2002. The leak from those tanks, and perhaps an underground pipeline, was described as "insignificant" a decade ago. Six years later that radioactive dribble had swelled up into a "continuous plume" of highly radioactive Cesium-137.

Obviously, there's been a major radioactive breach from those tanks, but to date the Department of Energy has refused to publicly report the incident. Even though it was reported by their own geologists.

A few hundred yards away, a tank called TY-102, the third largest tank at Hanford, is also leaking. Radioactive water is draining out of this single-hulled container and a broken subsurface pipe into what geologists call the "vadose zone," the stratum of subsurface soil just above the water table. In an internal 1998 report, the Grand Junction Office of the DOE detected significant contamination forty-two to fifty-two feet below the surface, and concluded in a memo to Hanford managers that the "high levels of gamma radiation" came from "a subsurface source" of Cesium-137, which likely resulted from leakage from tank TY-102."

This alarming report was swiftly buried by Hanford officials. So, too, was the evidence of leakage at tanks TY-103 and TY-106. Instead, the DOE publicly declared that portion of the tank farm to be "controlled, clean and stable."

No surprises here. The long-standing strategy of the DOE has been to conceal any evidence of radioactive leaking at Hanford, a policy that was excoriated in a 1980 internal review by the department's Inspector General, which concluded that "Hanford's existing waste management policies and practices have themselves sufficed to keep publicity about possible tank leaks to a minimum."

Needless to say, the Reagan years didn't augur a new forthrightness from the people who run Hanford. Seven years and several congressional hearings after the Inspector General's report was released, bureaucratic cover-up and public denial were still the DOE's operational reflex to any disturbing data bubbling up out of Hanford's boreholes. By 1987, Hanford officials had learned an important lesson in the art of concealment: The easiest way to avoid bad press and public hostility is to simply stop monitoring sites that seemed the most likely to produce unpleasant information.

It is now clear that the tanks began leaking as early as 1956, only a few years after the Atomic Energy Commission began pumping the poisonous sludge into the giant subterranean containers. It is also clear that the federal government covered up evidence of those leaks since the moment it learned of them.

How many tanks are leaking? How far has the contamination spread? The DOE isn't talking. It isn't even looking for answers. But geologists estimated that the faster migrating contaminants, such as uranium, will move from the groundwater beneath Hanford's central plateau to the Columbia in something like twenty-five years. That means that the first traces of radiated water could have started seeping into the Columbia in 2001.

This reckless strategy persists. In a document called "Official Characterization Plan of Hanford"—essentially a kind of 3-D map of contamination at the site—the DOE chose not to include Cobalt-60, a highly radioactive material that is present at deep levels across the tank farm. In addition, the Hanford plan fails to mention the fact that its own surveys have shown large amounts of Cesium-137 and Cobalt-60 forming radioactive pools in the geological stratum, called the plio-pleistocene unit, the last barrier between Hanford's soils and water table.

If the DOE remains locked onto this course it will never acknowledge or even investigate the potentially lethal flow of radioactivity toward the great river of the West. That's because the managers of Hanford say they will only research potential leaks if they detect a level of contamination several times higher than that ever recorded at Hanford—a standard clearly designed to shield them from ever having to pursue any subsurface leak investigation or publicly admit the existence of such leaks.

To help Hanford's managers avoid ever discovering such embarrassing leaks, the site plan calls for them to drill the penetrometer holes, through which contamination is measured, only to a depth of forty feet—or two feet above the bottom of the tanks, guaranteeing that they will avoid picking up any radioactive traces from the region of the most dangerous contamination.

There's a reason the Hanford managers want the public to believe that most of the contamination at the site is limited to the surface terrain. Theoretically, the topsoil can be scooped up and, with large government contracts, transferred to a more secure site or zapped into a glass-like substance through the big vitrification center now under construction. There's no way to de-contaminate groundwater or the Columbia River. Their only hope for containment is to contain the issue politically by plumbing the leaks from whistleblowers.

There's no question that the subsurface leakage is serious, extensive, and dangerous. The internal survey of Hanford by the Grand Junction Office detected high levels of C-137 deeper than 100 feet below the surface—and sixty feet deeper than the current plan calls for probing. That report concluded that both C-137 and CO-60 had "reached groundwater in this area of the tank farm."

Consider this. C-137 is a slow traveling contaminant. How far have faster moving radioactive materials, such as uranium, spread? No one knows. No one is even looking.

The DOE and Hanford's contractors want to close down the C Quadrant of the tank farm and declare it cleaned up, even though more than 10 percent of the waste at that site remains in tanks with documented leaks. There is mounting evidence that a plume of Tritium-contaminated sludge has recently penetrated the groundwater there as well.

John Brodeur is one of the nation's top environmental engineers and a world-class geologist. In 1997, after a whistleblower at Hanford disclosed evidence that the groundwater beneath the central plateau had been contaminated by plumes of radioactivity, Hazel O'Leary commissioned Brodeur to investigate how far the contamination had spread. It proved to be a nearly impossible assignment since the DOE and its contractors had taken extreme measures to conceal the data or avoid collecting it entirely.

A decade later, Brodeur has once again been asked to assess the situation at one of the most contaminated sites on earth, this time for the environmental group Heart of the Northwest. His conclusions are disturbing.

"There remains much that we don't know about the subsurface contamination plumes at Hanford," says John Brodeur. "The only way to solve this dilemma is to identify what we don't know up front and get it out on the table for discussion. This is difficult to do in the chilling work environment where bad data are commonplace, lies of omission are standard practice and people lose their jobs because they disagreed with some of the long-held institutional myths at Hanford."

RICHLAND, WASHINGTON.

Ecological Warfare: White Death in Iraq

THE ECOLOGICAL EFFECTS OF WAR, LIKE ITS HORRIFIC TOLL ON HUMAN life, are exponential. When the Bush Administration and their Congressional allies sent US troops in to Iraq to topple Saddam's regime, they not only ordered these men and women to commit crimes against humanity, they also commanded them to perpetrate crimes against nature.

The first Gulf War had a dire effect on the environment. As CNN reported in 1999, "Iraq was responsible for intentionally releasing some 11 million barrels of oil into the Arabian Gulf from January to May 1991, oiling more than 800 miles of Kuwaiti and Saudi Arabian coastline. The amount of oil released was categorized as twenty times larger than the Exxon Valdez spill in Alaska and twice as large as the previous world record oil spill. The cost of cleanup has been estimated at more than $700 million."

During the build up to George W. Bush's invasion of Iraq, Saddam loyalists promised to light oil fields afire, hoping to expose what they claimed was the US's underlying motive for attacking their country: oil. The US architects of the Iraq war surely knew this was a potential reality once they entered Baghdad. Hostilities in Kuwait resulted in the discharge of an estimated 7 million barrels of oil, culminating in the world's largest oil spill in January of 1991. The United Nations later calculated that of Kuwait's 1,330 active oil wells, half had been set ablaze. The pungent fumes and smoke from those dark billowing flames spread for hundreds of miles and had horrible effects on human and environmental health. Saddam Hussein was rightly denounced as a ferocious villain for ordering his retreating troops to destroy Kuwaiti oil fields.

However, the United States military was also responsible for much of the environmental devastation of the first Gulf War. In the early 1990s, the US sank at least eighty crude oil ships to the bottom of the Persian Gulf, partly to uphold the UN's economic sanctions against Iraq. Vast crude oil slicks formed, killing an unknown number of seabirds and aquatic life, while wreaking havoc on local fishing and resort communities.

During the first Gulf War, cruise missiles and months of bombing by US and British planes left behind an even more deadly and insidious legacy: tons of shell casings, bullets, and bomb fragments laced with depleted uranium. In all, the US hit Iraqi targets with more than 970 radioactive bombs and missiles.

More than fifteen years later, the health consequences from this radioactive bombing campaign are beginning to come into focus. And they are dire. Iraqi physicians call it "the white death"—leukemia. Since 1990, the incident rate of leukemia in Iraq has grown by more than 600 percent. The situation was compounded by Iraq's forced isolation and the sadistic sanctions regime—once described by former UN Secretary General Kofi Annan as "a humanitarian crisis" that made detection and treatment of the cancers all the more difficult.

Most of the leukemia and cancer victims aren't soldiers. They are civilians. Depleted uranium is a rather benign sounding name for uranium-238, the trace elements left behind when the fissionable material is extracted from uranium-235 for use in nuclear reactors and weapons. For decades, this waste was a radioactive nuisance, piling up at plutonium processing plants across the country. By the late 1980s, there were nearly a billion tons of it.

Then weapons designers at the Pentagon came up with a use for these tailings. They could be molded into bullets and bombs. The material was free, and there was plenty at hand. Also uranium is a heavy metal, denser than lead. This makes it perfect for use in armor-penetrating weapons, designed to destroy tanks, armored-personnel carriers, and bunkers.

When the tank-busting bombs explode, the depleted uranium oxidizes into microscopic fragments that float through the air like carcinogenic dust, and is carried on the desert winds for decades. When inhaled, the lethal bits stick to the fibers of the lungs, and eventually begin to wreak havoc on the body, showing themselves in the form of tumors, hemorrhages, ravaged immune systems, and leukemias.

It didn't take long for medical teams in the region to detect cancer clusters near the bomb-sites. The leukemia rate in Sarajevo, pummeled by American bombs in 1996, tripled in five years following the bombings. But it's not just the Serbs who are ill and dying. NATO and UN peacekeepers in the region are also coming down with cancer.

The Pentagon has shuffled through a variety of rationales and excuses. First, the Defense Department shrugged off concerns about Depleted Uranium, calling them wild conspiracy theories by peace activists, environmentalists, and Iraqi propagandists. When the US's NATO allies demanded that the US disclose the chemical and metallic properties of its munitions, the Pentagon refused. Depleted uranium has a half-life of more than 4-billion years. Approximately the age of the Earth. Thousand of acres of land in the Balkans, Kuwait, and southern Iraq have been contaminated forever.

Speaking of depleted uranium (DU) and other war-related disasters, prior to the 2003 invasion of Iraq, former chief UN weapons inspector, Hans Blix, predicted that the environmental consequences of the Iraq war could, in fact, be more ominous than the issue of war and peace itself. Despite this admission, the US made no public attempts to assess the environmental risks that the war would inflict.

Blix was right. On the second day of President Bush's invasion of Iraq it was reported by the *New York Times* and the BBC that Iraqi forces had set fire to several of the country's large oil wells. Five days later in the Rumaila oilfields, six-dozen wellheads were set ablaze. The dense black smoke rose high in the southern sky of Iraq, fanning a clear signal that the US invasion had again ignited an environmental tragedy. Shortly after the initial invasion, the United Nations Environment Program's (UNEP) satellite data showed that a significant amount of toxic smoke had been emitted from burning oils wells. This smoldering oil was laced with poisonous chemicals such as mercury, sulfur and furans, which can cause serious damage to human, as well as ecosystem, health.

According to Friends of the Earth, the fallout from burning oil debris, like that of the first Gulf War, has created a toxic sea surface that has affected the health of birds and marine life. One area that has been greatly impacted is the Sea of Oman, which connects the Arabian Sea to the Persian Gulf by way of the Strait of Hormuz. This waterway is one of the most productive marine habitats in the world. In fact, the Global Environment Fund contends that the region "plays a significant role in sustaining the life cycle of marine turtle populations in the whole North-Western Indo Pacific region." Of the world's seven species of marine turtles, five are found in the Sea of Oman and four of those five are listed as "endangered" with the other listed as "threatened."

The future indeed looks bleak for the ecosystems and biodiversity of Iraq, but the consequences of the US military invasion will not only be confined to the war-stricken country. The Gulf shores, according to BirdLife's Mike Evans, is "one of the top five sites in the world for wader birds, and a key refueling area for hundreds of thousands of migrating water birds." The UN Environment Program claims that thirty-three wetland areas in Iraq are of vital importance to the survival of various bird species. These wetlands, the UN claims, are also particularly vulnerable to pollution from munitions fallout, as well as oil wells that have been sabotaged.

Mike Evans also maintains that the current Iraq war could destroy what's left of the Mesopotamian marshes on the lower Tigris and Euphrates rivers. Following the war of 1991, Saddam removed dissidents who had built homes in the marshes by digging large canals along the two rivers so that they would have access to their waters. Thousands of people were displaced and the communities ruined.

The construction of dams upstream on the once roaring Tigris and Euphrates has dried up more than 90 percent of the marshes and has led to extinction for several animals. Water buffalo, foxes, waterfowl, and boar have disappeared. "What remains of the fragile marshes, and the 20,000 people who still live off them, will lie right in the path of forces heading towards Baghdad from the south," wrote Fred Pearce in the *New Scientist* prior to Bush's invasion in 2003. The true effect this war has had on these wetlands and its inhabitants is still not known.

The destruction of Iraqi's infrastructure has had substantial public health implications as well. Bombed out industrial plants and factories have polluted ground water. The damage to sewage-treatment plants—with reports that raw sewage formed massive pools of muck in the streets of Baghdad immediately after Bush's "Shock and Awe" campaign—is also likely poisoning rivers as well as humans. Cases of typhoid among Iraqi citizens have risen tenfold since 1991, largely due to polluted drinking water.

That number has almost certainly increased more in the past few years following the ousting of Saddam. In fact, during the 1990s, while Iraq was under sanctions, UN officials in Baghdad agreed that the root cause of child mortality and other health problems was no longer simply lack of food and medicine, but the lack of clean water (freely available in all parts of the country prior to the first Gulf War) and electrical power (the lack of which had predictable consequences for hospitals and water-pumping systems). By the middle of 1999, a large proportion of the 21.9 percent of contracts vetoed by the UN's US-dominated sanctions committee were integral to the efforts to repair the failing water and sewage systems.

The real cumulative impact of US military action in Iraq, past and present, won't be known for years, perhaps decades, to come. Stopping this war now will not only save lives, it will also help to rescue what's left of Iraq's fragile environment.

WITH JOSHUA FRANK.

PART TWO

Way Out West

But for my children, I would
   have them keep their distance
   from the thickening center; corruption
Never has been compulsory,
   when the cities lie at the monster's
   feet there are left the mountains.

—from "Shine, Perishing Republic"
Robinson Jeffers

Dark Mesas in an Ancient Light

I AM LOST IN A LABYRINTH OF STONE. I ONLY KNOW I MUST GO DOWN. I MUST follow the striated pink slickrock. Down and down this tight side canyon, disoriented by an elegant confusion of landforms: arches and hoodoos; dry falls and rock shelters; graben and needles; rimrock, chimneys, and swells.

Each step down the canyon takes you back in time. The place seems ageless. But the terrain changes day-by-day, shedding pieces of itself. It is a paradox of the landscape: the river plays the role of both geological architect and archaeologist: unearthing and altering the shape of the Colorado Plateau on a scale both massive and intricate.

Any attempt to understand the desert Southwest forces you to confront stark complexities, both ecological and personal: the meaning of its openness and silence; the green course of swift rivers in an arid, red land; the genocide and enforced poverty still pressed on its native peoples; the violent rush of rage that overcame me one night walking in the wild desert of the Santa Catalina Mountains at the sight of the lights of Tucson, burning like a perpetual explosion on the dark horizon.

My goal today is the confluence of the Colorado and Green rivers. I don't give a damn that I might be off track. The solution is obvious: go down, down inexorably to the river. I walk in a tumbleweed manner, stumbling over rocks. The heat is violent, draining my stamina, pampered for years by the cool, maritime climate of western Oregon.

Here the air is thin and flat. The humidity hovers at a mere two percent, sucking the moisture out of you. My lips chap, crack, bleed. They say the unrelenting glare of the sun reflecting off the red bones of rock can flip your consciousness as slyly and absolutely as any hit of mescalin. I open myself to it.

In a state of near delusion, it strikes me that the Southwest is a writhing, sexual landscape. Here the earth exposes itself in mesas, pinnacles, and sinuous slot canyons; in the flesh and blood tones of the sandstone; in the cool, lime-colored light of the ponderosa forests (what's left of them); and the unrepressed exuberance of the desert suddenly in bloom. Here the land seduces the senses and mocks them.

I am far from the first Anglo to strain at this obvious metaphor, naturally. My favorite writer, D. H. Lawrence, spent many years in Taos and several more traveling through Mexico. He was enthralled and repelled by the "blood nature" of the desert. Terry Tempest Williams writes arrestingly about the "erotics of place." The paintings of Georgia O'Keefe—her landscapes of canyons and mesas near Abiquiu, not the overtly sexualized flowers—vibrate with a consuming passion. Eliot Porter's photographs, especially those of the lost Glen Canyon and the rugged crenellations of the Sangre de Cristo Mountains near his home in Tesuque, evoke similar sensualities.

The fact that we come to this realization as an epiphany is a sad measure of how far we've removed ourselves from the rhythms of the land. The native people of the Southwest never knew such distance from the living landscape. Black Mesa and the strangely blue Chuska Mountains are not merely metaphors of the female and male deities for the Navajo, but tangible places of creative powers—as Mount Graham is to the San Carlos Apache, despite the gross indignity of a deep space telescope on the crown of the holy sky island. Similarly, the sipapu (the hole in the ground from which "the people" emerged) entrenched near the center of every kiva built by the Anasazi and their descendents in the Pueblo tribes is quite literally understood as a vaginal passageway of the sensate Earth.

The ragged sound of thunder shudders across the sky. That a slot canyon is a dangerous place to find oneself in during a sudden rainstorm is apparent even to an alien forest dweller like me. I scramble up the sun-warmed Cedar Mesa sandstone to a ledge about fifty feet above the creek bed.

Lightning fissures down out of a single menacing storm cloud embedded in a sky of absolute clarity. There is a small rock shelter a few hundred feet up the canyon, a perfect cover to ride out this desert tempest.

As a cool rain begins to fall, I notice that the slanting wall of the cliff is covered with petroglyphs. Dozens of pictures and symbols, ghost stories carved into rock. Some are clearly recognizable, others ancient and mysterious: bighorn sheep, coyote, lizards, the initials CJ '91 deeply chiseled with sophomoric bravado on top of a strange spiral 500 years old, men on horses in conquistador-style hats, circles within circles, tiny red handprints, floating armless, near-human figures.

A familiar image haunts the lower portion of the panel, the proud sign of an archaic fertility symbol etched into the dark desert varnish that coats the sandstone walls like a swipe of dried blood. Yes, it is Kokopeli, the hunchbacked flute-player, his wild hair standing up straight like the antennae of an insect, his engorged phallus cocked at an assertive and defiant 45 degree angle. He is the ubiquitous kachina of the pueblo people, who, in their wide migrations, have left his image on rock walls from Tierra del Fuego to northern Alberta.

This petroglyph panel is a historical tapestry of the Southwest woven onto stone—a silent meeting place for diverse threads of people who have lived upon this land, a place where cultures speak across centuries.

* * *

I finally reach the Colorado. But bad memories flood back. The last time I touched its waters was on a rented houseboat, rendered nearly senseless by a dozen bottles of Negro Modelo, floating above the blue void of Lake Powell.

Lake Powell: a place people come to inebriate themselves against the violence that has been done to the land. It is even a Mecca, of sorts, for radical environmentalists, a place we gather to vent our sour nihilism. Glen Canyon Dam: the correlate for every foul thing we've been doing to this country all these many years.

Yet, there is an undeniable, if repulsive, beauty to the dam itself: its cool sweep of blonde stone, its assertion of power over the forces of nature, the old themes of dominance and submission. A fascist architecture that would humble Albert Speer himself.

Glen Canyon Dam is there for a reason, a reason that exposes the tragic flaw in environmental politics. David Brower's admonition that environmentalists "never trade a place you know for one you don't" came through bitter experience. Brower himself crafted the deal that doomed Glen Canyon as a way of saving the stunning canyons of Dinosaur National Monument.

And the compulsive pattern of deal-making persists. The trade-off for a free-flowing Colorado through Marble Canyon was more nuclear power plants and uranium mining. The construction of the grim power plants at Page and Four Corners that burn coal gouged from the heart of Black Mesa and spew out the fly-ash in black stains visible from the international space station. Go to the North Rim of the Grand Canyon where, even on a good day, the view has been drained of color, smudged. It's like looking at the great chasm through a funeral veil. What the hell have we done?

Power follows property, said John Adams. And so it does. But in the desert Southwest, property follows water. Here water is power. Geronimo knew that well. Recall his dazzling defenses of places like Apache Springs. The philanderer and water-vampire Floyd Dominy (the J. Edgar Hoover-like head of the Bureau of Reclamation during the glory days of dam building in the arid west) grasped the political power of water. So did Mo Udall and Bruce Babbitt, whose reputations as "conservationists" will be forever darkened by their obdurate support of grotesque water—stealing schemes such as the Central Arizona Project. Impound the water and tame the electorate is the numbing mantra of Southwestern politics.

Follow the money, Deep Throat advised. In the Southwest, if you want to divine the truth, follow the water. Sooner or later you'll end up at a cow. More than 80 percent of the water diverted from the Colorado River goes for agricultural irrigation. And that means cattle. The water goes largely to multi-millionaire ranchers and ranches owned by transnational corporations and banks. The water no longer goes to the rural Hispanics, Apache, Hopi, and Navajo, who had developed a truly sustainable grazing and small agriculture based on the ancient system of acequias and other indigenous irrigation systems.

The ancient Hohokam village known as Los Muertos was served for ten centuries by a six-mile long canal diverting water from the Salt River to corn and squash fields. Eventually, a thirty-year drought struck the Southwest. The Salt River dried up and even the gentle agriculture of the Hohokam overtapped the dwindling resource. The city was abandoned.

Marc Reisner observes in his book *Cadillac Desert* that that same problem afflicts the entire Southwest today. But it is a problem that has been engineered in less than fifty years, not a millennium. The technological uses of the Colorado River are killing the land at both ends: through the submersion of places such as Glen Canyon and Flaming Gorge and the salinization of millions of acres of irrigated farmland in an arid climate. Watering the desert didn't transform Arizona into Iowa, but rendered it into a kind of post-modern Carthage. Technology wounds, says the New Mexico writer Chellis Glendenning. In an arid climate, the wounded land heals slowly, bearing deep scars that defy concealment.

In the end, the transfer of water is a transfer of power, property, and wealth. The infuriating entanglement of western water laws is a deliberate confusion, a cravenly-designed impediment to the appropriate and equitable allocation of resources, to real land reform and to the preservation of the desert rivers themselves. While the obstacles to such an ecological revolution may be profound, the way back is simple: Make the water stay with the land.

* * *

It tells you something about the politics of the Southwest that one of the wildest places in the region is the White Sands Missile Range. But it tells us more about the macerating nature of cows. Patriot missiles don't pack near the wallop on the ecology of the desert as a bovine herd grazing on full-automatic.

One of the main problems with domestic livestock grazing is its omnipresence on the landscape. More than 96 percent of the publicly owned lands in the Southwest (excluding the national parks and military lands) are under grazing permits. No place is immune. Not even the world's first wilderness reserve, the Gila Wilderness Area, can escape the scourge of cows, stock tanks, and ranching roads. These days real cowboys ride Chevy trucks, not palominos.

The impacts of grazing on desert wildlife are staggering. According *Grazing to Extinction*, a report written by the ecologist John Horning, grazing is the primary cause of decline in the populations of seventy-six species of fish and wildlife that are either listed under, or candidates for listing under, the Endangered Species Act. Cows and sheep are a contributing factor in the slide toward extinction of at least another 270 species. This is not to mention the bloody toll exacted on fragile populations of desert predators by hired killers from Animal Damage Control for the psychic benefit of western ranchers.

The cherished myths of the west are engraved so deeply on our consciousness that our perspective of how the land should look is distorted in unexpected ways. For example, many of us nurtured on the films of Howard Hawks and John Ford assume as a matter of course that the rock-strewn, barren banks are the natural aesthetic conditions of rivers such as the Rio Grande and San Juan. In fact, the rivers of the Southwest should flow through verdant sleeves of willow and cottonwoods trees. The fact that these riverine forests were largely eliminated from the landscape by the 1930s without, for the most part, ever suffering the bite of a chainsaw, illustrates the devastating consequences of livestock grazing on ecological fragile riparian areas.

Some of what has been lost is nearly unseen, but may be critical to the functioning of the desert system itself. Take cryptogamic crust, a kind of blue-green algae that weaves through the desert floor in thin black webs. The cryptogamic crust is the connective tissue that holds the desert together, similar to the mycchorizal fungi that underlies and nourishes the ancient forests of the Pacific Northwest. But intensive livestock grazing destroys this "living soil" and permanently impairs the ecological resilience of the land. Now extensive patches of cryptogamic crust can only be found on isolated mesa tops or in ungrazed parklands, such as Arches or the Maze district of Canyonlands.

Sooner or later the deconstructionist of western myths must take on the rancher and the folklore of the rugged individualist. There is a particular subspecies of the western rancher who remains blithely ignorant of the fact that his "lifestyle" is maintained by the generosity of the same federal government he despises. The average ranching family in the Southwest receives more than $25,000 a year in federal subsidies, yet squeals at even the most modest attempt to reform grazing practices on federal lands as an attack on inviolate property rights. The historian Bernard DeVoto best captured the attitude of the welfare rancher toward the federal government: "Get out, and send us money."

What has changed since DeVoto's time is the increasingly hostile demeanor of the ranchers and the object of their aggression: environmentalists have replaced the feds as the new target for cowboy angst. One of the most violent epicenters in the backlash against environmentalism is Catron County, New Mexico, which my friend Karl Hess, the libertarian environmentalist and author of *Visions Upon the Land*, calls "Cartoon County." And indeed it would be funny, if the reality were not so vicious. Here a brutal paranoia has spread like some strange virus from a 1950s' science fiction film. The ranchers of southern New Mexico and Arizona have become bitter allies in a violent campaign against local environmentalists, who form the scapegoats for all of their financial, social, and sexual problems.

The ranchers have adopted the litany of victimology. And some of them may indeed be victims. But not victims of environmentalists. The real agents of their misery, such as it is, are the banks squeezing their mortgages and a government that promised them more than the land could ever deliver.

"The war on the West may be a media event," says my friend Pat Wolff, a long-time veteran of the environmental wars in the Southwest. "But the climate of violence in New Mexico and Arizona is real. And it is intense. The scary thing is the level of tolerance given to the violent outbursts of ranchers, loggers, and miners." Like many environmentalists in the region, Wolff was regularly threatened—often in public. Rarely are the threats investigated and often the most virulent ranchers are portrayed as iconic figures in the local media. In 1993, my friend, the Navajo environmentalist Leroy Jackson, was found dead in his car on the Brazos Cliffs in northern New Mexico. He was on his way to Washington, DC to testify about the logging of sacred lands in the Chuska Mountains. His death was almost certainly the result of foul play. The cops didn't even launch an investigation, ruling his death a suicide. The dangers are real.

* * *

The conquest of the Southwest began with the search for gold and rapidly expanded to baser minerals: silver, copper, uranium, molybdenum, coal. Shafts were dug and blasted into nearly every mountain range in the region. Some mines ran for decades, others ran out in months.

What the mining companies left behind were not the ruins of a vanished culture, but a toxic legacy of greed—a gored and disemboweled landscape heaped with tailings piles and mining wastes, the fatal detritus of the private engorgement of the public's lands, left to leach for decades into the Southwest's precious waters.

The violence wrought upon the land accompanied a similar violence inflicted on the native people of the region. It began with Francisco Vazquez de Coronado storming Zuni Pueblo in 1540, mistaking the sun-burnished adobe walls for the golden city of Cibola. His marauders were vigorously repelled by the Bow Priests of the Zuni. Pueblos 1; Entrada 0.

But the Spanish didn't relent. One by one the pueblos fell to Spanish control. By 1598 each had been conquered—all, that is, except for Acoma, perched on its high mesa in western New Mexico. The following year the power-maddened Juan de Oñate ordered his troops out with instructions to subdue Acoma Pueblo. The Acoma people greeted the conquistadors with corn-pollen and turkey feathers. But the Castillans demanded tribute; they demanded gold. When the Acoma refused, the Spanish killers corralled the men, chopped off one of each of their feet (500 in all), and pitched the tribal leaders over the steep cliffs to their deaths.

It didn't end there, of course. In 1863, when the gold and silver miners demanded free access to the mountains of southern New Mexico and Arizona, federal troops were sent out to annihilate the Apache, who refused to settle on reservations. Smithsonian "collectors" accompanied the troops. They photographed the mutilated bodies of dead Indians, decapitated the corpses, marked the skulls, and sent them packed in boxes back to Washington. The great Apache leader Magnus Colorados was finally captured, publicly bull-whipped, and murdered. General Nelson Miles led 5,000 soldiers in the final pursuit of Geronimo and his thirty-seven warriors. The rest of the Apache were forcibly relocated to reservations, which were managed for decades as concentration camps.

The oppression continues, but in more insidious ways: Tribal councils are infiltrated by government snitches and corporate stooges. Budgets are bankrupted, resources exhausted. Thousands of Navajo are forcibly evicted from Big Mountain, while Black Mesa, their sacred mountain, is strip-mined by Peabody Coal. The tribal forests are logged at a voracious pace under the lash of the Bureau of Indian Affairs. The Mescalero Apaches are offered a nuclear waste dump as a way to enhance their "quality of life," while the San Carlos Apaches have their sacred Mt. Graham desecrated by the construction of deep space telescopes. Religious concerns about the sacred nature of Mt. Graham are dismissed as "primitive" emotions, and opponents are smeared as part of a "Jewish conspiracy."

The rural Hispanics of New Mexico have been victimized by a second conquest as brutal and oppressive as that conducted against the Pueblos, Navajo, and Apache. Land claims have been abrogated; water rights stolen. Since its earliest days in the Southwest, the Forest Service has used the rubric of "conservation" as a pretext for the acculturation of Hispanics and the dispossession of their property and their basic rights to use commonly-held lands. A modern day enclosure movement. Urban environmentalists share some of the culpability for these past wrongs.

In fact, all of the federal land management agencies have placed a template of homogeneity over the Hispanic people of the region—the cultural equivalent of even-aged management. To date, there have been few efforts to redress these abuses. No reparations have been paid. Little land has been returned.

This savage history of conquest is ameliorated only by the enduring beauty of the landscape and by a persistent culture of resistance, a spirited defense of the land that dates back to the first stream of arrows launched at Coronado by the Zuni warriors in 1540 and continued through Reies Tijerina's 1968 raid on the Tierra Amarilla courthouse—in an attempt to assert land and water rights granted, but never honored, in the Treaty of Guadelupe Hidalgo—to the Apache Survival Coalition's vigorous defense of Mt. Graham from the rampages of the University of Arizona and the Vatican. Radical environmentalism came of age in the deserts and rivers of the Southwest: Aldo Leopold, Black Mesa Defense, Ed Abbey, Doug Peacock, Earth First!, and El Partido

Verde, a political movement linking progressive environmentalists with other social justice movements.

* * *

The town is Nuevo Casa Grande in the Chihuahua province of northern Mexico, 100 miles or so southwest of El Paso. It is an old place with a new name. We are sitting outside a dusty cantina made of mud the color of salmon flesh. The finger traces of its builders streak the walls. The window and door frames are turquoise, the paint peeling off in blue scales.

The waitress has left us dark bottles of home-brewed beer and basket of chile peppers, poblanos and serranos, little green sticks of dynamite. We eat them until our mouths burn with an exquisite pain.

Some ethno pharmacologists swear that you can hallucinate this way. But being novices, and wanting later to amble in a nearly erect manner across ancient ruins outside town, my friend Fremont and I decide to linger on the bright edges of consciousness, here in this beautiful and tragic place, where macaws in wicker cages hang above us like cackling white blooms. These birds of the jungle were sacred to the Anasazi, Hohokam, and other people of the northern desert. I have seen petroglyphs of macaws carved into pink sandstone cliffs high above the San Juan River in Colorado, a thousand miles away from the nearest rainforest.

The complexities of these ancient trading networks are astounding to me, but they shouldn't be. The indigenous culture of Mexico was every bit as advanced as the Egyptians or the Athenians—more advanced in many ways, particularly in its relatively benign relationship to the land.

We are waiting on a man to lead us through Paquimé, the large complex of ruins of one of pre-Columbian America's most sophisticated cities, located a few miles outside town. For nearly 1,000 years, Paquimé was the ruling cultural and political center of northern Mexico. It was the nexus in a vast web of trade and commerce that extended in a 500-mile radius. Its architecture and agronomic practices were exported north to the Mimbres and Pueblos of New Mexico and Arizona. So were its macaws. In fact, the breeding and trading of birds may have been the main source of wealth for this city of 20,000 people.

A wind blows from the east. The fumes from a Pemex plant invade the air. It is a suffocating sensation, with each breath a black clotting of the lungs. Finally, an archaic truck rattles to a halt in front of our table. A small, wiry man climbs out of the driver's side window. His dark face is fissured with wrinkles. He has a beautiful smile. He has no teeth.

His name is José Lopez. He is a mestizo from Oputo, a small village on the Rio de Bavispe, seventy miles to the west. He has worked many jobs. He says he has logged timber in the Sierra Madre for Champion, International. He has stitched soles on running shoes, getting $2 for a 14-hour day. He worked in the Pemex refinery, until he fell and broke his back. It has almost healed, he says. Now he does odds and ends. He leads tourists to Paquimé. He speaks English. He is seventy-eight years old.

We climb in the back, careful not to put too much weight on the truck bed's thin crust of rust, and rumble down a narrow dirt road, casting behind us a billowing plume of smoke and dust. We watch the chilling disparities between life in rural Mexico and rural New Mexico, one of the poorest regions in the US, unscroll before us: children huddled on the roadside under red, woven blankets; women with wooden buckets of water carried for miles from the hideously polluted Casa Grandes River to tin shacks in barrios beside open sewers; men working the dry bean fields under a blistering sun.

The Peruvian novelist Mario Vargas Llosa called Mexico "the land of the perfect dictatorship." It is a dictatorship that has been created, propped up, anointed, and rewarded by the US government for nearly a century, ever since Black Jack Pershing busted across the border in 1917, vowing to bring back Pancho Villa "in an iron cage."

We have logged their forests; drained their oil fields; fixed their elections; threatened to seize their treasury; sent them our sweatshops, our drug financiers, and *maquiladoras*. For the last decade or so NAFTA has been at work, grinding away at the Mexico's poor and indigenous people. In return, we have attempted to seal our border against the "scourge of brown immigrants."

José brings the truck to a halt on the crest of a small hill overlooking a sprawling labyrinth of stone structures. The hill itself, José says with a slightly creepy edge to his voice, is a ceremonial mound. The ruins of Paquimé are thirty times the size of the celebrated Pueblo Bonito at Chaco Canyon, the largest Anasazi site in the American Southwest. Paquimé once featured condominium-like structures six stories tall, dozens of Mayan-like ball fields, temples, warehouses, marketplaces, and plazas. Now it is empty and crumbling, a city of ghosts.

We descend into the ruin, passing down narrow corridors and steep staircases to a subterranean layer, more than ten feet below the surface. Around 1350, Paquimé was hit by a series of catastrophes: an earthquake, a meteor strike, and finally, an assault by a well-armed enemy, perhaps the Aztecs. The city was abandoned by 1400 and never reinhabited.

José is telling the story of Paquimé in a vault that once stored beans, squash, chiles, peyote, and maize, when we are startled by a hollow buzzing, an insect sound, like the drone of a cicada. José motions us to stay still, while he performs a strange ballet across the floor into a dark corner of the room. Moments later he emerges into the filtered light holding a pure white rattlesnake, its tail twisting around his thin forearms. (Did he keep it here to impress the tourists? A conjuror's pet? If so, it worked.)

José rubs the flesh of the rattlesnake against our cheeks. This is not a ritualistic act, but an offering of experience. The snake is warm and smooth. I can feel the beating of its heart. Then José places the snake on the cold stone floor. It coils, then uncoils and vanishes into the fractured wall. José lights a cigarette and coughs. "It's all going to go as it did before," he says. "First the Indians, then the forest." Then he leaves us, alone in the deep silence of the sandstone ruins.

* * *

The libertarian economist John Baden used to quip that "even God wouldn't try to grow trees in Utah." The same maxim can be applied to the rest of the Southwest. You can cut down the primary forest, but you'll have a helluva time getting it to ever come back. There are 500-acre clearcuts on the Carson National Forest in northern New Mexico (one of the moister parts of the region), logged in the early 1960s, where the replanted trees remain shorter than your shoulders. It's a dry land and it's getting drier.

Desert forests, the green embroidery of the Southwestern landscape, are intimately tied to two features: water and elevation. The abstract concept of biological corridors is vividly expressed here on the face of the land itself, as the riparian forests (what's left of them) form thin veins through the vast deserts, linking the denser forests of distant mountain ranges. In the Pacific Northwest, the lower you go, the bigger the trees. That trend is reversed in the Southwest, where the deep forests of Mt. Graham float on a sky island a mile above the Arizona desert.

These factors create complex forest ecosystems that are extremely vulnerable to external influences, partially accounting for the paucity of old-growth in New Mexico and Arizona. In fact, the only region of the country with less old-growth forest than the Southwest is the southern coastal plain, now on its fourth generation of monocultural plantations.

Of course, the main reason the Southwest lacks old growth is the mission of the Forest Service, which has waged a merciless onslaught against the region's forests for the past forty years. On the surface, the agency's timber sale program appears to be an exercise in economic irrationality, since it loses nearly $10 million every year. In reality, of course, this largesse translated into corporate entitlements for companies like Duke City Lumber, Kaibab Forest Products, and Stone Forest Industries, whose mills served as the charnel houses for the forests of the Southwest, annually grinding up about 500 million board feet of public timber.

The presence of any significant chunks of old-growth forest in the Southwest today is largely due to the determined efforts of two tireless environmentalists: Robin Silver and Sam Hitt. Using the declining populations of Mexican spotted owls and northern goshawks as a legal wedge, Hitt and Silver teamed up with a pair of courageous scientists, Cole Crocker-Bedford and Peter Stacey, to craft a barrage of appeals, lawsuits, and Endangered Species Act petitions that eventually paralyzed the agency into something like submission.

Meanwhile, the "managed" forests of the region are sprucing up. And I don't mean they are getting cleaner. Less than a century ago, the forests of the Mogollon Rim, for example, were among the most exquisite on the continent: cool and open stands of big yellow-bellied ponderosa pines. Today these forests have been transformed into a cluttered thicket of spruce and piss-fir. It is the old story of mismanagement played out on a bioregional scale: grazing, high-grading, and fire suppression.

The ecosystem has been terraformed, inverted. But the forest is aiming to right itself on its own volition. The fuel is building up. The fires will come. There will be no stopping them. And the once and future forest will rise up out of the ashes like a true phoenix. Burn, baby, burn.

* * *

Once again I am drawn back, almost as if down the pathways of a dream, to the image of Old Oraibi at dusk, a dark mesa in an ancient light. Oraibi, sacred city of the Hopi, is one of the oldest continuously inhabited communities in North America. Here a complex society and agriculture co-evolved with a parched landscape of sand and stone. Here is a community that has sustained itself under the harshest conditions of nature, internal strife, and cultural aggression. The survival of Oraibi derives from a cultivated wisdom about the desert, an intimate knowledge of its limitations and capabilities.

"Together we realize the dangers of losing our land and our culture," the late Hopi elder Thomas Banyacya told me years ago. "We must come together will all people to protect this land or it will die."

There are answers here to question I have not yet learned to ask. They involve the nature of paradox: pacifism and resistance; despair and hope; poverty and wealth; change and tradition; freedom and responsibility; wilderness and community.

Standing at the base of Oraibi as the orange sun eases below Third Mesa, I am overwhelmed by the irresistible power of this place, by a fierce love for the land, by an unyielding desire for justice for its people.

Taos.

The Killing of Leroy Jackson

THE NAVAJO ENVIRONMENTALIST LEROY JACKSON HAD BEEN MISSING FOR eight days when an anonymous tip led New Mexico state police to a white van, its windows concealed by towels and blankets, parked at a rest stop atop the Brazos Cliffs south of Chama, New Mexico. The doors were locked; a putrid odor emanated from inside.

Patrolman Ted Ulibari broke the driver's door window and looked inside. In the back seat, under a thick wool blanket, he found the sprawled body of Leroy Jackson. He had been dead for days.

Jackson was the charismatic leader of Dine CARE, an environmental group of traditionalists on the big Navajo reservation. He was also my friend. Jackson was on his way from Taos to Washington, DC, where he planned to confront the Clinton administration over logging in the old-growth ponderosa pine forests in the Chuska Mountains, a mysterious and beautiful blue range that rises out of the high desert in northern Arizona and New Mexico. The Chuskas are a sacred place for the Navajo and Hopi, an earthly anchor of their complex cosmology.

Only days before Jackson disappeared, he had spoken out against the logging plans at a public hearing in Window Rock, Arizona. The Bureau of Indian Affairs (BIA) had just requested an exemption from the Endangered Species Act, which would allow the Navajo Forest Products Industries to clearcut the old-growth forest habitat of the Mexican spotted owl, a threatened species, in the Chuska Mountains near Jackson's home.

In the exemption request to the US Fish and Wildlife Service, the BIA had arrogantly claimed that because owls are "symbols of death" to some Navajo, the extirpation of the bird from reservation lands could be legally justified on religious and cultural grounds. During the hearing, Jackson eviscerated the Bureau for promoting a racist ruse to sanction the destruction of sacred forestlands.

More critically, Jackson hinted publicly at possible corrupt practices by the tribal logging company and officials at the BIA. He urged the Navajo Nation to return to its traditional respect for the land and to support practices that preserved local jobs and forests.

Jackson's remarks were greeted with angry gestures and threats of violence from loggers and millworkers. He received threats from Navajo Forest Products Industries (NFPI) executives and from employees at the Bureau of Indian Affairs. Leroy and his wife Adella, a nurse, were rudely awakened by late-night phone calls threatening to burn down their home. Jackson dismissed them at the time, but these and other threats led many of Jackson's closest friends to conclude that he was assassinated because of his environmental activism.

Although initial reports indicated that blood, possibly in large quantities, was found at the scene, state police later said that there were no obvious signs of foul play. A cursory autopsy ruled out most natural causes of death, including stroke, heart attack, and carbon monoxide poisoning. The results of a toxicology report showed trace quantities of marijuana and methadone in Jackson's blood and tissue. Even though Jackson was not a known drug user, the police swiftly dismissed his mysterious death as a drug overdose.

Jackson's friends claimed that the investigation into his death was cursory at best and pointed to irregularities and possible cover-ups. For example, the police refused to look into several credible reports that Jackson's van had not been parked at the Brazos overlook during the preceding week. The police also failed to photograph the crime scene or dust the van for fingerprints. For nearly a week, police left the van outside in a Chama parking lot before towing it to the crime lab in Santa Fe.

Although the New Mexico state police told Jackson's wife, Adella Begay, that only a small amount of blood was found on a pillow near Jackson's body, a source who was at the scene shortly after the van was discovered said the interior "looked staged. His body was posed and there was blood on the carpets and the seats."

Responding to a request from Jackson's friends, Bill Richardson, then the congressman representing northern New Mexico, sent a letter to the director of the FBI asking the agency to investigate the circumstances surrounding Jackson's death. In his letter, Richardson noted the recent threats Jackson had received for his environmental activism and suggested that, "a major crime may have been committed." Ultimately, the FBI declined to launch an inquiry, citing that the state police had concluded that Jackson had overdosed on methadone.

At Jackson's burial, his friends vowed to continue the search for his killer and to intensify the fight to protect the old forests on the Navajo reservation. "Those who killed Leroy thought they could silence him," said Earl Tulley, a traditionalist Navajo who co-founded Dine CARE with Jackson. "But they only made his cause stronger than when he was alive."

I met Leroy Jackson three times and talked to him often on the phone. We were friends. Kindred spirits. His voice radiated a rare combination of power, eloquence, and humility.

Leroy Jackson cared about his culture and the Navajo people as much as those forests on the slopes of the Chuskas. Indeed, for Jackson, the future of the Navajo forests was inseparably tied to the future of the Navajo people and their religion. That's what motivated his struggle.

The last time I spoke to Jackson was about two months before his death. He described in sharp detail plans by the Bureau of Indian Affairs and Navajo Forest Products Industries to clearcut much of the last remaining old-growth ponderosa pine forest on the Big Reservation.

Jackson was angry, but not discouraged. He explained that his new alliance of traditionalist Navajo leaders and energetic young activists was growing in strength and power on the reservation. He believed that Dine CARE was on the verge of dramatically reshaping logging practices on Navajo lands.

"They are going after the heart of the old forest in the sacred mountains," Jackson told me. "But they will not get it. There is a new respect for the old ways."

Ultimately, Jackson was aiming to change something much broader and more fundamental than simply the layout of a timber sale. Like other traditionalists, Jackson understood that outside forces, including the BIA, uranium and coal companies, oil and gas corporations, and the timber firms, had assiduously corrupted the Navajo tribal council. Under the banner of jobs, sovereignty, and future prosperity, these forces had begun stripping the reservation of its natural resources and cultural and spiritual heritage. This path had put millions in the pockets of the corporations, a few tribal leaders and some officials at the BIA, but had left the reservation itself impoverished: economically, ecologically, and culturally.

In response, Jackson and his companions were seeking a return to traditional Navajo values of the land and its use. This was dangerous ground and Jackson knew it. He told me about weekly death threats and about how loggers had hung him in effigy from their trucks the previous summer.

I remember telling him to be cautious. Yes, most hardcore environmentalists get threatened and we treat the threats almost as badges of honor—something to laugh and brag about, but not lose much sleep over. But I warned him that in the Southwest it's different. There, the threats have a history of being backed up by violence.

I wasn't telling Jackson anything that he didn't already know intimately. One of the last times we spoke he told me that he believed he would probably die in the fight to save the Chuskas.

* * *

Leroy Jackson was buried under ancient ponderosa pines high in the Chuska Mountains, the way to the burial site marked by pink ribbons. Some were tied to trees and shrubs, others to root-wads and slash left by the extensive clearcutting, testimonial to the Chuska's ignoble claim as the most intensely logged range in the Southwest.

Under a soft wind, looking out over the blue mountains, etched in the autumnal hue of aspens turning gold, the Navajo traditionalist John Redhouse spoke about Leroy's life: "Leroy was no different from the other Dine warriors and patriots who gave their lives. He took a vow to protect the male deity represented by the Chuskas and to preserve balance and harmony for the Navajo people. He saw that the Navajo tribe has not shared this vision, that they have pursued the white man's values. We will continue his struggle. It is a struggle for our destiny and our future."

WINDOW ROCK.

Anatomy of a Swindle:
Land Fraud as Government Policy

AS YOU DRIVE ACROSS CENTRAL UTAH ON INTERSTATE 70, YOU ARE LIKELY to be captivated by a golden bulge of sandstone shimmering in the sun to the south. This is the San Rafael Swell, a knot of canyons, domes and cliffs the marks the beginning of the redrock country of the Four Corners region. The old desert rat Edward Abbey praised the Swell as one of the most austere and beautiful places in the desert Southwest.

Naturally, the Swell, underlain with coal seams and pools of oil, has also been long prized by other less aesthetically-minded interests: strip miners and oil and gas companies.

Much of the area lies under the jurisdiction of the Bureau of Land Management (BLM), never known as the greenest of federal agencies. Still, because most of the Swell remains in a roadless and relatively unscathed condition it has been difficult for the BLM to get away with simply opening it up to mining and drilling. Lawsuits and endangered species keep getting in the way. Environmentalists have long sought to turn the area into a wilderness or national park.

Enter Steven Griles, deputy Secretary of Interior in the Bush administration and former lobbyist for oil and mining interests. Already under investigation for bullying the Bureau of Land Management on behalf of his former oil industry clients, Griles placed himself at the epicenter of a new scandal involving the proposed swap of more than 135,000 acres of land in the heart of the San Rafael Swell with the state of Utah, in exchange for parcels of state-owned land totaling 108,000 acres.

The deal, which was reluctantly shelved by the Bush White House following a scathing internal review by the Interior department's Inspector General, would have bilked the federal government out of ten of millions of dollars and opened habitat for rare species to unrestricted plunder.

Under a scheme hatched by Utah congressmen Chris Cannon and James Hansen, more than 130,000 acres of BLM land in the Swell would have been handed to the state of Utah in exchange for 107,000 acres of state lands. The congressmen promoted the deal as "fair value exchange," meaning that the market value of the lands being traded was roughly equal, a requirement of federal land law. To rub salt in the wound, the deal was pitched as an environmentally benign transaction.

But this was a crock and most people inside the BLM knew it. Biologists warned that the federal lands harbored the desert tortoise, an endangered species, and thus could not be traded away. Geologists disclosed that the federal land contained a trove of minerals and natural gas deposits, while the state lands were nearly worthless economically and offered little in the way of ecological value. One BLM officer in Utah noted that the oil, gas, coal, and shale deposits alone on the federal lands "could bring in hundreds of millions of dollars."

Agency land appraisers fired off internal memos saying that the appraisals had been deliberately cooked to make the grossly inequitable deal appear like a bargain for the feds. One memo said that the official appraisal, approved by Griles, was "one-sided and inaccurate." The appraisal approved by Griles and his cohorts valued the state and federal lands at about $35 million each. But BLM appraisers in Utah determined that the federal lands were worth at least $117 million more than the state lands.

In an internal memo to BLM director Kathleen Clarke, Dave Cavanagh, the agency's chief land appraiser, pointed out that the deal "generously inflated the value of the state lands to the disadvantage of the BLM." He also warned that public statements by officials in the Interior department, which stated that the deal had been scrutinized by independent appraisers, was "potentially misleading to the public." One of the most astonishing things about this memo is the fact that Cavanagh has himself been under fire from environmental groups for his role in approving bogus appraisals for other land deals.

The BLM's Clarke dismissed the concerns of her line officers, concealed the real numbers from skeptical members of congress, such as Rep. Nick Rahall, the West Virginia Democrat, and pursued the deal anyway. Word came down from Clarke's office that dissenters were to shut up and stop putting their complaints about the deal in writing. Efforts to shred the paper trail exposing the deal ensued.

Clarke was a former top aide to both Rep. James Hanson, former head of the House Resources Committee, and former Utah governor and Bush EPA director Mike Leavitt, a notorious anti-environmentalist who believes that all federal lands should be turned over to the states.

Clarke maintained that she recused herself from all matters related to the deal in order to avoid a conflict of interest. But the IG report revealed that in March of 2002, Clarke met with Sally Wisely, the BLM's top officer in Utah. Wisely told the IG's investigators that she had requested the meeting in order to relay her fears that the deal was being rushed through without enough attention being given to the concerns of the appraisers and geologists. Clarke told Wisely that it was a done deal.

But Clarke was just a stooge for Griles, who for all practical purposes ran the BLM like a private fiefdom and supply depot for his clients. Since taking office Griles pursued a course of privatizing the federal estate through land swaps, where federal lands rich in timber, minerals and oil are traded away for beat-over private and state lands. After the transfers, the lands, now free from the vexations of federal environmental laws, are easier for extractive industries to exploit with dispatch.

Griles' lieutenant in the Utah land exchange was Thomas Fulton, the deputy assistant secretary of Interior for Lands and Minerals Management. Fulton handled the negotiations with the state of Utah and the congressional delegation and ended up as the fall guy in the affair. The IG report fingered Fulton for providing false information to other Department of Interior officials (i.e., Interior Secretary Gale Norton) and members of congress. Fulton was removed from his position and sent into bureaucratic exile planning the BLM's commemoration of the bi-centennial of the Lewis and Clark expedition.

In the summer of 2002, BLM appraiser Kent Wilkinson went public with his objections to the deal. The whistleblower said that the swindle was one of the most one-sided land deals since the sale of Manhattan. "This is like Enron all over again," Wilkinson wrote in a broadcast email to journalists, which accompanied his analysis of the deal. "They're cooking the books and it's all to the detriment of the public."

Wilkinson's revelations prompted a public fit from Rep. Chris Cannon, the pudgy Utah congressman. Cannon called Wilkinson a publicity-seeking liar and a stooge of environmentalists. The congressman summoned the appraiser's boss to his office and demanded that "strong measures" be taken against the whistleblower for insubordination. "I want to make sure they get slapped hard, because they're acting inappropriately," Cannon blustered.

With a congressional bounty on his head, Wilkinson brought his concerns to Public Employees for Environmental Responsibility (PEER), a whistleblower protection group and one of the worthiest environmental outfits inside the Beltway.

PEER went on the offensive against Cannon and recruited help from Jack McDonald, the former chief appraiser for the BLM in Utah. "This is just another rip-off," McDonald told the *Washington Post*. "What does it tell you when an agency suppresses its own professionals? The agency's got something to hide."

But none of this stopped Cannon from proceeding with the deal. He pushed the swindle through the House in the fall of 2003 without debate, but Congress adjourned before the senate could act on it.

Don't look for any prosecutions to emerge from this affair, though. John Ashcroft passed on pressing any criminal charges against Griles, Clark, and Fulton for the swindle.

But the land exchanges go on, many with similar accounting hi-jinks and lopsided appraisals. In 2004 alone, more than a million acres of federal land was secretly traded away to states, private land-owners, and corporations. This is the dream of the

Sagebrush Rebels finally come true: the federal estate is steadily being turned over to private hands unencumbered by noisome environmental regulations.

"Despite some pretty damning revelations of what these people have done, you don't get a very good idea of what's going to happen to them," said Janine Blaeloch, director of the Seattle-based Western Lands Exchange Project, the only group in the nation fighting these rip-offs (and one of the best environmental groups of any kind). "This case shows how poisonous these land deals are, especially in places like Utah where the politicians want to privatize all public lands."

GREEN RIVER, UTAH.

Fear and Firewood in New Mexico

THE FIRST SNOWS OF FALL DUSTED THE HIGH VALLEYS OF NORTHERN New Mexico's Sangre de Cristo Mountains about the same time many residents of this beautiful and rugged landscape received an ominous letter from a man called Leonard Lucero. Lucero's letter warned that because of a federal court ruling on the Mexican spotted owl in a suit brought by environmentalists, many people would now be prohibited from gathering firewood from the Carson National Forest.

The letter hit its target, sparking angry protests and menacing telephone calls to New Mexico environmentalists Sam Hitt and Joanie Berde. Lucero is not a Wise-Use agitator. He's supervisor of the Carson National Forest, part of the new, kinder, and gentler Forest Service. Lucero is not a newcomer to the agency, however. Indeed, he owns a particularly vicious resumé, capped, perhaps, by his orchestration of the massacre at Millennium Grove, where he permitted Willamette Industries to clearcut the oldest trees in Oregon on Easter weekend 1985, even though he knew a federal court had issued an injunction against the sale.

In New Mexico, Lucero got away with his outrageous provocations. Newspapers throughout the state editorialized against the injunction. Even Bill Richardson condemned the ruling. Richardson, at least moderately sympathetic to environmental causes, wrote a blistering letter to environmentalists chastising them for their insensitivity to the rural poor and to the "custom" and "culture" of the communities of northern New Mexico. Richardson closed by threatening a sufficiency language rider to bypass the Endangered Species Act unless environmentalists allowed firewood cutting to resume.

But Richardson was misinformed. The fuel wood crisis had little to do with insensitive environmentalists. A year before the dramatic ruling on the Mexican Spotted Owl, Sam Hitt's group Forest Guardians, for example, had raised $35,000 to buy firewood-splitting equipment for a small Hispanic logging company based in Vallecitos. Instead, the current situation is due almost entirely to the entrenched malfeasance of the Forest Service.

In response to Federal Judge Carl Muecke's order to halt timber cutting, the Forest Service chose to shut down virtually everything, including firewood and Christmas tree cutting. J. Fife Symington III, governor of Arizona, delivered the message: environmentalists are arrogant grinches, holding Christmas hostage. It was a deliberate strategy to generate a violent backlash against the owl and its proponents. Lucero know that the firewood issue carried a cultural resonance, and he exploited it. Moreover, the agency has learned its lessons from similar injunctions, particularly in Idaho where outrage generated by timber and mining companies caused the Wilderness Society and Pacific Rivers Council to drop an injunction protecting salmon habitat. The lesson: find a scapegoat and make them feel political pain.

To understand how firewood could erupt into an angry uprising, you must delve into the complex social history of northern New Mexico. Much of this terrain remains in dispute, entangled in broken treaties, sophisticated swindles, and thousands of promises betrayed by the federal government. This is the country where, in 1967, Reies Lopez Tijerina and his comrades in the Alianza Federal de las Mercedes (Federal Alliance of Free City States) seized the courthouse at Tierra Amarillo in a desperate act of symbolic defiance, a violent call for the return of Spanish land grants secured to Hispanics in the Treaty of Guadaloupe Hidalgo. Much of that land is now part of the Carson National Forest. The Alianza's courthouse raid ended in a fierce gun battle, Tijerina's arrest, and a resentment that still seethes.

It is this festering animosity that Lucero and his PR flack Gary Schiff, attempted to stoke and redirect at environmentalists. Soon after Judge Muecke imposed his injunction, Schiff took to local radio stations and said the people responsible for the firewood shutdown were Sam Hitt, Joanie Berde, and the Forest Conservation Council's John Talberth. They were the reason, Schiff intoned, some people might not have enough wood to get themselves through a harsh winter. The implication was clear: pressure them and the injunction might be dropped.

Joanie Berde lives in the small village of Llano, a battered collection of old adobes perched above the Rio Santa Barbara near the Picuris Pueblo. Here Berde runs Carson Forest Watch, an environmental group that monitors Forest Service activities in northern New Mexico. She was a plaintiff in the spotted owl suit that led to Judge Muecke's injunction. But Berde's not just an environmentalist. She's worked hard to form alliances with rural Hispanics, often sacrificing a more aggressive environmental posture to maintain a bridge of trust in her community. Those ties were severely tested when Berde became a prime target of the Forest Service's campaign of misinformation and intimidation.

"I was worried about Joanie," confessed Sam Hitt. "Llano is an isolated community in an area where shootings are not uncommon. I truly feared that the rantings of Lucero and Schiff might motivate someone to harm her or to torch her house."

Berde says she fielded numerous harassing phone calls and was told by her neighbors to be cautious, that resentment against her was spreading. After some initial apprehensions about her personal safety, however, a more profound concern began to emerge: that the firewood debacle might ignite a backlash against environmental protection in the region. "Shutting down the firewood program turned the little guys against us," Berde says. "They wondered why environmentalists were releasing large timber sales to big companies like Duke City, but they couldn't get their firewood. It was a difficult contradiction to rationalize."

What Berde wants to explain is that the Carson's fuelwood program simply isn't sustainable. It's a problem the Forest Service has been aware of since at least 1977, when the Peñasco District of the Carson estimated that firewood was being logged off at more than seven times the sustainable rate. Even so, the Forest Service took no action. In fact, the Carson remains the only national forest with an unregulated personal fuelwood program. For decades, local residents have been able to cut as much firewood as they want, wherever they want.

Of course, people from the villages of northern New Mexico have been gathering firewood for centuries. Then, as now, piñon was the preferred species. It was plentiful, dried quickly, and burned slowly. Generations of firewood-cutting on the old *ejidos* (communal lands) had caused minimal ecological damage. But the advent of the chainsaw and pickup truck changed the cutting patterns, opening up the mid-elevation ponderosa stands and the high spruce/fire forests, and making commercial exploitation possible.

But the current bleak situation also owes a lot to Forest Service social engineering efforts, beginning in the 1950s and 1960s, to turn rural Hispanics from graziers into loggers. The Forest Service's motives were not entirely benign in this matter. Agency leaders believed that if they could entice Hispanics into relinquishing their sheep herds, there would be less reason to press the old land claims against the Forest Service. That's why the agency created the Vallecitos Sustained-Yield Unit, a disastrous experiment on the Carson that promised a steady flow of timber to a locally-owned sawmill. But the Duke City mill ended up in the hands of a British corporation, Hanson PLC, which opened and closed it according to the inscrutable rhythms of distant economic forces.

The Forest Service set up small commercial firewood operations in Hispanic communities. "The wood co-ops prospered for a time," writes William deBuys in *Enchantment and Exploitation*, his extraordinary history of the Sangre de Cristo region. "But most developed serious management problems and ceased operating by the early 70s...and the indiscriminate cutting continued."

By the mid-70s, then, the Forest Service knew it should have acted decisively to restrict firewood cutting. Instead, it backed off, taking a blindly *laissez-faire* approach. As a result, the volume of fuelwood cut from the Carson has nearly doubled since 1976. For the past three years, the Carson has given away about 30 million board feet of fuelwood a year—that's about three times the size of its commercial timber sale program. But as the cut increased, the number of permits declined. Much of the firewood is being resold in Taos, Santa Fe, and Albuquerque, where burgeoning development has created a lucrative black market in federal fuelwood.

Rampant firewood cutting has shorn gaping ecological holes in the Carson, now a nearly snagless forest. There is little downed woody debris left, especially in riparian areas where it is important for trout and other aquatic species. And, yes, the Mexican spotted owl is threatened by further firewood logging. So are other species that depend on standing dead trees, particularly cavity-nesting songbirds.

But the crisis is not just ecological, it's also cultural. Subsistence fuelwood gathering by rural Hispanics in northern New Mexico is threatened, but not by spotted owls or environmentalists. The problem resides with the Forest Service, which betrayed its commitment to both the environment and rural communities by siding with affluent commercial interests. When its mismanagement of the public's forests was exposed by a federal judge, the first reflex of the Forest Service was to shift the blame to environmentalists, to smear them in an shameful campaign of harassment and intimidation. This is the Forest Service as Bill Clinton and Jack Ward Thomas redesigned it, not James Watt.

But Joanie Berde remains confident the tactic will eventually backfire on the agency. "Ultimately, people will realize that the Forest Service has lied to them once again," Berde said. "It's our challenge, as environmentalists, to demonstrate that the future of rural communities in northern New Mexico is tied to the health of our forests."

LLANO, NEW MEXICO.

Pray to Play: Bush's Faith-Based National Parks

THE VIEW FROM THE SOUTH RIM OF THE GRAND CANYON, SMOGGED UP AS it is these days, still retains the power to prompt even the most secular of visitors into transcendentalist reveries as they cast their eyes toward Shiva's Temple and Wotan's Throne. Now tourists at the federal park in northern Arizona will be greeted with scriptural passages affixed to park signs to help interpret the religious experience of gazing into God's mighty chasm.

In the fall of 2003, Donald Murphy, deputy director of the National Park Service, ordered three bronze plaques featuring quotes from Psalms 68:4, 66:4, and 104:24 placed on viewing platforms on the south rim of the Canyon. The plaques were made and donated by the Evangelical Sisterhood of Mary in Phoenix, who live in a convent called Canaan in the Desert. The convent was founded in 1963 by Mother Basilea, who visited the Sinai where the nun said she conversed with the Supreme Deity about the moral decline of the western world.

The nuns' website warns that an "avalanche of moral decay is upon us... our society is disintegrating." As evidence, the nuns point to the removal of Judge Roy Moore's monument to the 10 Commandments in the lobby of the Alabama Supreme Court and to the heretical appearance of the Dalai Lama at the National Cathedral, "another illustration of how God's commandments are pushed aside, step by step. May Jesus help us and guard our hearts!"

At the urging of the sisters, Murphy overturned a decision to ban the plaques by the Park's superintendent, who contended the religious messages violated the US Constitution.

That's not all. Now, after soaking in the grandeur of the canyon, visitors can retire to the Park bookstore where they can browse through the diaries of John Wesley Powell, Edward Abbey's *Down the River*, historian Stephen Pyne's excellent *How the Canyon Became Grand*, and numerous volumes on the geology of the canyon. After all, the Grand Canyon has long been viewed as a kind of living encyclopedia of geological forces, a layered history of the Earth that debunked fundamentalist dogma on the age of the earth. "Nowhere on the earth's surface, so far as we know, are the secrets of its structure revealed as here," wrote the great American geologist John Strong Newberry.

But starting in the summer of 2003, the Park's bookstore began offering a volume titled *The Grand Canyon: a Different View*. The view found in those pages is indeed different. This book of lavish photographs and essays presents the creationist account of the origins of the great canyon of the Colorado River. It's edited by Tom Vail, a river guide, who offers Christian float trips through the canyon. "For years, as a Colorado River guide I told people how the Grand Canyon was formed over the evolutionary time scale of millions of years," Vail writes in the introduction to the book. "Then I met the Lord. Now, I have 'a different view' of the Canyon, which, according to a biblical time scale, can't possibly be more than about a few thousand years old."

One of the contributors is creation "scientist" Dr. Gary Parker who observes: "Where did the Grand Canyon itself come from? The Flood may have stacked the rock like a giant layer cake, but what cut the cake? One thing is sure: the Colorado River did not do it."

Earlier in the year, the Bush administration prevented park rangers from publishing a rebuttal to the book for use by interpretive staff and seasonal employees who are often confronted during tours by creationist zealots.

In southern California, a similar battle rages over a Latin cross erected on the Sunrise Rocks in the Mojave National Preserve. Apparently, the cross was erected by the Veterans of Foreign Wars and has since become a site for sunrise Easter services and a meeting ground for Wise-Use ranchers associated with the Christian Identity movement.

In December 2000, Park Service managers agreed to remove the cross, based on advice from the Justice Department that the icon violated the Constitution and Park Service regulations. But the Park Service backed down after Congressman Jerry Lewis, the right wing zealot from San Diego, intervened. The ACLU sued the Park Service in March of 2001 and won an injunction. The Bush Administration appealed and the case remains pending before the Ninth Circuit Court of Appeals.

Meanwhile, in the nation's capital the Park Service has bowed to pressure from the religious right to rewrite the history of protests on the national mall. Since 1995, the interpretive center at the Lincoln Memorial in Washington has shown an eight-minute long film depicting various demonstrations and gatherings at the monument, including anti-war protests, concerts, and Martin Luther King's most famous speech. In 2004, the Park Service acquiesced to demands from Christian groups to edit out footage of anti-Vietnam War protests and images of gay rights and pro-choice demonstrations. In a letter to the Park Service, the Christian groups charged that the film implied that "Lincoln would have supported homosexual and abortion 'rights' as well as feminism."

The Park Service HQ responded that they would edit the film to present a "more balanced" version. The revamped film includes footage of rallies by anti-abortion and Christian groups, such as the Promisekeepers, and shots of a pro-Gulf War demonstration. Neither of these events took place at the Lincoln Memorial.

"The Park Service leadership now caters exclusively to conservative Christian fundamentalist groups," says Jeff Ruch, director of Public Employees for Environmental Responsibility. "The Bush Administration appears to be sponsoring a program of Faith-Based Parks."

What's next? Live reenactments of the witch trials at Salem National Historical Park?

FLAGSTAFF.

How the West Was Eaten

COWS YOU SAY? IS THERE REALLY A BOVINE THREAT? WELL, FOR THOSE of you who believe that logging is the dominant threat to our public lands, think again. The Forest Service and the Bureau of Land Management control about 320 million races in the West. Grazing allotments cover 260 million acres or 82 percent of these lands, lands that have suffered from a century of malign neglect and outright abuse.

In the arid West, political and economic power derives from the control of water. (Check out Donald Worster's masterful *Rivers of Empire* for a damning explication of this reality.) Most of the water in the West goes not to satiate the thirst of people, but cows. Ironically, cows don't treat the West's most treasured resource very well. Yes, cows do kill salmon and trout and other aquatic species. Spawning beds are trampled, riparian vegetation is devoured, streambanks mangled.

Cows are also the chief source of pollution in the waters of the Interior. Most of the coliform and salmonella bacteria and giardia present in Western streams is discharged by cows. Consider this: cows release about 1,000 tons of excrement into Western waters every day. The situation is so ripe that environmental groups in Oregon, the trial balloon state, sued the Forest Service alleging that current grazing practices violate the Clean Water Act. The environmentalist want the Forest Service to get a Section 404 discharge permit for livestock allotments, a permit usually required for power plants, factories, and slaughterhouses.

Riparian areas cover about one percent of the total federal lands in the West, but represent vital habitat for about 75 percent of the native flora and fauna of the region. More than 80 percent of the riparian habitat on BLM lands is now in a degraded ecological condition, primarily due to domestic livestock grazing.

The rangelands themselves are in a similar state. Native grasses and plants are systematically replaced with species more favorable to livestock. Fire is excluded. Juniper and brushlands uprooted through chaining operations, and larkspur and other plants sprayed with pesticides. The native grasslands of the Great Basin have almost been eliminated by decades of overgrazing, leaving behind a battered legacy of exotic grasses, woody scrubland, and neo-deserts of scorched earth. In sum, the range ecosystems of the West have undergone a wholesale ecological conversion.

The fragmentation of Western rangelands is extreme. For example, nearly every grazing allotment is fenced, often with barbed wire, posing significant barriers for the migration routes of elk, deer, bison, and pronghorn. A conservative estimate from the BLM suggests that there are at least 300,000 miles of fence zigzagging across federal lands in the West. More realistic estimates put the figure closer to 500,000 miles. No one knows for sure.

Perhaps the ugliest aspect of public-lands ranching is its relentless war on the native predators of the West, including grizzlies, wolves, cougar, and coyotes. Even though livestock losses to predation total less than 2 percent per year, there is an entire agency of the federal government set up to act as a mercenary army for Western ranchers: Animal Damage Control (AKA, Wildlife Services). Over the past several decades, ADC killers have exacted a terrible toll on already depleted populations of Western predators. Each year, ADC killers track, trap, poison, gas, or shoot 135,000 mammals and more than two million birds. Last year alone, the agency killed more than 80,000 coyotes on public lands, a number as staggering as it is repulsive.

Never mind the fact that there are more cows on public lands than pronghorn, more domestic sheep than bighorns or mountain goats. There are more predator control agents than there are wolves, more ranchers than grizzlies, more range "scientists" than sockeye salmon in the Snake River basin. "The livestock industry is the last wildlife-genocide program in the United States," says Bruce Apple, of Rest the West.

The list of indigenous species threatened by cattle and sheep grazing on public lands is long and growing: willow flycatchers, Lahotan cutthroat trout, burrowing owls, pygmy ferruginous owls, Sage grouse, Dakota skipper butterflies, redband trout, loach minnows, and spikedace to name only a few. This is to say nothing of the lethal diseases passed from cattle and sheep to rare native species, such as bighorns and mountain goats. Huge holes are been riven into the natural fabric of the West by industrial ranching and no one wants to talk about it.

Take roads for an example. There's a nearly unanimous opinion among ecologists that roads pose one of the gravest threats to biological diversity in the American West. There are already more than 250,000 miles of ranching roads crisscrossing public lands, cutting across trout streams, elk calving grounds, and grizzly habitat. More are being bulldozed every year. Most of these roads are substandard, unplanned, and quietly (and sometimes not so quietly) eroded away, clogging the precious waters of the arid West and posing even further risks to bull trout, chinook salmon, and westslope cutthroat trout.

Then there's issue of wildlands. Quite simply, cows and sheep can go where log skidders, chokesetters and hard rock miners can't: wilderness areas, riparian strips, and other so-called natural preserves, including Great Basin National Park.

In 1993, former Arizona government Bruce Babbitt arrived in Washington, DC as Bill Clinton's Interior Secretary. Having resigned his position as head of the League of Conservation Voters, Babbitt quickly promised his pals in the environmental movement that he would move swiftly to reform outdated and destructive practices on the federal lands over which he now had control.

Babbitt left the starting gate in February 1993 hot-to-trot, tucking into Clinton's first budget request a scheme to reform grazing, mining and timber practices on public lands. At the time, these initiatives received a lot of adulatory press, but upon reflection it was a monumental miscalculation to invite Congress (even one controlled by Democrats) to authorize actions that Babbitt could have taken alone administratively.

The result was predictable. A posse of Western senators, led by the Montana Democrat Max Baucus, met with White House chief of staff Mack McLarty (a former energy executive) in late March of that year and demanded that the reforms, tentative as they were, be stripped from the budget. McLarty quickly assented, tossing the proposals on the political scrapheap with the other progressive casualties of Clinton's rookie months, right alongside Lani Guinier, gays in the military, and the humane treatment of Haitian refugees. All early warning signs, to anyone paying attention, that the political center was veering sharply back into the old groove on the corporate right.

At the time, Babbitt claimed ignorance of the decision to delete his public land reform package from the budget and, in fact, engaged in some very public posturing and pouting about being overruled by higher levels of the administration. The image, reinforced by a sycophantic profile in the *New York Times Magazine*, was of Babbitt standing tall against the despoilers of the West, only to be shot in the back by White House politicos. Yet, it turns out that Babbitt was far from innocent in this matter. Indeed, as Interior Secretary and personal confidant to Clinton, he circulated freely in the administration's control booth. Indeed, Babbitt's maneuvers were entirely characteristic of the politician. During his tenure at the Interior Department, Babbitt developed a distinctive pattern of behavior: initiate a cautious policy advance, retreat frantically at the first hint of opposition, then call a self-exculpating press conference to blame others (superiors, subordinates, associates, and interest groups) for his own mistakes and failures. When things went wrong, Babbitt always seemed to be AWOL. Pity his assistant secretaries and agency heads, who served as Babbitt's personal stable of scapegoats.

Duly chastened, Babbitt promised to "return to the West and listen to the people"— that is, the ranchers. He set up a series of grazing town halls held in Colorado, Montana, New Mexico, and Nevada. Opponents of federal grazing practices were largely excluded from these meetings. Instead, Babbitt was exposed to the unyielding recalcitrance of Western governors and congressional potentates, who lectured Babbitt that his timid plan would destroy the cultural equilibrium of the West.

The by-product of those Town Hall sessions was the publication of a report dubbed, "Rangeland '94." This document represented a significantly scaled back series of reforms of public land grazing practices, designed mainly to raise the BLM's standards up to the same level as those governing Forest Service lands. The report also called for a modest hike in grazing fees.

Even so, the new proposal failed to satisfy Western ranchers, who claimed (ludicrously) that it represented a taking of their water and property rights. Western senators, Democrat and Republican, launched a filibuster against the Interior Appropriations bill aimed at crushing the new range plan. Senator Malcolm Wallop, the Wyoming Republican, threw a particularly vulgar tantrum on the senate floor, alleging that anti-grazing environmentalists planned "a cultural cleansing of Wyoming, not unlike the Serbian rape of Bosnia."

Eventually, another compromise was worked out between Babbitt, Rep. George Miller, and Senator Harry Reid, in which Babbitt agreed to adopt a more limited set of reforms by late winter of 1995. The package was pulled from the bill. The filibuster was dropped and Babbitt prepared to move forward administratively.

Then along came NAFTA with Clinton short on votes and desperate to bargain with anyone. Scenting blood, several Western congressmen, led by Rep. Bob Smith, an Oregon Republic who owned a federal grazing permit, threatened to withdraw their support for NAFTA unless the Clinton White House agree to even further water down its range plan. Another deal was cut.

But the ranchers, the Western governors, and their backers remained unmollified. They wanted a trophy, a head. "Jim Baca must go," declared Cecil Andrus, the Democratic governor of Idaho, pronouncing a political death sentence for the embattled director of the Bureau of Land Management. "He's too aggressive and abrasive. Babbitt will never be able to gain the trust of ranchers with Baca in there."

So Babbitt gave his former friend Jim Baca the boot, then left DC in a plane for some Kissinger-like shuttle diplomacy, landing in Carson City, Nevada; Cheyenne, Wyoming; and Boise, Idaho. The capitulation was total. He devised a new set of public land ranching rules, measures briskly circumcised to fit the preconditions set by the Democratic fraternity of Western governors, led by Andrus, Roy Romer of Colorado, and Nevada's Mike Sullivan. If Babbitt felt humiliated, he didn't show it. Instead, he solicited letters from each of the governors to be included in the Interior Department press releases announcing the demise of his reform package. Listen to the words of chief instigator Andrus about Babbitt: "He came, he listened, he made changes to make it more workable in the Rocky Mountain West."

How workable? Workable enough that when the Bush administration arrived on the scene in 2001, they barely had to adjust a single component of the Babbitt plan to fashion it to their liking. And the changes they made were mostly for show to placate the Wise Use ultras.

Rancho Deluxe

How many public lands ranchers are there, you ask? Good question. For all of their political clout, you'd think the West was coppiced with them. In reality, there are only about 20,000 permittees on Forest Service and BLM lands. This is about five-tenths of 1 percent of the population of the West and less than 4 percent of the population of Wyoming, the most sparsely populated state in the US. Looked at another way, they could all be comfortably corralled in four of the new maximum security prisons constructed after passage of the latest bi-partisan crime bill.

The political power of Western livestock ranchers is also totally disproportionate to their waning economic influence. Thomas Power, chair of the economics department at the University of Montana, says that "ranching, despite its colorful association with the 'old West,' is not a dominant part of the contemporary Western economies. Ranching directly provides less than half of one percent of all the income received by Westerners. Ranching on federal lands is responsible for even less economic activity: One dollar out of every $2,500 of income received."

Who are these rangelords? Are they the small, family ranchers promoted by Babbitt and Bush alike as the crusty cultural icons of the American West? Sure, there are some small ranchers and a few ranching families who actually depend on the running of stock across the public range for a living. But the vast majority of grazing allotments reside with a small fraction of permittees, including some of the richest families in America, multinational corporations, regional utilities, media celebrities (such as Sam Donaldson), and several politicians.

Even those small family ranches aren't really owned by the ranchers, but by banks. The value of these ranches, most of which are mortgaged to the hilt, doesn't derive from the base property (i.e., the land actually owned by the rancher), but from the exclusive access to thousands of adjacent acres of public land, the water rights, and the nominal grazing fees. The public subsidies are treated as private capital.

Raise the grazing fees to market rates or enact tough regulations reducing the number cattle or sheep on a given allotment and where and when they can graze and the value of the ranch plummets, leaving the banks holding a half empty bag. Banks and financiers don't tolerate such loses. Witness the Keating Five (three-fifths of whom were Westerners) or the fate of Jim Baca.

So, at a time when the Democrats controlled the executive branch, both houses of congress, and most of the state houses in the West, how did the best chance to reform grazing policy in the last sixty years collapse with such finality? The most charitable interpretation, once advanced by many diehard Babbitt boosters, had the Interior Secretary playing something of a confidence game on the Western governors. The loosely constructed theory goes like this: Babbitt really believed in the fundamental reform of Western public land policy, but he caved in to commercial interests in the early days of Clintontime in order to enact more sweeping changes in Clinton's second term, when the administration would be less vulnerable politically. Under this scenario, a lame duck presidency was to have been Babbitt's ticket back to environmental redemption.

That theory went bust pretty quick. The Democrats lost control of the House, then the Senate. The Clinton administration, following the political charts of Dick Morris, swerved even farther to the right, making a string of deals with the Gingrich gang and publicly betraying the aspirations of the White House's most ardent supporters. Grazing reform was a dead issue.

Babbitt, whose own family owns large ranches in Arizona, fit the profile of another Western character familiar to readers of Mark Twain: the con man. Babbitt survived through eight years of Clintontime because he was able to run the same confidence trick on the same collection of dupes, over and over again: conflict-aversive conservationists and an eclectic collection of neo-liberals, devout communitarians, and social idealists, who were willing to suspend their disbelief in the fervent hope that meaningful dialogue with good ranchers could finally engineer a better future for the American West. Babbitt cynically played to these folks' inbred longing for a return to an Age of Innocence, where a kind of rural primitivism will prevail and the pastoral West will be lovingly cared for by the enlightened conservationists and small ranchers, a place where the New Forestry really is sustainable and the obligatory forms of mining are truly benign. Babbitt, of course, knew this was bullshit. His victims, though, continue to pursue these romantic fantasies.

But Babbitt, more than any Interior Secretary since fellow Arizonan Stuart Udall, was an expert at finding soft spots and exploiting them. He relentlessly evoked the cherished cliché of the Western rancher as a working model of ecological sensitivity, a particularly characterization. By what distorted measure is the preservation of the culture of Western ranching deemed a public value? Any serious historian of the West will explain that ranching is basically a kind of internal colonialism, a way to stake a claim on the land, first as a means to dispossess and exterminate Native peoples, then as a tool to evict poor Hispanics across the Southwest, and finally as a way to exert and maintain private rights over the public commons.

Public lands ranching is a peculiarly American form of social welfare. To qualify, you just need to get yourself a base ranch adjacent to some the most scenic landscapes in North America. Many ranchers came by their properties through primogeniture, a quaint medieval custom still common throughout much of the rural West. If you're a second son, a daughter, or a latecomer, don't despair: you can simply buy a ranch with a grazing permit, as billionaire potato king J.R. Simplot did. It's easy. No background checks or means-testing required. A million bucks should get you started.

Rest assured, your public subsidies are guaranteed—by senate filibuster, if necessary. Ranching subsidies are an untouchable form of welfare, right up there with the depletion allowance and the F-22 fighter. And guess what? It's guilt free. Nobody complains that your subsidies came at the expense of Headstart or aid to mothers with dependent children. Or that you take your profits from the subsidies and spend it on a case of Jack Daniels, a chunk of crystal meth, a night at the Mustang Ranch, a week at the roulette tables in Reno—or donate it all to Operation Rescue or the Sahara Club. (The most outlandish fables about profligate welfare queens have nothing on the average slob rancher.) Hell, do it right and somebody might even promote you as a cultural hero, a damn fine role model for future generations.

The Western ranching fraternity is more homogenous than the Royal Order of the Moose: landed, white, male, and politically conservative to a reactionary and vicious degree. It is not culturally, ethnically, or racially representative of America and never has been. Shouldn't there be equal access to this federal grazing largesse, these hundreds of millions in annual subsidies to well-off white geezers? A creative litigator might be able to demonstrate that federal grazing policies violate the Civil Rights Act.

Strip away the Stetsons, bolo ties, and rattlesnake-skin boots. Why should we view Western ranchers differently than the tobacco farmers of the Southeast? And what about their political benefactors? Is there are fundamental difference between, say, Max Baucus and Saxby Chambliss? Robert Bennett and Trent Lott? (Okay, Lott and Baucus have fewer bad hair days.) All annually raid the federal treasury to sustain industries that degrade the environment, ravage public health, and enervate the economy. Federal tobacco subsidies amount to about $100 million a year; grazing subsidies may exceed a billion a year. No wonder there's so little congressional support for a single-payer health care system: passage of such a plan might actually force the Cow and Cigarette Caucus to choose between the health of the citizenry and their allegiance to political porkbarrel.

Some argue that the rancher is rooted to place, that he loves the land, holds a unique reverence for its contours, beauty, rhythms. The rancher, they say, is one of Wallace Stegner's "stickers," not an itinerant booster or commercial migrant, like the cut-and-run logger. He doesn't leave behind radioactive tailings piles or slopes of stumps in his wake, but gently tends and grooms the landscape, improving Nature's defects, year after year, generation after generation.

But take away the subsidies, the nearly free forage, the roads, the even cheaper water that magically appears from nowhere in the middle of the high desert, the tax breaks, predator control, abeyances from environmental standards, and disproportionate political clout when any thing else goes against him, such as drought, rangefires, bad investments. Then charge them for the gruesome externalities of their "avocation" and then see how many stick around for the hardscrabble lifestyle that remains. Federal subsidies and political protection are the Velcro for most of these guys, not the view of the Wind River Range. Still the myths persist, proving, perhaps, that the suspension of disbelief was the very essence of Babbittry.

A Larkspur Rebellion

In the end, the Clinton administration's decision not pursue real reform of the management of Western rangelands represents one of the most glaring failures in a decade filled with similar capitulations to those who howled against any meager restraint on their freedom to exploit. Clinton could have crushed the grazing lobby if he wanted to—and no group deserved to be crushed more than the rangelords of the West. But they backed down. And that was that. Yes, Babbitt has much to answer for, but not as much as the environmental groups that went along for the ride with him.

Twelve years down the road of compromise, where are the big greens? Grazing, even though it remains the dominate and most destructive use of the public estate, is scarcely on the radar screen of the national environmental lobby—no doubt, because it's hard to fundraise around. When they have managed to mention the topic, it's been to call for a hike in grazing fees. They have largely avoided the issue of land abuse caused by livestock grazing. The Sierra Club, for example, finds it difficult to call for an end to grazing wilderness areas and actually supported the inclusion of grazing allotments in Great Basin National Park. Grazing reform, many green lobbyists argue, simply can't be marketed to the American public. It lacks the visceral imagery of clearcut forests or oil wells sprouting up along the Rocky Mountain front.

Motivated mainly by social and community concerns, some local conservation groups, such as the High Country Citizens Alliance, continue to cling to the consensus approach, pleading with cattlemen to simply improve poor grazing practices rather than seeking the removal of cows and sheep from degraded and/or ecologically fragile lands or grizzly habitat.

Yet, there is some cause for hope. There's something of a rebellion taking root in the Interior West, where a growing contingent of hardcore environmentalists, many of them unaligned with any big green group, are calling for radical changes in federal rangeland policy: the end of subsidies, the end of predator control, the end of livestock grazing on public lands altogether. Call it the Larkspur Rebellion, larkspur being a native plant poisonous to cattle.

These anti-grazing militants are the outsiders of the environmental movement: Clarke Abbey and Susan Schock, Pat Wolff and Tom Skeele, Lynn Jacobs and Michael Robinson, George Wuerthner and Kathy Myron. Their boots are muddy from fieldwork and they've rarely, if ever, been invited into corporate headquarters of the National Audubon Society or the NRDC. They were among the first to see through the Clinton administration's attempts to greenwash its public land policies. They fought the Bush administration from the first day. The repeated betrayals over the years by politicians and environmental big wigs have merely strengthened their resolve to resist token reforms and to advocate real change. Reform won't work. There's only one answer left. Leave the land alone. Let it heal itself.

SILVER CITY, NEW MEXICO.

In the Realm of the Grizzly Kings

Tomorrow will open again, the sky wide
as the mouth of a wild girl, friable
clouds you lose yourself to. You are lost
in miles of land without people, without
one fear of being found, in the dash
of rabbits, soar of antelope, swirl
merge and clatter of streams.

—from "Driving Montana"
Richard Hugo

IN JUNE 1877, A FISTFUL OF NON-TREATY NEZ PERCE LASHED BACK AGAINST the forces (miners, ranchers, and missionaries) conspiring to evict them from their traditional lands in the Hells Canyon and Salmon River country of central Idaho and eastern Oregon. The young warriors (mostly hot-headed teenagers) killed eighteen white settlers, bringing down upon their people the full wrath of the US Army, which was, of course, looking for any excuse to incarcerate or exterminate the tribe. Thus began the most amazing journey and ruthless pursuit in American history.

Shortly after the killings, the leaders of the Nez Perce bands, Looking Glass, White Bird, and Joseph, led their 300 warriors and 500 women, children, and elders across the Salmon and Clearwater Rivers and up the deep ponderosa, Doug-fir, and lodgepole forests of the Lochsa Canyon to the rugged Bitterroot Range, chased most of the way by the one-armed, demented fundamentalist Gen. Otis Howard. Their goal was the buffalo country north of the Canadian border and a possible union with the Sioux visionary Sitting Bull.

The dissident Nez Perce, loaded with dried salmon and buffalo robes, single-shot rifles, and their lodgepoles, quickly traversed the steep and treacherous Lolo trail, where Looking Glass skirted the band past an inept blockade at Lolo Hot Springs, known as Fort Fizzle. From there, they traveled down into the stunning Bitterroot Valley, then across the spiny Anaconda Mountains to a campsite along the Big Hole River, perhaps the world's most exquisite trout stream.

As the Nez Perce regrouped and rested, they were cruelly ambushed in a pre-dawn raid led by Col. John Gibbon that left the carnage of slaughtered women, children, and elders. Miraculously, the Nez Perce recovered behind Ollokot and Wounded Head and inflicted heavy casualties on the overconfident troops. Lean Elk led the shattered band away to the south across Bannock Pass; east to Henry's Fork, where they gathered camas root and raided General Howard's camp for horses and supplies; and then over the tall Targhee Pass and into the Yellowstone country.

The Nez Perce sped across the central plateau, hugging the rim of the Grand Canyon of the Yellowstone, and then made the slow, torturous crossing of the Absaroka Range, their travel impeded by dense forest and heavy treefall. When it appeared they might finally be caught between converging federal troops, the renegades descended the treacherously steep "Dead Indian Hill" undetected by Col. Samuel Sturgis' spies. Then the Nez Perce dropped into the dark and narrow slot of the Clark's Fork Canyon deftly evading the ambush plotted by the comically pompous colonel.

The Clark's Fork Canyon opened to a fast, grueling route north along the Rocky Mountain Front, across the Musselshell River and through the Judith Gap. The journey came to a bloody dénouement on the wind-brushed buffalo plains of northern Montana in the shadow of the Bear Paw Mountains, when General Nelson Miles unleashed this howitzers and cavalry on the weary Nez Perce who were encamped by Snake Creek only a few hours ride from the Canadian border.

Ollokot, Lean Elk, and Looking Glass were killed in the battle, along with 120 others. Chief Joseph, later canonized for his pacifism by white historians, surrendered to be imprisoned on the dusty Colville Reservation in eastern Washington. But the old chief White Bird, who refused even to consider giving up to the marauders in blue uniforms, quietly escaped with 200 other Nez Perce renegades to the wilds and relative freedom of the Canadian Rockies.

* * *

The escape route of the non-treaty Nez Perce roughly transects the bioregion now known was the Northern Rockies, a terrain that remains as hostile as it is enchanting. From Hells Canyon to the asbestos plants of Libby, the Chinese Wall to the Berkeley Pit, the Northern Rockies is a region of extremes—extremes in climate and geography, culture and politics. It is a haven for writers and artists, as well as white supremacists and conspiracy theorists; it's a region that gave rise to Earth First!, as well as some of the most virulent strains of the Wise-Use Movement.

In a bitter irony, perhaps symbolic of the region, the gray wolf was returned amid international fanfare to Yellowstone at the same time the grizzly seemed destined to make its final exit from the park.

The Rockies are the ecological spinal column of North America, a crookbacked corridor down which our native wildness flows. Unlike the coastal forest of the Pacific Northwest—a ragged and tattered ecosystem in need of major reconstructive ecological surgery—the wildlands of the Northern Rockies retain a certain native wholeness and exert an imposing primal presence on the totality of the landscape. Today, wildlands, not clearcuts, still define the states of Idaho and Montana.

Here, the opportunity exists to preserve complete ecosystems. There are roadless areas in Idaho the size of some of the original colonies. Some of them share grizzlies, wolves, and salmon. Beyond the smelter stacks, strip mines, and ski resorts, Lewis and Clark might still recognize much of western Montana. But each year this wilderness is being inexorably shaved away by the forces of corporate greed, bureaucratic malfeasance, political expediency, and social indifference. Each year secret ranges like the Yaak or the Missions, the Selkirks or the Crazies are being cut into fragments and islands, shattered images of their former selves, lengthening forever the forested synapses across which the sparks of life must jump.

Like the tragic saga of the renegade Nez Perce, the recent history of the Northern Rockies must be read with a mixture of hope and despair.

* * *

The national forests got their start in the Northern Rockies with the designation of the Shoshone Forest Reserve in 1897 and were managed in a largely custodial fashion until the 1950s, a period when district rangers really were rangers, riding right off the pages of Ivan Doig and Norman Maclean. These forests got their comeuppance in 1970 when the forestry and wildlife faculty of Montana State University conducted an investigation of the agency's management of forests in western Montana, revealing to the public what insiders had known for twenty years: the depletion of private timber stocks and the post-World War II housing boom instigated an era of timber primacy on the national forests.

The Bolle Report, named after Montana State University's Dean, Arnold Bolle, documented grisly patterns of overcutting, regeneration failures, decimated wildlife habitat, and destroyed trout fisheries. In many ways the Bolle Report was the first real evidence of the Forest Service's betrayal of the public trust and its progressive multiple-use mission promoted by Gifford Pinchot. "Multiple-use management, in fact, does not exist as the governing principle" for the agency, the Bolle Report concluded sharply.

The Bolle Report, and the Forest Service's continued mismanagement of the national forests in Montana and Idaho, led to the famous Church Hearings of 1971 and new conservation guidelines, the Randolph Bill, and ultimately the National Forest Management Act and the decade-long debacle of national forest planning, generated during the Reagan and Bush years.

These congressionally-mandated forest plans changed nothing in the Northern Rockies. In some cases the forest plans actually proposed doubling the historic logging rates, and established an "advance roading" strategy designed to settle the wilderness debate once and for all. Thus was the James Watt-John Crowell vision for industrial wood production on the national forests brought to life. Ironically, the agency midwife for most of these plans was then-Regional Forester James Overbay, who would return to the region as deputy chief in 1991 to lead the crackdown on reformist Regional Forester John Mumma and several renegade forest supervisors who said that meeting the forest plan timber targets would force them to break the law.

On top of these problems, harvesting timber in most of the Northern Rockies is an exceedingly irrational economic proposition, unless, of course, the government is writing the checks. The Forest Service's own accounting records bear this out. From 1990 to 2005, timber sales on national forest lands in Montana, Idaho, and Wyoming squandered more than a billion dollars—not to mention the monumental losses in environmental values, such as salmon, trout, and elk habitat.

The Forest Service goes to extraordinary lengths to justify and conceal these losses from a disbelieving public. For example, the Gallatin and Flathead National Forests in Montana have promoted new timber sales in grizzly bear habitat in order to raise money to close other logging roads also in bear habitat.

On the Idaho Panhandle Forests, the Forest Service justified new timber sales and roads in one watershed in order to raise funds to restore the damage done to another watershed by previous clearcutting.

The Clearwater National Forest in Idaho (perhaps the most landslide prone forest in the country) boasted in their forest plan that the clearcutting of the current forest would yield a kind of super-forest of tomorrow, where trees would grow 600 feet tall.

The Boise Forest claims its aggressive salvage sale program in roadless land is actually a forest health operation designed to preserve the wild character of western Idaho forests.

Believe it or not, that's the way natural resources bureaucracy really works in the Northern Rockies. These incidents are the rule not the exception. For forty years in the Northern Rockies the Forest Service has simply been cutting by numbers, meeting targets, building its budget, pleasing local politicians.

By the late 1980s, after repeated attempts at reform and little success in the courts, it appeared that the political forces driving the overcutting of the national forests in the Northern Rockies might be beyond therapy.

* * *

The impetus for corrective change in the region came from the parallel development of two forces: grassroots environmental groups, such as the Alliance for the Wild Rockies, and the internal Forest Service reform movement.

The evidence of unraveling ecosystems in the Northern Rockies had been steadily compiled by agency scientists, but buried year after year by obedient line officers. The evidence was left to fester in the files of the Forest Service until the early 1990s when the whole crisis burst open like an infected wound.

First came the so-called Sundance Letter to Forest Service chief F. Dale Robertson in which the supervisors of Region 1 forests described the Forest Service as "an out-of-control agency" that had strayed from its multiple-use mission by devoting too much staff and budget to timber sales and roads. This letter gave birth to an internal Forest Service reform movement, but it came back to haunt the careers of those who signed it. They became the targets of hardliners inside the agency and right-wing politicians looking for convenient scapegoats for the depleted resources of the region.

At the same moment, timber sales in the Northern Rockies began to bottom out, dropping 30 to 50 percent below forest plan targets. Several factors contributed to the decline in logging volume, including the overcutting of private lands on the checkboard landscape which triggered a moratorium on federal sales in overstressed watersheds, grossly exaggerated yield tables, regeneration failures, and conflicts with grizzlies, trout, and elk. Of course, the intractable problem was that the forest plan targets, themselves, were unsustainable. On some forests, such as the Lolo, Flathead, and Kootenai, the allowable sale quantities were nearly twice the sustainable logging rate of the forest plan standards and guidelines—and that's if you buy the increasingly dubious notion that any rate of logging in these dry forests is ecologically sustainable.

Meanwhile, bad ecological news continued to surface with reports of phantom forests on the Kootenai, ravaged watersheds on the Clearwater, destroyed grizzly habitat on the Targhee, all deliberately leaked to environmentalists or the press by Forest Service whistleblowers. None of this washed well with the Idaho and Montana Congressional delegations, the chief's office, or then Assistant Secretary of Agriculture John Beuter, who contended that the targets were "required management objectives" that must be met, regardless of the consequences for grizzlies or trout.

Senator Larry Craig, the closet-case from Idaho, made the delegation's concerns starkly clear in a bullying letter to Robertson: "You have a serious management problem that must be addressed. It is my hope that you will move to assure that targets are met and line officers held accountable for their targets."

Back in Missoula, John Mumma, the renegade regional forester for the Rockies, stood his ground. Mumma maintained that to meet the targets would force him and his supervisors to violate the law. This virtuous stance killed his career. Mumma was publicly scolded by James Overbay and was soon informed by Associate Chief George Leonard that this position was untenable and that he could either retire or accept a directed reassignment to DC. Mumma opted for retirement and told his compelling story to a largely indifferent Congress.

But the crackdown didn't end there. At the insistent prodding of Craig and Senator Conrad Burns of Montana, the Office of Inspector General launched covert criminal investigations against many of the reformist supervisors. One by one the whistleblowers were forced into early retirements, transferred out of the region, or compelled into directed reassignments to desk jobs in DC. The list of casualties is a long one: Tom Kovalicky, Bertha Gilliam, Fred Trevey, Win Green, Van Elsbernd.

The beat went on. The purge of Northern Rockies reformers continued through the Clinton administration with the forced retirements of Helena forest supervisor Ernie Nunn and the Custer's Curtis Bates. Under Bush, timber hardliners remained firmly in control of the regional office and in command of the key timber producing forests in the region.

* * *

The Northern Rockies is also home to one of the intellectual bastions of the privatization movement: Bozeman, Montana. Bozeman houses both the Foundation for Research on Economics and the Environment (FREE) and the Political Economic Research Center (PERC). Both outfits contend that most environmental problems in the West, including wilderness, water, and forest management, derive from a lack of defined property rights for natural resources. This is the Second Coming of the Sagebrush Rebellion, and it promotes that the only way to save the environment is to sell it.

PERC, whose top economist once told me that if the grizzly's "present net value" dropped to zero it should be driven to extinction, regularly attacks with some ferocity the public land ideals of the progressive era, dropping subtle hints along the way about the patriotism of environmentalists. Reading their publications you could be seduced into believing that Al Gore, Leonardo DiCaprio, and the managers of Yellowstone National Park (not to mention real environmental militants like Mike Roselle and Steve Kelly) pose a bigger threat to the ecosystems of the Northern Rockies than the W. R. Grace Co. or Boise-Cascade.

There is a clever cultural calculus at work in the free-market think tanks of the West that goes something like this: Environmentalists support regulations; Regulation requires Big Government; Big Government equals Socialism; Environmentalists are Socialists; Socialism is un-American; Environmentalists are un-American. This is exactly the kind of western neo-McCarthyism that plays well in the hinterlands.

FREE's John Baden, for example, gained some notoriety for his use of the watermelon as a metaphor for environmentalists: *Green on the outside, red on the inside.* He even produced a watermelon tie that was a hot item at gatherings of the free-marketeers, where, Windsor-knotted, they would all sip wine, toast Milton Friedman, and long for the days when the philosophy of John Locke was in its ascendancy.

Of course, many of the same corporations and foundations that support PERC and FREE also quietly fund People for the West and other more proletarian Wise-Use groups that are pursuing the property-rights cause in much more strident tones. It goes without saying that these same corporations, such as Chevron, Arco, and Amoco, stand to reap enormous economic benefits if the shock troops of the Wise-Use movement are successful in weakening federal laws and regulations.

It is a game that utilizes themes and symbols of insecurity, loaded signifiers, as my deconstructionist friends would say, that when pressed can ignite loathing and rage in a population that is terrified of change. The xenophobia card is played repeatedly by corporate-types and their agents from Cheyenne to Spokane. The rhetoric of entrenched nativism is articulated by figures widely regarded as social liberals, such as Senator Max Baucus.

"With increasing frequency, out-of-state members think they know what is best for Montana and the American West," Baucus said after his wilderness bill failed to skate through Congress in 1992. He blamed the defeat on the machinations of Hollywood celebrities, English majors, and eastern politicians.

Another example of how the subtle manipulation of images can distort reality is the rapid demise of the Yellowstone Vision document, a relatively tame and inoffensive attempt by the Park Service and Forest Service to establish a framework for managing the Greater Yellowstone Ecosystem. For the privatizers and the Wise-Use movement, the Vision document became an objective correlative for everything that was wrong with ecosystem management: It was a proposal hatched by radical scientists, environmentalists, and bureaucrats designed to lock up everything near Yellowstone, including private lands.

Naturally, nothing could be further from the truth. After all, the Vision document was generated under the first Bush administration. But highly paid Wise-Use provocateurs (one was a former lobbyist for Saudi Arabia) transformed the real anxieties of loggers, ranchers, and others who work at the margins of the Western resource economy into an extreme animus at environmentalists and the Park Service. Ultimately, these vitriolic attacks destroyed not only the Vision document, but also the careers of nearly everyone associated with it, including Lorraine Mintzmeyer, regional director of the Park Service, whose directed reassignment to Philadelphia was apparently engineered by John Sununu himself, then G.H.W. Bush's chief of staff.

As in most of the West, politicians and business leaders tout the Northern Rockies as a region of self-made men. Untrue. Indeed, it is the oligarchy of large corporations that continues to reap the liberal benefits of federal subsidies and public resources. These same companies routinely shaft and exploit their own laborers. Don't worry about our workers, Anaconda Copper and Champion International said, they're the rugged individuals of the American West.

A kind of corporate imperialism has been played out in the Northern Rockies over the past 100 years—a strategy for control, power, and commodification of cultures and resources that started with a campaign of genocide against the native peoples of the region and is now ending with a mop-up assault on the region's native ecosystem.

In the Northern Rockies, free enterprise was given free rein, backed by government guns, dams, and subsidies. To assume that the same free-market forces can correct this history of abuse and annihilation is to engage in a kind of economic surrealism. Want a reality check? Take a flight over the "private" timberlands of northwestern Montana and Idaho, the ecological equivalent of electroshock therapy for the uninitiated.

* * *

In the summer of 2002, I took a stomach-churning plane ride over the battered Mission Range in northwestern Montana. As the tiny Twin-engine Otter rose and plummeted through the vicious air pockets above the rugged mountains, I looked down on a legacy of lesions on the landscape, 640-acre chunks of raw, stripped forest, and felt my pulse pounding at the perfidy of Plum Creek Timber. Laid open below me was evidence of the corporation's audacious acquisitiveness, a thirty-year-long search and destroy mission on their own lands, aimed solely at turning trees into fast cash. Grizzly and mill worker, bull trout and timber faller be damned.

Company officials brazenly admitted that they were basically liquidating their own forest holdings, cutting trees at twice the sustained-yield rate. Plum Creek's chief executive for the Northern Region boasted in 1990: "We have never said we were on a sustained-yield program. Let's get to the heart of it. Sure it is extensively logged, but what is wrong with that?"

And Plum Creek wasn't alone. The other beneficiaries of the federal largesse known as the Northern Pacific Railroad Lands Grant (Champion International, Potlatch, and Boise-Cascade) joined in the clearcutting frenzy. Champion, eager to raise cash to build new mills and plants in the Southeast, blitzed its 800,000 acres at an even faster rate and then turned around and sold its land holdings to Plum Creek and its mills to Stimson Lumber, a Portland-based log exporter.

After annihilating its own land, driving dozens of small mill owners out of business, exporting millions of board feet to Asian markets, and other egregious enterprises, Plum Creek got a big dividend: the opportunity to cut even more on the national forests. The corporation is now the driving force behind calls to open more roadless areas to logging.

With its acquisition of Champion International's lands, Plum Creek positioned itself to be the sole timber operator in western Montana. The problem was its image. Unless the suppurating wounds to its public reputation were spruced up, the state of Montana might actually enact a state forest practices act. Or even worse: there might be a move in the Congress to take back the railroad grant lands from Plum Creek entirely. Such a move is called revestment, and Congress not only has the power to make such as seizure, it also has the moral obligation to do so.

So corporate officials finally admitted that something indeed had gone wrong. Sure, they'd made some bad moves in the past, but these lapses were more the fault of the times, an imperfect corporate understanding of ecosystem management, than of any ill intent. With more than 95 percent of its own forests logged off in Montana, Plum Creek Timber was prepared to be penitent.

Plum Creek's "environmental forestry" practices duly came under the imprimatur of the new forestry guru-for-hire Jerry Franklin, who taught the company how to feather the edges of its clearcuts and to leave behind more spindly trees per acre than Bill Arthur, the Sierra Club poobah who infamously clearcut his own land in eastern Washington and compounded the outrage by selling the timber to a log exporter. *Highgrading with a conscience? Enlightened deforestation?*

Plum Creek is not the only company to seek out a corporate facelift. Potlatch, long regarded as the Darth Vader of Idaho forest lands, boldly announced that it too is changing its ways and is planning to enter into an operational compact with the Forest Service to merge their Geographical Information Systems in an attempt to better manage the totality of the checkerboard landscape. Natch.

Plum Creek and Potlatch have also hired PR firms to spin stories of how their timber practices now harmonize with the needs of bull trout, wolves, and grizzly bears. All this gives new meaning to the term chop-logic.

* * *

How's this for a conundrum: Idaho and Montana remain wild because they haven't passed state-wide wilderness bills. In the West, the political objective of wilderness legislation is not so much to protect as to release, not so much to preserve as to secure land for logging and development unencumbered by the wilderness issue. Environmentalists bear serious complicity in this manner.

For decades the organizing principle of wildland politics in the Northern Rockies has been what I call non-confrontational incrementalism. Wilderness proposals were carefully calibrated to the prevailing political balance of the region, and sought only to draw protective lines around those roadless areas that lacked significant timber, range, and mineral resources. Wilderness on the rocks, my friend Howie Wolke calls it.

Ultimately, this approach collided against biological reality and the growing grass-roots environmental movement, which sought to use wilderness as a means to protect ecosystems. The top heavy national green groups, however, failed to alter their historic approach and, in 1990, signed off on the Lolo-Kootenai Accords, a compromised wilderness proposal for the two western Montana forests that contained "hard release" language designed to shield logging in non-wilderness roadless areas from legal challenges. The language, which later surfaced in Max Baucus' proposed wilderness bill, was developed by timber industry lawyer Steve Quarrles and attorneys for the (drum roll, please) National Wildlife Federation.

The Lolo-Kootenai Accords created upheavals and fractures in the environmental movement in the Northern Rockies, left the leadership of traditional groups riven by internal dissent, and, most importantly, led to the rise of the Alliance for the Wild Rockies and the development of the Northern Rockies Ecosystem Protection Act (NREPA), a 20-million-acre multi-state wilderness and wildlands restoration proposal. NREPA evolved as the striking counterpoint to decades of statewide, rocks-and-ice wilderness proposals that traded off ecological integrity and big wilderness concepts for favored hiking trails and political expediency.

Not surprisingly, the national environmental groups actively lobbied against introduction of NREPA. The Sierra Club even threatened to excommunicate renegade Club groups and chapters in Montana, Illinois, and New York that were supporting the bill.

Still, the political agenda for wilderness in Montana and Idaho continues to be set by the state's congressional delegations. They ritually offer up bills that release more than 70 percent of the remaining wildlands to development, fail to secure water rights for designated wilderness areas, and contain questionable release language that may limit citizens' access to the courts.

Some environmentalists, scrambling for any kind of crumbs, argue that these kinds of bills should be supported in order to secure at least some protection for threatened areas. But the statewide wilderness release bills lose any attractiveness they might have on the surface when viewed in the context of what is being lost. These measures are legislative anachronisms, throwbacks to the days of ecological segregationism, when old-growth forests were excluded from wilderness areas as a matter of political fiat.

While environmental groups in the Northern Rockies appear to be congealing around NREPA, a bitter residue of tension remains, particularly in the leadership of the national organizations. The problem for the reactionary forces in the Sierra Club, National Wildlife Federation, and National Audubon—the traditional envoys of incrementalism—is a profound one: How to affect the appearance of thinking big, while continuing to act small.

The solution, as crafted by Audubon's Brock Evans and the Club's Larry Mehlhaf, is to publicly endorse NREPA, do nothing to support it, then quietly back the puny piecemeal bills anyway. This is the intrinsic inertia of incrementalism at work.

* * *

A few final thoughts about the grizzly.

There is no question that the grizzly is in worse shape now than when it was listed as a threatened species thirty years ago. Its habitat has been steadily eroded by hundreds of thousands of acres of clearcuts, roads, subdivisions, and oil developments. Each year dozens are shot with impunity just because they acted like bears. Others are regularly tracked down, trapped, weighed, prodded, radio-collared, linked up with global positioning satellites, relocated when they stray beyond political boundaries, and injected with tranquilizers that when mixed with the destruction coming down around them, like a bad hallucination, simply drive many bears insane.

Among other gross deficiencies, the Fish and Wildlife Service's recovery plan for the bear, devised in Clintontime, represents a terrible negation of the nature of the grizzly. Compromise and consensus, the recurrent mantras of the Democrats and their green automatons, are not only alien to the bear, they are lethal to the bear's future as a species.

And now, under Bush the Younger, the bill came due for the great bear. The Yellowstone grizzly, clinging to a perilous existence in the region of the park, in the winter of 2007, was magically deemed recovered and was duly stripped of the meager protections it had enjoyed under the Endangered Species Act. And now the bear haters have their sights set on delisting the dwindling population of bears that prowl the Northern Continental Divide as well.

Have conservationists failed in one of our most important domestic missions? Hell, yes they have. By consistently conforming to the accepted political reality and repeatedly endorsing state wilderness proposals that militate against the very kind of dramatic change needed to protect the bear.

The grizzly is not merely a symbol of wildness; it is wildness personified. In the Northern Rockies, a "wilderness" without at least the hope of being traversed by the great bear is not truly wild. The ultimate test of the vitality of the region and the American environmental movement will be whether or not we can save the grizzly and its habitat. NREPA may not be enough, but its head and its heart are in the right place.

In the end, however, I believe we're going to have to draw a line. A line from Challis, Idaho to Whitefish, Montana. Call it a radius. Within this circle beats the wild heart of North America. *It's still not too late to save it all.*

* * *

Late June, Nez Perce Creek, Yellowstone. I was closely following the path the renegade Nez Perce took 115 years ago, a trail that permitted them to leave behind the homicidal Gen. Howard. Even then, Yellowstone, already a national park, stood as a sanctuary of freedom and wilderness.

Black storm clouds piled up over the Madison Range. I dropped down to a small bench by the stream to await the onslaught of the storm and watched the Yellowstone cutthroat angle themselves against the swirling current before rising to snatch newly hatched salmonflies. Jolted by thunder, I looked up the ridge and caught sight of my first Yellowstone grizzly: a young bear standing on a downed fir tree, digging playfully at the decaying wood. As lightning bolts shattered the sky, she rose on her hind legs, and turned her dished face towards me, her reddish coat flecked with gold, an image of bristling defiance.

A damn fool, all I could think of then was capturing a photo of the grizzly in this wild and distant place, but I stumbled and fell into the creek trying to unsheathe my camera. The cold current tugged at my legs, pulling me into the deep pool where the cutthroat had been feeding. When I finally regained my footing, dragged my pack out of the frigid stream, and looked back up the slope, she was gone: vanished into the amber light.

Bozeman.

Yellowstone: The Vision Thing; Or How Sununu Shrank the Ecosystem

YELLOWSTONE. THE WORD ITSELF RINGS WITH WILDNESS. AMERICA'S first and largest park. Home to grizzly and bison, bubbling mud pots, and steaming geyser basins. But, in fact, the high plateaus and mountains of Yellowstone Park are only a central core of a much larger ecosystem, an ecosystem that spills over into six national forests in three different regions, Grand Teton National Park, the Rockefeller Parkway, and two federal wildlife refuges. The Greater Yellowstone Ecosystem also includes hundreds of thousands of acres of state lands, private and Indian lands, and lands managed by the BLM.

The management implications of this landownership pattern are complex, convoluted, and violently controversial. For example bison, which carry brucellosis, a disease that sometimes causes miscarriages in domestic cattle, often stray out of the park onto private rangelands and grazing allotments on national forest lands. Annual bison hunts at the park boundaries—designed to cull the bison herds and stop the spread of the disease—have outraged animal rights activists and most environmentalists. Conversely, many ranchers intensely opposed efforts to reintroduce the gray wolf to Yellowstone, fearing the wolves will migrate out of the park and prey on sheep and cattle.

Geothermal energy developments outside the park boundaries, like those at the Church Universal and Triumphant ranch in Montana, threaten Yellowstone's world-famous geyser basins and other thermal features. Clearcutting, roadbuilding, and oil and gas development on national forest lands surrounding the park have contributed to the decline of grizzly bear populations.

Forest fires sweep across all boundaries. Indeed some of the blame for the intensity of the 1987 Yellowstone fires has been leveled at the Forest Service's aggressive fire suppression strategy. Others pointed fingers at the Park Service's let-burn philosophy. While the fires may have been good for the ecosystem, they blackened the reputations of both agencies.

Commercial developments in the parks—such as the Fishing Bridge complex—remain in place in prime grizzly habitat, despite agreements to remove them. Conservationists charge that Fishing Bridge and other questionable developments, such as the airport runway extension at Grand Teton Park (the only national park with its own airport), continue to proliferate throughout the region as a result of direct political interference in the management of the parks and adjacent forests.

The image of Yellowstone as wilderness or ecosystem increasingly seems more of an American myth than a reality. In fact, Yellowstone is a political landscape in which ecological forces are warped and bent to serve a variety of often conflicting bureaucratic, political, and economic demands. To make matters worse, or at least more convoluted, the land itself, the 12 million acres known as Greater Yellowstone, is managed by numerous different entities with often radically different objectives. The diversity of the ecosystem is rivaled only by the diversity of its managers.

* * *

As a result of these and other conflicts, in the early 1960s, the Park Service and Forest Service formed the Greater Yellowstone Coordinating Committee (GYCC), a task force with representatives from both agencies, each of the states, the BLM, and Fish and Wildlife Service. The GYCC was designed to provide a working relationship for the "integrated" management of the Greater Yellowstone area.

For decades, however, the GYCC snoozed away as dormant as the Yellowstone caldera. The agencies communicated only when they had too, usually when there were problems with grizzly bears or when politicians, like Senator Alan Simpson of Wyoming, demanded that park roads be opened to trucks hauling timber off national forest lands.

Two events worked to raise the profile of the Greater Yellowstone region. First, the forest plans for the national forest in Greater Yellowstone started to emerge in the early and mid-1980s. Most forests scheduled increased logging and roadbuilding near park borders and full-scale oil and gas develop of the Overthrust Belt.

Second, the Greater Yellowstone Coalition emerged as one of the first and most effective of the new crop of regional grassroots organizations. Greater Yellowstone Coalition began to aggressively advance the idea that the ecological health of America's oldest national park depended on how the 8 million acres of surrounding lands were managed.

Congress held hearings about Greater Yellowstone in 1985. The Congressional Research Service (CRS) and the House Subcommittee on Public Lands and National Parks and Recreation, harshly criticized the Park Service and Forest Service for the lack of coordinated planning and information on the Greater Yellowstone Area. The CRS report said that developments on Forest Service lands were threatening "the values of the entire Yellowstone area."

As a result of the hearings, the Greater Yellowstone Coordinating Committee began to compile the various management plans and objectives of each forest and park.

In 1987, the GYCC released a 240-page report, entitled "An Aggregation of National Park and Forest Service Management Plans," which provided an overview of the often-divergent management directions of the various forests and parks and called for a more formalized relationship between the Greater Yellowstone forests and parks. The report also suggested the need for an interagency document that would describe a future "vision" for the Greater Yellowstone area and ways that vision could be achieved through "coordinated management goals."

Initial Visions

In 1988, the Greater Yellowstone Coordinating Committee, which was co-chaired by Lorraine Mintzmayer, regional director of the National Park Service for the Rocky Mountain Region, and Gary Carghill, regional forester for the Forest Service's Rocky Mountain Region, began work on what was to become known as the Yellowstone Vision Statement.

"The Yellowstone vision document was not simply to be a regional plan or decision document—it was intended to be a study of the conditions of the areas involved and a formalization of coordinated, guiding principles," Mintzmeyer said. "It was to be a model for interagency cooperation in this area and a model for other areas, well into the next century."

When the seventy-page draft report was released in August 1990, it was hailed by the agencies and some environmentalists as the first ecosystem approach to public land management in the country. The Vision Statement provided three overriding goals for the management of the Greater Yellowstone Area:

Conserve a sense of naturalness and maintain ecosystem integrity throughout Greater Yellowstone; Encourage opportunities that are biologically and economically sustainable; Improve coordination and inter-agency cooperation in Greater Yellowstone.

The Vision statement subdivided these goals into some fairly specific objectives. For example, the goal to conserve a "sense of naturalness" throughout the area included mechanisms to protect geothermal features, fish and wildlife, air and water quality, biological diversity, and cultural resources.

The sustainable development goal outlined ways to reform range and timber management practices on national forest lands, and offered proposals for working with local communities to help diversify their economies. It also established a formalized process for consultation and coordinated planning between the agencies.

While the philosophy of the Vision may lean more toward the "natural management" paradigm of the Park Service, the document reads like a run-of-the-mill forest plan. It is general and obtuse, filled with loopholes and tendentious language.

Still, the document provided a pathway for change, perhaps the only way the Forest Service could be dragged through the process. Even so, there were indications early on that the Forest Service was not exactly eager to have its plans reviewed by the Park Service. After all, from the Forest Service's point of view it seemed a one-way street—there wasn't much chance that the Forest Service was going to change the Park Service's management of Yellowstone or Grand Teton.

James Caswell, supervisor of eastern Idaho's Targhee National Forest, was apparently one of those who thought the Vision was too restrictive, that it imposed too much of the Park Service's philosophy on the Forest Service.

Shortly after the release of the draft Vision, Caswell griped: "This is by no means the final product. I was on the team that wrote it, and my copy is full of red ink."

The Firestorm

While some agency officials and conservationists praised the Vision statement as a revolutionary document, others noted that much of the language in the report was vague and non-binding.

"The Vision report was non-binding, a kind of sweeping, but vague policy agenda that outlined how the various land management agencies can cooperate to protect the region's wildlife and biological diversity," said Scott Garland, public lands director for the Jackson Hole Alliance.

The Vision report was unilaterally condemned by members of the Wyoming, Idaho and Montana congressional delegations. Congressman Ron Marlenee and Senator Conrad Burns attacked the report as "a blueprint" for preservation. Burns said that he believed the Park Service was attempting to extend its management philosophy onto national forests lands. "They're planning on creating a 12 million acre park," Burns said.

The Wyoming Heritage Foundation—a coalition of industry groups—and People for the West led most of the opposition to the Vision report. "Yellowstone National Park is not endangered," the group charged after the release of the draft report. "Common sense tells you that. Jobs and local economies will be endangered if the Vision policies are approved."

The most vitriolic opponents of the Vision statement were corporate landowners within the Greater Yellowstone Area who contended that the report would place restrictions on private developments in the Yellowstone area.

From Vision to Framework

The final version of the report, which no longer contained the word "Vision" in its title, was released on September 11, 1991. The new report—now called "A Framework for Coordination of National Parks and National Forests in the Greater Yellowstone Area" and sliced from seventy pages to eleven—eliminated all references to biological diversity, ecosystem management, and the preservation of a sense of naturalness that highlighted the Vision statement.

The "Framework" called for a balance between the preservation of natural values and resource development. "Resource protection and resource use are not inherently mutually exclusive," the report concludes.

Lorraine Mintzmayer, who received her directed reassignment shortly before the release of the new Yellowstone report, alleged in her testimony before the House Civil Service Subcommittee that White House Chief of Staff John Sununu considered the original Vision statement a complete "disaster" from a political perspective and ordered that it be completely redrafted with decisive input from the political office of the Bush White House.

Much of the political pressure apparently came from Wyoming Senator Alan Simpson, who convened a meeting with Assistant Secretary of Agriculture James Moseley, Gary Carghill, and Scott Sewell then the Principal Deputy Assistant Secretary for Fish, Wildlife.

Mintzmayer, who was in Washington, DC at the time, was intentionally not invited to the meeting, where Simpson outlined his objections to the report and demanded that it be gutted or simply trashed altogether.

Soon after this meeting, apparently, Simpson—whom Ed Lewis, executive director of the Greater Yellowstone Coalition, described as having "a deep personal desire to micromanage Yellowstone Park"—contacted White House Chief John Sununu to complain about the Vision report and Mintzmeyer's leadership.

Mintzmayer recounted a meeting she had with Scott Sewell and Parks for the Department of Interior on October 5, 1990, where Sewell said that, "significant political contacts and pressure had been made to the White House and the Secretary regarding the Vision document."

Sewell blamed Mintzmayer personally for the political problems caused by the draft Vision statement and informed her that he had been "delegated by the Department" to personally rewrite the Yellowstone report.

Mintzmayer told me the Yellowstone Vision statement had been sheared down to a mere "brochure" that had little or no basis in scientific research and had little utility or credibility for professional land managers.

Both the White House and the Department of the Interior flatly denied that Sununu discussed the Yellowstone Vision statement with Sewell. The Interior Department also claimed that Mintzmayer's removal was unrelated to her role in the preparation of the draft Yellowstone report.

For his part, Marlenee also denied charges by conservationists that he had used political influence to have the report altered or that he played a role in the directed reassignments of Mintzmayer and John Mumma. However, his office confirmed that he helped arrange and provide transportation for ranchers and loggers to the contentious hearings in Montana on the Yellowstone Vision report.

"They've considerably scoped down the Yellowstone report and have met some of our concerns, but we're still not entirely pleased with its direction," Marlenee said.

"The final document completely fails to establish a set of principles to ensure ecological sensitivity and coordinated management of greater Yellowstone," charged Ed Lewis. "Political interference, apparently directed from the highest levels of government, has led to the complete abandonment of the concept of ecosystem management which was featured in the draft."

Saving Face

The revised "Framework" was publicly defended by several forest supervisors in the Greater Yellowstone area. Brian Stout, supervisor of the Bridger-Teton National Forest, said that criticism of the report's elimination of the words "naturalness" and "biodiversity" were overstated.

"What we're talking about is maintaining scenic values," Stout said. "It was never about limiting timber harvesting, grazing, or oil and gas leasing. The goal was to continue multiple-use activities in a way that preserves other values."

Privately, several forest supervisors and deputies said that they were disappointed that the report had been "gutted" and were concerned that the manner in which the report was altered indicated a troubling trend toward politicization of natural management decisions.

"It appears that any significant decision we make will be subjected to a kind of political litmus test," one supervisor told me. "And if you stand up you better be prepared to take a hit."

Park Service officials expressed similar concerns. "Any major decision, whether it deals with concessionaires, outfitters, or restrictions on overgrazing, now appears to be lifted out of the hands of professional managers and into the hands of politicians and political appointees," a Yellowstone Park official told me. "It seems that even the director of the Park Service and Secretary Lujan are often out of the loop on these decisions."

This official supported Mintzmayer's allegation that John Sununu and his deputies in the White House had worked directly with the deputy secretary of Interior for Fish, Wildlife and Parks on the redrafting of the Yellowstone document and other matters relating to development in the national parks.

The Yellowstone Vision document is dead. And among the causalities are the best regional Park Service director and the Forest Service's best regional forester. Other reformers inside both agencies were forced to lay low. But perhaps there is a more fundamental casualty, the old progressive ideal espoused by Gifford Pinchot and other public land managers, that scientifically trained managers paid by the public would automatically act in the public interest.

It should now be obvious that even when high-level agency officials develop innovative ecosystem management scenarios, ideas that invariably conflict with the dominant political paradigm, politics will prevail—often with disastrous consequences for the ecosystem and its few remaining bureaucratic defenders.

Moose, Wyoming.

Fire in the West: a Triptych

1. Smokey's Priggish Paw: The True Cause of Western Fires

THE BIG FIRES THAT DEVOURED FORESTS FROM COLORADO TO THE PACIFIC Northwest in the fall of 1994 coincided with the 50th anniversary of Smokey the Bear. The Forest Service's famous mascot with his ursine injunction "Only You Can Prevent Forest Fires," has been a PR triumph for the agency, but a biological disaster for the forests.

Under the guise of national security (Japanese incendiarists) the timber companies pushed the Forest Service (and thus Smokey) into big time fire suppression half a century ago during the Second World War, because they didn't want their standing assets (trees) to go up in flames. The result is over-fueled forests that periodically erupt into lethal infernos.

Long before Smokey ever raised his priggish paw, these forests, particularly in the arid Interior West, had known a history of burning and intentional manipulation through fire. American Indians were expert at it. The Forest Service's fire suppression program—a big subsidy to the timber industry and recreation communities such as Glenwood Springs, Colorado and Bozeman, Montana—promulgated the idea that forest fires were bad. They're not. Many western tree species, such as Ponderosa Pine, are dependent on fire for germination of their seeds.

Suppress the fires and the Ponderosa get out-competed by trees like spruce, which are far more susceptible to insects and disease. Net result: dying forests, as in the Sierras and on the east slope of the Cascade Mountains, overloaded with fuel and waiting for the first lightning strike, faulty muffler, or arsonist to set them off.

Forests do well with intermittent small fires, which have a cleansing effect and create patches of different-aged forests. This enhances the diversity of habitat. Such fires also burn out pests and brush, and make nutrients available. The big, stand-replacing blazes that result from long-term fire suppression have the reverse effect, consuming everything, scorching the soil, and reducing diversity.

Having successfully endangered the forests' long-term health by zealous fire suppression, the Forest Service then kills off the stricken patient with salvage timber sales, gouging logging roads into roadless areas, and hauling out post-fire timber in the name of recuperation.

Aside from the notorious uses of "salvage" to evade regulatory procedures and inhibitions on logging in wildlands or endangered species habitat, the trees that survive fires, standing or downed, are the nutrient capital of the new forest. In relation to the 1980 eruption of Mount St. Helens in Washington's Gifford Pinchot National Forest, the portion of the damaged forest that was subjected to salvage logging is coming back at a far slower pace than that which was left alone. A similar story is unfolding in the Yellowstone ecosystem, where recovery from the 1985 fires is proceeding much faster inside the national park than in the surrounding national forests, which were blitzed by salvage logging.

These big fires in the Rockies set the stage for the salvage logging onslaught by the Forest Service, under its disappointing chief, Jack Ward Thomas. In the name of "ecosystem management," a good notion that can be perverted to any fell purpose, Thomas and his minions have given the green light for a widespread attack on public forests. Thomas worked in concert with the big timber reps in Congress (Tom Foley, Larry Craig, Bob Packwood, Pat Williams, and Slade Gorton), who howled about the lethal infernos that must be averted by ferocious thinning and logging regimes.

From the crest of the Cascades to the crest of the Rockies, the whole western interior of the country is being sacrificed to these salvage logging operations under the deceptive banner of ecosystem management. What we are talking about here is more than 10 million acres of roadless forest, salmon and trout streams, and grizzly habitat. The main excuse for unleashing one of the biggest chainsaw frenzies in the nation's history is "forest health." In other words, the idea that we must destroy the forest in order to save it. Some of the worst firestorms—actual and potential—are caused by the timber industry's indiscriminate use of biocides, such as Garlon, to kill commercially undesirable trees and vegetation. Result: vast acreages of timber just waiting to erupt.

When Jack Ward Thomas was made chief, many environmentalists cheered, reckoning that Thomas' background as a biologist augured a more preservation-oriented approach. Instead, Thomas moved swiftly against Forest Service whistleblowers who raised the alarm about the agency's sanctioning of over-logging and give-away timber sales to big logging outfits with ties to the administration. Ominously, Thomas put the vast upper Columbia River Basin region in the hands of Steve Mealey, supervisor of the Boise National Forest and notorious manipulator of the "salvage sale emergency" provision as an excuse to log in roadless areas.

These onslaughts on what remains of the authentic national forests were resisted at two levels. In the frontlines are demonstrators in such areas as Cove/Mallard, a remote roadless area in Idaho's Nez Perce National Forest, sitting down in front of logging trucks.

And in Congress support continues to mount for the Northern Rockies Ecosystem Protection Act, sponsored by the Alliance for the Wild Rockies. This bill, in the works for more than a decade, would permanently protect the remaining roadless areas in Montana, Idaho, and Wyoming, thus putting a stake through the heart of what the late, great Edward Abbey used to call "this ursine bore," Smokey the Bear. Not a moment too soon.

2. Firestarter

If you believe what the Forest Service interrogators say, Terry Lynn Barton, a Forest Service employee, started the big fire in Colorado's Pike National Forest by burning a letter from her estranged husband. Maybe so, but it might also be that Terry Lynn started the fire by igniting her pay stub—at least metaphorically.

After eighteen years of dedicated service, Terry Lynn Barton's monthly pay was $1,485, which tots up to $17,820 a year. Try raising two kids on that in the greater metropolitan area of Denver. She's being described in the press as "a Forest Service technician," which is FS speak for all-purpose manual laborers cleaning up campgrounds, trail maintenance, and kindred grunt work.

Forget the Edward Abbeys, Jack Kerouacs, and Gary Snyders of the forest fire watchtowers, turning out literature while communing with nature and scanning the ridge lines for tell-tale plumes. The Forest Service, part of the USDA, has long been notorious for exploiting its bottom-rung workers more than any other agency. The laborers are often forced to live in squalid housing under fairly harsh conditions, with scant benefits.

These grunts are the ones who have to deal with visitors angered at having to pay as much as $40 in annual passes for visits to forests in a particular area. Having ponied up the money these visitors often find nature's temple criss-crossed with logging roads, scarred by clear cuts or the new, RV-friendly rec sites blessed by recent administrations.

From the anguish and outrage of Barton's superiors you'd think that the Forest Service has always regarded fire as the devil's work.

A little perspective: this particular Colorado fire burned across something over 100,000 acres. The implication is that all these acres are blackened zones of ash and carbonized stumps. Not so. Many of those acres will have suffered minor scorching. And of course healthy forests need fires as a natural and frequent catalyst to regeneration, particularly in the conifer forests in Colorado.

But the Forest Service's policy has been to suppress all fires, immediately. In the middle and long term this policy leads to huge fuel loads which, when the inevitable conflagration does come, then burst out into the kinds of large scale burns that we are now seeing across the West.

Responsibility for fires stretches far higher up the bureaucratic chain than poor Ms. Barton. Since the days of Gifford Pinchot the Forest Service has seen fire-suppression as a sure way to get a blank check from Congress. Fire-suppression gets the Service the big ticket items: planes, helicopters, and so forth. Fire suppression is used to justify the Service's road building budget and, of course, its logging programs.

The Forest Service says all fires are bad and need to be suppressed with the help of huge disbursements from Congress plus public vigilance. All children have the self-righteous smirk of Smokey the Bear dinned into their psyches, said bear being conjured into icon status sixty years ago after the incredible popularity of that noted fire-fugitive, Bambi.

So the Forest Service needs fires, and diligently sets them each year, under the rubric of Controlled Burn, or Prescribed Fire. These regularly surge out of control, as in the Los Alamos forests a couple of years ago, which was started by the Park Service in Bandolier National Monument. The Forest Service bigwigs okay fires and then summon ill-paid fighters to do the dangerous work. Far more prudent would be to let the fires run, but that of course would leave idle all the costly fire-fighting machinery and expose the Forest Service to the wrath of the real estate industry, which has raised million dollar homes in areas certain to see a blaze some day.

Terry Lynn Barton, portrayed in the press as the John Walker Lindh of Colorado, faced years in prison, while the timber industry licks its lips at the prospect of "salvage logging" the Colorado forests. "Light it and log it," as the old phrase goes. Once a forest burns, existing restrictions go out the window, the Forest Service offers up 100,000 acres for salvage logging, and in go the timber companies, hauling out the timber, immune to environmental restrictions. You don't think timber companies have been setting fires for years, often with Forest Service complicity?

3. Just a Match Away: Fire Sale in So Cal

Sooner or later all big fires become political events.

Even before becalmed Santa Ana winds and mountain sleet quenched the blazes in southern California, politicians from both parties raced to exploit the charred landscape for their own advantage—a kind of political looting while the embers still glowed.

Republicans, naturally, pointed an incendiary finger at environmentalists, rehashing their tired mantra that restrictions on logging had provided the kindling for the inferno that consumed 3,600 homes (largely in Republican districts) and took twenty human lives (the non-human body count will never be tallied).

Not to be outdone, Democrats parroted a similar line, but in more bombastic tones. They tried to affix the blame on George W. Bush, alleging that our chainsaw president had rebuffed desperate pleas from Gray Davis for money to finance the logging off of beetle-nibbled forests in the parched San Bernadino Mountains.

So here the two parties converge once again, harmonized in their fatuous contention that more logging will prevent forest conflagrations. It didn't take long for this unity, soldered by the flames of southern California, to find a way to express itself in Congress.

On Halloween Eve of 2003, the Senate passed the so-called Healthy Forest Initiative with just a paltry fourteen votes of dissent. This bill is the no-holds-barred logging plan crafted by Bush's forest czar, Mark Rey, a former ace timber-industry lobbyist who now oversees the Forest Service from his perch as Deputy Secretary of Agriculture. Using fire prevention as a pretext, the legislation authorizes a kind of pre-emptive strike of logging across more than 20 million acres of federal lands. It also exempts the blitzkrieg of cutting from adherence to most environmental laws, and shields it from legal challenges by pesky green groups.

Although environmentalists roundly derided the plan as a gift to big timber, it was embraced and championed in the senate by a cohort of top rank Democrats, including California's Dianne Feinstein, Oregon's Ron Wyden, and Montana's Max Baucus, the political playmate of celeb enviro Robert Redford. The version of the bill that passed the senate was spun as a compromise brokered by these three luminaries. In fact, the logging legislation was essentially the same bill that Rey dreamed up for Bush and his backers in big timber and the building industry. Except the Democrats were more generous, increasing the funding for the $2.9 billion plan by $289 million more than even the White House requested.

Feinstein, long a favorite of the Sierra Club, was the lead perpetrator of soothing myths about the bill. "This legislation is not a logging bill," Feinstein said. "This legislation would merely allow the brush to be cleared out." She makes it sound like a weekend clean up operation, when the reality is more akin to the silvicultural equivalent of Shock and Awe.

There's no money in clearing brush or thinning small trees. And let's be clear, the Healthy Forests Initiative, which should land in the PR Hall of Fame in the category of "most deceptively titled bills," is all about making money for timber companies. Feinstein's legislation underwrites the logging of big trees, many of them in roadless areas far removed from even the most advanced tentacles of suburban sprawl. In exchange, she doles out to complacent environmentalists—the Pavlovian dogs of the political establishment—a few tiny old-growth reserves as morsels, knowing that they can always be logged later. Hush puppies, indeed.

So the timber industry didn't have to break a sweat to achieve their fondest objective. Politicians from both parties, along with the media, did their work for them. The public fears fire more than other natural events, such as earthquakes or tornadoes.

Fires seem preventable. People want to believe there's a political fix, and congress is anxious to feed that illusion.

But the forests and chaparral of southern California are meant to burn. This is an ecosystem born, reared, and shaped by fire. Once or twice every twenty years for the past 10 millennia these forests and scrublands have been scorched with fires at least as intense as those which blazed this autumn.

Logging off big (or little) trees won't alter that ecological reality in the least, except, perhaps, to exacerbate it. Wildland fires are linked most firmly to periods of prolonged drought. The longer the drought, the bigger the fires. Indeed, logging will simply remove from the forest the hardiest trees, the very ones that have survived previous fires. In their place will come new logging roads which will open up tempting new avenues for forests arsonists.

The fires may also come more frequently because of economic factors. During recessions, arson-sparked forest fires become more common. At least three of the big California fires were deliberately set. Firefighting, which is almost useless in combating forest fires, is big business. And increasingly it's a corporate business. Under Clinton and Bush, firefighting has been privatized. That business needs fires—the bigger the better—in order to prosper. A government subsidy is just a match away. Firefighting and military expenditures are the last remnants of Keynesian economics thriving in the American system these days. Congress blindly writes blank checks for both enterprises regardless of their utility.

Of course, global warming also plays a role. The West is becoming drier and hotter. In the future, scrubland and forest fires will become more frequent, more intense, and burn longer than in the past. But don't expect action from the current crop of politicians on that front either. The congress is more likely to hand out tax breaks for designer SUVs than to give a dime to solar energy or raise fuel-efficiency standards. In the post-9/11 landscape, Bush has made the conspicuous burning of fossil fuels a patriotic emblem of American manliness.

Simply put: fire can't be excluded from these ecosystems, but the endless march of subdivisions and mountain resorts can be halted. (Indeed, wildfires might be thought of as a naturopathic remedy of sorts, a kind of ecological radiation treatment for the cancer of urban sprawl.) Of course, none of the politicians on the scene today will entertain notions of even the least restriction on further development of the shrinking forests, deserts, and chaparral of the arid and fire-prone West. Instead, they try to pacify the developers and homeowners with the comforting illusion that smart-bomb logging and beefed up firefighting can keep the inevitable infernos in check. It's a dangerous delusion that cost twenty lives in the fires and left thousands displaced.

The rich will survive to build again, bigger and sturdier structures, with irrigated lawns, swimming pools and tile roofs. The insurance companies are pressed by politicians to pay up in full so that the building trades can prosper.

But what will become of the poor and uninsured, the true human victims of these autumn fires? One calculation by the *Los Angeles Times* estimated that 32 percent of the residents evacuated from the southern California fires were welfare recipients, which means they were impoverished women and children. How many more were poor men? Elderly? Migrant workers? The desperate people who tend the homes of the Riverside and Big Bear elites. Where will they end up?

The final victim in all of this is environmental movement itself. It is clearly defunct at the operational level. The green establishment vowed that stopping the Healthy Forest Initiative was their top legislative priority. But their campaign, which tried to lay all the blame on Bush and his gang of Republican ultras, was reduced to cinders with those California fires and the carrion feeders of the Democratic Party. They got creamed eighty to fourteen, betrayed by legislators, including Feinstein, Wyden, Boxer, Murray, and Baucus, who they had previously certified as champions of the green cause.

The big greens can't even go down fighting. With the blood still fresh on the floor from the slaughter in the senate, a representative from the Wilderness Society told the *Idaho Statesman* that the legislation "offers workable solutions to forest problems, as long as the government follows through with its promises." There you have it. With one move, the Wilderness Society yanked the rug from beneath the grassroots greens and at the same time stamped its imprimatur on logging as a tool to fight forest fires.

Given a chance, the forests of the San Bernadinos will recover. The same can't be said for the credibility of the Sierra Club and the Wilderness Society.

Ashes to ashes, dust to dust.

RIVERSIDE.

Steal a Tree, Go to Jail;
Steal a Forest, Meet the President:
The Politics of Timber Theft

STEALING TREES IS AS OLD AS THE KING'S TIMBER RESERVES. THE SANC-
tions for such sylvan thievery have always been harsh. In medieval England, it
meant public torture and slow death. In the US, the levy was a kind of financial death penalty: triple damages plus serious jail time.

A couple of years ago, two tree poachers drove a log truck onto a small farm in
central Indiana after midnight, cut down two 100-year old black walnut trees in the
small woodlot, loaded the pilfered trunks onto their truck and fled across a cornfield.
The county sheriff caught them when their truck stalled in the field and sank in the
mud. It turns out that the men had been hired by a local sawmill owner, who was set
to sell the lumber to a German timber broker. All three men were tried and convicted
of tree theft.

The black walnut trees, highly prized by German furniture makers, were valued at
$150,000 each. The men were hit with $900,000 in fines and three years of jail time.

Contrast this with evidence coming out of a trial in Portland, Oregon, concerning timber theft on a massive scale. According to internal documents from the US
Forest Service, more than 10 percent of all trees cut off of the national forests are stolen,
usually by timber companies that deliberately log outside the boundaries of timber
sales offered by the agency. The annual toll involves hundreds of thousands of trees
valued at more than $100 million.

The situation was so rife with theft and fraud that in 1991 Congress set up a Timber
Theft Task Force to investigate tree stealing on federal lands. The ten-person team
launched three probes: timber theft on the ground, accounting fraud, and complicity
and obstruction of justice by Forest Service managers.

The team won an early victory. In 1993, the Columbia River Scaling Bureau, a supposedly independent accounting agency that measures and values timber logged off
the national forests in Oregon and Washington, was convicted of fraud. The Bureau
deliberately undervalued logs in return for kickbacks from timber companies. The firm
was hit with a $3.2 million fine.

But this was just a tune up for much bigger fish, namely the largest privately-owned
timber company in the world: Weyerhaeuser. The covert investigation was code-named

"Rodeo." The task force soon compiled evidence that Weyerhaeuser had illegally cut more than 88,000 trees off of the Winema National Forest in southern Oregon. The pilfered trees were valued at more than $5 million. Moreover, investigators suspected that managers in at least three different Forest Service offices had gotten wind of the investigation, tipped off Weyerhaeuser, destroyed documents, and tried to silence agency whistleblowers.

As the investigation picked up steam in the spring of 1995, the head of the task force, Al Marion, traveled to Denver for a secret meeting with the chief of the Forest Service, Jack Ward Thomas, hand-picked for the position by Bill Clinton. Thomas, a wildlife biologist, had won the job after his role in spearheading Option 9, the infamous Clinton forest con job that restarted logging in the ancient forests of the Pacific Northwest.

Marion outlined the investigation for Thomas and Manny Martinez, his newly-appointed deputy for law enforcement. The lead investigator told Thomas that the evidence was compelling and that there would be a good probability of criminal convictions and recovery of large civil fines.

According to notes from the session taken by Martinez, Thomas told Marion that he would give his team "eighteen months to finish the cases" and promised them an additional $300,000 to pursue the investigation. In the next few weeks, the team developed new leads suggesting that Weyerhaeuser's tree theft was systematic and may have been occurring on three other national forests in the region. One estimate suggested that Weyerhaeuser might have been illegally logging more than 33,000 trees a month.

Most of the tree stealing done by Weyerhaeuser occurred in so-called salvage sales, where only dead and dying trees were meant to be cut. Instead, Weyerhaeuser crews, often operating at night, logged off thousands of healthy ponderosa pines and hauled them off to mills under cover of darkness.

On other occasions, timber theft investigators alleged, Weyerhaeuser crews logged off green trees in open daylight under the nose of Forest Service officials and then buried the green trees in stacks of dead lodgepole pines.

"They bundled the trees, sometimes twenty trees to a bundle," says Dennis Shrader, the lead investigator in the Rodeo case. "I estimated that as many as ten trees per bundle were green trees."

Yet, just as the task force was closing in on its culprits, its work came to a crashing halt. Less than four weeks after the Denver meeting with Jack Ward Thomas, Marion received a bizarre letter from the chief thanking him for his service and disbanding the task force immediately. The letter was hand delivered by Martinez.

Marion and his colleagues were out of a job. Thomas ordered their files seized and locked in a vault, where they remained for the next ten months. Marion retired rather than be relocated to West Virginia. Shrader, the head of the Weyerhaeuser investigation, was reassigned to a desk job in a storage closet in the Portland office of the Forest Service.

Why did Thomas pull the plug? It now seems evident that the order came directly from the White House in order to protect Weyerhaeuser executives, who were long-time friends and backers of Clinton, his chief of staff Mac McLarty, and his top White House counsel Bruce Lindsay.

In the 1960s, Seattle-based Weyerhaeuser, enticed by cheap land prices and non-union labor, began buying up forestland in the southeast. By the time Bill Clinton was elected governor in 1978, Weyerhaeuser was the largest landowner in Arkansas. During Governor Clinton's idealistic first term, he tried to curtail the roughshod logging practices of the timber industry in the state by placing limits on clearcutting, aerial pesticide spraying, and logging near streams and rivers. The new regulations riled Weyerhaeuser, which poured money into the campaign of Clinton's rival Frank White. Clinton lost and retreated to a corporate law firm in Little Rock run by his pal Bruce Lindsay to lick his wounds and plot his return to power.

Lindsay soon introduced the humbled Clinton to Jack Creighton, Weyerhaeuser's CEO. Clinton confessed his mistakes and pledged to devote himself to protecting Weyerhaeuser's interests should he ever return to the governor's mansion. The timber giant accepted Clinton's apologies, invested heavily in his re-election bid, and remained a faithful political sponsor over the next twenty years.

When local Forest Service officials tipped Weyerhaeuser to the criminal probe on the Winema Forest, Weyerhaeuser executives complained to their two protectors in the Clinton inner circle, McLarty and Lindsay. The White House instructed political appointees in the Department of Agriculture to tell Thomas to kill the investigation. And it was so.

"The bottom line is that Weyerhaeuser is one of the largest companies in the world," says Shrader. "When you've got an organization that large and with that kind of clout and that amount of resources, they are able to apply political pressure."

While Thomas may have intervened in order to save Weyerhaeuser, his decision to terminate the task force entirely had the effect of halting every other timber fraud investigation then under way.

Up in southeast Alaska a two-year long probe by the task force had uncovered an even grander timber theft scheme unfurling on the Tongass National Forest, the nation's largest publicly-owned forest. Investigator Steven Slagowski had been presented with compelling evidence that large rafts of timber logged off the Tongass by the Ketchikan Pulp Company, owned by Louisiana-Pacific, were routinely disappearing at night before they could be scaled and inventoried by Forest Service workers. The timber ended up being sold to lucrative Asian markets in violation of federal laws requiring the logs to be sent to Alaskan mills.

This was just one of a number of scams on the Tongass uncovered by Slagowski and his colleagues in 1994. He estimated that as much as one out of every three trees logged from the Tongass was illegally cut. In some cases, entire islands were clearcut with the timber companies paying little or nothing for the trees. The illegal cutting often occurred in endangered species habitat. Slagowski noted that nesting sites for bald eagles and marbled murrelets, a small forest-nesting seabird, were both routinely clearcut. "It was theft of unprecedented proportions," says Slagowski.

As in Oregon, the Tongass timber theft ring thrived with the collusion of Forest Service officials—many of them high ranking. Forest Service managers routinely gave advance warning to targets of the investigation and the regional office, based in Juneau, twice convened secret "vulnerability assessment teams." On both occasions, the teams included managers suspected of either being complicit with the timber thieves or participating in the cover-up.

Most of these facts emerged through a lawsuit filed with the US Merit Systems Protection Board (MSPB) by five members of the task force who are seeking the return of their jobs. The MSPB is a federal administrative court charged with hearing claims brought by federal whistleblowers who have suffered retaliation for exposing government corruption.

These days, instead of going after multi-million dollar timber theft rings, Forest Service law enforcement teams spend their time arresting environmental protesters, pulling up pot plants, and harassing poor Hispanics in northern New Mexico who gather firewood from federal forests without a permit.

"Since 1995, ongoing investigations have been disrupted or are simply gathering dust," says Tom Devine, a lawyer at the Government Accountability Project, which represented Marion and five other whistleblowers from the quashed task force. "No new major fraud cases have been opened and only small, firewood theft cases are being investigated."

Steal a tree for firewood go to jail. Steal an entire forest of trees and ship the logs to Japan and watch your company's stock soar.

The Bush administration, naturally, sees no compelling reason to restart an investigation into white-collar crime in the forest. Instead, they have moved to make it easier for timber companies to legally steal trees from the public lands. In November 2003, Bush signed the deceptively-titled "Healthy Forests Initiative," which prescribes wholesale clearcutting of public forests immune from legal challenge and environmental strictures—all in the name of fire prevention.

A couple of weeks later, Bush issued an executive order opening 300,000 acres of ancient forest on the Tongass to logging. Clinton had deferred logging on these lands, but rejected pleas from environmentalists to permanently protect the temperate rainforest from cutting. Bush exploited the loophole at the request of Alaska's Senator Ted

Stevens, who has strip mined the appropriations process to enrich himself, his family, and his son's clients, including timber companies operating on the Tongass.

None of this logging will have to take place under the cover of darkness.

KETCHIKAN.

W Marks the Spot: Bait and Switch in the Bitterroot

L IKE RUMSFELD'S PENTAGON, THE FOREST SERVICE UNDER GEORGE W. Bush runs on PR, corporate cronyism, an obsession with secrecy, and the rapid-fire deployment of fabricated justifications for cutting down old-growth forests.

In Bush's war on the wild, the trees themselves are portrayed as standing weapons of mass destruction, which must be leveled by chainsaws before they ignite into raging wildfires that threaten to incinerate the towns of the rural West. Such is spin, anyway.

Much of this struggle has played out in Montana, where Bush's chainsaw crusade has been blessed by the state's leading Democrat, Senator Max Baucus, an obedient wind-up doll for the timber giants in Big Sky country.

Ground zero in this war is the Bitterroot National Forest, a 1.6 million acre chunk of public land, adorned with Ponderosa pine, serrated mountain peaks, and alpine lakes that sprawls along the spine of the Continental Divide in western Montana.

Beneath the rugged peaks and park-like forests lies the Bitterroot Valley, once the province of working cattle ranches. In the last few decades, though, the ranchers have been pushed out and the valley taken over by the super-rich, who have built multi-million dollar weekend retreats, ornamented with private airstrips and helicopter pads, from which they survey their boutique ranches and decamp for fly-fishing expeditions on the Big Hole River. The Bitterroot Valley, meandering southward from Missoula, is swiftly becoming one of the most elite strips of real estate in the Rocky Mountains— Montana's version of the grotesque compounds defacing Jackson Hole.

By and large, the people who can afford to own land in the Bitterroot these days are richer than those nameless executives who brunched with Dick Cheney during the conclaves of his energy task force. Perhaps that explains why the Bush administration has chosen to make the Bitterroot National Forest an ecological version of their assault on Fallujah.

There's money in that valley. Lots of it. And the Lear Jet Rancheros who own most of the land there now are terrible pyrophobes, fearful that their rustic palaces, ludicrously implanted on the fatal fringe of one of the most fire prone forests in the West, will be annihilated in a wall of flames.

So the Bush administration opted for a pre-emptive strike, with bulldozers and chainsaws serving as ecological cruise missiles.

On December 3, 2003, Bush signed into law the cunningly titled "Healthy Forests Restoration Act." This bill, a kind of War Powers Act against old-growth forests, was adeptly maneuvered through congress by Mark Rey, Bush's Undersecretary of Agriculture in charge of the Forest Service, who once toiled the mean blocks of K Street in DC as the timber industry's top lobbyist.

Offering fantastical claims about the coming sylvan inferno, Rey, with the timely connivance of a few key Democrats, was able to intimidate the congress into giving the Bush administration a free hand to assault western forests without having to abide by the troublesome constraints of environmental laws, such as the Endangered Species Act and National Environmental Policy Act.

All of this in the name of saving the forest from itself.

One of the first assault plans to emerge from this Act is slated for a swath of old-growth forest along the East Fork of the Bitterroot River, close to the pass where the Nez Perce, under the leadership of Chief Joseph and Looking Glass, executed their dramatic escape from the murderous troops of the Seventh Infantry into the Big Hole valley. Lewis and Clark also poked around in these canyons and forests. The area has a profound historical resonance. No matter.

The Bitterroot logging plan targeted an area near the town of Sula. Forest Service officials contended that their timber cutting scheme is designed to serve as a protective buffer for this bucolic hamlet, a kind of levee of stumps against the coming firestorm. Under the Forest Service plan, more than 4,000 acres of prime old-growth forest, posing little or no fire threat, were opened to industrial logging, while the agency offered to do only a token amount of work that might qualify as fire-protection or ecological restoration.

But many long-time residents and environmentalists didn't immediately swallow the Forest Service's apocalyptic rants.

In the Rockies, the Forest Service's veracity ratings rank somewhere between that of Bush and Plum Creek Timber. Perhaps the old-timers and greens in western Montana understood that clearcutting generally increases the risk of big wildfires, instead of dampening it. Perhaps they feared logging would flush tons of sediment into the fabulous trout streams of the East Fork. Perhaps they suspected that the logging would destroy habitat for the elk, goshawk, bear, and wolves that roam these forests. Perhaps they suspected that instead of aiding the economy of the Bitterroot Valley, the money from the timber sales would end up in the coffers a couple politically-wired timber companies.

In a rare coalition, greens, local foresters and firefighters, hunters and fly-fishers came together and drafted their own homegrown plan for protecting the town of Sula from wildfires and for restoring parts of the Bitterroot Forest and its streams that had been mangled by past logging and roadbuilding projects. They called this the Community Protection and Local Economy Alternative.

Although some environmentalists believed even this plan was too generous with blade application, it enjoyed widespread community support. Even so, the Bitterroot's Forest Supervisor, Dave Bull, arbitrarily yanked out all mention of watershed restoration and road closures from the citizens' alternative, claiming that the Healthy Forests law doesn't allow any kind of restoration work that isn't directly tied to logging. This policy nicely mimics the Bush administration policy on birth control, which prohibits federal-funded programs from mentioning the word "condom"—except to describe the failure rates of the prophylactics. Bull was apparently acting on orders from his boss, timber supremo Mark Rey, who moonlights as Undersecretary of Agriculture.

Sensing rejection in the wind, the Bush administration summoned a PR team, working in tandem with the Montana Logging Association, to help market the clearcutting plan. Still the Forest Service and its allies' desperate fear-mongering about catastrophic fires sweeping down the valley with genocidal intent didn't sell to the locals. According to internal documents pried out of the Forest Service using the Freedom of Information Act, we know that the public almost unanimously rejected the agency's war plan for the Bitterroot. When the Bitterroot plan was presented for public inspection, it generated an impressive 10,000 individual comments. It turns out that 98 percent of those comments opposed the Forest Service plan and supported the restoration alternative prepared by local citizens. The Forest Service tried to bury these results and scuffed their feet at releasing them under the FOIA, an act the Bush gang desperately wants to obliterate in the name of national security.

Here's were the story takes a brutish turn, and where the Bush administration's pious encomia to democracy, collaborative experiments, and local control once again proved to ring hollow. That very same FOIA request also brought with it an unexpected trove of papers proving that the solicitation of public input was nothing more than a choreographed charade. At the precise moment the agency was supposed to be considering the views of locals and deliberating over the ecological merits of the competing plans, the Forest Service had secretly dispatched a kind of special operations force into the Bitterroot Forest, armed with cans of spray paint, which they used to covertly mark stands of old-growth trees targeted for the chainsaws. This operation cost the agency $162,000 of public money.

In other words, the fix was in. The public debate over the impending destruction of the West's premier forests was a theatrical exercise, like Colin Powell's vaporous musings before the United Nations.

"The marking of these logging units before a decision had officially been made shows explicitly that the Bush administration's so-called 'collaborative' efforts were simply a bait and switch con game," said local resident Larry Campbell, a member of Friends of the Bitterroot.

There's a final irony here. After learning of the preemptive targeting of the old-growth stands along the East Fork of the Bitterroot River, environmentalists went out to inspect the doomed groves for themselves. Usually, the condemned trees are marked with an X. Here in the Bitterroot, though, the Forest Service spray-painted the big, yellow-bellied Ponderosas, some more than 400 years old, with an all-too familiar brand: "W."

SULA, MONTANA.

Frightening Tales of Endangered Species

CHUCK CUSHMAN WAS ON A ROLL. HIS RUDDY FACE ENFLAMED TO IMPERIAL purple as he unleashed a horror story about the dastardly practices of the Fish and Wildlife Service's "endangered species strike force." It seems that back in February of 1994 a black helicopter swooped down on a rice paddy in Kern County, California. Twenty-five armed federal agents emerged from the chopper and swarmed across the plantation, arresting the owner, a certain Taung Ming-Lin, a hard-working, commie-hating Taiwanese rice farmer, for having accidentally killed, yes, an endangered rat.

The feds seized his tractor, confiscated his plow, and sent Mr. Ming-Lin off to the federal penitentiary. Then the bank foreclosed on his farm. "That was the whole point of the operation," Chuckman thundered. "The feds wanted that property for themselves. Another case of empire building, pure and simple."

Cushman, insurance salesman turned anti-green crusader, head of the American Land Rights Association and star carnival barker of Wise-Use confabs across the country, wasn't finished. He next spun the sad tale of poor Ben Cone, who had the distinct misfortune to own property in North Carolina, a state where property rights were once sacrosanct—until, that is, the red-cockaded woodpecker showed up. When federal wildlife snoops discovered the endangered bird on Cone's land (or planted it there, according to other versions of the tragic tale), they immediately cordoned off more than 1,000 acres of the Cone estate, prohibiting any kind of development whatsoever. The men in black, Chuckman roared, even forced Cone to hire a wildlife biologist to develop a monitoring plan for the useless woodpecker. The price? Nearly $10,000. That's right, Chuckman sneered. Ten grand out of Ben Cone's own pocket.

Until the red-cockaded woodpecker came along, Chuckman reported to the rapt crowd of loggers and miners and ORV-driving Christians, Cone was a responsible logger, managing his little plot of woods with tender care. But that protection area for the woodpecker, that green zone, if you will, cost Cone nearly $2 million. To recoup these loses and to prevent the red-cockaded woodpecker from expanding its range and placing even more of his property off-limits to "management," Cone, Chuckman said with a shake of his head, was left with no choice but clearcut the rest of his land. "See the perverse incentives at work?" Chuckman asked. "Now, some environmentalist will probably come along and accuse him of being a land-raper, when the feds left him no choice."

Next he told the horrifying tale of the southern California hospital that was halted in order to protect eight endangered sand flies. Then Chuckman related the shocking news that federal agents were responsible for devastating wildfires in California that destroyed hundreds of homes because use of lawnmowers was banned to protect endangered rats. Even geese are tortured to protect useless rare species, Chuckman said, as he recounted how federal Fish and Wildlife agents descended on a flock of Canadian geese in Utah and forced them to vomit to see if their stomachs contained the endangered Kanab ambersnail.

Cushman wasn't the only one telling such stories. The Timber Industry Labor Management Committee and the anti-environmental National Wilderness Institute had a few of their own. Have you heard about how the red-cockaded woodpecker, the Al Qaeda of the avian kingdom, threatens our national security? Apparently, these stealthy woodpeckers have secretly invaded patches of old growth forests that have miraculously survived the chainsaw at Fort Bragg military base in North Carolina. The presence of these invaders has paralyzed the Army's plans to construct a desperately needed new detention facility. To make matters worse, the woodpeckers have interfered with Army training exercises and weapons testing.

Then there is the depressing tale from the Florida Keys, where the Fish and Wildlife Service's timid efforts to provide a sanctuary for the last 400 or so Key deer, a species nearing oblivion, have apparently place elementary school children at grave risk. How could this be? Well, according to the National Wilderness Institute, the feds nixed plans for the construction of a new elementary school because it might impinge upon an 8,000-acre Key deer preserve. Now the kids must be bussed down thirty miles of dangerous swamp road around the preserve.

If that doesn't rile up you, perhaps the story of the Texas widow will stir your anti-environmental passions. As the president of the National Cattlemen's Association told the Senate Environment and Public Works Committee, it was only weeks after her late husband's estate was settled when Mary Rector had the extreme misfortune to find a pair of golden-cheeked warblers nesting in her hedgerow. Mrs. Rector wanted to mow down that unsightly tangle of thorny shrubs and subdivide her property in a manner good Texans have been doing for generations. But then, suddenly, Fish and Wildlife agents rushed in, stilling the bulldozers and threatening to prosecute the distraught widow unless she left the diminutive songbirds to nest in peace.

Then the head of the Alliance for America stepped to the microphone to tell the senators of the agonizing fate of the Shepard family, whose family enterprise was shut down to protect a catfish. For more than 100 years, the Shepards of Kansas had been mining gravel out of the bed of the Neosho River. Then the feds shattered the family dream. Their gravel scooping days were over. All because of the madtom catfish.

Then there's story of Michael Rowe, the California man whose home was ruined for the sake of a single rat! For years, Rowe had put away money to build an addition to the one-bedroom home on his twenty-acre ranch near Winchester. Then he discovered that his house site was within a study area for the Stephens kangaroo rat. Rowe could have hired a biologist for $5,000, but if he found a single rat on the property his addition would be deemed illegal. If no rats were found, a missive from the American Land Rights Association said, Rowe would then have to pay the government $40,000 for a rat reserve elsewhere. In essence, the Rowe dream house was destroyed by fed overlords before it left the drawing board.

These anecdotes, and dozens more just like them, seem to be heart-wrenching stories of small landowners, all deeply versed in the works of Jefferson and Wendell Berry no doubt, threatened by an aggressive and indifferent federal government that places the rights of rats and flies above the well-being of people. These are, of course, industry counter-myths, sensationalist narratives illustrating the ways endangered species and their advocates menace humanity.

Curiously, not one of these horror stories is quite true. And most are patently false. The Texas widow, for example, was advised only that an endangered species was found on her property. The Fish and Wildlife Service didn't stop her from wiping out the nesting birds by clearing a swath thirty feet wide and a mile long, nor did the agency prevent her from subdividing the ranch for more than a cool million.

In the Florida Keys, the elementary school was indeed built in Key deer habitat, and the endangered species' population is plummeting. Today only 255 remain in that locale.

The US Army achieved a decisive victory over the red-cockaded woodpecker in the battle at Fort Bragg. The massive new facility is now operational and tanks are once again blasting away in woodpecker habitat.

Mr. Cone, the sensitive logger, did indeed clearcut his 2,000 acres of North Carolina pine forest for a handsome profit, with no interference from the Fish and Wildlife Service.

As for Mr. Rowe, the California man terrorized by the kangaroo rat, his problems started with Riverside County Habitat Conservation Planning Agency, which had designated part of his property as a kangaroo rat study area. The county had agreed not to grant any grading permits within such study areas unless a biologist demonstrated that it was not being used by kangaroo rats. In the case of Mr. Rowe's property, the cost of hiring a biologist would not have been $5,000, but a more modest $500. Indeed, a Fish and Wildlife Service agent offered to conduct the study for free, but Rowe declined. The mitigation fee for the rat reserves was not $40,000, but a mere $1,000, with the money going into a reserve acquisition fund. Mr. Rowe's home was not destroyed. Indeed, it is still occupied.

As for the hospital in Colton, California supposedly put on hold for sake of the eight sand flies, the construction of the building was never halted. An agreement was reached between the developer and the Feds regarding the sand flies before construction began. The developer agreed to set aside 10.27 acres near the hospital as a reserve for the species. The hospital site is seventy-six acres in size, thus the fly habitat constitutes only 13 percent of the total acreage. The hospital is now fully operational. The sand flies aren't doing nearly as well.

In Kansas, the woes suffered by the Shepard family's gravel mining operation were also exaggerated for senatorial consumption. The state of Kansas listed the Neosho River madtom catfish as a threatened species in 1978. State biologists temporarily halted gravel scooping operations by the Shepards until they could determine what, precisely, was needed to protect the fish during spawning time. Alternate sites in the river continued to be available for gravel mining. Mining continues. Catfish continue to decline.

Taung Ming-Lin, the Kern County rice farmer, was informed when he purchased his plantation that it contained habitat for several endangered species, including the Tipton kangaroo rat, San Joaquin kit fox, and blunt-nosed leopard lizard. Ming-Lin was told that he would need a state permit before he developed his property. The farmer ignored this advisory and two subsequent instructions and proceed to grade, plow, and flood the fields. When federal and state wildlife agents came to investigate (in jeeps, not black helicopters), they discovered several kangaroo rat corpses, charged Ming-Lin with violating the Endangered Species Act and seized a small tractor and disc. Six months later, after Ming-Lin agreed to wait six more months before resuming his farming operations, obtain the necessary permits (allowing him, in effect, to legally kill endangered species), and donate $5,000 to an endangered species protection program in Kern County, the government dropped the charges. His farm was not foreclosed on. In fact, it's being farmed today.

On the surface these Tales of the Endangered Species Act Run Amok might appear to be little more than rural legends, evidence of a kind of infectious ecological paranoia in the backwoods. Certainly, various versions of these stories have been spun for years on Liars Benches in small town across the South and the West.

But the political reach of these tall tales extends far beyond the backwaters and bayous of the Republic. In fact, they represent a carefully calculated campaign against the Endangered Species Act hatched by PR firms and lobbyists on behalf of real estate moguls, timber and mining companies, and their Wise-Use movement front groups. These anecdotal fragments have been stitched together into a potent counter-story, designed to implant anxieties in the common folk, to foster anger and rebellion against phantom oppressors.

Imprinted on the national consciousness by the daily diatribes of Rush Limbaugh and the twisted reporting of ABC's John Stoessel, large segments of the American public now accept these tales as facts. It's gone far beyond owls versus loggers. Now obscure species such as the pearly-shelled pocket mussel and the fairy shrimp are portrayed as the brutal instruments of Big Brother.

These manufactured tragedies have developed a stronger currency in the past decade or so, partly due to the reactionary political climate that has descended over the country, the white rural male backlash against the government, and the rise of an anti-nature Christian Right. The bureaucratic bunglings of the Clinton and Bush administrations have helped foment the unrest.

But widespread popular acceptance of these endangered species myths has most of all to do with the hard, and handsomely remunerated, work of powerhouse public relations firms such as Burston-Marsteller and Edelman PR, which have precisely choreographed the telling of these stories in the popular press, across the talk radio airwaves, and in tear-stained testimony on Capitol Hill.

Under the guidance of these gurus of consumer consciousness, the once enormously popular Endangered Species Act has been portrayed as a law born of good intentions that has been horribly abused by an insensitive federal government backed by nature-worshipping environmentalists. Thus, reality is inverted. The David and Goliath struggle is no longer about the grizzly bear against the chainsaws of timber giant Plum Creek, the sockeye salmon against the unforgiving hydrodams of Columbia, or the peregrine falcon versus the toxic ravages of DDT.

In the corporate counter-myth, the Endangered Species Act, backed by armed agents of the bloated federal government, is suffocating the small farmer's hopes of living out his Jeffersonian dream, undermining the grizzled rancher seeking to defend Manifest Destiny, and bankrupting the kindly widow who only wanted to put the grandkids through college.

In fact, 99 percent of the time when the Endangered Species Act clicks into action it simply pits one branch of the federal government against another: the Fish and Wildlife Service tries to halt Forest Service logging and road-building plans or the National Marine Fisheries Service lodges a protest against some outlandish scheme the Corps of Engineers has for killing off yet another river. And nine times out of ten, the wildlife advocates lose these inter-agency confrontations. The timber sales are logged, the roads are built, the dams flood the canyon and the spawning beds—seldom with any alterations. In over twenty-five years, only about ten projects have been entirely halted due to conflicts with an endangered species. Ten out of tens of thousands.

Private landowners only enter the picture when they are receiving some kind of federal subsidy or when they commit especially egregious violations of the law, usually involving the killing of a listed species. Even then the fines are puny. And even hefty fines won't stop the slide toward extinction.

All this being said, the challenge for environmentalists is not to construct counter-counter-myths. Nor is it to join in yet another lavish media campaign, developed by some competitor of Burston-Marsteller, defending the existing Endangered Species Act. The real challenge is simply to speak the truth.

Environmentalists need to come right out and say it straight: the Endangered Species Act is a well-intentioned failure. Not because it places animals over people, but because it is almost totally ineffective. The law, passed in 1973 in the reign of good King Richard Nixon, friend to all living things, was one of the most important pieces of environmental legislation in the nation's history. Now it is dying. At its best, America's premier environmental law is little more than a final, frail safety net, a kind of welfare program for wildlife, designed to drive species down to their minimum viable populations and keep them there. It is an over-packed ark, leaking at every seam.

Saving the Endangered Species Act is not enough. The law needs to be thoroughly overhauled, substantially strengthened with tough sanctions for violators, and most importantly, tied directly to the protection of ecosystems and public lands.

The chances of this happening are almost nil. Why? Because the annual political spats over the future of the Act serve the purposes of both parties and their constituents. Even the big environmental groups have a financial stake in this fake fight over the future of the law. The law has been sitting in limbo since the Carter era. And predictably, every year, the industry groups offer up a bill to gut the Act. The Democrats counter with a weak compromise and the green groups will issue emergency fundraising alerts to save the law. Stalemate occurs. The green groups will raise more millions claiming victory, and the developers will continue to invade endangered species habitat with a winning record of 10,000 wins to ten losses. Because a fiction known as the Endangered Species Act will still be around, the pro-industry Wise Use Movement will still be able to raise money to fight it. As for the corporations, if they log, mine, or build on public lands they will still receive billions in taxpayer subsidies, and if they choose not to log, mine, or build on their own properties they can claim ecological harm or a "takings" and get millions more in compensation.

So there you have it. A win-win solution for everyone except the spotted owl, Mexican wolf, grizzly, salmon, and all those other species soon to disappear from the face of the Earth or be preserved in test tubes in some genetic zoo. And that sad saga is no tall tale.

Washington, DC.

Is the Eagle Really Back?

IT'S BECOMING AN ANNUAL RITUAL. WHEN THE JULY 4TH HOLIDAY ROLLS around, it's time for the incumbent in the White House to showboat his environmental credentials. In the summer of 2000, Bill Clinton made a grand expedition over to the tidal basin in Washington, DC, where, with Bruce Babbitt by his side, the president mc'd a lavish ceremony announcing the removal of the bald eagle from the endangered species list.

"The American bald eagle is now back from the brink of extinction, thriving in virtually every state of the union," President Clinton declared. "I can think of no better way to honor the birth of our nation than by celebrating the rebirth of our proudest living symbol."

On the surface, the numbers are impressive. In 1963, there were only 465 breeding pairs of bald eagles in the lower-forty-eight states, according to numbers supplied by the Fish and Wildlife Service. (This is figure almost certainly low, since much of the Mississippi delta and North Woods were not surveyed.) By 2000, the Service claims there may be as many as 12,000 eagles in the US. Of course, 5,000 breeding pairs is still a far cry from the 500,000 birds estimated to have lived in the continental US in the mid-1800s.

Typically, Bruce Babbitt used the occasion of the eagle's delisting to tout his own insidious tinkering with the Endangered Species Act. "America was the first nation on earth to pass a comprehensive law protecting endangered species, the Endangered Species Act, and once again we have shown that this landmark law works," Babbitt said. "Today the American bald eagle is back. The bald eagle joins a growing list of other once-imperiled species that are on the road to recovery."

Of course, Babbitt neglected to mention that under his watch the grizzly bear, marbled murrelet, coho salmon, California gnatcatcher, and northern spotted owl have continued to slide ever closer toward extinction—mainly because he chose to cut deals with developers rather than enforce the law for the benefit of rare species.

The bald eagle population has rebounded somewhat, largely due to the decision to ban the sale of DDT in the US, a move that was made when Clinton was still eligible for the draft. Since most eagles aren't migratory, the fact that a loophole in the law allowed US chemical companies to continue dumping their toxic supplies across the developing world didn't devastate their populations. Other raptors and migratory fish-eating birds haven't been so fortunate. Witness the recent declines in osprey, marsh hawk, and black shouldered kite populations.

But even the comeback of the eagle is vastly overstated. After all, a species that has "recovered" to less than 2 percent of its natural population size should hardly be something to brag about. This is especially true because the bald eagle, unlike other imperiled species, has benefited from a wide range of special laws beyond the ESA, including the Migratory Bird Treaty Act and the Bald Eagle Protection Act of 1940. The big raptor has done well in the Great Lakes region, but remains in a perilous state throughout much of the interior West, where logging of old-growth riparian habitat, poisonous run-off from mining operations, and dewatering of streams has kept the eagle on the ropes. It's the old story: where the issue is habitat, species continue to decline because the government, particularly the Clinton/Gore/Babbitt regime, does little to enforce the law when it conflicts with the economic interests of land developers and timber companies.

Take the eagles of Klamath Lake, in south-central Oregon. This marshy area on the Cascade Range's eastern front used to be a haven for nesting and migrating eagles. Now the lakeshore is being mercilessly gobbled up by developers, and the bird's numbers are dropping. Removing the eagle from the list makes it easier for big-time developers to carve even more deeply into the little old-growth that remains. A case in point is the mammoth ski/golf resort planned for Pelican Butte, adjacent to a bald eagle sanctuary. The developers have hired wildlife biologist Jack Ward Thomas, former chief of the Forest Service, to flack for them. With the eagle off the endangered species list, Thomas' job just got much less complicated.

In Babbitt's home ground, the desert Southwest, the situation is even more dire. The desert bald eagle is small and unique. The southwest hosts only about fifty breeding pairs, down from over 500 pairs fifty years ago. These birds have keenly adapted to the smothering heat of the region by nesting in the winter. Fledglings leave the nest in the spring, much earlier than northern eagles, before the summer heat peaks. Even so, the fledgling mortality rate has been high in recent years and appears to be getting worse. In the past decade, more than 75 percent of the young desert eagles have died before they've reached four years old, the average breeding age.

On top of this, nesting eagles are raising fewer and fewer chicks. In 1998, for example, forty pairs of desert eagles produced twenty-three nestlings, for a nest productivity rating of 0.59. This is down from a nest productivity rating of 0.68 in 1997 and 0.85 in 1996.

The ecological threats to the desert eagles were mounting at the very moment Clinton and Babbitt, eager for an uplifting summer photo-op, moved to shred the legal protections for the national bird. Nearly 30 percent of the species' habitat in Arizona is slated for development. "Only the Endangered Species Act mandates enforceable evaluation of these projects," warns Dr. Robin Silver, of Phoenix-based Southwest Center for Biological Diversity. "Without the protection of the Endangered Species Act there will be nothing to stand between the desert eagle and extinction."

KLAMATH FALLS.

Clinton Versus the Spotted Owl

Part One: Cutting It Down the Middle

WHEN JACK WARD THOMAS HANDED PRESIDENT BILL CLINTON THE final copy of his plan for the ancient forests of the Pacific Northwest Forest, Clinton asked only one question: "How much timber will it cut?"

With this revealing query began the bizarre final chapter in the saga of Clinton's adventure in the rainforests of the Northwest, the home of the salmon and the spotted owl.

In the final two weeks of April 1994, the Clinton administration saw its strategy to reinitiate timber sales in Northwest forests come to a shocking fruition, when most of the key environmental groups in the region agreed to lift the three-year old federal injunction prohibiting new timber sales in spotted owl habitat. At the same moment, one of the nation's largest forest products companies announced its glowing support for Clinton's forest plan.

Watch how neatly the pattern of events unfolded.

On April 14, 1994, the Clinton administration submitted the Record of Decision for its Northwest forest plan to federal Judge William Dwyer in Seattle. A disturbing codicil to the original plan (widely known as Option 9), the 200-page Record of Decision granted a series of last-minute concessions to timber interests that were designed to accelerate the preparation of new timber sales in old-growth and keep the plan's annual timber sale above the one billion board foot mark—the psychological barrier demanded by the timber industry.

The animals pay the price. For example, in order to meet the politically-driven cut levels, the final document shrank protection of the rare Marbled Murrelet by 250,000 acres in southern Oregon alone. The Marbled Murrelet is a chunky sea-faring bird that nests only in old-growth forests near the Pacific Ocean. It is listed as a threatened species. The diminished Murrelet was specifically tailored to clear the way for several enormous timber sales slated for the Siskiyou National Forest. Some of these sales, including the hotly contested Sugarloaf sale, are located in roadless areas.

Despite the intense uproar from the public and the scientific community over the prospect of logging and roadbuilding inside these ancient forest reserves, the Clinton plan greenlights thinning and salvage logging inside these supposedly sacrosanct areas without being subject to a detailed environmental assessment. This change was geared toward accelerating logging in the Oregon Coast Range and the Olympic Peninsula, the two areas where the Spotted Owl is most vulnerable to local extinction.

Most seriously, the final document dramatically weakened the standards for watershed analysis in order to "fast-track" logging operations in key basins. Back in 1993, Clinton and Bruce Babbitt hailed these detailed environmental assessments as the analytical and procedural cornerstone of the new ecosystem management approach. The basin-wide reviews were supposed to force timber sale planners to closely scrutinize the effects of logging and roadbuilding on entire watersheds. In fact, the group of scientists that peer-reviewed the draft Clinton plan concluded that these watershed assessment were "critical to the eventual success of adaptive management." But with a stroke of the pen, Thomas and Clinton wiped them away.

As Clinton was taking with one hand, he was giving with the other. On April 15, 1994, a band of timber executives announced that they would not oppose the implementation of the new Clinton plan in court, opting instead for a "congressional strategy." This meant that the industry planned to beg their congressional clients—men like Senator Mark Hatfield and House Speaker Tom Foley—to simply inscribe into law higher timber sales levels for the region than are called for under the Option 9 scheme and to insure that, once the levels are set, they remain immune from judicial scrutiny.

Forest Service chief Jack Ward Thomas indicated that he "might have a personal preference for timber targets" set by congress. This is where the slippery nature of Clintonism turns opaque. Instead of fighting for the ecological integrity of their own forest plan, they sent up a smoke signal to congress begging them to subvert it.

But this was a tall order. For starters, Congress didn't want to take the blame for Clinton's failures. Sen. George Mitchell told Bruce Babbitt point blank that he would fight any effort by the administration to shield its plan from legal review. Even traditional architects of so-called sufficiency legislation (laws that set timber and road-building targets and free activities from compliance with environmental statutes) displayed a distinct lack of enthusiasm for this approach without having an explicit and public nod of support from Clinton himself—a commitment that the president was unwilling to make.

Meanwhile, the federal courts had already struck a blow to the legality of the approach used to craft Clinton's logging plan. In March 1994, in a suit brought by the Native Forest Council, Federal Judge Thomas Jackson ruled that the secretive process used to develop Option 9 violated the Federal Advisory Committee Act, or FACA. Along with the Freedom of Information Act, FACA stands as one of the pillars of open government. It requires that all advisory panels to the federal government contain balanced representation, hold public hearings, and make their deliberative records open to public review. Judge Jackson ruled that the Clinton approach violated each of these requirements.

This case laid the legal groundwork for the substantive challenges to future timber sales offered under the Clinton plan. For example, FACA seemed likely to be a fruitful angle of attack against the consensus-based planning processes that are proliferating under the Adaptive Management approach. The response of the Clinton administration was to test congressional sentiment for a repeal of FACA. Sound familiar?

On April 19, several of the environmental plaintiffs in the Spotted Owl lawsuits declared their dissatisfaction with the Clinton plan at a press conference in Washington, DC. "The plan has come a long way politically, but falls short ecologically," charged Andy Kerr, conservation director of the Oregon Natural Resources Department. "It fails to protect hundreds of species identified as dependent on old-growth forests, placing many at risk of extinction. Clearly, this doesn't meet President Clinton's own standard that the plan be scientifically credible and legally responsible."

Kerr and Julie Norman, director of Headwaters, a southern Oregon conservation group, vowed that the environmentalists would mount a full-blown legal assault on the Clinton forest plan. She said the legal challenge would focus on "salmon, economics, and some owl claims."

Here's where things turn mysterious. One short day after these brawny pronouncements, Judge William Dwyer convened a status conference on the case in Seattle. At this hearing, the Forest Service officially requested that the injunction on new timber sales in Spotted Owl habitat be dissolved. The agency's attorneys claimed that merely by filing the new plan with the court they had fully complied with the judge's orders. At that point, Sierra Club Legal Defense Fund's attorney shocked the court by telling Dwyer that the eleven environmental groups represented by his law firm would not oppose the Clinton administration's request to lift the injunction and begin logging in old-growth again. He said that while the environmentalists might file an "amended complaint" to the old lawsuit, they were unlikely to seek a new injunction.

This was the second capitulation by the green lawyers to Clinton in less than a year. In September of 1993, in "a gesture of goodwill" to the Clinton administration, the environmentalists agreed to allow logging with fifty-four timber sales in old-growth forests vital to the survival of the Spotted Owl. It was at that point that the Forest Conservation Council, a Santa Fe-based group, split from the coalition and got new lawyers to press the fight.

And as the Sierra Club Legal Defense Fund offered to give up the entire injunction, only the Forest Conservation Council and the Native Forest Council of Eugene, Oregon demonstrated any resistance to the Clinton crowd's political pressure to surrender the hard-won legal victory. The Native Forest Council was not a plaintiff in the original suit, but was granted *amicus* status by the court. Both organizations filed briefs with Judge Dwyer voicing strenuous objections to the release of the injunction. They argued that the burden of proof should lie with Clinton's Forest Service to demonstrate that it is in compliance with the judge's orders. But those suits were a long shot, a final protestation of a politically-driven sellout.

With the injunction lifted, the Forest Service began implementing the Clinton logging plan in June of 1994. The agency told the court it was ready to put forward 165 million board feet of timber in owl habitat during the summer—the first new timber sales since the G.H.W. Bush administration.

On April 21, Weyerhaeuser fulfilled its end of the bargain. The timber giant's executive vice-president declared that the company was satisfied with the Clinton logging plan and pledged to defend it in Congress or the courts "by any means necessary." You know you're in deep trouble when corporate executives start quoting Malcolm X.

But Weyerhaeuser's support for the Clinton plan shouldn't have come as a surprise. The company, along with other industrial forest land owners, such as Plum Creek, ITT-Rayonier, Simpson and Georgia-Pacific, were the clear winners in the Option 9 sweepstakes. After all, these corporations had already been the financial beneficiaries of declining federal timber sales. As the price of lumber soared, so did their profits. The Clinton plan's permanent restrictions on the rate of federal land logging substantially increases the long-term value of their own holdings.

More importantly for Weyerhaeuser, under the generous provisions of the Clinton administration's new 4(d) Rule, industrial forest land owners were largely exempted from the Endangered Species Act's strict prohibition against the "incidental taking" (that is, killing) of a listed species. This regressive rule punishes small landowners, but allows these multinational timber titans to continue clearcutting unabated in Spotted Owl habitat on their own lands, even when it ravages the owl's already declining population.

Of course, the biggest victory for companies such as Weyerhaeuser and Plum Creek came when the Clinton administration stiff-armed environmentalists and labor leaders by refusing to stem the flow of raw log exports from private, corporate, and industrial lands in the Northwest. Even though the owl takes the rap, these exports are the leading cause of job loss in the timber sector.

For years, environmental strategists had plotted the ultimate crack-up of the timber monolith, pitting private landowners against public timber buyers (such as Louisiana-Pacific), domestic millers against log exporters. Well, the fissures finally came, but they didn't unfold the way many expected—the most socially and environmentally deviant corporations emerged as unscathed victors.

What do we make of this odd accumulation of events, this carefully executed endgame to the Northwest forest crisis? Some grassroots environmentalists and labor organizers for the pulp and paper workers' union charge that a three-way deal was cut between mainstream green groups, log exporters, and the Clinton administration. From a distance, the pattern to this rapid denouement seemed horribly prearranged.

But the conspiracy falters on one salient point: the environmentalists received nothing for their gestures of goodwill, their reluctant dealmaking. Option 9 degenerated with every concession; it didn't improve. In the end, only the lawyers made out. Trees for fees.

No, the bizarre and tragic conclusion to the Northwest forest fight simply revealed the fundamental nature of the Clinton approach and its abiding allegiance to corporate culture. If Clinton and Al Gore really shared an interest in protecting American timber workers and the ecology of the temperate rainforests of the Pacific Northwest, there was an obvious solution: end commercial logging on public lands and terminate the export of unprocessed logs to overseas ports. But Clinton didn't align himself with the owl, the working stiffs, or the grassroots. He sided with the suits.

Part Two: Long Time Coming, Long Time Gone

The plaintive voices on my answering machine repeated the same incredulous refrain: "What the hell's going on here? Can you believe what they did?"

Frankly, no, I couldn't believe it. Although I had known for weeks that the environmentalist plaintiffs in the Spotted Owl lawsuits would not ask Judge William Dwyer to maintain his injunction against logging in ancient forests after the Clinton administration submitted its final flawed plan for the public forests of the Pacific Northwest, it still didn't make any sense.

After all, the Dwyer decision was the *Brown v. Board of Education* of environmental lawsuits, a revolutionary ruling handed down during the first Bush administration that seemed destined to subvert the exploitative paradigm of public lands management that had dominated the national forests since Nixon was vice-president. Yet, it was impossible to imagine Thurgood Marshall, who had successfully argued *Brown* and a wave of other civil rights cases, relinquishing the court's order based on mere promises from the government to seek a degree of integration in a mere 60 percent of the segregated school districts of Topeka, Kansas—a rough parallel of the Clinton forest plan's moderate level of protection for 60 percent of the region's old-growth forests. Under the Clinton plan, logging is permitted even inside ancient forest reserves, which is like having white's only history classes in a black-dominated high school.

The Dwyer injunction was the only real lever of power by which the environmental movement could move the top-heavy Clinton administration, a looming deterrent against political backsliding and double-dealing. Then, suddenly, it was gone—simply discarded, jettisoned away. Why?

The environmentalists involved offered disparate explanations, none entirely satisfying. Some cited a lack of funds; others admitted to a queasiness over their ultimate chances of success for keeping the injunction in place. Some described it as the politic thing to do. All agreed that they were following the sagacious advice of their attorneys at the Sierra Club Legal Defense Fund, or SCLDF.

Andy Kerr, conservation director for the Oregon Natural Resources Council, suggested that the Dwyer injunction had simply run its course. Owls are out, salmon are in.

"We need to recast the whole issue," Kerr told me. "We need to move beyond owls and look at mollusks, salmon, log exports. We might be able to win a bigger victory in the future."

Behind the tangled web of legalisms, Kerr admits that ancient forests will be lost in the interim. Exactly how much is a matter of intense debate. The Forest Service has a decade of timber sales on the shelf, the bulldozers ready to roll. Many of these sales have already been tweaked to conform to the Clinton logging rules. In addition, the timber industry holds contracts on another billion board feet of prime old-growth timber. Over the course of the Clinton presidency, the Forest Service could log 50,000 acres of old-growth timber inside ancient forest reserves.

Another environmentalist plaintiff raised the specter of a sufficiency rider as the prime motivation for dropping the Dwyer injunction. He explained that a continuance of the injunction might provoke "hostile elements" in the Congress into shielding the Clinton plan from any future legal challenges under the Endangered Species Act. I reminded him of the Deal of Shame, where the plaintiffs in the owl suits traded their acquiescence to forty-four timber sales in ancient forests for a commitment from Clinton and Bruce Babbitt to veto any new restrictions on judicial review.

"Yes, but that doesn't mean they'll keep their promises," he rejoined.

Exactly my point.

In its defense, the lawyers at SCLDF offered nothing substantial either, opting instead for legal sophistry and recombinant rationalizations, as spiraling and impenetrable to the naked eye as a strand of DNA. Attorney Todd True reportedly told his clients that the Dwyer injunction "had outlived its usefulness." He claimed that it would simply be more convenient and efficient to start a new round of litigation focusing on adaptive management and ecosystem protection.

This is hardly a persuasive argument. One of the key elements of the 1992 Dwyer ruling was the judge's finding that the Bush owl plan did not secure protection of other old-growth obligate species, for which the owl was meant to be an indicator. In short, Dwyer himself opened the legal door for these broader ecosystem-level issues.

The lawyers also told their clients that they were unprepared to argue the legal deficiencies of the Clinton plan before Judge Dwyer. They claimed that they needed "several weeks of discovery" to craft their briefs. Yet the basic outlines of the Clinton plan had been clear for nearly ten months and it had only deteriorated since its unveiling—plenty of time to deconstruct its numerous legal vulnerabilities.

SCLDF's handling of the Dwyer injunction brought into sharp question the cogency of the once mighty law firm's legal and political advice. In August 1993, when SCLDF lawyers advised their clients to submit to Clinton's demand that dozens of timber sales in critical habitat for the owl be released, they argued that the injunction would be dissolved automatically once a new Environmental Impact Statement was prepared for the Clinton forest plan. The advice was questionable, but it became a sinister, self-fulfilling prophecy.

Even Dwyer displayed a certain disgruntled disbelief at the cavalier treatment of his injunction, a ruling that led to death threats against him.

Understood properly, these concessions amounted to a series of political, not legal, calculations aimed at appeasing officials, such as Al Gore and Bruce Babbitt, inside the Clinton administration. It was the calculus of a trade-off. In order to save more forest in the future, they argued, some old-growth stands had to be consigned away today. This strategy eerily mirrored the essential gambit of Option 9 itself. In each case, a certainty was sacrificed for an improbability.

At its root, the essence of the Spotted Owl case was this: for more than a decade after it was clear that the spotted owl was at risk of extinction, the federal government had systematically sidestepped, ignored, violated, and subverted the law in order to meet its own politically-drive timber targets, debauching the native forest ecosystems of the Pacific Northwest in the process. In an extraordinary series of rulings from a Reagan-appointed judge, Judge Dwyer denounced this deviant pattern of behavior in the harshest terms and meted out the strongest punishment available to him: a permanent injunction halting all new timber sales in old-growth forest. It was a deliciously draconian decision.

So what had really changed since 1991? The Clinton plan remains a political construct, lacking scientific credibility and legal merit. A federal court in Washington had already ruled that the secretive process used to develop the Clinton plan was fatally flawed, and violated the basic principles of open government. Meanwhile, nineteen of the nation's leading forest ecologists attacked the Clinton plan for being worse for the Spotted Owl than the recovery plan drafted during the Bush administration. The ecologists predicted ominously that the Clinton plan would not save the owl from extinction. Option 9 has gotten worse since they reviewed it.

If there's an upside to any of this, it may be that the restarting of the chainsaws will awaken grassroots forest activists in the Northwest, many of whom had been lulled into a kind of complacent senescence by the lack of new timber sales to organize around. But what a price to pay.

If you're lucky enough to own a copy of Judge Dwyer's original injunction, hold on to it. They won't be making them like that one any more.

Recount in the Forests: Bush Puts Out a Contract on the Spotted Owl

EVERY SUMMER FOR THE PAST DECADE YOUNG BIOLOGISTS HAVE HEADED OFF into the mossy forests of the Pacific Northwest to call spotted owls. Every year the birders get fewer and fewer responses. The spotted owl, which thrives only in the oldest of forests, is in a downward spiral toward extinction. Take the rainforests of Washington's Olympic Peninsula. There, the owls, isolated in a desert of clearcuts and sprawl, are rapidly disappearing. According to the most recent surveys, these Olympic peninsula owls have declined by more than half in the last decade alone. At this rate the secretive bird may well become extinct by 2010.

In the Cascade Range of western Washington and Oregon, the owls, jeopardized by continued logging on private and federal forest lands, aren't doing any better. Populations are plummeting at a rate of 5 to 8 percent every year. Give the owl in those tattered mountains another twenty-five years at most, unless all logging stops.

So the numbers just weren't adding up right for Bush, who promised the timber industry that he would reinvigorate logging across the owl's habitat. Through its first four years, the Bush administration has produced far less timber for its clients than did the Clinton administration. The natives were getting restless.

With the numbers stacked against them, the Bush team simply attacked the counters. Sound familiar? Remember Palm Beach County? The Bush White House relentlessly parrots one of the most paranoid accusations of big timber: that the Fish and Wildlife Service is intentionally undercounting the spotted owl population in order to suppress logging on federal lands in the Pacific Northwest. The Fish and Wildlife Service, the Bush flacks charged, is too biased in favor of protecting...you guessed it...wildlife. This must come as a shock to both environmental groups and the agency, which is facing dozens of lawsuits for not moving fast enough to protect a slate of vanishing species, from the gray wolf and grizzly to the northern goshawk and bull trout.

So for the first time ever, the Bush administration hired private firms to assess the status of two bird species threatened by logging in the northwest: the spotted owl and the marbled murrelet. The spotted owl was listed as threatened under the Endangered Species Act in 1990 and the murrelet, a small sea-bird that nests in ancient coastal forests, in 1992.

The two private firms were paid about $800,000 for the biological reviews of the status of the birds. These aren't just any private consulting firms either. Both have sturdy financial ties to the timber industry. The status of the spotted owl was reviewed by the Sustainable Ecosystems Institute (SEI), a mercenary ecology firm for big timber. In 2003 alone, the Institute received more than $270,000 from Pacific Lumber, roughly 44 percent of its total revenue. Pacific Lumber, corporate molester of the redwoods of northern California, hired Sustainable Ecosystems to review the status of the marbled murrelet on company-owned redwood forest lands in Humboldt and Mendocino counties. But Pacific Lumber isn't SEI's only client in big timber. Sustainable Ecosystems has also received money from Boise-Cascade, Weyerhaeuser, Potlatch, and Rayonier. The firm's website refers to these timber giants warmly as "sponsors and partners."

The genius behind this scheme to privatize the spotted owl recount was Mark Rey, the Paul Wolfowitz of the chainsaw brigades. Rey, once the most feared timber industry lobbyist on the Hill, is now deputy secretary of agriculture overseeing the Forest Service. He has been at war against the owl and its defenders for twenty years: orchestrating numerous industry lawsuits, directing campaign contributions to pro-timber legislators, drafting legislation that exempted logging in owl habitat from compliance with environmental laws.

The owl recount resulted from a 2002 lawsuit that Rey helped concoct with his former clients at the American Forest Resource Council and the Western Council of Industrial Workers, a union under the thumb of big timber bosses.

In early 2001, the Bush administration ordered the Fish and Wildlife Service to halt status reviews of owl and murrelet populations, which are required every five years by the Endangered Species Act. The administration claimed poverty: it simply didn't have enough money to conduct a proper evaluation. Then Rey urged his cohorts in the timber industry to sue the government to compel the review. The industry sued and won. It was a calculated gamble. To get more than a trickle of timber flowing from federal forests, the industry needs the owl delisted. But the population trends all point down, and steeply down at that. Thus, there was the risk that an unbiased review by the Fish and Wildlife Service might lead to the owl being upgraded to an endangered species, greatly expanding restrictions on logging, roadbuilding, and other developments across the region, even on private land.

That's when Rey floated the scheme of taking the reviews from the hands of the Fish and Wildlife Service and giving it to a private outfit with ties to the timber industry. Big timber pinned its hopes on two factors that certainly wouldn't survive scrutiny by biologists at the Fish and Wildlife Service. First, it introduced spotted owl surveys conducted by the industry, which purported to show a thriving population of young owls in cut-over forests in Oregon and northern California—these are surveys widely regarded as junk science by most ecologists. Second, the industry desperately wanted the population of the California spotted owl (a distinct species inhabiting the Sierra

Nevada range) to be double counted as part of the northern spotted owl population. Seen one owl, seen them all.

The private review team was headed by discredited forest ecologist Jerry Franklin. Franklin, once the dean of Forest Service researchers, cashed in his reputation during the 1990s for a position at the University of Washington school of forestry, a program lavishly underwritten by Weyerhaeuser. He was later called upon by Bill Clinton to head up the team that developed the infamous Option 9 plan for northwest forests—a plan that legitimized continued logging in spotted owl habitat. The decline of the owl has been steeper under Franklin's plan than it was during the logging frenzy of the Reagan and Bush the Father years. Fresh from this triumph, Franklin began to hire himself out as a consultant to any timber company that would have him.

Like David Kay and his band of weapons hunters in Iraq, Franklin and the Bush owl hit squads scoured the forests of the Northwest for birds that simply aren't there, ghost owls.

All this was part and parcel of a larger Bush project to privatize the work of natural resource agencies, from Park Service interpreters to firefighters. The move serves cherished objectives of the corporate cabal now running the White House: neuter the agencies, break the power of the federal employees union, and transfer crucial work to compliant outside contractors. These contracts, often handed out to political patrons of the Bush crowd, come with an unwritten codicil: produce the results the administration wants or risk losing future deals. You're either with us or against us. It doesn't take long for that lesson to be drilled home to jittery bureaucrats.

It could have been different. In 1990, the spotted owl won a chance at survival when federal (and Reagan-appointed) Judge William Dwyer, slapped an injunction on all logging in the owl's habitat. It was a courageous decision that prompted a freshet of death threats. Dwyer shrugged them off. The enviros largely cowered and finally caved when confronted with political blackmail by Clinton. They relinquished the hard-won injunction and sanctioned Jerry Franklin's logging plan, which condemned the owl to smaller and smaller micro-reserves of ancient forest that serve as little more than a kind of ecological death row.

Then big greens, now foraging for grants on salmon and the boondoggle of "restoration forestry," turned their back on the spotted owl, once their totemic species. To continue to press for protection of the owl and its habitat would have meant an aggressive confrontation with Clinton and Bruce Babbitt. And they wanted none of that. "We haven't actively focused on the spotted owl in several years," confessed Heath Packard of the National Audubon Society. This is a damning admission given that the Audubon Society had raised millions on behalf of the owl and stood mute as the bird slid toward statistical death in a slow motion extinction.

So after two decades of fierce warfare in the forests of the Pacific Northwest, the spotted owl and dozens of other species that cling to the last fragments of ancient forests appear doomed. Bush will get the blame, but the fingerprints on the death warrant are indelibly bi-partisan.

FORKS, WASHINGTON.

The Bear Minimum: The Grizzly and the Fate of the Rocky Mountain West

THE ONE TRUE SYMBOL OF WILDERNESS TODAY IS THE GRIZZLY BEAR, *Ursus arctos horribilis*. Grizzlies and humans (Doug Peacock, excepted) just don't get along. More humans, less bears; less bears, less wilderness. And since the larger part of American history has been that of humans subduing wilderness, the great bears have not fared well.

Thirty years ago, the mighty grizzly bear of the American Rocky Mountains landed on the Endangered Species list. It was one of the first animals singled out for this dubious citation.

By 1973, the giant bears, which once ruled the great plains and Rocky Mountains from the Dakotas to California and struck terror into the Lewis and Clark expedition and many who followed, existed only in a few patches of isolated and still-wild land in Montana and Wyoming: greater Yellowstone, Glacier National Park, and the Bob Marshall Wilderness, the Cabinet Mountains, the Selkirks, and the Swan Range.

Even in these last remote refuges, the bear was hardly thriving. Perhaps 350 bears remained in Yellowstone. Then the Park Service closed the open dump, a stable source of food, and the population dropped. The Cabinet-Yaak, Selkirk and Swan populations totaled less than 200 bears combined. The healthiest population existed in the chunks of wilderness in and around Glacier National Park, which tallied perhaps 500 bears in the early 1970s. But this was something of an illusion, since the Glacier population was being buffeted by Canadian bears crossing the border to escape the merciless hunting campaigns of the north. Grizzly refugees.

Extinction loomed as a real possibility for the greatest living symbol of the American Rockies.

It still does.

From the time the bear was listed, the state of Montana clamored to have the bear removed, particularly in the Glacier area, where it wanted to auction off lucrative grizzly bear hunts. The Forest Service, which manages most of the bear's habitat in the region, griped that if taken literally, the Endangered Species Act protections would put a serious dent in its annual timber sale offerings. The agency refused to interpret the act literally. The Park Service, which manages Yellowstone and Glacier, liked having the bear as an attraction, but chafed at suggestions that the agency should scale back its plans to construct resorts for tourists in bear habitat. When, inevitably, tourists got mauled and dismembered by irritated bears, the Park Service, whose mission is to protect wildlife, sent assassination teams out to track down the killer bears and dispatch them.

Across much of Montana, federal land is checker boarded with private holdings, a legacy of the railroad land grants. This was, of course, one of the greatest government sanctioned rip-offs of all time, where the railroad barons were given alternating sections of federal land as an inducement for the construction of the trans-continental railroads. In secret deals, the railroads eventually sold off these lushly timbered parcels to big timber companies. The deals were covert because, under the terms of the land grants, the land was supposed to revert to the federal government if they weren't needed for the construction of the railroad corridors.

For decades, the railroad grant lands were owned by two timber giants, Plum Creek and Champion International. Through the 1960s, the timber companies did little logging on these mountainous lands. They were remote and the timber wasn't that valuable. Then beginning the late 1970s two things happened. The Forest Service began building roads into these lands, thus reducing the logging costs for Plum Creek and Champion. And the price of timber soared.

The timber companies struck while the iron was hot. Over the next ten years, Plum Creek and Champion went on a logging frenzy, cutting without restraint. By the end of the 1980s, more than 2 million acres of forest, most of it prime grizzly habitat, had been liquidated. Reporter Richard Manning unearthed internal memos from executives at both companies that revealed each had logged off more than 90 percent of its holdings. So much for sustainable forestry.

Predictably, both firms began to shut down their operations in the Rockies, closing the mills and laying off thousands of workers despite their repeated pledges to stay in Montana for the long haul. Champion left Montana altogether, moving to the southeast and Mexico. Plum Creek stuck around, but transformed itself from timber company to real estate developer, turning its clearcut forests into wilderness ranchettes and mountain subdivisions.

Meanwhile, the Fish and Wildlife Service, the federal agency charged with ensuring the bear's survival, took a *laissez-faire* approach toward *Ursus horribilis*, partly on its on initiative, partly at the insistence of Wyoming/Montana/Idaho congressional junta. Under the strictures of the Endangered Species Act, the Fish and Wildlife Service is tasked with identifying the lands that are considered essential for the survival of a listed species and designating those lands as critical habitat. These lands are then considered sacrosanct and the agency is permitted to prohibit any activities therein, which might harm the species.

With the grizzly, this never happened. The Fish and Wildlife Service neglected to designate critical habitat, and their decision was backed by a congressional rider that prevented environmental groups from suing the agency for violating the law. Without a critical habitat designation, it was almost impossible to challenge incursions into the bear's last redoubts.

Not that they would have sued, mind you. Nationally and locally, environmental groups considered the grizzly politically toxic. It threatened to put them in conflict with some of their favored politicians in the region, most notably Senator Max Baucus.

So the grizzly never had much of a chance. Its habitat was under assault by loggers, miners, oil companies and real estate barons, while the bureaucrats and NGOs charged with looking out for its survival took a pass.

This all changed in 1990 when a group of young and radical greens came together in Missoula and formed the Alliance for the Wild Rockies. Headed by Mike Bader, a former Yellowstone Park ranger who had conducted extensive research on grizzlies, the Alliance unleashed a barrage of lawsuits on behalf of the bear. It frontally attacked Democratic politicians, like Baucus, Bill Clinton, and Representative Pat Williams, who spouted green rhetoric, but worked to undermine the bear at every turn, often through the noxious practice of congressional riders to appropriations bills which shielded destructive logging schemes from environmental challenges in the federal courts.

What other groups in the region took as a liability, the Alliance seized on as a calling card. More than any other animal in North America, the grizzly craves large expanses of roadless terrain. The Northern Rockies are the only place in the lower-forty-eight with grizzlies and a sizable chunk of wilderness—about 16 million acres spread across Idaho, Wyoming, and Montana. Protect the bear and you could save most of this land from the chainsaw and oil wells. Save the roadless areas and you ensure a future for the grizzly and dozens of other species, such as the bull trout, lynx, Pacific fisher, and gray wolf.

But it turns out you have to go beyond merely saving the roadless areas and wildernesses. They are now islands, isolated refuges in a sea of clearcuts, ranchettes, and oil patches. To give the grizzly a real shot, these archipelagos of forest need to be linked together through a network of wildland corridors that are off-limits to logging, road building, mining, and oil development. That's the logic behind the Northern Rockies Ecosystem Protection Act (NREPA).

NREPA, or something even bigger, may be the last chance to save the grizzly. The news has not be good for the great bear. In early 2007, the Bush administration moved to strip the Yellowstone bear population of its protections under the endangered species. This unwelcome event occurred despite the fact that several sinister internal assessments have concluded that the grizzly faces dire threats in all three of its final strongholds, a crisis brought on by *Homo sapiens voracissius*. Otherwise known as ranchers, timber companies, and the oil and gas industry.

If there's been one human subspecies more antipathetic to *Ursus horribilis* than any other, its probably been the bear's supposed protector: *Homo bureaucraticus*, aka the federal lands bureaucrat, who sees the irascible bear as an unmitigated nuisance. That's because grizzlies are the original sylvan Luddites, frightening tourists (occasionally taking one out), shredding pretty North Face tents, rummaging around dumpsters at local resorts, and generally raising hell in the neighborhood.

You can hardly blame the bear. One example: after the grizzly was put on the endangered species list, the Park Service approved the huge Grant Village resort complex on the western shore of Yellowstone Lake, right in the middle of prime grizzly fishing habitat. In exchange, the Park Service promised to dismantle the Fishing Bridge campground on the other side of the lake, also favored habitat for the bear. Enter Senator Alan Simpson, who put a stop to that. So the bears went fishing for cutthroat trout as they have done since time immemorial and got caught up in the tourist traffic. First time ursine intruders get drugged up with sodium pentothal (which turn many into psychotics) and airlifted to remote, troutless regions of the park. Two strikes and you're out. Repeat offenders are shot to death. In 2004, nineteen grizzlies were killed in the Yellowstone region, half of them by wildlife and Park Service officials.

So after thirty years of this, the Feds have had enough. They've pronounced their work done and have moved to de-list the grizzly in Yellowstone. The rationale for such de-listing is an old stratagem of *Homo bureaucraticus*, namely: a robust declaration of victory. The Bush administration (following a template laid down in Clintontime) declared flatly that the government believes it has "achieved recovery plan goals for the Yellowstone ecosystem." And then washed their hands of the blood.

Grizzlies, for obvious reasons, are hard to count, except for the ones you've dispatched. But most non-government scientists believe there are fewer female grizzlies in the Yellowstone and Glacier regions now than there were when the bear was first listed. In fact, of the nineteen bears killed in Yellowstone in 2004, ten were adult females, some leaving behind cubs that soon perished as well. Does this mean the Endangered Species Act is a failure? No. It means that federal bureaucrats have lacked the will to enforce the law.

To truly defend the bear, those bureaucrats would have been forced to confront the designs of some of the most ruthless lobbies in America—for whom *Ursus horribilis* has been an irksome obstruction to making money. The grizzly stands in the path of oil and gas companies such as Chevron, which wants to sink wells in the Rocky Mountain Front east of Glacier Park; in the path of Boise-Cascade and Plum Creek Timber, which wants to log off the remaining six million acres of wild forest in the Northern Rockies; in the path of Club Yellowstone, and other elite ski resorts; in the path of mining companies, who want to excavate giant holes in the Absaroka and Pioneer Mountain' ranges in search of gold.

.Facing these opponents, where may the beleaguered grizzly turn for succor, aside from an unwary hiker? An apparent ally would seem to be the wildlife lobby, but here too peril lurks in the path of *Ursus horribilis*. A few years ago someone sent me an internal memo from the National Wildlife Federation that set forth a plan for establishing a "grizzly recovery zone" in central Idaho. The plan was written in consort with Defenders of Wildlife and, yes, two timber industry groups. Alas, the Idaho grizzlies won't, in all likelihood, be given much chance to recover. Plowing through the virtually impenetrable prose of the memorandum, we find that these two conservation groups placed some codicils on the tails of their plan. For example, oversight of the recovery zone was to be partially surrendered to local boards, dominated by such disinterested parties as Potlatch Timber and Hecla Mining.

The bear's status under the scheme is somewhat of a giveaway, as any alert *Ursus horribilis* skimming the contents would speedily realize. The intent is to reclassify the great bear as "a non essential experimental population," which means the bears could be killed by any rancher or hunter claiming thereafter that their lives or livestock were at risk.

Characteristically, this cautious approach surrenders the fruits of a tremendous legal victory for the Endangered Species Act in the so-called Sweet Home case by the Supreme Court. The court ruled that destruction of a listed species' habitat is the same as killing the species outright. But in their "fair compromise" with industry, the neo-liberal green's conceded that the notion of "harm" should not be understood to include "any actions that modify grizzly habitat." In other words, the grizzly should not be considered an impediment to timber sales or gold mines. They were expendable.

Under these perilous conditions, give the grizzly another fifty years at most in the lower-forty-eight. The only hope for their survival resides in legislation, like NREPA, that locks up huge chunks of land away from the bulldozer and the chainsaw, locks the land up tight as inviolate wilderness, with no exceptions. No wilderness, no grizzlies. No grizzlies, no real wilderness.

Kalispell.

High Line Fever: A Trip Across the Dark Side of Montana

LIKE MANY OTHER AMERICAN WRITERS, JOHN STEINBECK WAS DRAWN TO Montana. Steinbeck described the allure of the Big Sky state in *Travels with Charley*: "I am in love with Montana. For other states I have admiration, respect, recognition, even some affection, but with Montana it is love and it's difficult to analyze love when you're in it. The scale is huge, but not overpowering, The land is rich with grass and color, and the mountains are the kind I would create if mountains were ever put on my agenda. Montana seems to me to be what a small boy would think Texas is like from hearing Texans." I know what Steinbeck meant.

But Montana also has a dark side. I came here to see both. As field work for an investigation into the mining industry, Larry Tuttle, who runs the Center for Environmental Equity in Portland, and I hit the road to visit three mining sites: Zortman-Landusky next to the Ft. Belknap Reservation in the Little Rockies, the old Iron Mike mine on the Continental Divide, and the planned McDonald gold project along the Blackfoot River.

I flew from Portland into Great Falls, the Missouri River town at the base of the Rocky Mountain Front. The airport is large for a city this small. That's because it is connected to Malstrom Air Force Base, a command post for the nation's nuclear arsenal. The day I arrived the commander of the air base held a press conference pleading for a new generation of Minuteman missiles, "the old crop having gone out of date." In the West, airports and prisons often seem to be neighbors. The Great Falls prison is a shadeless compound situated next to the Malstrom AFB, where prisoners, many of them Indians, are subjected to the perpetual thunder of fighter jets and commercial airliners landing and taking off. The Air Force jets are coming in 24-hours a day, one flight every twenty minutes. It's difficult to imagine anyone getting used to the sound or being able to sleep through the night. That's why the prison was put there, according to Steve Leach, a prison rights activist in Billings. "Those overflights are considered a form of punishment."

Great Falls is an industrial town that bears the scars of the old Anaconda copper smelter that polluted the city for decades and dumped toxins and heavy metals into the Missouri. Even the falls, which caused Lewis and Clark some of their most anxious moments, are gone now, submerged beneath a series of useless dams erected by that most destructive of federal agencies, the Army Corps of Engineers. Before leaving, we toured the new Lewis and Clark Museum, which drapes over the canyon rim near where the Corps of Discovery had made the most treacherous portage of their journey. As such museums go, this isn't a bad one. Lewis is presented as the manic-depressive he was, while Clark comes off as the more stable and humane of the two. The Indians are treated with respect, particularly Sacagawea who is reverentially presented as the Mother Teresa of the Lemhi Shoshone (though Indians may more rightly view her as a Mata Hari). The tribes aren't patronized, though the difficult subject of genocide doesn't get mentioned. The museum, operated by the US Forest Service, makes much of the fact that Lewis and Clark were first-rate ethnographers and naturalists, though it neglects to discuss the despicable uses people like John Jacob Astor, Phillip Sheridan, George Crook, and James J. Hill would soon put to their information. I was surprised to learn that Lewis and Clark had brought with them a primitive small pox vaccine; it turned out to be as useless as Lewis' folding-iron canoe, the medicine dissolving during the first spill into the Missouri.

As we pulled out of Great Falls onto Highway 89 north toward Ft. Benton, I picked up a copy of the *Great Falls Tribune,* one of America's best daily newspapers. The lead story was an all-too familiar one. The previous day federal animal killers with the USDA's Animal Damage Control program tracked down three wolves on the Rocky Mountain Front near Choteau and shot them from a helicopter. Their crime: they were suspected of killing two lambs and injuring a calf. The killing operation cost more than $15,000. The lambs and calf were valued at less than $750. Two weeks earlier, three more wolves had been captured in the Bitterroot valley, south of Missoula, again for harassing sheep. One of the wolves died, apparently strangled to death by the government trapper. There's something terribly amiss here. These wolves, whose predations on livestock are minimal, should have been given a medal for knocking off a lamb every now and then, not stuck with a bounty on their heads. There is a lamb glut in the US, partially due to a flood of post NAFTA/GATT imports from Canada, Australia, and New Zealand. And, through a fund administered by the Defenders of Wildlife, ranchers are fully compensated (at higher than current market value rate) for each cow or sheep killed by grizzlies or wolves.

So why kill the wolves, if the pressure isn't coming from the ranchers? It has little to do with economics and everything to do with politics. The Bush administration wants to demonstrate that, under its flexible application of the Endangered Species Act, predators that get out of hand will be given the death penalty. No questions asked; no quarter given. In the Ninemile Valley, north of Missoula, ranchers have come to look with pride and affection on the two packs denning on their lands. They feel protective of the wolves. One of them told me: "I'll be damned if I'll let the feds know where those pups are. Surest way for them to get killed."

There is another factor at work as well. The Feds would just as soon see the wolf and grizzly made the scapegoat for the economic problems of the ranchers, problems that are really the result of the trade policies pushed by neoliberals and neocons. The ranchers know this, even though the media feign ignorance. George McClellan owns a 1,500-acre cattle ranch in the Kettle Range of eastern Washington. McClellan runs a fine-looking, clean operation. If anyone should be making a profit in this business, it's him. But he's about to sell out. Beef prices have tumbled since enactment of NAFTA and have never recovered. On top of that, a monopoly exists in the meatpacking industry. "We've got only one place to sell our beef," McClellan says. "That's IBP. They tell you the price. You take it or leave it. Well, I worked my ass off last year and still lost $6,000." What's going to happen to this rangeland when people like McClellan give it up? Who's left: the big corporations, ranchettes owned by Microsoft execs (complete with Lear jet landing strips), gated communities along trout streams, and the slob rancher.

This is Blackfoot Country, land that once belonged to the most feared of the northern plains Indians. It's an austere, wind-battered terrain of rolling plains of shortgrasses, pronghorn, and cutthroat trout streams. It was near one of those streams, the Marias River, that the Plains Indian wars began when Meriwether Lewis and part of his expedition stumbled across a Blackfoot encampment and shot their way out, killing a young Indian and wounding several others. The grizzlies used to wander down here from their mountain dens sixty miles to the west. Now the Blackfoot are mustered on a small reservation at Browning, the bears rarely venture past the boundaries of Glacier Park and the landscape is covered with fields of wheat and alfalfa and pock-marked by underground missile silos, the prairie-dogs of the nuclear age.

At the town of Havre, Route 87 joins with Highway 2, the road they call the High-Line. It parallels the Canadian border, running alongside the sweeping meanders of the Milk River, past small marshes alive with frantic flights of killdeer plovers and yellow headed blackbirds, and through railroad towns like Chinook and Malta that haven't changed all that much in sixty years, except for the neon profusion of casinos. The casinos and state-sponsored slots and video poker machines are one more blast at the Indians, who had just begun to see a new trickle of money find its way to them.

From Havre (pronounced "have-her") the crumpled outline of the Bear Paw Mountains frames the southern horizon. This is where Chief Joseph and his Nez Perce tribe's thrilling escape from their pursuers in the US Cavalry came to its abrupt and bloody conclusion, just forty miles from the sanctuary of Alberta. They had stopped for a few days here on an alluvial bench near the Milk River, exhausted from a dozen battles along the 1,500-mile trek that took them from eastern Oregon, across Idaho, up the steep Bitterroot Mountains, through the Big Hole and the Yellowstone Country, and up the Rocky Mountain front. Joseph and his fellow Nez Perce leaders mistakenly believed they had eluded the mad pursuit of Gen. Nelson Miles. But Miles had finally tracked them down, set up cannons on a ridge above their camp, and fired upon them with Howitzers and deadly Hotchkiss guns in the early morning. The Nez Perce warriors could have easily escaped across the river to Canada that day, but Miles knew they would never abandon the women and children at the camp. Joseph surrendered and the Nez Perce were marshaled onto two small reservations in Idaho and Washington.

In the last few years there has been an attempt by revisionist historians to redeem Miles' career and shift the blame for the brutal treatment of the Indians to his rival, George Crook. To those who know his career, though, Miles remains one of the true bastards of the West. It was to Miles that Gen. William T. Sherman wrote this infamous letter, outlining what can best be described as a kind of ur-Phoenix program: "If some of the worst Indians could be executed I doubt not the results would be good—but that is impossible after surrender under conditions. Rather remove all to a safe place and then reduce them to a helpless condition." The real genocide against the American Indians occurred not on the battlefield, but on the reservation. Miles got his start killing Indians during the Red River Wars against the Comanche and Southern Cheyenne. The general's preferred tactic was to kill their horses, burn their lodges, and destroy their crops. Miles shipped the leaders of the Cheyenne tribes off to prison in Florida, where he later sent Geronimo. Miles had a hand in the assassination of both Sitting Bull and Crazy Horse. He played competing Sioux chiefs, such as Red Cloud and American Horse, against each other. He betrayed the Crow, who he had used as a surrogate army against both the Sioux and the northern Cheyenne. After the Indian wars, Miles hired out his troops as strike busters, highlighted by a particularly vicious assault on the Pullman workers in 1894.

We turned south at Malta, a town the mining industry claims as one of its dependents. It's hard to detect where those benefits have trickled down. Malta looks just like all the other towns on the High Line, dusty, weather-scarred, economically depressed. As with Havre, Harlem, Zurich, and Chinook, the biggest action seems to be at the grain elevators, which, a gas attendant tells me, "are holding wheat from back in the Carter administration. Keep it at 53 degrees and it'll stay forever." Of course, that's a big problem. All the grain elevators have been full for twenty years and nobody's been buying much for ten.

Our destination is the Little Rocky Mountains, an island range that rises like a pod of humpback whales out of the Great Plains. The entrance to the Little Rockies rivals that of any national park. There are slot canyons, natural bridges, caves, rock shelters, and towering walls of limestone. Most of the Little Rockies are part of the Ft. Belknap Indian Reservation, the place where the Assiniboine and Gros Ventre Tribes were confined by Miles and his cronies in 1876. But the southern tip of the range was swindled from the Indians in the early 1900s when gold nuggets were found glistening in some of the creeks. Pick-ax miners and dredging operations came and went over the next seventy years, then in 1979, Reno-based Pegasus Gold acquired the site, called Zortman-Landusky, and began to excavate the biggest open pit gold mine in Montana.

The top 1,000 feet of two mountain peaks were sheared off and two 800-foot deep pits were carved into the earth. The rock was crushed and placed on heap-leach pads, some of them more than 600-feet tall, and then doused with a sodium cyanide solution. The sodium cyanide is purchased in 100-gallon barrels from DuPont, whose stake in the new chemical mining boom is largely hidden but very profitable. It is mixed with water and then sprayed on the mounds of crushed rock. The gold is leached out-at the rate of .12 ounces per ton. And, in theory, the cyanide-laced water drains into holding ponds. Despite the enormous size of the project, an environmental impact statement was never completed for the mine.

The mine went at it full-blast for more than fifteen years. The mine itself isn't on Indian lands and it employed few people from the Reservation, but since operations began, it has forever altered the lives of the Gros Ventre and Assiniboine who live there. We hiked up Mission Creek Canyon, which cuts through the reservation from the small town of Hays back toward the mine. The gaping void of the mine is visible from nearly every spot on the reservation, including the tribe's sundance site, and it literally engulfs Mission Peak, a sacred site. Before the mine went in, Mission Creek was a world-class trout stream. Then in the mid-1980s, the fish began to die. "We found them floating belly up, hundreds of them," says Joe Azure of Red Thunder. "We took them to a toxicologist and found they were loaded with toxins and heavy metals from the mine."

The Indians mobilized against Pegasus, joining forces with anti-mining organizers Jim Jensen and Will Patric to oppose an expansion of the mine in 1994. Pegasus responded to the opposition by blackmail, threatening that if the company wasn't allowed to dig another two pits it would halt operations entirely and fire its 280 workers. The strong-arm tactics worked. The Interior Department and the state of Montana both approved the expansion in 1996. The Indians and the enviros sued, but before a final decision could be reached, the price of gold began its plunge. Pegasus shut down the mine and filed for bankruptcy protection. The mine workers were laid off, but Pegasus' lawyers went before US Bankruptcy Judge Gregg Zive and asked for $5.5 million in bonuses for the company's top executives. The judge approved the request, but reduced the amount to a cool $5 million. "We need to induce employees to continue working during difficult times," explained Pegasus' lawyer Mark Thompson. Of course, the execs (including the CEO) banked the money and quickly ran off to other firms.

Meanwhile, the big hole at Zortman-Landusky remains and it is leaking acid, arsenic, cyanide, and other heavy metals. The cleanup of the site is now the responsibility of the state of Montana and its taxpayers. The price tag is estimated at more than $100 million, but most agree that won't begin to repair the damage.

From the Little Rockies we headed south into the Missouri Breaks, a labyrinth of hidden canyons on the southern flack of a rare undammed stretch of the Missouri. Today, this region is part of the Charlie Russell National Wildlife Refuge. Russell was an untrained painter who lived in Missoula. His exuberant watercolors of the Old West and the Blackfoot Indians rival anything produced by the more popular Frederic Remington. For those who've never been on a wildlife refuge in the West and wonder if you can actually see a lot of animals, the answer is yes: cows. Most national wildlife refuges are leased for livestock grazing and the Russell was no different. For the next eighty miles, cows were our constant companions. Where ORVs and dirtbikes were prohibited in order to protect prairie dog colonies, cows were given a free pass. As we left the refuge, we turned back for one last look at the Little Rockies a hundred miles to the north. Even from here the mine was visible, shining like a hideous grimace on the horizon.

As we crossed the Rockies on our way to Missoula, we descended into the small hamlet of Lincoln, the redoubt of Ted Kaczynski. We ran into the woman who cut Ted's hair after he was arrested. She now refers to herself as the Unabarber. Kaczynski wasn't a total recluse. In fact, he was a familiar character in town. He used to pedal his bike down to the library, a fine-looking structure about the size of the average two-car garage in some midwestern city like Toledo, Ohio. After Kaczynski was nabbed, much commentary was made about how Kaczynski must of have been deranged, because he lived in such a "cramped and dingy" shack. But the Unabomber's cabin is a pretty fair replica of many other houses in Lincoln, which real estate agents refer to as "idyllic retreats," put on the market at $100,000, and find lots of buyers for. Kaczynski lived at the foot of Dalton Mountain and from his road I'm told he had a sweeping view of the Blackfoot River valley and a pair of buttes a few miles to the west called Seven-Up Pete.

Some say the thing that really pissed off Kaczynski during his years in Lincoln was the plan by mining giants Phelps Dodge and Canyon Resources to demolish the Seven-Up Pete buttes with a new gold mine that would dwarf in scale even the Zortman-Landusky pit. It was after the proposals were announced, these folks say, that Ted K. began showing up at environmental gatherings. The Seven-Up Pete plan was certainly outrageous. It called for the two 600-feet tall buttes to be leveled and replaced with a gaping hole 1,200-feet deep. Waste rock would be piled up in 800-foot tall mounds. The cyanide heap-leach pads would sprawl over 900-hundred acres of land. All of it right next to the Blackfoot River, perhaps the world's most famous trout stream.

These are the sacred waters of Norman Maclean, the river of his book *A River Runs Through It*. Half of the land for the mine is owned by the state of Montana, the other half is part of a ranch owned by one of Montana's most famous families: the Baucuses. The ranch is run by John Baucus; his brother Max is the senior US senator for Montana, a fashionable liberal who has the backing of Hollywood stars like Robert Redford. The Baucus family stood to make more than $14 million from leasing out this portion of their ranch for a smelter and a giant mound of lethal mining waste.

Just outside Missoula we stop in a little bar called Trixie's where cowboys, loggers, fly-fishers, and river runners mingle, amicably it appears. Trixie was a rodeo showgirl in the '40s known for her rope tricks and trick riding. After dark, Trixie, it is said, put her rope to more Sadean purposes and the establishment earned a reputation as one of the more rambunctious whorehouses in the West. Today, the bar serves thick and bloody hamburgers saddled with mountains of ranch fries and ice-cold bottles of Coors. Trixie's is a micro-brew-free saloon. Shortly after the feds hauled Ted K. away, Trixie's began offering a popular t-shirt: "If you want a drink come to Trixie's, if you want to get bombed go to Lincoln."

GREAT FALLS, MONTANA.

PART THREE

Politicians and Other Rank Strangers

"The developer is what he is. No further punishment is necessary."
—Edward Abbey

Glory Boy and the Snail Darter:
Al Gore, the Early Days

WHAT WE NOW RECOGNIZE AS "THE GORE STYLE" WAS FASHIONED IN the earliest days of his political career. The young congressman picked out safe issues on which to cut a posture. He'd fully digested the lessons of his own masters' thesis, that television had shifted the balance of power from the Congress to the Executive branch. He became a zealous promoter of TV cameras in Congress and contrived to be the first to speak to those cameras from the House floor. Characteristically, his premier message concerned the therapeutic value of filming House proceedings on a day-to-day basis: "It is a solution for the lack of confidence in government." Anyone who has watched C-Span for the past twenty years would surely come to precisely the opposite conclusion.

Gore would seize on an issue that could be easily exported to the Sunday talk shows, such as children's nightwear treated with Tris, a flame retardant that turned out to be carcinogenic. Those particular hearings in May of 1977 were the first to bring young Rep. Gore onto the network news shows, and he made full use of the opportunity. "Did it trouble you," he howled theatrically at one industry executive, "that the children of this country might have tumors, carcinogenic or otherwise, produced by the chemical that would be used in all this sleepwear?"

From perilous nightwear he turned his attention to infant formula, another sure-fire TV grabber, where he and the shapely Tipper discoursed on the virtues of breast-feeding. On the heels of fiery sermons against Nestlé for its infant formula, came Gore's efforts to enact a national organ transplant database. This talent for converting minor issues into major TV opportunities was no doubt what prompted Gore's enthusiasm for Clinton's pollster Dick Morris when the latter arrived to bail out the Clinton White House in 1995 and 1996.

"Around Washington he's what we call 'a glory boy,'" a Democratic Party insider told Gore Vidal. "He gets to the House and starts running for the Senate. He gets to the Senate and starts running for the White House. There's no time left to do any of the real work the rest of us have to do."

The legislative venue for Gore's grandstanding was the House Commerce Committee's subcommittee on oversight and investigation. Gore had lobbied strongly to be appointed to this subcommittee, correctly assaying its screen-time potential. In short order he developed an inquisitorial style, matched off the floor by his mercilessly abusive treatment of his staff. His sponsor was the powerful Michigan Democrat John Dingell, the auto industry's greatest friend on Capitol Hill and, later, the most virulent opponent of clean air legislation. Dingell can himself be a merciless interrogator and evidently saw Gore's potential. Gore would describe himself later as Dingell's spear-carrier.

Gore's skills at self-promotion carried his name into the news and afforded him a certain national reputation as a crusading liberal. But at the substantive legislative level Gore remained emphatically on the center-right. Take the issue that perhaps defines the Democratic Party's social mission more than any other: labor rights. In the dawn of the Carter presidency, with Democrats controlling both houses, a bill came before the House aimed at expanding unions' picketing rights. Famously in America, one has the right to strike (barely), but not the right to win, because picketing—a vital component of any serious strike—is so circumscribed by legal restrictions it is effectively useless as a coercive tool in many fights with employers. So this vote was a big one. The AFL-CIO felt confident of victory, but it missed the fact that newly arrived Democrats like Gore felt no loyalty to labor and were intent on advertising that disposition to their business contributors. Gore provided one of the crucial votes that turned back labor's bill.

As a House member Gore was virtually a poster boy for the National Rifle Association. In 1978 he voted to block funding for the implementation of new federal handgun regulations, explaining many years later that, "when I represented a rural farm district in the House of Representatives there wasn't a problem [with handguns] perceived by my constituents." In 1985, after he had moved from representing the crackers in the 4th District to being the junior senator for all the people of Tennessee, he voted for what the NRA called "the most significant pro-gunners' bill in the last quarter-century"...

As a Congressman, Gore spoke of his belief in "the fetus' right to life." He was a relentless supporter of the Hyde amendment, which banned federal funding for abortions for poor women. In one early version of Hyde's bill, there was language allowing exceptions to the ban in the case of rape. Gore voted against that.

The most far reaching of all the measures dreamed up by the conservative right to undercut *Roe v. Wade* was an amendment put forward by a Michigan Republican, Mark Siljander, in 1984. It carried a one-two punch. First, it defined the fetus as a person from the moment of conception. Second, it denied federal funding to any hospital or clinic that performed an abortion. Gearing up for his Senate run that year, Gore was one of seventy-four Democrats to vote for Siljander's ultimately unsuccessful measure.

Those votes returned to haunt Gore as his political ambitions went national and he bid for more support than he'd ever needed in the 4th District or even the entire Volunteer State. By 1988 he was brazenly rewriting his political biography. He and his staff were well aware that his votes against choice—only four years earlier—would be brought up by his opponents. "Since there's a record of that vote," an aide told *US News & World Report* in March of 1988, "what we have to do is deny, deny, deny."

The problem returned briefly in 1992 and again in the Democratic primaries in 2000, when Bill Bradley, challenging Gore for the nomination, used the occasion of a debate in the Apollo Theater in Harlem, to flourish and then read out a letter Gore had written to a Tennessee constituent in 1984, in which had stated: "It is my deep personal conviction that abortion is wrong. I hope that some day we will see the current out-rageously large number of abortions drop sharply. Let me assure you that I share your belief that innocent human life must be protected and I have an open mind on how to further this goal."

When confronted with contradictions between his pretensions and his deeds, Gore reflexively performs a ritual of numbed incantation. "I believe a woman ought to have the right to choose," he kept repeating to his interlocutors in 1992, and he did the same thing at the Apollo in 2000. Someone less rigid could have said, "Look, I've evolved." Freed from his lawyers, Bill Clinton can go through such a routine effortlessly. But Gore, the perfect child of demanding parents, can never admit error, even in retro-spect. In 1988, even as both Al and Tipper issued their fabrications about their use of marijuana, Tipper said, "It was either admit it or lie, and we would never lie."

One unlovely hoof print after another tracks its way across Gore's legislative voting record. In the 1980s, when the IRS proposed new regulations denying tax-exempt status to private schools that barred black students, Gore was among those in Congress who tried to undermine the regulations.

Likewise, in Gore's supposed devotion to the environment, there has always been a vast rift between stirring proclamation and legislative reality. Back in the late 1970s, two of the hottest environmental battles concerned the Clinch River Breeder Reactor and the Tellico Dam, both within the purview of the TVA. As it was planned, the Clinch River reactor was not only a $3 billion boondoggle of the first water, but was also desta-bilizing in terms of the arms race, since it was scheduled to produce weapons-grade plutonium. The Congressional battle over the planned reactor stretched from the mid-1970s to 1983, when, amid growing national disquiet about nuclear power, it went down to defeat.

Gore was a fanatic defender of the reactor, the most ardent of all the Tennessee congressional delegation. When the Republicans briefly captured the Senate in 1981, the senior senator from Tennessee, Howard Baker, became majority leader and made protection of the Clinch River project one of his priorities. He and Gore kept the fight going until the end. Arkansas' Senator, Dale Bumpers, gave an entertaining account of this in a 1997 speech: "I remember in 1981, Republicans took over this place and Howard Baker, the senator from Tennessee and one of the finest men ever to serve in this body, became majority leader. I was trying to keep any additional nuclear plants from being licensed—and it was not a tough chore. A lot of people had made up their minds at that point that the nuclear option was not a good one. I fought for about four years to kill the Clinch River Breeder reactor. But I was up against the majority leader. And as everybody here knows, as the old revenuer said, when they announced *United States v. Jones*, he turned to his lawyer and said, "Them don't sound like very fair odds to me." And it was not very fair odds to go up against the majority leader on the Clinch River Breeder, which was going to be built in his beloved Tennessee. Howard Baker could always just pull out that one extra vote he needed. The vote was always close, but you are majority leader, you know, you can just call somebody over and say, 'I need your vote,' and you usually get it. Finally, one year I was ahead by about six or seven votes as the votes were being cast, and I think Senator Baker decided that he was done for, and he turned everybody loose that had committed to him [those] who did not really like the idea of the Clinch River Breeder Reactor and only voted for it to accommodate him. He turned them loose, and I think we won that day by about seventy to thirty. Happily, that was the end of the Clinch River Breeder."

In 1984, Al Gore took Baker's Senate seat and, over the next eight years, voted for the nuclear lobby 55 percent of the time. As vice president and author of *Earth in the Balance* (which stays fairly mute on the topic of nuclear power) Gore, along with his former legislative staffer, Energy Department Assistant Secretary Thomas Grumbly, tried to bring the Clinch River scheme to life again as the Fast Flux Test Facility in the Hanford nuclear reservation in the State of Washington.

Then there was the Tellico Dam, the first big test of America's greatest environmental law, the Endangered Species Act. A law passed in 1973 during the Nixon presidency, which also saw creation of the Environmental Protection Agency. The dam, on the Little Tennessee River, was 95 percent complete when biologists discovered the imperiled snail darter species still clinging on in the stretches of the river that were to become the reservoir behind the dam. Environmentalists brought suit against the dam project, and eventually the Supreme Court ruled that the Endangered Species Act required that the dam not be completed.

The Little Tennessee was one of the few wild rivers left in the state unmolested by the TVA. The dam wasn't needed for flood control and wouldn't generate power. All it would do was store water and divert it to another dam nearby. The recreation benefits were negative, since the Little Tennessee was a famous trout stream and popular with canoeists. In fact, the only purposes of the dam were to line the pockets of the cement producers and construction nabobs of Tennessee, and to afford an amenity for the "Timberlake" community being planned by Boeing. As Mark Reisner puts it in his book *Cadillac Desert*, "It was like deciding to put a 50,000 seat Superdome in the middle of Wyoming and then building a city of 150,000 around it to justify its existence."

Shocked that the Act could threaten huge pork barrel projects, the very lifeblood of Congress, the legislators set up the so-called "God Squad," which would pass judgment on species-endangering schemes, using cost-benefit analysis as the standard. In the case of the snail darter, the God Squad, led by economist Charles Schultze, did its homework. "Here is a project that is 95 percent complete," Schultze concluded, "and if one takes just the cost of finishing it against the benefits, it doesn't pay."

The fight over the snail darter was fierce and bitter because the stakes were so high. If the pro-dam forces could win a waiver of the Endangered Species Act here, then such a waiver would inevitably be the first of many. Gore was among the leaders in the effort to get this waiver, and in the end Congress exempted the dam from compliance and overturned the Supreme Court's injunction. As the defenders of the snail darter predicted, the path to destruction of the Endangered Species Act now lay open, and first down that path had been none other than Al Gore.

After he and the other pork-barrelers got the vote that exempted the dam, Gore announced triumphantly, "It was unfortunate that the controversy over the snail darter was used to delay completion of the dam after it was virtually finished. I am glad the Congress has now ended this controversy once and for all."

How Gore, Howard Baker, and James Duncan (the Republican Congressman in whose district the dam was located) consummated their awful victory was vividly described by Representative Bob Edgar, a Democrat from suburban Philadelphia: He recounts how on June 18, 1979, Gore and his colleague Duncan pushed through, as a rider to the appropriations bill, a measure allowing the Tellico Dam to go forward. "Duncan walked in waving a piece of paper. He said, 'Mr. Speaker! Mr. Speaker! I have an amendment to offer to the public works appropriation bill.' Tom Bevill and John Myers [two dreadful reps] of the Appropriations Committee both happened to be there. I wonder why. Bevill says, 'I've seen the amendment. It's good.' Myers says, 'I've seen the amendment. It's a good one.' And that was that. It was approved by voice vote! No one even knew what they were voting for! They were voting to exempt Tellico Dam from all laws! They punched a loophole big enough to shove a $100 million dam through it, and then they scattered threats all through Congress so that we couldn't muster the votes to shove it back out. I tried—lots of people tried—but we couldn't get that rider out of the bill. The speeches I heard on the floor were the angriest I've heard in elective office. They got their dam. That is the democratic process at work."

The foes of the dam had one last hope, that President Jimmy Carter would veto the bill. But Carter too was bushwhacked. The Baker-Gore forces threatened to withhold support for the Panama Canal Treaty, which Carter was fighting for at the time.

Gore supported a scheme to transplant some of the snail darters to the nearby Hiwassee and Holston rivers, where they survived. But the larger damage was done. As David Brower, America's greatest environmentalist, said in retrospect, "This was the beginning of the end of the Endangered Species Act." After the snail darter came other species and other waivers, the most notorious of them engineered under the auspices of Vice President Gore. In the Pacific Northwest the spotted owl and marbled murrelet, in the Southeast the red-cockaded woodpecker, in Southern California the gnatcatcher—all were as chaff under the chariot wheels of the timber and real estate industries, who successfully lobbied the vice president and his minions for the all-important waivers. Like refugees in wartime, imperiled species were assigned one holding pen after another, issued temporary "safe" passes, while Gore's appointments in the Interior Department and the Council on Environmental Quality felt the heat from developers and timber barons and crumbled.

The way American politics works, it took a reputed environmentalist to destroy America's best environmental law. In l98l, there wasn't a major environmental group in the country that didn't bugle its frantic alarums at the approach of the Reaganauts and that Beelzebub of the greens, James Watt, Reagan's Interior Secretary. The Sierra Club, the Wilderness Society, National Audubon, the Natural Resources Defense Council, all raised millions of dollars on the specter of Watt and the havoc he would wreak on environmental regulations. In fact, the pathetic and maladroit Watt never stood a chance. He set back the cause of environmental pillage by at least a decade.

But when Watt was gone and Reagan was gone and Bush was gone, the Democratic "greens" came back to power, and they accomplished triumphs that the Republicans had never dared dream possible. Gore, who had reinvented himself as an environmentalist, largely on the basis of *Earth in the Balance*, was embraced by the Big Green organizations. They used his entirely mythical green credentials as a way of getting their membership to overlook Bill Clinton's own adversarial relationship with nature while he was governor of Arkansas.

Yet consider Gore's record by Big Green's own criteria. Like all the major environmental organizations, the League of Conservation Voters functions as an outrider for the Democratic National Committee, and its annual ratings of Congress members are notoriously skewed against Republicans. Gore's lifetime rating from the League is 64 percent, meaning he was in sync with the League's positions two-thirds of the time. This is not much when you look at such green stars of the League as Patrick Leahy of Vermont, Tim Wirth of Colorado, George Miller of California, or even a Republican like the late John Chafee of Rhode Island, all of whom were consistently ranked in the 90s. The League's rating of Gore in his House years ran at an average of about 55 percent, with one year down at 30 percent, which put him in harness with such world-class predators as Don Young of Alaska.

Gore didn't make many friends in the House, but his propensity to techno-flatulence (e.g., "The government is just a big software program") soon prompted him to sniff out a kindred soul in the form of a pudgy young Congressman from suburban Atlanta who had a marvelous facility for rotund phrase-making on any issue to hand. From the time he was first elected, in 1978, Newt Gingrich was positioning himself with precisely the same blend of opportunism, albeit at a noisier level, as Al Gore was.

The two consecrated their amity in a group called the Congressional Clearing House on the Future. They met monthly, published a newsletter and hosted lectures by futurists and pop scientists including, Carl Sagan and Alvin Toffler. But these monthly klatches were not enough to satiate Gore and Gingrich's passions for heady chat about meta-technical trends, artificial intelligence, the population bomb, and extraterrestrial life (Gore believes ardently that We Are Not Alone). The two would meet for dinner at each other's houses. Poor Tipper, hoping for a romantic candle-lit evening with her spouse, would open the door to see the beaming, porcine features of the rising Republican star from Georgia on the doorstep. The relationship didn't end when Gore reached the Senate. In fact, in 1985, he and Gingrich co-authored a bill titled the Critical Trends Assessment Act. The legislation called for the creation of a White House Office on Futurism (WHOOF) to "study the effects of government policies on critical trends and alternative futures." In his career in Congress, Gore was rarely the principal author of a bill. This was an exception, albeit a doomed one. Although the two battled for WHOOF strenuously, it never went anywhere.

Soon after his arrival in Congress, Gore formed the Vietnam Veterans Caucus with John Murtaugh, Jim Jones, and Les Aspin. For Gore, the caucus opened up a useful avenue into hawkish Democratic circles, where men like Aspin and Sam Nunn were doing the Pentagon's work, proclaiming that "Vietnam Syndrome" was sabotaging the nation's vital sinews. Gore picked up the lingo quickly enough: "I think it is important to realize that we do have interests in the world that are important enough to defend, to stand up for. And we should not be so burned by the tragedy of Vietnam that we fail to recognize an interest that requires the assertion of force."

With such language, Gore established himself early on as "safe" from the point of view of the Pentagon and the national security complex. Safety meant never straying off the reservation on such issues as America's right to intervene anywhere it chooses. Gore backed Reagan's disastrous deployment of US Marines in Lebanon in 1983. He supported the invasion of that puissant Caribbean threat to the United States (population 240 million) by Grenada (population 80,000). He later chided his 1988 Democratic opponents for their failure to embrace this noble enterprise. At a time when many Democrats wanted to restrict the CIA's ability to undertake covert actions, Gore said he wouldn't "hesitate to overthrow a government with covert actions," a posture he ratified with his approval of the CIA's secret war in Afghanistan. This, the largest covert operation in the Agency's history, ultimately saddled Afghanistan with the Taliban fundamentalists, destroyers of cities, stoners of women, harborers of Bin Laden, and overseers of that country's rise in status to the eminence of world's largest exporter of opium and heroin to the United States and Europe.

The Nature of Ronald Reagan: Will the Earth Accept His Corpse?

N EARLY OCTOBER 1983, I FOUND MYSELF PACING THE TERMINAL AT THE OLD Weir Cook Airport in Indianapolis, awaiting the arrival of David Brower, the great environmentalist. Brower emerged from the plane, his face aglow with impish triumph. We hustled down the terminal to the airport bar where he imparted the momentous news that his nemesis James Watt, the messianic Secretary of Interior, had just been evicted from his post in the Reagan administration.

Watt had doomed himself by denouncing the members of the federal coal-leasing commission as "a black, a woman, two Jews, and a cripple." The commissioners had shown the audacity to resist Watt's demented shale-oil scheme, which sought to transform the Great Plains into a moonlike landscape of craters and toxic slush ponds. So, like Earl Butz before him, Watt's political obituary was written with a racist slur. It's probably fitting that he fell from such a self-inflicted trifle. After all, Watt was an instinctive and unrepentant bigot, just like his boss Reagan. Ask any Apache.

Of course, the Christian fundamentalist and apostle of strip-mining from Wyoming nearly lost his job over another bone-headed misdemeanor: his attempt to bar the Beach Boys from performing at a 4th of July concert on the National Mall. Reagan had to intervene personally on behalf of that All-American band, whose music could have provided the soundtrack for the sunny brand of trickle-down utopianism the president was trying to force-feed the country in those days. The Gipper, who, if nothing else, always demonstrated a keen PR sense, may well have lost confidence in Watt at that precise moment.

But the Interior Secretary, who once declared that the end of the Earth was so close at hand that there was no reason to fret about conserving ecosystems for the long haul, had been on the ropes from the beginning of his tenure, due, in large part, to the Dump Watt campaign initiated by Brower and his group, Friends of the Earth, only weeks after Watt's nomination was confirmed by the US senate. Within a few months, Friends of the Earth had gathered more than two million signatures on a petition calling for Watt's removal. In those days, the right to petition the government still seemed to stand for something.

Brower loathed Watt, but viewed him as a comical figure, a corrupt moralist sprung from the pages of a Thackeray novel. He reserved his real animosity for the appalling Reagan, the supreme Confidence Artist of American politics.

Unlike many progressives, Brower never wrote off Reagan as an incompetent and incoherent stooge. He knew better. Brower, the arch-druid, and Reagan, the union-busting snitch, had sparred with each other across the decades—first in California over parks and wild rivers, pesticide spraying, nuclear power, and the governor's brutal attacks on the peaceable citizens of Brower's hometown of Berkeley; and later around the globe over wilderness, endangered species, the illegal war on Nicaragua, and the proliferation of nuclear weapons.

During the pitched battles to save some of the world's largest trees, Brower and his cohorts goaded Reagan into making his infamous declaration: "Once you've seen one redwood, you've seen them all." That Zen koan-like pronouncement pretty much summed up Reagan's philosophy of environmental tokenism. Later, Reagan propounded the thesis that trees generated more air pollution than coal-fired power plants. For the Gipper, the only excuse for Nature was to serve as a backdrop for photo-ops, just like in his intros for *Death Valley Days*, the popular western TV series that served as a catwalk for the rollout of Reagan as a politician.

Brower viewed Reagan as a mean-spirited and calculating figure, entirely cognizant of and culpable for his crimes. He refused to allow the old man access to the twin escape hatches of plausible deniability and senile dementia.

Born a year apart, the two men were part of the same generation and both spent most of their lives in California. Yet, the tenor of their lives couldn't have been more different. In World War II, Brower served as an instructor for the famous 10th Mountain Division and returned home a pacifist. He didn't talk much about his war experience, preferring to brag about the number of Sierran peaks he'd bagged (seventy first ascents) or the wild rivers he'd floated.

Reagan spent World War II in Hollywood making racist propaganda films to inflame the fever for a war that tens of thousands of others would die fighting in. Years later he boasted (that is: lied) about liberating the Nazi death camps, even as he was forced to defend his demented decision to bestow presidential honors on the dead at the cemetery in Bitburg, Germany, final resting place for the blood-drenched butchers of the Waffen SS. Reagan possessed a special talent for the suspension of disbelief when it came to the facts of his own life. Perhaps, if the earth in Simi Valley refuses to receive his corpse, the custodians of Bitburg could erect a cenotaph for Reagan on those chilly grounds.

After a couple of hours spent draining Tanqueray-powered martinis at that airport bar in Indianapolis, some of the initial glow gradually dissipated from Brower's face. "You know, Jeffrey, we may soon come to miss old Watt," Brower predicted.

He was right, of course. James Watt proved to be the greatest fundraising gimmick the big environmental groups ever stumbled across, far outperforming panda calendars and postcards of baby Harp seals about to fall victim to the fur-trader's skull-crushing club. During Watt's tenure, the top ten environmental groups more than doubled their combined budgets, and for a brief time, became the most powerful public interest lobby on the Hill.

Watt's approach to the plunder of the planet seethed with an evangelical fervor. He brought with him to Washington a gang of libertarian missionaries, mostly veterans of the Coors-funded Mountain States Legal Foundation, who referred to themselves as "The Colorado Crazies." Their mission: privatize the public estate. Many of them were transparent crooks who ended up facing indictment and doing time in federal prison for self-dealing and public corruption. They gave away billions in public timber, coal, and oil to favored corporations, leaving behind toxic scars where there used to be wild forests, trout streams, and deserts. These thieves were part of the same claque of race-baiting zealots who demonized welfare mothers as swindlers of the public treasury.

Watt, who was himself charged with twenty-five felony counts of lying and obstruction of justice, never hid his rapine agenda behind soft, made-for-primetime rhetoric. He never preached about win-win solutions, ecological forestry, or sustainable development. From the beginning, James Watt's message was clear: grab it all, grab it now. God wills it so. The message was so high-pitched and unadulterated that it provoked a fierce global resistance that frustrated Watt at nearly every turn. In the end, he achieved almost nothing for the forces of darkness.

Soon, Watt's divinely-inspired vigilantism against nature would be replaced by a more calculating approach, a kinder and gentler path to exploitation, that reached a terrible crescendo under Clinton and Gore, a team which, according to Brower's expert calculation, did more damage to the American environment in their first four years in office than Reagan and Bush the Father accomplished in twelve years.

Still there's reason to miss Watt and Reagan. Their brazen contempt for the world inspired ordinary people to rise up against their government's leaders on behalf of the spotted owl and Yellowstone grizzly—rise up, and on occasion, actually rout them. Today even Watt's minions, like Steven Griles and Gale Norton, who are now directing the berserker environmental policies of the Bush the Younger administration, don't ride nearly as tall in the saddle as Reagan and Watt did in the early 1980s, when it seemed that real demons stalked the earth.

Fade to black.

Golden Parachutes: George Bush, Barrick Resources, and the Politics of Greed

AT THE PRECISE MOMENT GEORGE H. W. BUSH BURST BACK INTO THE headlines by renouncing the long-standing and ill-used membership in the National Rifle Association, the putative architect of the New World Order quietly sold his services to a much more invidious enterprise: American Barrick Resources Company.

In May 1994, I learned that Bush had signed on as a senior advisor on international affairs for this transnational mining company, breaching a promise he had made prior to leaving presidential office not to serve on any corporate boards. "President Bush doesn't do boards," Bush spokesman Jim McGrath told me. "This is the exception that proves the rule. President Bush is very concerned about avoiding any apparent conflicts of interest."

In fact, Bush's new position with Barrick may be a direct payoff for the special attention his administration lavished on the multi-billion-dollar Canadian company.

Barrick is the most profitable gold mining company in North America, owed largely to its ownership of the vast Goldstrike mine near Elko, Nevada. The 1,800-acre Goldstrike mine contains an estimated $10 billion worth of gold; yet, under the 1872 Mining Act, the land was "patented" by Barrick from the Bureau of Land Management (BLM) for less than $10,000. When Secretary of Interior Bruce Babbitt handed Barrick the title of the land in the spring of 1993, he called it the "greatest gold heist since Butch Cassidy"—a comment notable for its grotesque understatement.

In fact, Barrick's patenting of the Goldstrike mine was made possible by the Bush administration, which in the summer of 1992, secretly adopted a "fast-tracking" process to accelerate the Goldstrike mine's patent-approval. Under the traditional procedures of the BLM, patenting of mine claims takes two to four years and is overseen by officials at the BLM. The "fast-tracking" approach developed by the Bush administration allowed Barrack to hire an "independent" consultant to supervise an abridged approval process. The Goldstrike mine was patented in six months.

This was a triumphant maneuver. At the time, it appeared likely that the Congress would approve a mining reform bill ending patenting of federal lands and imposing a token 8 percent royalty on the value of minerals removed from federal lands. Ultimately, the bill failed by two votes. If the measure had passed, and Barrick had not been granted the fast track exemption, the Goldstrike mine would have been forced to pay the government about $80 million a year in royalty payments.

Barrick is owned by Horsham Corp., a Toronto-based holding company controlled by Canadian financier Peter Munk. Munk is close friends with former Canadian Prime Minister Brian Mulroney. It was Mulroney who recommended that Bush take the position as a senior advisor to Barrick. Mulroney and Bush developed an intimate personal relationship when forging both the US / Canada trade accords and the outlines of NAFTA.

Barrick spokesman William Bork told me that former-President Bush would advise the company on "geopolitical issues" as it explores new mining opportunities in the Third World. The former President may be particularly helpful in Barrick's pursuit of mining claims in the gold-laden mountains of Indonesia. A minor impediment to the swift extraction of this buried lucre is fierce opposition by native tribes in East Timor and Irian Jaya. For years, the Indonesian government has moved to brutally dislocate and suppress indigenous people in order to secure control of the country's rich oil, timber, and mineral resources, which it could then sell off to Western corporations. The result has been a genocidal campaign (actively supported by the Bush and Clinton administrations) leading to the deaths of more than 500,000 people. By some accounts, more than 20 percent of the indigenous population in the mining region has been slaughtered in the past twenty years. Bush's congenial relations with the Suharto regime helped speed Barrick's entry into this spooky landscape of gold and death.

Bush is joined on Barrick's senior advisory board by former-Senator Howard Baker (whose law firm represents corporations seeking to exploit natural resources in Siberia and other Asian countries) and Vernon Jordan, consigliore to Bill Clinton. Jordan, who headed the Clinton transition team and still spends (non-billable?) hours as President Bill's golfing partner, now presides as chief rainmaker at the notorious DC law firm of Akin, Gump, Strauss (as in former Democratic Party chairman and Ambassador to Russia Robert Strauss), Hauer & Feld.

One of the most powerful influence peddlers on Capitol Hill, Akin, Gump's client portfolio represents a dark list of transnational corporations and vicious government regimes, including Bechtel, the governments of Chile and Colombia, Enron, Loral, RJR Nabisco, and Westinghouse. Clearly there are no hands too dirty or bloody for this liberal firm to hold and wash.

It will be recalled that in the spring of 1993 Vernon Jordan was summoned to Houston for a consultation with Maxxam Corporation's CEO, Charles Hurwitz, ransacker of redwoods and S&Ls. Jordon's assignment was to use his influence with federal officials to shield the corporate raider from suffering a near certain indictment at the hands of Janet Reno's Justice Department for his role in the pillaging of the United Savings Association of Texas and the illegal raid on the Pacific Lumber Company.

Jordon also attempted to broker a federal buyout of the Headwaters redwood grove for the outlandish sum of one billion dollars.

Vernon Jordan proved his worth to Barrick in the early days of Clintontime when he got the White House to pressure Babbitt to back off his campaign to reform federal mining policies. During the early months of the Clinton administration, Babbitt was eager to push mining reform as a top priority at the Interior Department. By the summer of 1993, however, the Clinton administration had totally abandoned its commitment to end the give-away of federal minerals.

Most of the blame for this retreat was laid at the feet of Western governors and legislators, such as Cecil Andrus and Max Baucus. While they certainly were influential factors in the decision, a more decisive figure in this debacle was Vernon Jordon, who, according to a high level official at the Interior Department, personally advised President Clinton to delete mining reform from his political agenda.

Bush and Jordon are also useful front-men for Barrick as the company advances its interests in the international mineral marketplace. Outside the United States, Barrick's most profitable existing operations are the huge Nevada and El Tambo mines in Chile. The company acquired the El Tambo property during General Augusto Pinochet's wretched tenure as dictator. At the time of this deal, Pinochet's regime was loudly praised by the Bush administration for opening up Chile's economy to "western investment."

Currently, Jordan's firm, Akin, Gump, represents the new Chilean government (business-suited followers of Pinochet), and has judiciously advised them to accelerate the General's policies of selling off the country's vast forest and mineral resources at cheap prices to North American corporations. In return, Jordan (and Bush, for that matter) has actively promoted the inclusion of Chile (which he calls the "greatest democracy in South America") in a post-NAFTA free-trade pact—a move supported by Newt Gingrich.

Dismaying as these events may appear, such nefarious activities are standard operating procedure for the power elite in DC these days—people who sell their services to the highest bidder, regardless of the company's resumé of crimes against the environment and humanity. Indeed, the worse the rap sheet, the higher the consulting fees. In George Bush's case, the door revolves slowly, but lucratively.

Elko.

Ron Brown and the Steelhead: Mining the Politics of Gold

DRIVE UP THROUGH CENTRAL IDAHO, TAKE THE ROAD NORTHEAST OF Stanley and follow along the Salmon River's eastward sweep, where its fed by a thousand streams falling off the White Clouds, Lost River, and Lemhi Ranges.

There you'll see fly-fishermen casting for chinook salmon and steelhead trout, fish that have made the incredible 700-mile journey up from the mouth of the Columbia River to spawn in the high mountain waters. There aren't many of these fish now. In fact, it's a miracle they're here at all. The last hundred years in this region haven't been kind to them.

First there was the great gold rush of the late-19th century, whose mementos survive in the form of stripped hillsides, piles of toxic tailings, scoured and dredged streambeds—the detritus of the gold frenzy.

Then in the 1940s and 1950s came the era of the dams, big ones all the way from Bonneville to the "deepwater port" of Lewiston, Idaho. These sure didn't do the salmon much good.

Neither did the logging boom of the 1980s, clearcutting the mountainsides and cutting disastrous roads and skid trails into the fragile soils of the Idaho Batholith, which in turn set off landslides that wiped out entire runs and buried once clear streams under mounds of rock and silt.

But now salmon and steelhead that survive face a crisis born of a bureaucratic quirk that may finally doom them to extinction.

In the niceties of federal demarcation, the salmon falls under the pitiless sway of the Department of Commerce—headed in the early years of Clintontime by Ron Brown—rather than the potentially more merciful supervision of Bruce Babbitt's Interior Department.

These fish, you understand, are *anadromous*, a word of Greek etymology meaning that they run through the Interior Department's oversight of fresh water fish and out into the salt water realm of the Commerce Department.

Here it is that etymology spells extinction. When it comes to pleasing the captains of industry, there was scarce a man on earth more alert and responsive than Ron Brown.

The Salmon River chinook and steelhead, protected under the increasingly tattered umbrella of the Endangered Species Act, have now become an impediment in the onward rush of a new generation of gold miners.

These miners do not come in the form of those hardy prospectors of former times, equipped only with pickax and mule. Today they are mighty international conglomerates. At their sides are not mules, but legions of lawyers, lobbyists, and politicians—bought and paid for. In their hands are not pickaxes but capital equipment for modern extraction: dynamite, cyanide, giant bulldozers.

On Williams Creek, a tributary of the Salmon River, near the small town of Salmon, Idaho, is a 648-acre mining claim owned by FMC Gold Co., partially owned by South African gold and diamond giant, De Beers.

It has been the intention of FMC (which also manufactures the M-1 Tank) to take advantage of the archaic federal mining law of 1872, which allows mining company to claim title to public lands in the Salmon National Forest for $5 an acre and pay no royalties on the gold that they—in this case FMC—intend to extract.

Connoisseurs of the 1872 law have noted that shortly after being thumped from office, former President George H. W. Bush joined the board of American Barrick Resources, a Canadian-owned gold mining company that in 1993 received title to the Goldstrike Mine outside Elko, Nevada. This was also public land, administered by the federal Bureau of Land Management. The 1872 Mining Law allowed American Barrick the right to buy the title to the public property for $5,500 against expected revenues of over $10 billion. During Bush's term, reform of the old mining law seemed imminent, so Bush personally fast-tracked American Barrick's bid to lay claim to this mountain of public wealth. And Bush got his payback.

Back in Idaho, the only obstructions to FMC's garnering of an expected $300 million haul in gold were those above-mentioned *anadromous* fish.

The National Marine Fisheries Service (or NMFS, pronounced "nymphs") originally held that FMC's planned Beartrack Mine on Williams Creek would place these last chinook and steelhead in "extreme jeopardy" of extinction. Heap leach mining with cyanide, NFMS concluded, wasn't conducive to restoring fish habitat on the mighty Salmon River.

It's harder to get gold out of Idaho rock these days. There's not much of it left. In its blueprints for the Beartrack Mine, FMC plans to dig out a square mile of rock 800 feet deep, down to the water table. They will then crush the boulders, flush the resulting dirt and rubble through a mile-long pipe, heap it up, soak it with cyanide and garner .036 ounces of gold dust per ton of crushed rock.

To give a parallel in today's drug economy, that's like taking a gram of cocaine, mixing it in a ton of glucose powder, and then trying to recover and reconstitute the coke.

To their credit, the federal fish biologists held that fish don't do well in cyanide. FMC countered by saying the company would be real careful and would line its leach pits with a gigantic rubber diaper. The enviro crowd said: Hmmmmm.

It was a stand-off until March 7, 1994, when Ron Brown met with the corporate honchos of FMC, who gave him a piece of their mind on the topic of the fish cops at NMFS, a group not exactly known for beating up on corporate executives.

Shortly thereafter came a letter of appreciation from FMC corporate headquarters to Secretary Brown, thanking him profusely for expediting the approval process for the mine. The level of understanding and mutual esteem attained by FMC and Ron Brown remained a secret for some crucial months, until a salmon-friendly source at the National Marine Fisheries Service leaked highly incriminating memos to the press.

After Brown gave the nod to FMC, the chinook and steelhead had one last hope, in the imposing form of The Wilderness Society. Along with the Pacific Rivers Council, they, in late January 1995, successfully enjoined all logging, grazing, and mining activities, including the Beartrack Mine, in the Salmon National Forest. The fish cheered.

Then, a few weeks later, the Wilderness Society mysteriously ordered its lawyers back into federal court to beg for the hard-won injunction to be lifted. In some irritation, Federal Judge David Ezra agreed. The Wilderness Society—whose president Jon Roush was at that very moment logging $150,000 worth of timber off of his own environmentally-sensitive ranchland in Montana—never gave a satisfactory explanation for the somersault. A well-placed call from Ron Brown is not out of the realm of possibility.

And, for disclosure's sake, it must be noted that in the early 1990s, according to this "nonprofit" corporation's stock portfolio, the Wilderness Society owned several hundred shares of stock in, yes, FMC.

What Ron Brown should have known was this: the economic future of central Idaho lies in tourism, wilderness use, whitewater rafting, recreational fishing—if any fish survive. Heap leach cyanide mining won't help the people of Idaho in the long-term; it will only impoverish them.

When FMC leaves Williams Creek after a decade or so, all that will be left will be a big hole in the ground, a polluted water table and cyanide-laced tailings. Someone should put up a historic marking in homage to Ron Brown, and in memory of the fish.

BOISE.

An Inside Job: Cecil Andrus
and the Bull Trout

WHEN CECIL ANDRUS STEPPED DOWN AS GOVERNOR OF IDAHO, HE didn't let time hang heavy on his hands. Laden with plaudits from the Potato State's eco-crowd as the most environmentally sensitive official in Idaho's (admittedly bleak) history, Andrus made haste to accept invitations to join the boards of two mining companies, Coeur d'Alene and Nu-West, and a grocery store, Albertson's, which stocks cans of Rep. Helen Chenoweth's favorite brand of sockeye salmon—the dead kind.

Andrus, whose curriculum vitae boasts of a stint as Jimmy Carter's Interior Secretary and as an employee of the Wilderness Society (the logging outfit that truly cares), also hooked up with the Gallatin Group, a Seattle-based influence-peddling firm with a nefarious roster of clients from across the West.

Thus equipped with income-enhancing retainers, the former Idaho governor, who often poses in hip-waders knee deep in the Salmon River fly-casting for steelhead trout, set up the Andrus Center for Public Policy, a non-profit think tank on natural resource issues, lodged rent-free at Boise State University. Conflict resolution, Andrus claims, is the Center's operational specialty.

First up on the Andrus Center's agenda was the well-known troublemaker of the West, the bull trout. America's largest native freshwater trout, the bull is a species of immense significance to logging and mining interests in Idaho and Montana. You see, the bull trout is rapidly disappearing from rivers and lakes across its range, the victim of run-away clearcutting, water diversions, and gold mining operations using sodium cyanide.

Here the game begins. Any listing of the bull trout as an endangered species would greatly impede the designs of the extraction industries across a vast area stretching from the Pacific Coast of Oregon to the crest of the Rocky Mountains. Indeed, the economic significance of the bull trout makes the Northern Spotted Owl look downright low-rent in comparison.

As consequence of a petition filed by the Alliance for the Wild Rockies, federal scientists, after prolonged procedural foot-dragging, seemed finally poised to place the bull trout under the protections of the Endangered Species Act. At this fraught moment, with timber and mining companies aghast at the prospect of yet another lowly fish interrupting their predations, the ex-governor turned conflict-resolver sprang into action.

In a giant leap backwards to the "good neighbor" policy of James Watt, Cecil Andrus suggested that the bull trout's future would best be decided around a conference table of reasonable folk assembled by his Boise think-tank. Guess who came to dinner? That's right: executives from Plum Creek Timber, Potlatch Timber Company, and FMC Mining. Meanwhile, the invitation list was carefully culled of any malcontents, such as Mike Bader, Steve Kelly, and Keith Hammer—the very folks who had drafted the petition on behalf of the bull trout. When I asked Andrus why these conservationists were excluded, he sniffed: "We already know what their position is, and there's no give in it."

When the conference finally took place, it featured much corporate whining about the onerous nature of the Endangered Species Act and vigorous boasting from state officials about how much better served the bull trout would be under their enlightened stewardship. Then the event was loudly endorsed as a "model" by Andrus' former Wilderness Society boss, George Frampton, then number two at the Interior Department with special responsibility for fish and wildlife matters.

In a dense atmosphere of consensual harmony, Frampton's emissary to the affair, Mike Spear, declared that the Fish and Wildlife Service now felt no need to list the imperiled trout as endangered, and instead would consign its fate to the hands of individual states, such as Idaho. To this comforting pronouncement, Charles Grenier, a timber executive at Plum Creek, proclaimed gratefully: "That's the icing on the cake!"

But it turns out that Andrus wasn't the neutral master of ceremonies he claimed to be. A modest amount of digging through IRS filings discloses the fact that a top client of the Gallatin Group is, you guessed it, Plum Creek Timber. Plum Creek, it must be noted, owns 1.5 million acres of land in Washington, Idaho, and Montana that could have been deemed critical habitat for the bull trout. Another top client of the Gallatin Group is a consortium of aluminum companies drawing cheap power from hydro-dams on the Columbia and Snake Rivers, dams that have inundated thousands of miles of bull trout habitat. One of the key players in the aluminum axis is Kaiser Aluminum, owned by the Maxxam Corporation, which is controlled by the corporate raider Charles Hurwitz.

So here we have the spectacle of the benighted Cecil Andrus offering his supposedly impartial services to mediate the fate of the bull trout. He culls from his roundtable the trout's most vigorous defenders and caters to the fish's would-be executioners. A deal is summarily hatched with his buddies in the Clinton administration that will allow timber, mining, and water diversions at historic rates and will drive the bull trout to extinction throughout much of its range.

Meanwhile, Andrus doesn't disclose the fact that he sits on the boards of mining companies with a vested interest in the trout's extirpation and the he serves as lobbyist for corporations such as Plum Creek that have put the fish in its dire condition in the first place. In the business world, this is what is known as an inside job. It ought to be a crime.

BOISE.

The Political Science of
Jack Ward Thomas

Part One: Under New Management

I N LATE MARCH OF 1993, I RECEIVED A CALL FROM A HIGH-LEVEL OFFICIAL IN
the Washington, D.C. Office of the Forest Service. He told me that the new assistant Secretary of Agriculture Jim Lyons had just informed Forest Service chief F.
Dale Robertson that a new chief would be appointed within the next year. My source
predicted with a knowing chuckle that, "the next chief will have three first names."

Nine months later, in a dramatic break with tradition, research ecologist Jack Ward
Thomas, author of a ground-breaking report on the northern spotted owl and leader
of the team of scientists that developed Bill Clinton's plan for Pacific Northwest forests,
was named the new chief of the Forest Service.

Thomas, who is not a member of the Senior Executive Service (the elite corps of
high-level federal bureaucrats from which the past two chiefs have been selected)
became the first politically appointed chief in more than eighty years, a fact that has
irked many senior officers inside the embattled agency and some members of Congress,
including Rep. Bruce Vento of Minnesota and Sen. Mark Hatfield of Oregon.

"I am concerned about the Clinton administration's decision to politicize the Chief's
position," Hatfield fumed. Vento, a Democrat, voiced similar reservations and personally urged Vice-President Al Gore to allow Robertson to retire and then appoint a new
chief from within the ranks of the Senior Executive Service.

Most environmentalists, however, praised Thomas' appointment. "This is the most
sweeping change in the Forest Service since 1905, but there's still a lot of house cleaning to do," effused Andy Kerr, conservation director of the Oregon Natural Resources
Council. "Thomas will be confronted with an entrenched clearcutting cabal inside his
own agency that is vigorously supported by many members of Congress."

Meanwhile, Robertson, under increasing fire from a variety of fronts over the past
three years, leaves office as the first chief ousted for overtly political reasons since
President Howard Taft fired Gifford Pinchot in 1910, after Pinchot publicly denounced
Interior Secretary Richard Ballinger's giveaway of coal resources in Alaska. Many historians argue that Pinchot's dismissal forged the demise of the Taft presidency.

Associate Chief George Leonard, often called the shadow chief for his keen political instincts and fierce advocacy of the agency's timber program, was also removed from his position. Leonard will now serve out the remainder of his tenure under house arrest as a "special assistant" to Jim Lyons. Leonard's replacement, David Unger, the former associate deputy chief for the national forest system, had been appointed to the Forest Service, in a so-called politically embedded position, at the close of the Reagan presidency. For more than a month during the period between Robertson's dismissal and the appointment of Thomas, Unger served as "Acting Interim Chief."

The evictions of Leonard and Robertson appears to be the first step in a top-down purge of the agency that some insiders speculate may reach all the way down to the forest supervisor level. A so-called "hit list" of top-level Forest Service personnel has been circulating between national environmental groups and administration officials since soon after Clinton's election. Among the names on the hit-list: Deputy Chief James Overbay; Director of Timber management Dave Hessel; and a crop of regional foresters, including David Jolly (Region 1), Larry Henson (Region 3), John Lowe (Region 6), Floyd Marita (Region 9), and Michael Barton (Region 10).

Rumors of Robertson's impending dismissal and Thomas' impending appointment prompted seventy Forest Supervisors to write President Clinton urging him not to break with tradition by politicizing the chief's position: "We are aware of the effort to replace the Chief of the Forest Service with a political appointee. With all due respect, we oppose this course of action. It would set a precedent for all future administrations, making it possible for the currently correct special interest groups to control the National Forests." This letter was signed by several supervisors widely regarded as some of the agency's leading reformers, including Orville Daniels and Frank Voytas.

The most frequent criticism of Thomas, lodged (anonymously) by those in the upper hierarchies of the Forest Service, suggests that the biologist lacks the managerial skills and experience necessary to navigate the agency through the troubling days ahead—an era of sinking morale, budget shortfalls, and widespread lay-offs. But these claims were spurious and poorly-motivated.

Thomas is an adept manager and a facile motivator. Under extreme time deadlines and intense political scrutiny, Thomas organized, supervised, and nurtured three separate teams of independent-minded scientists into producing three of the most highly-acclaimed scientific policy documents in the history of modern ecology. By comparison, Dale Robertson's managerial style, like his patron Ronald Reagan's, seems negligent to the point of criminality.

At first the Clinton administration appeared as if it might placate the concerns of the supervisors and Congress by making Thomas attend the SES training academy for six months. Ultimately, however, Lyons prevailed on the White House to make the appointment immediately.

A staffer for the Senate Agriculture Committee told me: "Jim Lyons [former chief of staff for the House Agriculture Committee] has always believed that the Forest Service's problems were largely people-oriented. I think he plans a total house cleaning, replacing old-time timber beasts with new foresters, game managers with ecologists, and road engineers with watershed scientists."

However, on Thomas' second day as chief he rejected calls from environmentalists to replace two regional foresters widely considered ferocious timber beasts: Dave Jolly and Larry Henson. Thomas said: "Both men fulfilled their mission under the previous chief very well. I expect them to do the same now that their mission has changed slightly."

* * *

From a distance, Jack Ward Thomas bears a striking resemblance to Mikhail Gorbachev. And, like Gorbachev, Thomas, a twenty-eight-year Forest Service employee, is more properly seen as a reformist (not a radical or a revolutionary) with deep ties to the agency and its original conservation ethic, an ethic developed by early Forest Service leaders, including Pinchot, Aldo Leopold, and Robert Marshall.

Like Leopold, Thomas began his career in wildlife biology shooting hawks, coyotes, and other predators, a long way from his current status as one of the world's leading proponents of ecosystem management. Charting the evolution of Thomas' ecological ideology, from game manager to ecosystem planner, reveals much of his strategy for transforming the Forest Service.

Thomas spent a great deal of his career in the agency at the point where science and politics intersect; it is a career marked by several critical junctures where his scientific policy recommendations seemed consciously tailored to fit the boundaries of the existing political landscape.

An elk biologist by training and avocation, Thomas first gained national attention in the late 1970s when he authored *Wildlife Habitats in Managed Forests*, a book that dismantled many of the prevailing assumptions about wildlife management in the West. This study made two novel assertions: first, Thomas argued forcefully that old-growth and unmanaged forests were not biological deserts, but rich repositories of biodiversity; second, Thomas deconstructed the myth that aggressive timber management regimes benefited most wildlife, even big game species like elk and deer.

Like most of the non-commodity-oriented work produced by Forest Service research scientists, including Jerry Franklin and Barry Noon, the management recommendations in Thomas' book and dozens of other articles rarely translated into changes in how the national forests were managed. But if district rangers ignored Thomas' work, environmentalists devoured it, learning the basic elements of landscape ecology and then turning that research back on the agency through appeals and litigation.

* * *

In 1976, Congress was engaged in a heated debate over two competing bills designed to reform the management of the national forests. Angered by over cutting and destruction of wildlife habitat in his home state of West Virginia, Senator Jennings Randolph introduced a highly restrictive bill that would have required the Forest Service to preserve the natural diversity of plants and animals and prohibit any activities that might destroy fish and wildlife habitat. The Randolph bill enjoyed the support of some of the most powerful members of the Senate, including Frank Church, Lee Metcalf, and Dale Bumpers.

However, the Forest Service and timber industry voiced intense opposition to the Randolph bill, prompting Sen. Hubert Humphrey to introduce a much weaker piece of legislation that replaced strict regulations with broad and highly discretionary guidelines for forest management. Although the toothless legislation was later amended to contain a diversity section, the Humphrey bill never defined the meaning of "diversity" and its language on wildlife and habitat protection was much weaker than the restrictive standards of the Randolph bill.

As president of The Wildlife Society, Jack Ward Thomas made a controversial and pivotal decision to support the Humphrey bill, a decision that ultimately sealed its passage as the National Forest Management Act. Thomas later said he decided to support the Humphrey bill because he was convinced that its "diversity" provision would give wildlife biologists equal footing with timber managers in forest planning decisions. Thomas also helped to engineer a side-agreement allowing so-called K-V Funds (after the Knutson-Vandenberg Act) collected by the Forest Service from timber sale receipts, to be used for wildlife habitat improvement and other purposes—a move he believed would increase the anemic budgets for wildlife and other non-timber resources.

Thomas' endorsement of the Humphrey bill proved to be a stunning miscalculation for two reasons: first, the diversity provision of the law was totally unenforceable and did nothing to alter the subordinate position of wildlife biologists and other resource specialists; and, second, the expansion of the K-V Act became an insidious incentive to accelerate environmentally destructive timber sales.

Then in the late 1970s, Thomas played a key role in helping the Committee of Scientists and the Forest Service develop the wildlife and diversity regulations for the NFMA, the same regulations that would later entangle the Forest Service in Judge William Dwyer's court in Seattle and lead to Thomas' two most controversial assignments: drafting a conservation strategy for the northern spotted owl, and leading the team that developed President Clinton's plan for Northwest forests.

* * *

The only legitimate feature of the rightly reviled Section 318 to the 1990 Interior Appropriations Bill (the Rider from Hell), which consigned tens of thousands of acres of ancient forest to the chainsaw without compliance to federal environmental laws, was a little noticed provision calling for an interagency task force to develop a conservation plan for the northern spotted owl. Several members of the Northwest congressional delegations supported the task force under the belief that the team of scientists would finally demonstrate that the owl could survive in a managed forest landscape, thus averting its listing as a threatened species and, more importantly, keeping the cut at near historic levels. Thomas was named the team leader.

Six months later, the scientists rocked the Northwest when they released what came to be known as "The Thomas Report" (a 300-page "conservation strategy" later described as the most detailed examination of a single species in the history of ecology) which concluded that, unless drastic conservation measures were adopted, the spotted owl would be doomed to extinction in many parts of its range in less than fifty years.

The Thomas Report called for placing more than 6 million acres of forest into the Habitat Conservation Areas (where no commercial timber sales, salvage, or thinning could occur) and recommended the adoption of the so called 50-11-40 Rule to regulate harvesting on the managed landscape, including state and private lands. In all, timber harvests on the spotted owl forests were expected to fall by about a third from forest-plan levels.

As draconian as this may have seemed to some in the Northwest, the Thomas Report was actually a bare-bones strategy that attempted to balance political reality with the biology of the owl, a strategy that sacrificed 40 to 50 percent of the remaining owls and old growth in the region, with hope of growing enough old forest habitat inside the forest reserves to stabilize the owl's population by the year 2100.

Thomas crafted this compromise even as he admitted to a Congressional committee that "most, if not all, spotted owl experts agree that cessation of all old growth logging would be best for the owl."

Of course, for all his "pragmatism," Thomas was still vilified by the industry and the George H. W. Bush administration. Shortly after the Thomas Report was released, BLM director Cy Jamison played to the industry's wrath when he said: "I'm not going to allow a noose to be placed around the neck of the Northwest economy and then let Jack Ward Thomas be judge, jury, and hangman." After publicly denouncing Thomas, Jamison went on to pursue his own pernicious and ill-fated God Squad strategy, which sought to over-ride the Endangered Species Act and consign the owl to extinction for the good of the timber industry.

But Thomas' gambit, that some of the last old growth could be logged immediately in exchange for a more regulated forest in the future, became a guiding principle of the subsequent attempts to construct a management plan for Northwest forests, including the Gang of Four study, SAT Report, and most importantly, the FEMAT report that gave birth to Option 9, the Clinton forest plan.

* * *

During an early briefing on Option 9 to foresters and ecologists at Oregon State University, Jack Ward Thomas lifted the 1,800 page report above his head and pronounced: "This is not science, but a policy document written by scientists." But precisely how much of a role did "policy" demands, relayed to Thomas by Clinton administration politicos, play in shaping the forest plan?

We know that when Thomas took the initial eight alternatives developed by FEMAT to Washington, DC, Bruce Babbitt and Jim Lyons rejected each of them because none cut enough timber. So Thomas went back to Portland and, along with Jerry Franklin, quickly cobbled together Option 9, a forest management strategy that runs counter to many of Thomas' core ideals about protecting old growth and spotted owl habitat.

For example, Option 9 permits salvage logging and thinning to occur inside late-successional reserves, which Thomas had previously rejected as inappropriate. "We simply don't know how to recreate old growth," Thomas said in 1992. "Until we do, these activities should be restricted to the managed landscape." Option 9 also dropped the 50-11-40 Rule and *any* restrictions on private lands.

Did Thomas' knowledge that he was a leading contender for chief of the Forest Service in any way affect his decision to sign off on Option 9? Does Thomas really believe, as one of his fellow scientists suggested to me, that from the chief's office he could elevate the standing of biologists within the agency, and thereby improve Option 9 and other strategies from the inside out?

These are troubling questions that have no definitive answers. It does seem clear, however, that Jack Ward Thomas' brand of "political science" is emblematic of the direction Bruce Babbitt and Jim Lyons want to take the nation's public lands: toward an ethos of management without lines, consensus-based conservation agreements, and experimentation across the landscape.

Thomas told me that he expects logging, grazing and mining to continue to play an important role in the future of the national forests. "We cannot expect to sustain human life on this planet without exploitation of natural resources. The question is how it will be done."

Thus, while Thomas may want to transform the underlying mission of the Forest Service from multiple-use to ecosystem management, this does not foretell the end of widespread commodity development on the national forests. Instead, it may signal the institutionalization of ecological forestry and ecological grazing.

Of course, many of these changes will come at a high price to the environment and our nation's environmental laws. In the summary of the FEMAT report, Thomas confesses that we are now entering a period of ecological triage, where some species may have to be sacrificed and some laws must be altered to fit "everyday reality."

* * *

Jack Ward Thomas' ascendancy to chief was greeted with what one reporter called "universal accolades" from conservationists. In fact, many environmentalists are already acting like eager acolytes for Thomas' quest to impose "ecosystem management" as the new template governing resource exploitation on the national forests.

One ecstatic environmentalist declared that under the guiding triumvirate of Gore, Babbitt, and Thomas, America's public lands will finally become a place "where science reigns." *Excuse me,* but as Thomas himself has said: "I don't want to be part of a world where scientists make all the decisions."

Why? Forest ecology is subject to a kind of information entropy: the more we learn, the less we know. But does this imply conservationism and restraint? Or does it translate into adaptive management zones, new forestry, holistic research management (cows pretending to be bison), new perspectives, tread lightly, kinder and gentler cyanide heap leach mining? History says the latter.

Consider this. Soon after Thomas' appointment as chief, top timber industry lobbyist Jim Geisinger testified before Congress that the industry fully embraces the shift toward ecosystem management. Moreover, several respected ecologists told another congressional committee that from a "biodiversity perspective" the extinction of individual species is not necessarily a matter for concern, if the ecosystem itself continues to "function."

The terrain of our terminology has been colonized by industrial foresters, pork-barrel politicians, and federal bureaucrats. *Ecosystem management. Biodiversity.* The very meaning of these terms has already been corrupted to the point where they now become the justification for environmentally destructive and economically disastrous activities. It's going to be a hard fight winning them back.

From this vantage, the most important question was not whether Jack Ward Thomas was up to the job of being chief, but whether the environmental community is capable of defending the national forests under Thomas' tenure as chief and providing the kind of creative tension necessary to advance the cause of ecosystem protection, not management.

Part Two: Jack Ward Thomas Goes Downhill

Jack Ward Thomas, once touted by Al Gore as the nation's most accomplished ecologist, has now accepted a position as a PR flack for a ski developer. Thomas' task is to greenwash the environmental wreckage from the construction of a $37 million resort inside an ancient forest reserve on national forest lands in southern Oregon, about thirty miles north of Klamath Falls. The ski resort, located on Pelican Butte in the Winema National Forest, is inhabited by numerous rare wildlife species, including the northern spotted owl.

Landing Thomas to their side was quite a coup for the developers, the Jeld-Wen Corporation. Thomas is the former head of the Forest Service, the federal agency that made the decision to greenlight the resort. More importantly, the ski resort is slated for an area that Thomas himself has twice identified as vital wildlife habitat. The resort, which will sprawl over 5,200 acres, is entirely located inside habitat designated by the Fish and Wildlife Service as critical for the survival of the northern spotted owl. In 1990, Thomas led a team of federal biologists who identified the forest-dwelling owl's habitat and urged its protection.

More than half of the ski resort will be constructed inside an old-growth forest reserve, which Thomas himself mapped out and said should be permanently protected. At the time, Thomas was hand-picked by President Bill Clinton to head the team of scientists, who would develop the administration's Northwest Forest Plan—a plan designed to protect the spotted owl and other wildlife that live in the ancient forests of Oregon, Washington, and northern California. Thomas and the other scientists identified Pelican Butte as providing crucial habitat for thirty-four threatened or rare species, including the spotted owl, lynx, Pacific fisher, pine marten, and redband trout. Thomas' report advised that, "development of new facilities that may adversely affect [the old-growth reserve] should not be permitted."

Jeld-Wen's ambitious plan for the ski resort calls for the construction of eight chair-lifts, a T-bar lift, fifty-two downhill runs, eighteen Nordic ski trails, four snow-making ponds, three large lodges, numerous maintenance buildings and roads, and a 100-car gondola. All together, the resort would be the second largest in Oregon and one of the biggest in the Pacific Northwest.

The Forest Service, which Thomas led as chief from 1994 to 1997, has looked fondly on the project. Eager for new sources of money since its timber sale program hit the skids, the Forest Service published an environmental impact statement supporting the ski resort. The report downplayed the certain harm to endangered species, forest ecology, and water quality.

By accepting a position with Jeld-Wen, Thomas, a recipient of the Aldo Leopold Medal for Conservation and the Chuck Yeager Award, seems to be backtracking from advice that he gave to his fellow biologists about selling their services to industry. In 1986 Thomas gave a speech at the North American Wildlife Conference, where he warned that biologists shouldn't "perform professional services for anybody whose role or primary intent is to damage wildlife."

There's no doubt that the ski resort will have a devastating impact on wildlife. The Fish and Wildlife Service condemned the project, noting its adverse impact on the spotted owl and several species of rare fish that inhabit Pelican Butte's streams and nearby Klamath Lake. The Environmental Protection Agency also opposed the resort, noting the potential for pollution of streams from erosion and sewage spills. The development will also destroy, according to the Forest Service's own analysis, more than a quarter of the mountain's wolverine habitat. Wolverine populations are declining across the American west.

This is not the first time the Jeld-Wen Corporation has reached out to conservationists to help maneuver its plans past environmental regulators. In 1998, the company, which operates a golf resort at the foot of the mountain, recruited the Audubon Society to sanction its development. The company placed the following statement from Cindy Bradley, environmental educator for Audubon International, on its website: "The open space of a golf course is utilized not only by golfers, but is habitat for a variety of wildlife species. We welcome [Jeld-Wen's] commitment to the environment and to managing the golf course with wildlife in mind."

To many environmentalists the most shocking aspect of the ski resort is Jen-Weld's plan to build a 2,000-space parking lot in the bald eagle nesting and roosting area adjacent to the Upper Klamath National Wildlife Refuge. The area now supports more than 100 eagles. Ralph Opp, a wildlife biologist who helped write the recovery plan for the bald eagles at Pelican Butte, is outraged by the plan because he assumed that the area had been permanently protected. "That was the thinking," Opp said. "We're drawing a line at this point in time. We're setting this aside. But now we're compromising again. It sort of leaves a bad taste in my mouth that for the good of man and the economy we're going to chip away at this mountain that was set aside."

KLAMATH FALLS.

Stephen Breyer, Cancer Bonds, and the Origins of Neoliberal Environmentalism

A NY MAN ADMIRED BY BOTH SENATORS TED KENNEDY AND ORRIN HATCH can't be all good. And, in fact, Stephen Breyer's elevation to the highest bench illustrates concisely how, across the past twenty years, Kennedyesque liberalism and Hatchian conservatism have merged into a unified, pro-corporate posture.

Put more nastily, Breyer's ascent to the Supreme Court offers an unpleasing paradigm for the utter bankruptcy and degradation of that liberal tradition of which Kennedy is erroneously supposed to be the custodian and stout defender. Those with short memories often ascribe certain familiar features of the socio-economic landscape to the "Reagan Revolution." Such features center on the erosion of government regulations unwelcome to big business.

But the intellectual and political groundwork was done by Teddy Kennedy's people back in the 1970s. And Stephen Breyer was one of them. This was the launch time for the deregulation of airlines, trucking, and for the erosion of environmental victories won in the previous decade. Breyer and Alfred Kahn, another Kennedy man, predicted that, in the bracing combat of the unregulated free market, the inefficient and unproductive would go to the wall, airline services would become more flexible, cheaper, and above all, more profitable.

Any student of the real world could have told them—and many did—the true consequences of deregulation would be greater business concentration and higher prices. Consumers paid the price and so did Kennedy's core constituency, organized labor. The same thing happened in trucking, deregulated in 1980 on Kennedy's initiative. In the next decade, freight workers wages fell more than 25 percent.

In January of 1979, Breyer, then Kennedy's chief legislative counsel, published an extremely influential article in *Harvard Law Review*, in which he argued an old business favorite: Environmental hazards could best be dealt with by market mechanisms in which "rights" to pollute would be traded.

In other words, the country would be divided into zones and a pollution index would be established for each zone, with companies allowed a certain amount of pollution within the overall permissible limit. But if Company A uses only 25 percent of its "pollution rights," it can trade or sell the remaining 75 percent to Company B that has already reached its limit if they are in the same area. On paper, Company B would not be exceeding regulatory limits, though of course the people living next to Company B's plant would be dealing with higher levels of poisons.

To put it crudely, the Kennedy neoliberals wanted to organize a market in Cancer Bonds, offering relief to the Business Roundtable, which was screaming that in 1977 the operations of six regulatory agencies caused $2.65 billion in "incremental costs" to forty-eight major companies, about 10 percent of their total capital expenditure.

Thus, out of Kennedy's office came the initiative to replace environmental law compliance with "cost effective reforms," including pollution taxes and credits, effluent charges, and markets for pollution rights. As environmental economists Jim O'Connor and Daniel Faber put it, the scheme is designed to "increase capital's flexibility to meet regulatory requirements but continue polluting in a profitable manner."

The regulatory theory promoted by Breyer was transmuted into law in the Clean Air Act of 1990. In May of 1992, the Tennessee Valley Authority bought an estimated $2.5 million worth of credits from Wisconsin Power and Light, which didn't need them. This credit allowed TVA to exceed its limit of sulfur dioxide and other toxic emissions. As Benjamin Goldman shows in his useful book, *The Truth About Where You Live,* among those on the receiving end, Shelby County, Tennessee ranks twenty-second among all counties in the nation for excess deaths from lung cancer. Sheboygan County, Wisconsin ranks twenty-eighth from the bottom in the same category—an almost perfect reverse, mirroring the transfer of poisons from north to south, comfortable to poor, white to minority.

For Breyer, equity and the unregulated play of market forces move in harmony. His ascent to the Supreme Court owed everything to his patron, Ted Kennedy, in truth one of the most effective foes of the real interest of labor and environmentalists in the US Senate today. Small wonder Orrin Hatch is smiling.

For the environmental movement there are lessons in this history. The legislative triumphs of the late 1960s and early 1970s, many of them coming to pass in Nixon time, had indeed imposed constraints on corporate profitability. By the end of the 1970s, Congress had passed more than twenty major laws regulating consumer products, the environment and workplace conditions. Hence the corporate counterattack described above and ongoing to this day.

In the early and mid-1970s, environmentalists played the game of rising liberal expectations, assuming that their pluralist conception of the political economy would in turn permit, at both popular awareness and state policy levels, a new, environmentally aware attitude toward cost and regulation.

In the late 1970s, the corporate titans bit back and successfully set labor and environmentalists at each others' throats. Since a good many greens are middle class and essentially anti-labor in philosophical outlook, the antagonism was real. Also, by the end of the 1970s, mainstream environmentalism had moved from popular activism to managerial caution, with some groups, such as the Environmental Defense Fund, gladly endorsing and promoting the market-based theory of environmental regulation offered by Breyer in his chilling 1979 tract.

WITH ALEXANDER COCKBURN.

Adventures in the Endangered Skin Trade: Why Elephants Hate Neo-Liberals

ALL THROUGH THE REAGAN-BUSH YEARS, GREENS THUNDERED THEIR indignation at the Republicans' indifference to endangered species (other than beleaguered executives looking for a federal bail-out or for an indictment to be quashed). Nothing roused more passion than the slaughter of the world's few remaining elephants, leopards, rhinos and kindred species dear to the big game hunters' hearts.

And indeed both Reagan and Bush did thwart efforts to strengthen international protection for rare wildlife species. With the return to power of the Democrats in 1993, many environmentalists looked to Interior Secretary Bruce Babbitt to end the international trade in exotic animal trophies. By the end of 1993, deeds—as so often was the case in Clintontime—turned out to differ markedly from the promises.

A range of regulations govern big game hunting and the taking of trophies. These include the US Endangered Species Act and the Convention on International Trade in Endangered Species of Wild Fauna and Flora.

In theory, the Endangered Species Act allows only for import of listed species for scientific research or enhancement/survival of species. Under the threat of lawsuits from green groups, both Reagan and Bush more or less stuck to the letter of the law, with the corpses of such rare species being admitted primarily on the grounds (dubious or not) of scientific research. The relevant agency here is the Fish and Wildlife Service in the Interior Department. Its officials decide which listed species may be imported and whether these species are from approved countries. Between 1981 and 1992—the twelve years of Republican tenure of the White House—an average of 2,000 trophy animals belonging to species listed under the International Convention were imported each year.

With the arrival of the Democrats in 1993 came a new philosophy based on inane neo-liberal dogma. Theory here took the form of our old friend, the cash carrot. The idea has been that if the Fish and Wildlife Service charges hefty permit fees for the hunting of these species, it will provide a financial incentive to preserve their habitat. Some of the money is remitted to the relevant countries, which are meant to remit the money to their environmental bureaucracies, which in turn, crack down on poachers and protect existing stocks.

All of this twaddle betrays staggering ignorance of Third World conditions, where corruption means that the money is often immediately stolen, and where the governments themselves are broke. Mozambique, which has the famous Maputo Elephant Reserve, has been forced to lease the 3-million-acre eco-system to James Blanchard, the right-wing financier from Louisiana, who proposes to transform the preserve into a themed hunting park. Blanchard once financed RENAMO, the mercenary guerrilla force backed by the CIA and South Africa, which as part of its destruction of Mozambique in the 1980s, killed off 80 percent of the elephant population.

In the first year of Bruce Babbitt's supervision, imports of exotic species shot up from an average of 2,000 during the Reagan-Bush years to 17,953. The following year the number rose again, to 21,000. In 1992, Bush's last year, the Fish and Wildlife Service authorized the importation of 400 African elephant and leopard trophies. In 1994, the Clinton administration allowed 1,200 trophy imports of these two species.

Trophy hunting is a multi-billion dollar industry, where large white-owned safari outfits charge rich white people thousands of dollars to hunt rare wildlife in Africa. A typical trophy-hunting safari in Tanzania, for example, costs between $40,000 and $60,000. Little, if any, of this money stays in Tanzania. Most of it goes to the outfitters, which are often owned by American, European, or South African companies. For example, the Gellini outfitting company of Italy promises its clients "exclusive camps near the favorite hunting areas of Ernest Hemingway, led by first class professional hunters. Our luxury camps feature the best Italian cuisine served by waiters dressed in crisp whites, carrying fresh drinks." According to one survey, more than 60 percent of the clients of American safari outfitters are millionaires.

The typical safari hunt is neither exhausting nor dangerous. Most African elephants are shot from trucks near the borders of national parks. The favored method of hunting leopards and lions is to shoot them from blinds at night, as the animals are attracted to bait (usually zebra or impala) hung from trees. Bright spotlights are flashed on the cats to freeze them before the hunter makes the kill.

Many of the trophy imports into the United States come from South Africa, where endangered species, such as African lion, bontebok, and elephants are slaughtered on large privately-owned game ranches, some of which are more than a half million acres in size. Many of the rare animals offered for hunting in these places are trapped from the wild and then transported to enclosures in the game reserves. The Kido Game Ranch in South Africa advertises the opportunity to kill scimitar-horned oryx ($4,500), letchwe kafue ($1,600), addax ($4,700), and Pere David deer ($1,650)—not including taxidermy and gratuity.

The taxidermy costs are almost as expensive as the hunting permits themselves. A life-sized leopard mount costs nearly $2,500, the crafting of a zebra skin runs $1,500, a whole baboon costs $2,000, and the tab for a shoulder mounting of white rhino is about $4,000. Even animal novelties are not cheap. The stuffed penis of a cape buffalo (called a "pizzle cane") costs $225, an elephant footstool sells for $600, a map of Africa on an elephant ear goes for $925, a lion scrotum pouch costs $150, while a warthog skin beer mug can be made for $125.

A significant player in this story is Safari Club International, at whose annual convention in 1994 Babbitt was a speaker. These tour operators naturally relish the possibility of sharply raising the number of animals they can legally kill and import. Much of the recent increase in trophy hunting of threatened and endangered species can be attributed to Safari Club trophy competitions, where gold and diamond awards are presented to those hunters who have killed the greatest number of listed species. The 1995 winner was Dr. Gerald Wamock, MD, a radiologist from Portland, Oregon, who has bragged of killing 278 different species. During his acceptance speech, Dr. Wamock said he is now "going back to kill the same species with a muzzle loader."

Some of the Safari Club's high profile clients include General Chuck Yeagar, actor Steven Seagal, Rep. Billy Tauzin, Rep. Richard Pombo, Dan Quayle, General Gen. Norman Schwarzkopf, and the country singer Glen Campbell. The Safari Club is a powerful force in Washington, where its interests are advanced by lobbyist Ron Marlenee, the former congressman from Montana known for his extreme anti-environmental positions. The Club's political action committee doles out nearly a quarter of a million dollars a year. Its top recipient is the wild man from Alaska, Don Young who raked in more than $14,000 over the past two years. Young is working sedulously to forge new loopholes in the Endangered Species Act that will allow increased importation of trophy hunted endangered species.

In his speech before the Safari Club Babbitt, spoke favorably of the idea of auctioning exotic hunting permits to the highest bidder, saying "these auctions promise much needed currency benefits to argali habitat [the argali are endangered sheep in Khirgistan] and enlist area residents in on-the-ground effort to conserve the species."

Only Babbitt could babble such imbecilities with a hopeful countenance.

Ben Nighthorse Campbell:
A River Runs Through Him

"The dam is a con." —Jake Gittes, *Chinatown*

AS ANY FAN OF THE MOVIE *CHINATOWN* KNOWS, IN THE AMERICAN WEST one commodity reigns supreme. Not oil or timber, not gold or silicon chips, but water which flows its glistening way through the body politic, providing nourishment for corruption.

The latest politician caught in a crooked water grab is Colorado's Ben Nighthorse Campbell, the Harley-riding former Democrat who jumped the divide to the Republicans in the wake of the 1994 elections. The move didn't surprise observers who had followed Campbell's career. The senator had modeled himself after Wayne Aspinall, an anti-environmental congressman from western Colorado who orchestrated the spasm of dam-building, mining, and logging in the West in the late 1950s and 1960s. Campbell shared Aspinall's vision, but he's never exhibited his grandiose malignity. Campbell's politics have rarely risen above the petty and the personal.

In the summer of 1998, Campbell concocted a bill to transfer the federally-owned Vallecitos reservoir and dam, located in southern Colorado near Durango, to the privately-owned Pine River Irrigation District. As originally devised, the legislation would have sold the federal property to the ranching and development group for only $492,000, far below its market value. But by the time the bill had moved out of Campbell's committee, even that small sum had been excised and both the reservoir and the dam were offered on behalf of we-the-people to the Pine River organization for free. In a speech on the Senate floor, Campbell said the transfer was needed in order to give citizens "local control" over their water supplies. The bill flew through the Senate unanimously on a voice vote on October 8, 1998, but stalled when the Congress adjourned before the House could take up the legislation.

All of this is standard political fare, excepting one factor: Campbell concealed from his colleagues the fact that he was to be a beneficiary of the scheme. The senator was a major shareholder in the Pine River Irrigation District. The Irrigation District is really a collection of downstream ranchers and developers, of whom Campbell is the *primus inter pares*, AKA top dog.

Campbell is one of the Pine River group's largest landholders. His Nighthorse Ranch covers 267 acres of the Irrigation District. 90 percent of the landowners in the irrigation district own less than 100 acres. On his financial disclosure forms filed with the Clerk of the Congress, Campbell also modestly chose not to disclose the value of these holdings and the attendant water rights.

In theory, the US Senate has rules against this kind of brazen self-dealing. Senate Ethics Rule 37.4 prohibits a senator from introducing legislation "the principal purpose of which is to further his own pecuniary interest" or that of a "limited class" of which the senator or his family is a member.

But the Senate Ethics Committee didn't see it that way and ended up giving Campbell a mild tap on the wrist for his malfeasance. Campbell sustained the tap bravely, telling a town meeting in Colorado, "These charges were bullshit." Nor had the committee taken up the matter on its own initiative. It was forced to deal with it after a small but feisty Colorado environmental group, the Citizens' Progressive Alliance, filed a complaint alleging numerous violations of senate rules by Campbell. Thus challenged, the senate ethics committee sat on the complaint for months, then in November 1999 this august body of moral arbiters sent the Citizens' Alliance a letter dismissing the complaint. The committee used subtle reasoning to conclude that Campbell hadn't "technically" violated senate rules. In effect, the committee concluded that the Irrigation District, of which Campbell is a leading owner, didn't represent "a limited class."

In the view of Phil Doe, a Littleton, Colorado environmentalist who filed the complaint for the Alliance, "the ethics committee letter was gibberish. In fact, it's insulting. And it shows just how much of a club the senate is and how much each member can get away with."

On the Hill, Campbell is widely regarded as a bully, a senate version of Rep. Dick Armey. But in the aristocratic upper chamber, Campbell doesn't have Armey's clout and is mistrusted by both Republicans and Democrats. "Campbell is stupid, uninterested, and mean," a staffer for a Republican senator told me. "His staff spends most of its time cleaning up the messes he makes." Campbell, who has little influence on the Hill, prefers to throw his weight around back in Colorado, targeting reporters, environmentalists, and federal employees. In 1996, managers at the Ignacio, Colorado offices of the Bureau of Indian Affairs (BIA) lodged complaints with their superiors about Campbell's intimidation of their resource managers.

This show of senatorial clout was part of an effort to get the BIA to divert more of its limited water supplies to Campbell's ranch. Dan Breuninger, the head of the BIA's Southern Ute Agency, told the *Durango Herald* in an October 1998 story, that the senator "threatened [BIA employees] with the loss of their jobs."

Brueninger's predecessor, Tony Recker, had also heard complaints about Campbell's strong-armed tactics. "I've heard that the BIA area director has been talked to in a number of ways [by Campbell]," Recker said. When asked if he had been harassed by the senator, Recker clammed up. "I would rather not answer that question."

Such oafish behavior apparently runs in the family. The Campbells' neighbor, Jim Nall, claims he was threatened with a beating by Campbell's son. Nall sought and received a restraining order against Campbell Jr. And Campbell Sr. doesn't like the press much either. During a recent to Durango, the gallant senator met with the county council to discuss the Animas-La Plata dam and river diversion scheme and other legislative matters. Although Colorado sunshine laws require all government meetings to be open to the public, Campbell threw a fit when he espied a reporter from the *Durango Herald* planning to do his lawful job, covering the session. The senator demanded that the reporter be evicted from the room and the meeting held behind closed doors. Later Campbell said he didn't have anything against that particular reporter, but that he thought the publisher of the paper was "a scumbag."

During his senate floor speech, Campbell said the Pine River Irrigation District deal fit nicely with Al Gore's reinventing government scheme and that it was motivated by a desire "to save precious taxpayer dollars." The water rights alone are worth an estimated $2 billion. But that's not all the Irrigation District gets. More than 500 acres of now public land surrounding the reservoir and the dam are part of the deal. These lands are valued at more than $100 million, and this doesn't count lucrative oil and mineral rights to these lands that will also be transferred to the district. Plus, the Irrigation District will be given the right to charge license fees for boats and other recreational activities on the lake, which might put millions more into the District's accounts.

Campbell seems perpetually to be operating in murky legal waters. In reviewing the master contract between the Irrigation District and the US government, Phil Doe discovered a provision that Campbell and the senate ethics committee have ignored. The language expressly forbids any member of congress from benefiting from the contract.

Over the past thirteen years, Campbell has received subsidized federal water from the Vallecitos Project, subsidies that may be illegal under the terms of the contract. The Bureau of Reclamation estimates that the value of the subsidies is at least $277,000. But if the water going to Campbell was sold on the open market it would likely fetch more than one million dollars.

Yet the senator's benefits extend well beyond the water subsidies. Campbell personally lobbied the Department of Agriculture to provide low-interest loans and construction grants to the Irrigation District totaling $17 million. And he has bragged about his role in bringing home such bacon to his fellow shareholders. In a March 6, 1998 letter to the District, Campbell boasted that he had approached Agriculture Secretary Dan Glickman about securing more money for the Pine River Irrigation District and added that, "my position on the Committee on Appropriation allows me to work directly on the funding issue."

There is another aspect to this affair, which expands the level of intrigue and corruption much further, encompassing such environmental kingpins as Al Gore and Bruce Babbitt. Under the auspices of Gore's National Performance Review (NPR), also known as the "reinventing government" initiative, the sell-off of federal assets has accelerated swiftly since 1993. Although cast as a way to downsize government, in practice, the Gore Performance Review has put valuable federal properties up for sale at garage sale prices. Often these assets end up in the hands of political cronies of the administration. Take one of the great rip-offs of the 1990s: the sale of the Elk Hills petroleum reserve to Occidental Petroleum, a company with deep ties to the Gore family. Elk Hills, located near Bakersfield, is one of the top ten oil reserves in the US outside of Alaska, containing over one billion barrels of oil. Gore praised the privatization of the site, which also provides crucial wildlife habitat." With the sale of Elk Hills we are getting the government out of the oil business," said Gore piously proclaimed, in a somewhat crude rendition of the functions of government: "We're returning to the private sector those functions that can be more effectively performed in the private sector."

In a similar vein, Bruce Babbitt helped engineer a huge federal/private land swap, involving his family's ranch in northern Arizona, which will aid a sprawling theme-park development called Canyon Forest Village, located near the entrance to Grand Canyon Park. The Disneyland-style scheme is being built by Tommy DePaolo, one of Babbitt's former legal clients.

Although the Clinton crowd scarcely holds Ben Nighthorse Campbell in high esteem, especially after he jumped ship to the Republicans after the 1994 elections, they needed Campbell's support for another grandiose project: the Aminas-LaPlata water project, a multi-billion dollar scam now being hyped as a plan to give more water to the Southern Ute tribes. In fact the dam is designed to accelerate the development of the booming suburbs around Durango, Colorado. Babbitt once opposed the water impoundment project. Now he supports it as part of his legacy to the West (and a pay-off to his political patrons) and he summoned Campbell's help in pushing the project through. "We've been flimflammed," Ray Frost, a leader of the Southern Ute Tribe, told me. "Where will we ever come up with the $185 million to bring the water from the reservoir to the reservation? That water is meant for Durango."

Campbell, by the way, served on both the Senate appropriations committee and the energy and natural resources committee, which has jurisdiction over all western water projects.

In the True West, that's how the sweetest deals go down.

Durango.

In the Out Door:
Bruce Babbitt's Big Score

N O BETTER CASE FOR CYNICISM ABOUT POLITICS IS AVAILABLE THAT THE career of Bruce Babbitt, Interior Secretary in Clintontime, an era now bodied forth by major green groups in their fundraising material as a time when stewardship of the nation's natural resources can contrast finely with the pillage supposedly ushered in by the Cheney-Bush crowd.

Before leaving the Department of Interior, Babbitt promised that he wouldn't cash in on his years of government service by becoming a high-priced DC lawyer. Then he promptly took a job with Latham and Watkins, a big Washington law firm whose clients include some of the roughest environmental pillagers in the business. Babbitt defended his about-face by saying that he needs to make money to pay off his legal bills stemming from an independent counsel investigation into whether or not he committed perjury when he said he did not try to shake down Indian tribes for campaign contributions.

Within days of landing his new job as a counsel in the firm's Environmental Litigation shop, Babbitt could be found at the annual gathering of the Nuclear Energy Institute (NEI), the $3-billion lobbying arm of the nuclear industry, cheerleading for the planned Yucca Mountain Nuclear Waste Dump on Western Shoshone lands in Nevada. The Clinton administration opposed the dump, acting more out of a desire to keep Nevada Sen. Harry Reid happy than any sudden seizure of ecological conscience. "It's a safe, solid geologic repository," Babbitt proclaimed, evoking a standing ovation from the massed nukers, something even Dick Cheney had failed to do when he spoke to the NEI earlier that morning

Among Babbitt's present clients are two of the biggest developers on the California coast: the Hearst Ranch at San Simeon near Big Sur and Washington Mutual, developers of the Ahmanson Ranch in Ventura County. As Interior Secretary Babbitt resisted designating habitat for the red-legged frog and in late December of 2000, the Interior Department also decided against listing the San Fernando spineflower as an endangered species. The spineflower, an ankle high plant with delicate white flowers that resemble baby's breath, was declared to be extinct in 1929, until botanists found several thousand plants growing on the south slope of Laskey Mesa, where many of the shops and homes in the 5,500 Ahmanson ranch development are scheduled to be built.

Babbitt's association with the Hearsts presents an equally unattractive picture of yesterday's supposed protector of the environment, here abetting a scheme either to wreck the coastline below Hearst Castle south of Big Sur, or extort staggering sums from the feds and the State of California for leaving it alone—at least for the time being until, twenty-five years down the road, the costly conservation easements are forgotten and development commences.

During his tenure at Interior, Babbitt ushered through hundreds of complex lands swaps and federal buyouts of private property where potential development plans had been stymied by environmental restrictions. The deals often ended up with the developers getting much more money than their land is worth. The most high profile example was the Headwaters Redwood Forest bailout, where corporate raider Charles Hurwitz ran off with more than $480 million for land that an Interior Department land appraiser concluded had a market value of less than $100 million.

Under Babbitt's guidance, lawyers for the Hearst family are taking advantage of a new entirely legal scam whereby 19th century records known as certificates of compliance can be used for such purposes as creating ocean-front parcels and subdivisions, over-riding existing zoning restrictions, even though the original parcels may have been inland and on worthless terrain. Developers have been using the law as leverage to extort huge sums from conservation groups as the price for easements protecting the land.

Hearst lawyers have amassed a parcel of documents that could allow the corporation to chop the 83,000-acre ranch into 279 parcels and create oceanfront subdivisions. According to the *Los Angeles Times*, Steven Hearst has suggested that the Hearst Corporation may be willing to forego such plans if the government will pony up $300 million or more to buy them out.

Babbitt tetchily defends the use of these certificates of compliance to maximize the value of the land. "I would advise any client who is considering alternative uses to perfect their rights," claims Babbitt. "It's good, proper, and correct to do that." Yes, this is the Interior Secretary who, with Vice President Al Gore, railed against development that was eroding America's natural treasures. Is there a better argument than Babbitt for Ralph Nader's case that, on the practical level, the two parties are one, and that the despoliation continues whether Babbitt or Gale Norton run Interior or which one of them spins through the revolving door and goes to work for a firm like Latham and Watkins?

Big Sur.

Leave It to Leavitt: Meet David Broder's Favorite Polluter

A S A RULE, SECRETARIES OF THE INTERIOR DEPARTMENT COME FROM THE West and directors of the Environmental Protection Agency hail from the East. Ronald Reagan breached this cardinal political tenet by picking Anne Gorsuch Burford of Colorado to head his EPA department, with disastrous results. Burford resigned in disgrace and narrowly escaped indictment. Her top aide, the ridiculous Rita Levelle, wasn't so fortunate. She ended up doing time in federal prison for lying to congress, a fall girl for Burford.

Christie Todd Whitman, the ditzy director of the EPA under George W. Bush, abruptly resigned in late June of 2003 to return to New Jersey. There she mulled over a run for the US Senate—a project swiftly doomed following recent disclosures by the EPA's Inspector General that Whitman lied to the people of the New York City metro area after 9/11, as she pronounced the post-blast air safe to breathe, when, all the while, she knew it was contaminated with a deadly stew of toxins.

Many DC insiders presumed that Bush might try to dampen the bellows about his scandalously pro-polluter policies by tapping a slick fixer for the post, such as William K. Reilly, who commanded the agency during his father's administration. But no. Bush the Younger, following the flagitious advice of his political bantam Karl Rove, chose to follow in Reagan's inauspicious footsteps. He drafted Mike Leavitt, the rightwing governor of Utah.

Leavitt looked as surprised at the news of his nomination as Dan Quayle did when got the call from George Bush the first. After all, Mike Leavitt had never shown much interest in the EPA, outside of battling to keep its regulatory arms from stifling the smokestacks of Utah's polluters. As the leader of a renegade group of western governors, Leavitt sent a memo to the Bush transition team shortly after the 2000 election demanding that the new administration transfer most of the EPA's regulatory responsibilities to the states. He even pushed for Bush to give presidential backing to a constitutional amendment handing individual states control over federal lands and environmental issues. Leavitt christened this plan Enlibra, which sounds like a bizarre apparition from the Book of Mormon but boils down to the environmental version of welfare reform.

Of course, Enlibra had already been given a test-drive in Utah with unnerving results. Over the course of Leavitt's twelve years as governor, Utah outpaced nearly every other state in a dubious category: generation of toxic waste. By the end of his tenure, the Beehive State, the thirty-seventh most populous in the nation, ranked second in industrial pollution, trailing only Nevada.

But Utah may soon surpass its neighbor to the West, especially with Leavitt at the helm of EPA. Already, Utah boasts the two top polluters in the country: Kennecott Copper Company, located in Magna south of Salt Lake City, and USMagnesium Corp., whose deadly smelter towers over the shores of the Great Salt Lake in Rowley, Utah.

It's stiff competition, but USMagnesium may well rank as the sleaziest corporation in America. As the sole producer of magnesium in the US, the company is a true monopoly and acts like one. For years, its smelter was the most toxic smokestack in the world, belching chlorine-laden gas into the skies of the Salt Lake Valley.

USMagnesium is owned by Wall Street raider Ira Rennert, who refers to himself as "a financial Houdini"—an appellation he earned by bilking bondholders out of millions and skating away freely. From his Renco holding company, Rennert commands a slate of corporations, including lead and coal mines; a steel factory; and AM General, which manufactures both the military and SUV versions of the Humvee. In New York, Rennert is known mainly for building the biggest and gaudiest mansion in the Hamptons, a 66,000 square foot palace with twenty-nine bedrooms, thirty bathrooms, and two bowling alleys.

When EPA finally slapped USMagnesium, then called MagCorp, with a lawsuit in 2000, Rennert crashed the company, filing for bankruptcy instead of paying the fines. Leavitt, a dutiful recipient of Rennert's campaign contributions, lambasted the EPA for unfairly harassing one of Utah's finest corporate citizens. The governor repeatedly cited the bullying of MagCorp as an example of EPA regulatory overkill.

But Rennert the raider didn't seem too ruffled by it all. He swiftly reorganized the company, still under his control, as USMagnesium and deftly evaded liability for his environmental crimes, much to the dismay of EPA regulators. "We thought that bankruptcy might be a trick they would pull," said EPA attorney Martin Hestmark.

But Rennert's revamped company faces new charges. The BLM, far from the greenest agency in the government, claims that USMagnesium has been systematically stealing minerals from federal lands in the Salt Lake Basin. Meanwhile, the EPA is attacking USMagnesium on another front, accusing the company of sluicing toxic waste into unlined ditches feeding into a 400-acre pond of chemical sludge. The EPA wants the waste treated before it is disposed. Rennert contends that his company is exempted from such trifles by 150-year-old federal mining laws. Leavitt apparently agrees.

As governor, Leavitt's pet project was the Legacy Highway, a $1.9 billion four-lane monstrosity designed to feed the every-expanding sprawl of Salt Lake City. There was a problem from the start: the Great Salt Lake and hundreds of wetlands that form one of the great shorebird nesting grounds in North America. Leavitt ignored pleas from environmentalists to avoid the wetlands and began paving them over in 1997, saying that he was fulfilling the Mormon vision of Brigham Young to transform the desert into a grinding economic engine. A lawsuit filed by environmental groups and the mayor of Salt Lake City followed, and eventually the conservative 10th Circuit Court of Appeals slapped an injunction on Leavitt's highway, saying it violated federal clean water and wetland rules—regulations that the governor is now responsible for enforcing as head of the EPA.

In 1991, an outbreak of whirling disease struck Utah's trout population, killing thousands of fish, including rare native cutthroat trout. Whirling disease is the piscine equivalent of AIDS and now threatens native fish throughout the Rocky Mountain region, from New Mexico to Montana. The source of the contamination in Utah was traced back to the Rock Creek Ranch, a commercial trout hatchery owned by the Leavitt family. At the time, Mike Leavitt was director of the hatchery that spread the deadly infection. (He later resigned and turned the daily operations of the trout factory over to his brother.) The Utah Department of Wildlife Resources launched an investigation and found that the Leavitt business was operating without the mandated inspections and far beyond the scope of their license.

"It must be pointed out that the inappropriate transfer of live fish from [Road Creek Ranch] facilities not having the necessary fish health approval resulted in the transfer of *Myxobolus cerebralis* to other facilities," the finding noted. "The other private growers in the area were checked and found to be negative."

The Attorney General's Office filed charges against the Leavitt fish enterprise, citing more than thirty violations of state regulations. Leavitt resigned his position as hatchery director and his company pleaded "No Contest" to the charges.

Allegations later surfaced in the media that the Leavitt's had intentionally dumped whirling disease-infected trout into six Utah rivers. The motive? To wipe out native populations of cutthroat and rainbow trout. By this time, Leavitt was governor, and the head of the Division of Wildlife Resources felt uncomfortable in pursuing the matter. "I have not been able to take some of the actions I would have liked out of fear that I would do the Governor more harm than good," wrote Ted Stewart, director of Utah's Department of Natural Resources in 1996.

Stewart had ample reasons for caution. In 1994, Leavitt purged ten biologists in Utah's Department of Wildlife Resources, who had been holding up mining and logging plans because of concerns over rare wildlife. "I blame the political hacks from the governor on down," biologist Craig Miya told *High Country News* a few days after being fired. "They've gutted the agency for doing our jobs too damn well."

According to Todd Wilkinson's excellent book, *Science Under Siege*, the replacement biologists were warned "to refrain from identifying endangered species."

Even some corporations view Leavitt with contempt. In early 2003, the Outdoor Recreation Industry Association threatened to move its annual trade show out of Utah in protest of Leavitt's secret deal with Interior Secretary Gale Norton which prevented the BLM from designating any new wilderness study areas on federal land in Utah. The move opens up 6 million acres of roadless land to off-road vehicles, mining and oil leasing.

In April of that same year, Norton and Leavitt sealed another backroom deal, which Utah greens dubbed the "pave the parks" scam. Under this novel agreement, old hiking trails and wagon roads through national parks, wildlife refuges, and forests will now, through the magic of bureaucratic redesignation, be considered "constructed highways" and open to paving and attendant development. Leavitt loves his roads.

Although Leavitt frequently derides the DC elites, he does enjoy backing from a cadre of longtime Beltway insiders, headlined by *Washington Post* columnist David Broder. The increasingly addled Broder, who lately put George W. Bush on an intellectual par with FDR, anointed Leavitt as an energetic middle-grounder, although Broder admitted that he knew next to nothing about his environmental record in Utah. Nothing excites Broder, who describes himself "an unabashed Leavitt fan," like the middle-ground, even when the middle ground is chocked with dioxins and PCBs. Broder declined to disclose the level of cancer deaths he would find acceptable as a judicious act of political statesmanship.

Then there's Hillary Clinton. The senator from New York brayed to the press about the vile nature of Leavitt's record on the environment. She vowed to filibuster his nomination. Then only weeks later Clinton, and nearly every other Democrat in the senate, voted to confirm him as the new EPA director.

The fix was in.

SALT LAKE CITY.

Power, Profits and Extinction:
Killing Salmon with Paul O'Neill

PAUL O'NEILL, BUSH'S SECRETARY OF THE TREASURY, IS AN UNLIKELY apostle for the crusade to combat global warming. But for the past couple of years the former corporate executive has been preaching the virtues of moving away from fossil fuels. In 1998, while head of aluminum giant Alcoa, O'Neill gave a speech to the aluminum industry's trade association in which he named what he believed to be the world's two most pressing problems. "One is nuclear holocaust," he said. "The second is environmental: specifically, the issue of global climate change and the potential of global warming." O'Neill handed out copies of his 1998 speech at Bush's first cabinet meeting.

O'Neill, who just called for the abolition of the corporate income tax, is not an altruistic green. For more than a decade he ran one of the world's most rapacious timber giants, International Paper. However, he's a financial opportunist. While helming Alcoa, O'Neill correctly devined that new clean air rules could help the aluminum makers, which stood to profit if Detroit was forced to switch to lighter weight cars made with more aluminum.

More deviously, O'Neill also foresaw the possibility of making a killing by getting in on the front end of the new energy market, which he did for Alcoa, the company that he ran for a decade. In the process, he made himself a bundle of money.

Aluminum companies are the biggest energy hogs in the Pacific Northwest. The aluminum industry was lured to the Columbia River basin during the manufacturing frenzy of World War II, where it was given cheap federal power for arms manufacturing. But aluminum making is an incredibly inefficient industry. Even at current market rates, the Northwest Energy Coalition estimates that it takes anywhere from $2 to $5 worth of electricity to produce a single pound of aluminum, which then sells for only 70 cents.

These companies could never make it on their own, thus they turned to the Bonneville Power Administration (BPA) for help. BPA is the federal agency based in Portland, Oregon, which markets the hydropower from the federally operated dams in the Columbia River system and provides 46 percent of the electricity for Oregon, Washington, Idaho, and western Montana. It deals away 102 megawatts of power every day. In the past, BPA has sold the power at only the cost of generation with no mark up—one of the reasons that the Pacific Northwest has enjoyed the cheapest electric rates in the country, about $25 per megawatt hour. But the cheap power isn't shared equally. The biggest power gluttons, namely the aluminum smelters, get the lowest rates. These smelters buy 2,000 megawatts of power each day from BPA.

But even these below-market rates weren't enough to satiate Alcoa. In 1996, the aluminum companies convinced the Clinton administration to give them so-called remarketing rights that would allow them to purchase subsidized power from BPA then resell the power at market rates.

When energy prices surged in May of 2000 and California felt its first power crunch in decades, utilities scrambled to find new power at nearly any price. "Oregonians always feared that Californians would come for our water," says Larry Tuttle, director of the Portland-based Citizens for Environmental Equity. "But few realized that the first raid would be on water-power."

Because of these changes in contracts, the big companies were primed to cash in on California's misery. Thus, the aluminum companies promptly idled their plants, sent thousands of workers home and sold their subsidized power to California to capitalize on the skyrocketing rates. The profits are staggering. The aluminum companies have taken power that they bought for about $25 a megawatt hour and sold it on the wholesale market for between $200 and $1,000 a megawatt hour.

In 2002 alone, Alcoa made more than $250 million on BPA subsidized "load curtailments" designed to redirect power to California.

After being tapped as treasury secretary, Paul O'Neill chose not to immediately divest himself of $90 million in share and stock options in Alcoa. When asked if this presented a conflict of interest, O'Neill told *Meet the Press* that, "The ethics department lawyers said they thought it was OK for me to maintain these shares. You know, I can't imagine that, as treasury secretary, I'm going to have decisions come before me that have anything to do with this."

Ethical questions aside, it was a shrewd business move. Alcoa's first quarter earnings for 2001 were a company record $404 million—far surpassing Wall Street's expectations and $57 million more than the previous year. Since most of the company's plants had been idled, much of the windfall can be attributed to the remarketing of its federal power. Alcoa's stock rose by more than 7 percent during the same period, meaning that O'Neill's bankroll increased by $6 million.

And Alcoa's far from alone. According to a report by the Northwest congressional delegation, the aluminum companies Kaiser, Goldendale Northwest, and Columbia Falls—all with smelters in the Northwest—have profited the most from the resale of BPA power. Kaiser netted $426 million; Goldendale Northwest, $344 million; and Columbia Falls, $292 million according to the report, which analyzed data supplied by BPA.

Kaiser's refusal to share its unused power with the federal agency has put the BPA in the position of buying back power for up to twenty-two times more than it cost to produce it. Kaiser is controlled by the modern day robber baron Charles Hurwitz, the butcher of the California redwoods. In a nasty labor dispute, Kaiser had locked out workers at most of its plants at the same time as it was raking in millions from the resale of federal power. Typically, Kaiser is blissfully unrepentant about its profit-making off the energy crisis. "We are making significant revenue here," Peter Forsyth, Kaiser's vice-president for Northwest Regional Affairs, gloated. "Why give it up?"

Altogether these so-called Direct Service Industries have reaped approximately $1.7 billion off these remarketed power deals. And remember the rationale behind giving these companies preferential rates was that aluminum companies helped to industrialize the West and provide high-paying jobs in rural areas.

The prolonged drought that has gripped the Pacific Northwest for nearly five years has only compounded the problems. For much of 2001, for example, Los Angeles had received more rainfall than Seattle. Meanwhile, Portland was twelve inches short of its normal rainfall level and counting. The snowpack in the Northwest, which feeds the Columbia River system, was just 53 percent of normal, just shy of the all-time low of 1977. Run-off levels were also the second lowest in seventy-two years and streamflows were the third worst ever. The situation remains dire.

At the same time, the Pacific Northwest faces an 8,000-megawatt power deficit. "We are becoming increasingly concerned that this may be a long-term crisis," confessed Steve Wright, acting administrator for the BPA. "Meanwhile, Canadian reservoirs, which store half the Columbia basin's water, remain extremely low, which means we could start next year with less than a full tank."

With BPA short of power because of the drought, it was forced to go back to those same companies and at astronomical rates, buy back the power it just sold them for the cost of generation. As a result, the BPA depleted its coffers and faced bankruptcy.

While the big corporations and executives like O'Neill and Hurwitz made a killing, residential consumers were hit with blackouts, ruined salmon streams, and the prospect of rate increases of between 50 to 250 percent over current costs. There's a direct relationship. According to Oregon Congressman Peter Defazio, for every 100 megawatts of power BPA has to purchase to service the big aluminum companies, rates for other Northwest consumers increase by 10 percent.

The timing of all this couldn't have been worse for the salmon stocks that once ran the Columbia watershed in numbers seen nowhere else on earth, but which now teeter at the edge of extinction. The eight hydropower dams on the lower Snake and Columbia Rivers block passage to spawning grounds for migratory salmon and the migration to the ocean of young salmon and steelhead. Environmentalists, Indian tribes and most fish biologists believe that for the salmon to survive many of these dams will have to come down. But the Clinton administration decided not to anger the aluminum industry and instead opted for an "aggressive nonbreach strategy." The cornerstone of this approach was a plan to require the dam operators to increase the flow of water through the spillways, hoping to flush juvenile salmon safely downstream. The Bush administration followed up by deciding that the demand for increased power production trumped the needs of the salmon for better flows. Instead of flowing through fish passages, nearly all of the Columbia River water is being channeled into the giant hyrdoturbines.

The number of Snake River chinook, an endangered species, heading toward the ocean in 2001 was the third lowest on record. The dams are bound by court orders and a salmon recovery plan to provide enough spillwater to flush migrating salmon downstream. To circumvent this legal roadblock, the Bush administration, at the behest of Paul O'Neill, declared a power emergency, which enabled the US Army Corps of Engineers, which operates the dams, to override the salmon-recovery plan and send all of the water into the hydroturbines, which slice and dice the salmon like a giant cuisinart.

How bad is it? At the turn of the century more than 16 million salmon and steelhead spawned in the Columbia River system. Today, there are fewer than a million, and more than 90 percent of those are hatchery bred fish. The wild Columbia salmon are nearly extinct. The National Marine Fisheries Service estimates that the salmon death toll will climb by 13.3 percent because of the lack of flows—that's more than 133,000 fish.

Instead of giving the fish the flows they need to survive, which most fish scientists conclude will ultimately require the breaching of several dams, the aluminum industry and the BPA want to collect the fish in the upper basin, put them into barges or big trucks, and transport them past the dams.

One study estimates that 85 percent of the Snake River salmon will conduct their journey to the Pacific mostly on barges. But the barged salmon fare worse than the ones that face decimation in the giant hydro turbines. "This is no way to recover salmon," says Ted Koch, a federal fish biologist in Boise, Idaho. "We are lying to ourselves if we think that we are recovering salmon stocks and meeting power needs, too." Other federal fish biologists concur that the BPA's power-generating schemes will doom the world's most prolific salmon river. "What's happening makes me extremely nervous," says Howard Schaller, a salmon expert with the US Fish and Wildlife Service. "It makes me think that this region doesn't have the will to do what it needs to recover these fish."

The aluminum companies say that they have given the BPA millions of dollars a year to mitigate the damage their operations do to salmon and steelhead. But much of that money simply goes to hatcheries, not to save wild fish or their habitat. And, according to documents unearthed by environmental economist Karyn Moscowitz, the BPA spends more than $4.4 million every year on the Columbia Basin Law Enforcement Program, a four-state police force that patrols the Columbia and Snake largely harassing Indians trying to assert their salmon-fishing rights. The $4 million pays for about thirty-five full-time officers and deluxe state-of-the-art equipment, including airplanes, radar equipment, guns, and numerous vehicles and horses. "In 1995, the force made 1,484 arrests, but tracked only down 139 illegally caught salmon," says Moscowitz. "At a total of $3.6 million, BPA pays nearly $26,000 a fish for this program."

Peter DeFazio, however, advocates a plan that could aid both the salmon and Northwest power consumers. The congressman argues that the BPA must be forced to sever its contracts with the aluminum companies and reroute that power to residential consumers and provide fish. He pins much of the blame for the current crisis on the 1992 Energy Act, a federal deregulation bill fostered the freewheeling marketing of federally generated power. Defazio, one of only sixty house members to vote against the deregulation bill, has introduced legislation introduced to revoke the deregulation provision of the 1992 Energy Act and re-regulate the energy industry.

"These have been dark days for Californians, but an extremely profitable times for a few giant power marketers," said DeFazio. "Congress made a colossal mistake in allowing the deregulation of wholesale production and distribution of energy. It eliminated the mandate that generators serve the public and provide stable, affordable, and reliable at-cost power. We were left with private power buccaneers capitalizing on the energy crisis while we struggle to conserve, suffer from lost jobs, and brace for the lights to go out in our area. I continue to support regional energy price caps for a short-term solution, but I think we need an aggressive solution for the long run. We need to return to a regulated energy market, with stable, reliable, cost-based power."

The Rise and Fall of Richard Pombo

THE BANNER STRETCHED ACROSS THE ENTRANCE TO THE CROBAR—A trendy New York nightclub—proclaimed, "Welcome to the Pombo-Palooza." At the door, members of the Rockettes handed out cowboy hats to the A-list of invited guests. Inside, a model clad in rhinestone hot pants and a cleavage-enhancing top that might have chastened a Hooters waitress rode a mechanical bull. On the stage, the Charlie Daniels Band cut loose with fiddle-driven Southern funk as lobbyists and lawyers, politicians and tycoons danced the two-step and drank iridescent blue martinis.

Such was the scene in 2003 at Congressman Rick Pombo's coming out party. The young legislator from Tracy, California had just been appointed the new chairman of the House Resources Committee. At forty-two, he was the youngest chairman on Capitol Hill. George W. Bush couldn't attend the hoedown but he sent a herogram congratulating the congressman he calls "Marlboro Man."

That night money flowed faster than champagne. Before Charlie Daniels had finished his first set, Pombo's campaign war chest had been fattened by more than $250,000, courtesy of an assortment of real estate barons, oil and mining company executives, timber lobbyists, and casino operators. Many of these contributors would turn out to be the cream of lobbyist Jack Abramoff's clientele. (Abramoff now faces many years in prison for his corrupt dealings.) And that was just their opening bid. Over the next two and half years, Pombo's political accounts would be fattened by an additional $2 million from an ever-expanding retinue of lobbyists, real estate barons, and corporate PACs.

The arc of Richard Pombo's career is an unlikely success story. He is a college dropout from a dusty ranching town in California's Central Valley. He showed no particular flair for politics during his early days and, when given the chance, nearly bankrupted the family dairy ranch. Politics was a last resort, and even in this arena Pombo's future seemed uncertain: he was not a particularly gifted public speaker, nor possessed of an especially engaging personality.

Pombo likes to describe himself as a rancher. He strutted into congressional hearings in cowboy boots and a Stetson. He owns a ranch, but spends less time on it than Bush does clearing sagebrush in Crawford. Pombo did upload photos of himself on his website constructing a pink barn for his children's pet pigs over a Christmas break.

Pombo used to sport a thin *Brokeback Mountain* moustache. These days he brandishes a manly goatee. The new growth was detected shortly after the movie premiered.

Western myths aside, the Pombo family didn't make their fortune selling milk from their small herd of dairy cows. The Pombos got rich by buying up ranchlands and subdividing them into ranchettes for Bay Area commuters. As a member of congress, Pombo pushed for freeway projects that caused the value of properties owned by his family to soar.

Some thought that young Richard might get a job selling real estate for his uncle, who owned one of the largest brokerages in the Central Valley. But Pombo never passed the real estate exam.

Politically, however, his uncle proved to be a huge help. The red and white Pombo real estate signs are ubiquitous across the congressional district. Thus, Rick Pombo, a tubby and slick-haired man of Portuguese descent, enjoyed huge name recognition before he ever considered running for office.

Pombo has spun various tales about the event that prompted him to run for Congress. For years he claimed that he was enraged by plans to turn an abandoned railroad near his family ranch into a bicycle trail which—he fumed—would lead to the entire valley being designated a "viewshed" where development would be restricted. Later, Pombo said he ran for office because the family ranch had been designated "critical habitat" for the San Joaquin kit fox, the world's smallest wild canid and an endangered species.

Both stories are embellished to the point of fantasy. Pombo's ranch was never at risk from either action. The allegation about the kit fox driving his family from their homestead is particularly outlandish, since the feds have never designated critical habitat for the tiny vulpine. Real ranchers look kindly on the kit fox, since it feeds almost exclusively on rodents regarded as crop pests. In any event, the habitat designation wouldn't have restricted ranching operations, but developments. And, indeed, that's precisely what ticked off Pombo. He was forced to pay $5,137 into a regional conservation fund as an impact fee for houses he built on his "ranch." The houses went up; kit fox populations went down.

In 1992 Pombo won his seat in Congress after narrowly defeating Democrat Patty Garamendi, daughter of the hugely unpopular state insurance commissioner John Garamendi.

In 1996, Pombo published a book-length screed against the Endangered Species Act and environmentalists. Titled *This Land is Your Land*, the book was ghost written by rightwing columnist Joseph Farrah. Woody Guthrie wouldn't recognize many of the sentiments set forth in the Pombo-Farrah tract, which called for the dismantling of the Endangered Species Act and disposal of public lands to private interests. Though not a bestseller, the book acquired the allure of a Gnostic gospel among the "Wise Use" crowd, whose concept of wise use derives from God's commandment to Adam in the book of Genesis to pillage the earth's natural resources as he thinks fit. The book put Pombo on the ledger as an apex berserker in what Ron Arnold, the P.T. Barnum of the Wise Users, has billed as the War Against the Greens.

But the Wise Use Movement's backing of Pombo certainly doesn't explain his rise to power. The Wise Users have had their congressional champions in the past, notably Helen Chenoweth, of Idaho. But they've tended to labor in obscurity, deemed as coarse Visigoths even in their own party. For his first few years, Pombo toiled in a similar kind of isolation. His speeches at property rights confabs denouncing Bruce Babbitt as an agent of the United Nations and the reintroduction of wolves to Yellowstone as an example of "political paganism" garnered only the occasional comical notice in the gossip pages of the *Washington Post* and *Los Angeles Times*. Pombo's annual introduction of bills to dismantle the Endangered Species Act rarely attracted more than a few dozen co-sponsors and usually went extinct without a hearing.

In Bushtime, though, Pombo got on a roll. His McCarthyesque hearings on the dangers of "eco-terrorism," where environmentalists were hauled up before the House Resources Committee and forced to endure harangues from both Democrats and Republicans, culminated in the FBI's arrest of nearly a dozen environmental activists on charges of sabotage, conspiracy, and arson. Rod Coronado, an editor of the *Earth First! Journal* and probably the most famous animal rights activist in North America, was also arrested for giving a speech in 2003 at UC San Diego where he demonstrated how to make and use a Molotov cocktail.

Pombo's scheme to sell off millions of acres of federal forest and range lands, once considered political poison, was adopted by the Bush administration in the fall of 2006, with a proposal to dispose of 200,000 acres of public land to mining and timber companies and real estate speculators, all in the name of funding rural schools.

In 2005, Pombo came close to realizing his wildest dream when the House of Representatives passed his bill to annihilate the Endangered Species Act by a hefty margin of 229 to 193. Soon after this mighty triumph, the *Washington Times* announced the onset of "Pombomania" among young Republican ultras.

Ironically, Pombomania probably owed more to his enemies than to the shock troops of the property rights movement. Plucking bellicose quotes from his book and his stump speeches, the Sierra Club turned Pombo into the personification of environmental villainy. In dozens of mass fundraising appeals, Pombo was presented as the new James Watt, the dark agent of the looting of the public estate. Pombo glories in his role. "I'm their bogeyman," Pombo gloats. "They need me to raise money."

The Sierra Club's threat inflation of Pombo almost certainly factored into Tom DeLay's decision to catapult the congressman over the heads of more senior members to the chair of the Resources Committee, one of the most prized seats in Congress.

Pombo also got help from the Democrats. His rewrite of the Endangered Species Act, which eliminates the designation of "critical habitat" for listed species, sets in legal stone many of the practices implemented administratively by his former nemesis Bruce Babbitt when he served as Clinton's Interior Secretary.

In Clintontime, Babbitt simply refused to designate critical habitat for dozens of at-risk animals and plants, forcing environmental groups into court to compel the Fish and Wildlife Service to live up to its legal obligations. The suits were slow in coming while Clinton was in office, but they began to proliferate after Bush came to power.

Bush and Pombo used those lawsuits, most of which resulted in favorable verdicts for the greens, to charge that the law was outdated and was being exploited by militant environmentalists and litigation-happy lawyers. The Bush-Pombo team got some unexpected help from one of the liberal lions of the House, George Miller, the former chair of the House Natural Resources Committee. In the summer of 2006, Miller pronounced that the law needed to be reworked.

"There is a recognition that the current critical habitat arrangement doesn't work for a whole host of reasons," said Miller. "There are some in the environmental community who think the answer is just no to any change, and I think that's a problem."

At those words from a politician once regarded by greens as the most enlightened member of the House, critical habitat went extinct without a fight. There were warning signs of Miller's impending collapse. Shortly after the Democrats lost control of the House, Miller gave up his leadership position on the Resources committee. Friends said he was too tired to fight the likes of Don Young and Pombo.

Another congressional Democrat, Dennis Cardoza, Representative from California's 18th District, worked closely with Pombo to craft his assault on ESA—an assault that includes a provision that is likely to bankrupt the US Treasury faster than Halliburton's Iraq contracts. Pombo's bill instructed the federal government to pay off developers for not violating the law. Under this rule, the feds would have to compensate property owners for value of a "proposed use" for land inhabited by endangered species. It's a shakedown provision. A Central Valley rancher could propose to build a casino in kit fox habitat, and the feds would be required to pay out millions to keep them from building it. Then the next year the same landowner could come back with new plans for a golf course and get another payoff.

Sound absurd? A similar law was passed by the voters of Oregon in 2004. The law was initially stuck down by a state court as unconstitutional, but a few months later the Oregon Supreme Court reinstated the statute, which virtually wipes out the state's vaunted land-use planning regulations.

Fortunately, Pombo's bill ran aground in the Senate, where Lincoln Chafee, the Republican from Rhode Island, has vowed to keep the Endangered Species Act from being "Pomboized." (It may be a coincidence but one of the only zoos in the country that maintains a kit fox exhibit is the Chafee Zoological Gardens in Fresno.)

Chafee stood up against his fellow Republican, but you didn't hear similar objections from California's senior Senator Dianne Feinstein. Feinstein and Pombo have worked closely over the years on everything from water policy in the Central Valley (more water for farms, less for salmon) and logging in the High Sierra near Lake Tahoe. The real estate caucus sticks together.

During his campaign, Pombo targeted other laws for obliteration in the coming few years. At the top of his hit list was the National Environmental Policy Act, the law that requires Environmental Impact Statements for all federal projects.

It was a dramatic run, but, alas, Pombo did not survive to witness the promised land. The ethical noose fatally tightened around his political career.

Back in the 1990s, Pombo made rich sport of attacking Hillary Clinton for her role in the Travelgate affair. But it turned out that Pombo's office had its own travel-related problems. Pombo's political Svengali was a man called Steven Ding, who had long served as his chief of staff. When Pombo landed the Resource Committee chair, he also made Ding chief staffer for the committee. Ding was double dipping, getting paid by both the committee and Pombo's office.

Ding lives in Stockton and traveled back to California from DC every week. The House Resources Committee picked up the tab. From 2003 through 2004, Ding billed the committee $87,000 in commuter charges. Some of those visits may not have been to see Mrs. Ding. Even though he had two positions with Pombo, Ding enjoyed enough free time to also hire himself out as a private consultant to corporations and lobbyists seeking his insider knowledge. In 2005, Ding earned $57,000 in outside consulting fees. On four occasions, the House Ethics Committee has cited Ding for low-balling or failing entirely to report such outside remunerations.

Ding wasn't alone though. He was merely traveling down a trail that was blazed by his boss. Each year Pombo's office spends nearly twice as much on travel as do the offices of the adjacent congressional districts. The biggest freeloader was Pombo himself.

In the summer of 2005, Pombo took his family on a two-week vacation, touring the national parks in a rented RV. He sent the $5,000 bill to the Resources Committee. When Rep. Ellen Tauscher questioned the reimbursement, Pombo said he was doing research. And perhaps he was. A few weeks after he returned from his grand tour, Pombo's office leaked a white paper to the *Washington Times* calling on the Bush administration to sell off a dozen national parks.

What about Pombo's wife, Annette, whose recipe for Apple-Walnut Crosscut Pie was the most popular page on the congressman's website? Surely, Annette's travel expenses shouldn't have been covered by the committee? It turns out that since 2001

Pombo has paid his wife and his brother at least $465,000 in consulting fees from his campaign fund.

This wasn't Pombo's first infraction. In 2004, he used office funds to pay for the printing and mailing of a flier to a nationwide list of property rights fanatics urging them to write letters in support of Bush's plan to allow snowmobilers to run amok in Yellowstone Park. The Ethics Committee ruled that the flier violated the rules on franking and slashed his mail budget. Later that year, Pombo gave all of the Republican staffers on the Resources Committee a paid vacation in October so they could disperse across the country to work in GOP election campaigns—another ethical foul.

In October 2005, the Center for Public Integrity reported that Pombo had taken two overseas junkets to New Zealand and Japan. Both trips were paid for by a group called the International Foundation for Conservation of Natural Resources, which receives funding from bioengineering firms such as Monsanto and also from pro-whaling interests. Pombo did not report the trip on his income tax form, though the IRS considers overseas junkets gifts on which taxes must be paid.

"I really have no idea what is going on with that foundation," said Pombo, when confronted with the report. "Obviously I will have my accountant check into this." Even by the high standards of congressional evasiveness, this was a spectacular bout of memory loss. Pombo was a founder of the International Foundation for Conservation of Natural Resources and served as its chairman until July of 2005.

Then there's the Jack Abramoff connection. Like Bush, Pombo pretended to have only the foggiest recollection of the beleaguered super lobbyist. "I think I met the guy a few times," Pombo chirped. "But he never stepped foot in my office. Never lobbied me about anything."

Unfortunately for Pombo, Abramoff left a distinct paper trail across Capital Hill, with much of the forensic evidence found in the chambers of the Resource Committee, where the business of his clients was so often decided. Duane Gibson, a former top staffer on the Resource Committee, left the committee to work in Abramoff's firm, where he represented mining companies and Indian tribes. Gibson helped Pombo draft a legislative rider that would have transferred thousands of acres of prime federal lands to mining companies. Three months before Pombo inserted the measure in the budget bill, Gibson hosted a $1,000-a-head fundraiser for the congressman.

In 2002, Pombo went to bat for Charles Hurwitz, owner of Maxxam and infamous looter of redwoods and of Savings & Loans. Pombo and Tom Delay intimidated federal regulators into dropping an investigation of Hurwitz's banking practices. Most of the legal footwork was done by Gibson, who later came under legal scrutiny by federal prosecutors. Hurwitz, of course, was a top contributor to Pombo's campaign war chest.

Republicans were so worried about Pombo's ethical dilemmas that they recruited an old war-horse to challenge him in the primary: Pete McCloskey. McCloskey is a former congressman and a sponsor of the original version of the Endangered Species Act. McCloskey called Pombo the "Duke Cunningham of the environment," a reference to the now imprisoned congressman from San Diego who memorialized his menu of bribes on his congressional stationery.

Pombo fended off McCloskey, but he couldn't overcome the changes in his district that he had done so much to facilitate, as more and more Bay Area commuters (and Democratic voters) moved onto subdivisions sprouting up on the old ranches and farms of the Central Valley. This merciless demographic did him in. Sprawl bites the hand that feeds it.

Rich Pombo frittered away one of the safest seats in the House. He might have had a better chance of surviving if he had shaved the goatee and returned to that suggestive moustache.

MODESTO.

Howard's End: How Dean Lost It

WE FIND OURSELVES ON THE ERODING DOWN SLOPE OF EMPIRE. THE titans have fallen. We are now ruled by minor princelings: Al Gore, George W. Bush, John Forbes Kerry, Howard Dean. These are the days of the dauphins.

A republic in name, we now rigidly follow the laws of political primogeniture. The slushy predictability of our current politics may well be our unraveling. The world awaits a change in fortune, betting on the collapse of the behemoth.

If this arthritic republic falls, it will crumble from within, like so many other over-extended empires of old. The cracks are already showing up, unmaskable fissures in the foundations. The signs are abundant everywhere for those who still know how to read: In our phony politics, in our outsourced economy, in our looted and poisoned environment, in our corporatized culture that offers us bikini-clad women eating worms for entertainment, in our rotting schools, our burgeoning prison industry, our turnstile hospitals, our irredeemable racism, our executioners' gibbets where the most grue-some of political rituals are still played out in hiding. We are anxious to shed blood, but we can't stand to see it flow. Yet another birthmark of our perverted puritanism.

Scott Fitzgerald, our most prescient writer, foretold it all in the novel he wanted to title *Under the Red White and Blue*. The great wheel of fortune has come full swing. The promise of the republic, the green light that lured so many to these forested shores, has been squandered. Worse: pilfered. The financial aristocrats—the villains Jefferson and Franklin warned against at the very birth of this nation—are more powerful than they have ever been. Jay Gould is a petty crook compared to the likes of Ken Lay and Dick Cheney. The rich are different. They crack things up and not only get away with it, but are glamorized and idolized for the damage they've done and the billions they've looted. We worship the beasts that devour us. The rest of us are left to scavenge the rubble. Our politics offer us false choices and few true champions.

Where is the resistance to this ruination?

Don't look to the powerbrokers of the Democratic Party. These days the creaky cura-tors of the American left paint its opponents as maniacal demons. Hitler is the reflexive metaphor for any Republican. All the corroded left seems to know is the politics of hysteria. The purpose of this ritualized threat inflation is to make the pallid offerings of the Democratic Party seem credible. But Bush is not a fanged creature out of Bosch. He is stupid and dull, a banal frat boy, more Arendt's Eichmann than Hitler. In the frank assessment of his former Treasury Secretary Paul O'Neill, the President is blind, apathetic, and mute; just a hearing aid shy of being our political version of Tommy, minus the power chords. Bush doesn't or can't read the morning papers or briefing books. Condi Rice, the gorgon of the NSC, spoon-feeds him what she feels he needs to know in small portions that can be easily regurgitated. The real work is done by the coterie of neo-cons that swirl round him: Cheney, Rumsfeld, Rove, Wolfowitz, and Scooter Libby. In medieval times the cretinous sons of the elites were sent packing to the priesthood. These days they run for president and everyone prays for the best.

So now we are presented with Howard Dean, the latest incarnation of a maverick progressive. He is, of course, neither. But you can't mention that in mixed company. The image of Dean the pugilistic populist has already been manufactured and implanted into the popular consciousness. And everyone plays along, from the press to Dean's fellow Democrats, who yelp that he is a dangerous outsider bent on smashing the delicate balance of the Clinton years. Even Karl Rove slithers across the screen hissing homilies about the authentic Dean.

To point out the obvious is to risk ridicule. And ours is a society that fears ridicule as a mortal sin. But Howard Dean is not as billed, by his supporters or his detractors. The big trouble with Howard is that beneath the frothy veneer he's pretty much just like all the rest. Only shorter.

A review of Howard Dean's career doesn't reveal a resume of unparalleled mendacity, although Dean is a gifted liar and craven politician untroubled by matters of conscience even when it means betraying friends and allies. No. The fragrance here is something more unappetizing. The smell of rot.

Dean is shown to be a run-of-the-mill and mundane governor out of the Democratic mainstream. Beneath the layers of greasepaint, the Dean Minstrelsy Show is a political re-run underwritten by the same old sponsors. Not of George McGovern, god forbid, but of the same neo-liberal troupe that has cloned Gore, Lieberman, Kerry & Kerrey, Edwards, Breaux, Dodd, and the Clintons. Of course, Bill Clinton was freighted with a tragic flaw, which at least made his tenure somewhat, if not redeemable, at least diverting, though the play went on much too long. Clinton could be hated. Dean, even in angry man mode, evokes only a dull throbbing of the cortex. This is what entropy feels like.

He is sour and surly; grouchy and privileged. Dean is the Democrats' Bob Dole, sans the flinty Kansan's sense of humor, war record, and Viagra-fortified erections. Howard Dean seems about as erotically-charged as Nixon.

Dean is a Yanqui, in the oldest and most disreputable sense of the term—a true scion of Wall Street and old money. That's one reason he was able to raise so much cash, so quickly on the Internet. He's the Amazon.com of presidential candidates: a lot of money poured in early for insubstantial returns.

Dean ascended to power in the most self-consciously progressive state in the republic. A word or two about Vermont: I live in Oregon. Vermont could be our little sister state—only more homogenous and more uptight. It is blindingly white, wealthy, and snugly cocooned from the fractious rhythms of the republic. Ralph Nader could be elected governor in the Green Mountain state. But Howard Dean is no Ralph Nader. Therein lies part of the truth about Dr. Dean.

* * *

Howard Dean was raised on Park Avenue, as the son of a Wall Street broker who co-founded the Dean/Whitter securities firm. As a youth, Dean spent his summers in East Hampton and attended elite private academies, including a stint at a boarding school in England. In 1967, Dean entered Yale. By all accounts, his tenure there was as unremarkable as that of George W. Bush. Unlike, say, Al Gore, then plotting the trajectory of his political career with Martin Peretz at Harvard, neither Dean nor Bush seem to have been particularly ambitious collegians.

Even at Yale in the late 60s, Dean was cautious, vaguely anti-war, and pro-civil rights. But he refused to align himself with any particular movements on campus, saying that he "instinctively distrusted ideologues." More likely, Dean knew that any kind of radical association might impede the business career he was planning to pursue.

After Yale, Dean joined his father on Wall Street. He tried his hand at stock trading for a couple of years, made a bundle, got bored, and then went to medical school. Dean graduated from Albert Einstein Medical School in 1978 and fled to Vermont to undertake his residency. There he met his future wife, Judith Steinberg. They soon married and opened a medical practice together in Shelburne, Vermont.

Soon Dean grew bored with medicine and began to dabble in politics. In 1982, he was elected to the Vermont House of Representatives. By all accounts, it was a tenure undistinguished by any major accomplishment. Yet, four years later he ran for the position of lieutenant governor and won. He was elected to three consecutive terms of this largely ceremonial position. Then fate intervened. On August 14, 1991, Vermont's governor, Robert Snelling, was felled by a fatal heart attack. Dean sped to Montpelier upon hearing the news and later that day he was sworn in as the new governor.

Dean's first major initiative as governor set the tone for his political career. The Vermont economy had been hobbled by recession and Democrats in the state legislature were pushing a modest tax increase for social programs. The tax increase seemed ready to pass, then Dean intervened, siding with the Republicans. Instead of raising taxes, Dean lowered them. It was a sign of things to come.

Dean governed Vermont from the middle right. He fetishized balance budgets, achieving the holy balance on the backs of the needy and the powerless. He pandered to the police, backing draconian drug laws and even lending support to the death penalty. Dean backed Monsanto against environmentalists, organic farmers, and consumers. He trumpeted his own welfare reform plan that was as miserly as anything put forward by Tommy Thompson. A friend of nuclear power, Dean conspired with New England's other nuclear governors to unload the region's radioactive waste on a small and impoverished Hispanic town in west Texas called Sierra Blanca. And on and on.

Early in his presidential campaign, Dean's own mother ridiculed his presidential aspirations as "preposterous." Like George W., Dean was never his mother's favorite child, which may explain his tendency to throw political tantrums. These are the guys you really have to watch like a hawk.

After Dean vaulted to the front of a lethargic and uninspiring pack of Democratic competitors, he began making mistakes. It's so much easier to lope along as the underdog. Dean deadened much of his rustic appeal when he began to court the endorsements of party insiders, and losers at that: Al Gore, Jimmy Carter, Bill Bradley, Tom Harkin.

Then Dean famously solicited the votes of working class southern rednecks, but he offered them nothing except a kind of thinly-coded race-baiting. Dean lacks even the most basic rhetorical lingo to address the traumatic economic dislocations of the Bush/Clinton/Bush era. His economic agenda is scavenged from the wreckage of Paul Tsongas and Bill Bradley, offering only a kind of stern Yankee paternalism.

Aside from the Iraq war, the Dean schema is fetchingly elitist, gliding silently over the battered preterite of American society. Dr. Dean pushes policies sharply attuned to the appeasement of middle class anxieties, the nervy triangulated center. Hence the familiar concerns about crime, drugs, health care costs (as opposed to universal care), education, budget deficits. But with Dean the articulation of these centrist obsessions comes out sounding brittle and vaguely threatening. Clintonism shorn of empathy.

It's doubtful that many of Dean's former patients lament the fact that he abandoned his medical practice for politics. He has a stern bedside manner. This is a man, unlike Bill Clinton, who displays little compassion for those in pain. Take medical pot. Despite Dean's confession of youthful encounters with the divine weed, the doctor opposes giving cancer and AIDS patients the right to smoke marijuana to ease their suffering. His health care plan is almost as miserly, a brand of Hillary-lite.

* * *

Then came Iowa. First Dean lost the caucuses, then he lost his mind. I'm not talking about his Dexedrine-infused outburst following his defeat in the caucuses, an election that is rigged by party bigwigs to tilt toward establishment favorites like John Kerry and John Edwards.

Of course, Dean made big mistakes. Fatal ones. For starters, he attacked Dick Gephardt in Iowa. Bad move. Dean didn't have to win Iowa outright. If Dean finished second to Gephardt, he would have still been perceived as the winner. After all, Iowa was Gephardt's backyard. But Dean got greedy. He wanted a sweep. He was baited into making a mortally false move. Dean dropped his mask, revealing an unappetizing visage. People didn't like it. In the meantime, the affections of the voters drifted over to Kerry and Edwards.

After Iowa, the DNC powerbrokers snickered at the antics of the interloper they called "Dizzy Dean." The Dean threat was never ideological. He is a pure neo-liberal. Rather, it came from the fact that Dean didn't owe the Clinton establishment anything. He raised his own money from the mysterious precincts of the virtual world. He was intemperate, perhaps ungovernable.

Soon the carrion birds came circling, stripping plank after plank of his campaign themes as if he were the flayed corpse of Marsyas. The problem for Kerry and Clark and Edwards was that they were manufactured candidates, as engineered as a Monsanto soybean. The vitality of Dean's campaign pulsed from its very unpredictability. He is an eccentric centrist, given to unscripted outbursts like a Prozac-taker gone off his meds.

The plantation masters of the party fear nothing more than unpredictability. That's one reason why they were so desperate to, as one senior Democratic congressman put it, "McGovern" him.

Yet, the election and its aftermath proved Dean to be a hollow man. Aside from Joe Trippi's innovative campaign strategy and Dean's hammering of Bush on the Iraq war, he did not have much to offer. Dean didn't know how to speak to working people, had little to say to greens, and insulted blacks. Dean's anger seemed more shrill than authentic, and in the end, he didn't know how to fight. Finally, Dean even surrendered his own signature issue, admitting that the Iraq war wasn't really a paramount concern to Democratic voters. Sad, but true.

Then there was the pitiful spectacle of Dean dragging his wife, Judith, across the snowy cornfields and into the television studios. You could see how uncomfortable she was at each venue. There was a look of disgust on her face as she was pigeonholed into the role of dutiful wife by her own desperate husband and by hypocritical news celebrities like the disgusting Dianne Sawyer (who had a dalliance with Henry Kissinger when she was a debutante in the Nixon White House). Dean lost the election (and his credibility) right there.

Then it went straight downhill. Rarely has a front-running campaign, freighted with cash and an army of devoted volunteers, capsized so suddenly with so little provocation and not even the whiff scandal. The dull demise of Howard Dean makes one long for the salacious pleasures of Gary Hart, Donna Rice, and the Monkey Business.

There were more problems. His TV ads were inept. Joe Trippi got too much credit for building the Dean phenomenon and not enough blame for orchestrating a terrible series of commercials, which turned off voters across the nation. Trippi walked away from the wreckage with millions for his firm and acted as if his fingerprints weren't on the carnage.

Then Dean drove the final nail into his coffin by replacing Trippi with Roy Neel. Neel is a telecom lobbyist who exploited his cachet with the Clinton White House to maneuver the atrocious Telecommunications Act through congress in 1996, one of the greatest corporate giveaways of the Clinton/Gore era. Neel is the same Beltway savant who advised Gore not to contest his own election. Neel's function wasn't to resuscitate Dean's campaign but to ease it into extinction, limiting the damage to the Democratic Party and, if he could, rehabbing Dean's reputation among party loyalists. Dean went along with it all like a beaten puppy. The man has no pride.

By February 18th, it was all over. The plug was pulled on the Dean campaign. Having burned through money faster than Michael Jackson goes through lawyers, Dean found himself deep in debt. To bail his way out, Dean set up Democracy for America, a virtual think tank to keep the virtual Deaniacs from drifting into Naderland. It even won the endorsement of DNC kingpin Terry McAuliffe. The circle had been squared.

In mid-May, Howard Dean joined John Kerry for a strange campaign swing through the Pacific Northwest. They held hands, played hearts on the campaign bus, gushered effusions of praise on each other. There was no unsettling talk of the Iraq war or the PATRIOT Act or the sadistic horrors of Abu Ghraib. Instead, the candidate purred to the press about a "Kerry and Dean" administration. Dean smiled, half way to paying off his staggering campaign debts. Since Dean surrendered his run for the nomination, 354 US troops and more than 5,000 Iraqis had perished. Kerry vowed to keep the troops in Iraq for another four years. And the putative anti-war candidate said nothing about it. Perhaps Dean is future presidential material after all.

Suicide Right on the Stage:
The Demise of the Green Party

"Ignorance of remote causes disposeth men to attribute all events to the causes immediate and instrumental: for these are all the causes they perceive." — Thomas Hobbes, *Leviathan* (1651)

S O THIS IS WHAT ALTERNATIVE POLITICS IN AMERICA HAS DEGENERATED to: Pat LaMarche, the newly minted vice-presidential candidate of the Green Party, has announced that she might not even vote for herself in the fall elections. The Greens, always a skittish bunch, are so traumatized by the specter of Bush and Cheney that they've offered up their own party—born out of rage at decades of betrayal by Democrats from Carter to Clinton—as a kind of private contractor for the benefit of those very same Democratic Party power brokers.

Take a close look at what LaMarche, a not-ready-for-primetime radio "personality," had to say to her hometown newspaper in Maine only days after winning the nomination in Milwaukee.

"If the race is tight, I'll vote for Kerry," LaMarche said. "I love my country. But we should ask them that, because if Dick Cheney loved his country, he wouldn't be voting for himself."

This is the sound a political party makes as it commits suicide.

LaMarche's running mate, David Cobb, is no better. The obscure lawyer from Texas is a dull and spiritless candidate, handled by some truly unsavory advisors. In action, Cobb functions as a kind of bland political zombie from a Roger Corman flick, lumbering across the progressive landscape from Oregon to Wisconsin and back again, to the tune of his liberal political masters. The tune? The familiar refrain of "Anybody But Bush."

Bland, yes, but it worked, thanks to the likes of Medea Benjamin and the preposterous Ted Glick. At their recent convention in Milwaukee, the Green Party, heavily infiltrated by Democratic Party operatives, rejected the ticket of Ralph Nader and Peter Camejo in favor of the hollow campaign of Cobb and LaMarche.

This didn't harm Nader much. Indeed, it may liberate him. Free of the Green Party's encyclopedic platform, Nader could distill the themes of his campaign to the most potent elements (war, jobs, corruption, and the environment) and, unburdened by the concern of party building, Nader could focus his efforts only on the battleground states, where Kerry must either confront Nader's issues or lose the election. It's as simple as that.

The fatal damage in Milwaukee was done to the Green Party itself, where Cobb and his cohort sabotaged the aspirations of thousands of Greens who had labored for more than a decade to build their party into a national political force capable of winning a few seats here and there and, even more importantly, defeating Democrats who behave like Republicans (see: Al Gore). The fruits of all that intense grassroots organizing were destroyed in an instant.

But behold: the rebuffed Nader continued to poll nearly 6 percent without the Green Party behind him. Yet, you can't discern Cobb's numbers with an electron microscope. Of course, the bizarre irony is that's precisely the way Cobb and his backers want it.

So, the Greens have succeeded in doing what seemed impossible only months ago: they've made the quixotic campaign of Dennis Kucinich, which still chugs along claiming micro-victory after micro-victory long after the close of the primaries (indeed there have been more victories after the polls closed than before), seem like a credible political endeavor. Of course, Cobb and Kucinich share the same objective function: to lure progressives away from Nader and back into the charnel house of the Democratic Party.

But at least Kucinich remained a Democrat. Cobb and LaMarche were supposedly leaders of a political party that formed not in opposition to Republicans, but from outrage at the rightward drift of the Democratic Party. Apparently, the Green Party has not only lost its mind, it's lost its entire central nervous system, including the spine. Especially its spine. They've surrendered to the politics of fear. And once the white flag is raised there's little chance of recovering the ground you've given up.

Always nearly immobilized by an asphyxiating devotion to political correctness, the Green Party has now taken this obsession to its logical extreme by nominating a pair of political invertebrates to the top of its ticket. Under the false banner of the Cobb/Lamarche campaign, the Green Party is instructing its members to vote for its candidates only in states where their vote doesn't matter. This is the so-called safe state strategy.

Safe? Safe for whom? Not for Afghan or Iraqi citizens. Not for US troops. Not for the detainees at Gitmo, Bagram, or Abu Ghraib. Not for migrant farm laborers or steelworkers. Not for the welfare mother or the two million souls rotting in American prisons. Not for the spotted owl, the streams of Appalachia, or the rainforests of Alaska. Not for the residents of Cancer Alley or the peasants of Colombia or teen age girls slaving away in Nike's toxic Indonesia sneaker mills. Not for the Palestinians, the Lakota of Pine Ridge, or elementary school students from the hard streets of Oakland. Not for the hopeless denizens of death row or three strikers in for life for a gram of crack or gays hoping to unite in marriage or even cancer patients seeking simple herbal relief from excruciating pain.

A crucial player in this unsavory affair was Medea Benjamin, the diva of Global Exchange. In rationalizing her decisive vote backing the Cobb/Lamarche ticket, Benjamin emitted this profundity: "John Kerry is not George Bush." Apparently, that tiny sliver of genetic variation is all it comes down to these days.

Yes, Medea, you're right. Kerry is simply Kerry, a bona fide war criminal, with a record of political infamy that is just as malodorous as that of George Bush—only it's longer. Over the past four years, Kerry has been complicit in the enactment of some of Bush's most disgusting policies. Indeed, these days Kerry offers himself up mainly as a more competent manager of the Bush agenda, a steadier hand on the helm of the Empire.

Kerry stands unapologetically for nearly every issue that caused the Greens to bolt the Democratic Party. He was present at the founding of the Democratic Leadership Council, the claque of neo-liberals that seeks to purge the Democratic Party of every last vestige of progressivism and reshape it as a hawkish and pro-business party with a soft spot for abortion—essentially, a stingier version of the Rockefeller Republicans.

Kerry enthusiastically backed both of Bush's wars and now, at the very moment Bush is signaling a desire to retreat, the senator is calling for 25,000 new troops to be sent to Iraq, where under his plan the US military will remain entrenched for at least the next four years.

Kerry supported the PATRIOT Act without reservation or even much contemplation. Lest you conclude that this was a momentary aberration sparked by the post-9/11 hysteria, consider the fact that Kerry also voted for the two Clinton-era predecessors to the PATRIOT Act, the 1994 Crime Bill and the 1996 CounterTerrorism and Effective Death Penalty Act, which were just as bad.

Although he regularly hams it up in photo-ops with the barons of big labor, Kerry voted for NAFTA, the WTO and virtually every other job-slashing trade pact that has come before the senate. Kerry, who has courted and won the endorsement of nearly every police association in the nation, regularly calls for putting another 100,000 cops on the streets and even tougher criminal sanctions for victimless crimes. He refused to reconsider his fervid support for the insane war on drug users, which has destroyed families and clogged our prisons with more than 2 million people, many of them young black men, whom the draconian drug laws specifically target without mercy. Kerry backs the racist death penalty and minimum mandatory sentences. And so it goes.

The Congressional Black Caucus jeered Ralph Nader when he spoke to them about his campaign, a bizarre reception for a man who has been a tireless advocate for civil rights and poor people. If this group of legislators actually cared about the welfare of their constituents, instead of merely their sinecure within the party, they would hire the twin Dominatrixes of Abu Ghraib, Lynddie England and Sabrina Harman, to clip a dog leash on Kerry (who disgustingly said he'd like to become the second black president) and interrogate him about his dreadful record on civil rights when he comes calling seeking their support. Of course, they won't. The Congressional Black Caucus is perhaps the only political conclave with clout as vaporous as the Greens.

Kerry, and his top advisor Rand Beers (a veteran of the Clinton and Bush National Security Council), crafted Plan Colombia, the brutal and toxic war on Andean peasants, waged for the benefit of oil companies under the phony rubric of drug eradication. His scrawny energy plan, devoid of any real emphasis on conservation or solar power, calls for more offshore oil leasing, widespread natural gas drilling, transcontinental pipelines, and strip-mining for coal. His deficit-fixated economic policy, scripted by Wall Street bond tycoon Robert Rubin, is even more austere than Bill Clinton's.

Like Joe Lieberman, Kerry markets himself as a cultural prude, regularly chiding teens about the kind of clothes they wear, the music they listen to, and the movies they watch. But even Lieberman didn't go so far as to support the censorious Communications Decency Act. Kerry did. Fortunately, even the Bush Supreme Court had the sense to strike the law down, ruling that it trampled across the First Amendment.

All of this is standard fare for contemporary Democrats. But Kerry always goes the extra mile. The senator cast a crucial vote for Clinton's wretched bill to dismantle welfare for poor mothers and their children and, despite mounting evidence to the contrary, he continues to hail the mean-spirited measure as a tremendous success.

This is merely a précis of the grim resumé of the man the Green Party now supports through the proxy candidacy of David Cobb. The message of the Cobb campaign is: a vote for Cobb is a vote for Kerry. Translation: a vote for Cobb is a vote for war, and everything that goes along with it.

It's also a vote for political self-annihilation. David Cobb is the Jim Jones of the Green Party. Form a line and pass the Kool-Aid.

Risk-free voting? Don't bet your life on it.

Gale Norton in Slacks: Inside Dirk Kempthorne's Closet

A FTER SERVING FOR FIVE YEARS AS INTERIOR SECRETARY IN THE BUSH Cabinet, Gale Norton, protégé of James Watt, quietly stepped down from her post overseeing the ruination of the American West. Norton's sudden exit was almost certainly hastened by the widening fallout from the corruption probes into Jack Abramoff and the retinue of clients and the politicians and bureaucrats he then held on retainer. Abramoff, it will be recalled, performed some of his most extravagant shakedowns of clients, many of them destitute Indian tribes, seeking indulgences from the Interior Department.

Norton escaped being directly implicated in Abramoff's crimes of influence peddling and bribery. But her former chief deputy, super-lobbyist J. Steven Griles, who oversaw oil and gas leasing on federal lands while on the payroll of his lobbying firm, became a key target of the Abramoff investigation and even shuffled off to federal prison for his crimes.

In a series of emails remarkable for their braggadocio and name-dropping, Abramoff advised his clients to donate money to an industry front group, founded by Norton, that promotes the privatization and industrialization of federal lands. In return, Abramoff bragged that he could offer them unfettered access to the top officials at the Interior Department, where their fondest desires would be a favorable hearing from people like Griles. In one instance, Abramoff claimed that Griles promised to block an Indian casino proposal opposed by one of Abramoff's clients.

To replace Gale Norton, Bush called upon his old pal Dirk Kempthorne, the Idaho governor and former US Senator, who once cherished notions—fantastical though they may have been—of occupying the White House. In picking Kempthorne, Bush once again demonstrated the mindless consistency that would be one of his hallmarks as president. Far from moving to clean up an office sullied by corruption and inside-dealing, Bush tapped a man, who, over the course of his twenty years in politics, has taken more money from timber, big ag, mining and oil companies than any governor in the history of American politics.

Unlike many other western conservatives, Kempthorne doesn't hit up the religious right for money. He goes straight to the corporations who want something done in Boise: JR Simplot, the potato king; Boise-Cascade, the timber giant; mining companies, such as ASARCO, Hecla, and FMC Gold; and the power companies. And Kempthorne gives them what they want. Kempthorne is Jack Abramoff without the middleman, decision-maker and lobbyist rolled into one.

Over the years, one of Kempthorne's most loyal political patrons has been the Washington Group International (WGI), a Boise-based company that functions like a mini-Bechtel. During Kempthorne's tenure as governor, WGI contributed more money to the politician than any other interest. The company got immediate returns on its investment. With an assist from Kempthorne, WGI won the lucrative contract to manage Idaho's highways. The federal government scuttled the deal, saying the contract had been awarded illegally. The contract went up for bid again and, miraculously, Kempthorne once again picked WGI for the job.

With Idaho mired in a decade-long drought, water has become as contentious a political issue as oil in Alaska. Farmers, ranchers, and Idaho's powerful sports-fishing industry formed a rare coalition last year, intent on reforming Idaho's archaic water laws to give more water to ranchers and salmon. The bill moved through the state legislature with surprising speed, much to the irritation of the Idaho Power Company, the state's biggest water hog. Even Idaho Power's threat to jack up electric rates by millions of dollars didn't stall progress of the bill. So the company turned to Kempthorne, who flattened the bill with a veto. Idaho Power is Kempthorne's second largest political contributor.

The phone giant Qwest is Kempthorne's fourth biggest contributor. In 2004, Qwest approached Kempthorne with an urgent plea: the deregulation of pricing for landline phones in Idaho. When Kempthorne sent a message to the Idaho state legislature urging the body to bow to Qwest's desires, it was met with a certain measure of hostility by Idaho residents, who viewed with some skepticism the phone company's contention that such a move would save them money in the long-run. Even members of Kempthorne's party balked and the bill went down to a narrow defeat. Over the next few months, Kempthorne disciplined recalcitrant Republicans and, when the session opened in early 2005, the Qwest bailout bill sailed through and was signed into law by the governor.

This is run-of-the-mill *quid pro quo* politics. But Kempthorne has been implicated in a more pungent scandal that may yet lead to criminal indictments of political and business associates: In 1999, a group of investors with close ties to Kempthorne fronted a scheme to build a satellite campus for the University of Idaho in downtown Boise. The project was named University Place and it called for the construction of three large buildings on prime real estate in the heart of the city.

Questions about the economic viability of the University Place project were swept aside by two of Kempthorne's closest friends, Phil Reberger and Roy Eiguren. All three men were University of Idaho alums and members of the University of Idaho Foundation, the institution responsible for financing the development. At the time of the University Place deal, Reberger, who had managed every one of Kempthorne's political campaigns, served as the governor's chief of staff. He also had a seat on the foundation board and had been appointed by Kempthorne to the Idaho State Building Authority.

Eiguren, who is one of Kempthorne's top individual donors, served as the Foundation's vice-president at the same time that he worked as a lobbyist for the project in the state legislature. He is also a senior partner in Givens Purlsey, a top Boise law firm that represented Capital Partners, the California construction company picked to build the project.

Financing for the development was a problem from the beginning for the cash-strapped university. So Kempthorne, Reberger, and Eiguren hatched two schemes: first they would entice the Idaho legislature to approve $163 million in state-backed bonds to fund the construction. Then they would ensure that the Idaho Department of Water relocate into one of the buildings, as a prime tenant and a key element in the viability of the project.

Both of these maneuvers may have skirted state and federal laws. A 2003 investigation by the Idaho state attorney general's office determined that the bid to move the Water Department into University Place may have been rigged from the top.

Meanwhile, the project proved to be a financial catastrophe, which compelled the university's president, Robert Hoover, to resign in disgrace and left the University Foundation $26 million in debt. The debt was mysteriously repaid in a secret settlement earlier this year. The federal Department of Justice has quietly opened a criminal investigation into the affair.

Kempthorne's nomination was momentarily blocked by Florida Senator Bill Nelson, who begged for the governor's assurance that he not open the Florida coastline to oil drilling. Kempthorne told the senator he would make no such pledge. Indeed, he brayed that his top priority would be to expand drilling for oil across all federal lands, including off shore reserves. Nelson wobbled and the Democrats Maginot Line crumbled once again. Kempthorne sailed through the Interior committee without a vote against him and scarcely one probing question about the corruption scandal that shadows his every footstep. A week later the entire senate took a test vote on his nomination: only eight Democrats voted no. A few minutes later his nomination was approved on a voice vote without dissent.

And that's how Dirk Kempthorne, one of the most environmentally hostile visigoths in the West, came to occupy the office once inhabited by the legendary swindler Albert Fall.

Kempthorne should feel right at home.

Boise.

Michael Brown's Flirtations with Disaster

FOR THOSE OF YOU WAITING ON THE EMERGENCE OF KARL ROVE'S New Orleans strategy, it already came and went: Blame it on Brownie.

Admittedly, this bit of misdirection doesn't qualify as vintage Rove. But then Rove, who was tapped by Bush to head the reconstruction program, may have personal reasons for keeping the deepening New Orleans scandal on the front pages. At least it takes the heat off of his own travails, as Special Prosecutor Patrick Fitzgerald prepares to lay out his case before the federal grand jury in Arlington.

So Mike Brown, the fabulously inept director of FEMA, now joins Paul O'Neill and Richard Clarke as another flattened figure of Bush administration road kill.

Of course, Brown is a convenient and deserving patsy.

Prior to joining the Bush team, the high point of Brown's career had been his tenure as executive director of the International Arabian Horse Association. Like his patron George Bush, Brown proved to be an inept businessman. In a few brief years, Brown had wrecked the once venerable organization, bankrupted its accounts and opened it up to a flood of lawsuits. One former member of the group called Brown's management of the organization "an unmitigated, total fucking disaster."

When Brown himself became a target of lawsuits, he passed the hat to collect cash for a legal defense fund to fend off angry litigants. Soon he raised $50,000. Then he was fired. Brown pocketed the money and never looked back.

The International Arabian Horse Association was Mike Brown's Harken Oil. Although the board ousted Brown, the eviction came too late for the horse people. The horse group has never recovered. Indeed, it has dissolved as an organization. But Brown went on to greater things, like helping to supervise the drowning of America's greatest city.

A quick scan of Mike Brown's resumé gives the impression that he was at least marginally qualified for the FEMA position. After all, Brown claimed to have been the director of emergency management operations for Edmonds, Oklahoma, population 68,000.

But this brawny assignment turns out to have been a feat of vita inflation. According to the former mayor of Edmonds, "Mike was more of an intern. He didn't have anyone reporting to him."

Other than that, Brown's professional career is vaporous. As a lawyer, Brown represented a small oil company, a smaller drilling company, and a family-run insurance brokerage. He did a lot of family estate planning and, yes, was once named "political science teacher of the year at Central State College." Central State, as in the oil patch of Oklahoma. But even this position turns out to have been a mirage. Brown never taught anything, let alone political science, at Central State College. He was a student there. But there's no trace evidence that he won any academic laurels at this Harvard of the Heartland.

Brown got the FEMA post courtesy of his college roommate, Joe Allbaugh. Allbaugh is one of Bush's longtime political wranglers. Among other feats, Allbaugh helped cover up the document trail detailing Bush's desertion from the National Guard. In return for these services of political camouflage, Allbaugh was rewarded with the head of FEMA, an agency for which he had descried a profound loathing.

Deploying Gingrichian bombast, Allbaugh denounced FEMA as a "bloated entitle-ment program." He quickly set out to dismantle it. The first move, in the wake of 9/11, was to strip FEMA of its cabinet level status and subsume it under the auspices of the terror-obsessed Department of Homeland Security, where the agency was kept on a tight choke-collared leash by Michael Chertoff, perhaps the least empathetic person in the Bush cabinet.

In a few short years, Allbaugh had transformed FEMA from a crisis agency that dis-tributed aid to disaster victims into a corporate welfare service that hands out big gov-ernment checks to a coterie contractors with political ties to the Bush White House.

When his work was done, Allbaugh tapped his old buddy Mike Brown to supervise the newly dilapidated agency, while Allbaugh went on to commandeer a few compa-nies that stood at the front of the FEMA welfare line, their hands out for the reception of fat reconstruction checks. Allbaugh-allied firms were some of the first to cash in on the corporate looting of New Orleans.

Of course, Joe Allbaugh is hardly alone in this respect. His predecessor, James Lee Witt, who headed FEMA under Clinton and is put forth by Democrats as a model disaster czar, traded in his FEMA credentials for a high-paying gig with the insurance industry, lobbying congress to help companies like All State wiggle out of paying off their claims in the wake of hurricanes and other natural reckonings.

At the urging of the Bush White House, Michael Brown stocked the upper echelons of FEMA with people a lot like himself. FEMA became a kind of patronage-holding pen for talentless cronies of the Bush gang, a role the monastery once served for the dim-witted sons of the aristocracy during the Middle Ages. (Now the intellectually limited scions of the wealthy land spots as the figureheads of FEMA or the Oval Office.)

Take Brown's chief of staff, Patrick Rhode. You might think that because Brown had no experience managing a disaster relief agency he might tap the expertise of someone who did. You'd be wrong. A detailed look at Rhode's job history reveals not the slightest hint of any experience with floodwaters, hurricanes, earthquakes, or tornadoes. His only encounter with disasters had been a stint with the Bush 2000 campaign. Rhode parlayed that service into a plum slot as a special assistant to the President and deputy director of National Advance Operations, a position he assumed in January 2001. Brown plucked him from the White House to join FEMA in 2004.

Brown's number three man was Scott Morris. Before becoming deputy chief of staff at FEMA, Morris worked as a press officer for the 2004 Bush campaign. Prior to that, Morris labored for an Austin, Texas company called Maverick Media, which produced political commercials for the Bush 2000 campaign. Again there's not even trace evidence that Morris has any experience with natural disasters beyond turning them into photo-ops for Bush and Cheney.

What's crucial to understand about Bush's FEMA is that it didn't fail at its task in New Orleans; under Bush, FEMA was no longer a disaster relief agency, but a cleanup and reconstruction-funding agency. With this in mind, it was only natural that Mike Brown waited to act until all the damage had been done. His role wasn't to throw life rafts to people drowning in shit-saturated water, but to dole out contracts to favored companies for the rebuilding of the city.

Perhaps Mike Brown's fatal mistake was that he flinched on camera and dared to show a little sadness and empathy for those who went down in the flood. That humane slip may have signed his bureaucratic death warrant.

George W. Bush is often praised by the press for his loyalty. One wonders why. It's obvious that the Bush family code goes precisely the other way. Bush demands absolute fealty, while he's willing to sacrifice almost anyone (except his hateful mother) to protect his own ass.

As the rubble and rotting corpses of New Orleans are laid at his feet, the hapless Mike Brown finds he is the latest refugee from the Bush administration to learn this cruel lesson.

New Orleans.

The Green Imposter:
When Al Gore was Veep

THE OFFICIAL VERSION OF THE POLITICAL BATTLES OVER THE ENVIRONment in the late 1990s goes something like this:

As the Republican Visigoths swept into control of the 104th Congress in January of 1995, trembling greens predicted that not an old-growth tree, not an endangered species would be spared. The Republicans' threats were terrible to behold. They proposed to open the Arctic National Wildlife Refuge to oil drilling. They vowed to establish a commission to shut down several national parks, to relax standards on the production and disposal of toxic waste, to turn over enforcement of clean water and air standards to the states. They uttered fearsome threats against the Endangered Species Act. They boasted of plans to double the amount of logging in the National Forests.

Then, the official myth goes on, the president, Gore, and the national greens fought off the Visigoths.

American politics thrives on simple legends of virtue combating vice. As regards the environment, the Republican ultras did not carry all before them. They didn't need to. Clinton and Gore had already done most of the dirty work themselves. The real story begins back in the early days of the administration, when Clinton and Gore had what might be called an environmental mandate and a Democratic Congress to help them move through major initiatives. But the initiatives never happened. Instead, those early years were marked by a series of retreats, reversals, and betrayals that prompted David Brower, the grand old man of American environmentalism, the arch druid himself, to conclude that "Gore and Clinton had done more harm to the environment than Reagan and Bush combined."

The first environmental promise Al Gore made in the 1992 campaign, he soon broke. It involved the WTI hazardous waste incinerator in East Liverpool, Ohio, built on a floodplain near the Ohio River. The plant, one of the largest of its kind in the world, was scheduled to burn 70,000 tons of hazardous waste a year in a spot only 350 feet from the nearest house. A few hundred yards away is East Elementary School, which sits on a ridge nearly eye-level with the top of the smokestack.

On July 19, 1992, Gore gave one of his first campaign speeches on the environment— across the river from the incinerator site, in Weirton, West Virginia. He hammered the Bush Administration for its plans to give the toxic waste burner a federal air permit. "The very idea is just unbelievable to me," Gore said. "I'll tell you this, a Clinton-Gore

Administration is going to give you an environmental presidency to deal with these problems. We'll be on your side for a change." Clinton made similar pronouncements on his swing through the Buckeye State.

Shortly after the election, Gore assured neighbors of the incinerator that he hadn't forgotten about them. "Serious questions concerning the safety of the East Liverpool, Ohio hazardous waste incinerator must be answered before the plant may begin operation," Gore wrote. "The new Clinton/Gore administration will not issue the plant a test burn permit until all questions concerning compliance with the plant have been answered."

But that never happened. Instead, the EPA quietly granted the WTI facility its test burn permit. The tests failed twice. In one, the incinerator eradicated only 7 percent of the mercury found in the waste when it was supposed to burn away 99.9 percent. A few weeks later, the EPA granted WTI a commercial permit anyway. They didn't tell the public about the failed tests until afterward.

Gore claimed his hands were tied by the Bush Administration, who had promised WTI the permit only a few weeks before the Clinton team took office. But by one account, William Reilly, Bush's EPA director, met with Gore's top environmental aide, Katie McGinty, in January 1993 and asked her if he should begin the process of approving the permit. He says McGinty told him to proceed. McGinty said later that she had no recollection of the meeting.

Gore persisted in maintaining that there was nothing he could do about it once the permit was granted. A 1994 report on the matter from the General Accounting Office flatly contradicted him, saying the plant could be shut down on numerous grounds, including repeated violations of its permit.

"This was Clinton and Gore's first environmental promise, and it was their first promise-breaker," says Terri Swearington, a registered nurse from Chester, West Virginia, just across the Ohio River from the incinerator. Swearington, who won the Goldman Prize in 1997 for her work organizing opposition to WTI, has hounded Gore ever since, and during the 2000 campaign she was banned by Gore staffers from appearing at events featuring the vice president.

The decision to go soft on WTI may have had something to do with its powerful financial backer. The construction of the incinerator was partially financed by Jackson Stephens, the Arkansas investment king who helped bankroll the Clinton-Gore campaign. According to EPA whistleblower Hugh Kaufman, during the period when the WTI financing package was being put together, Stephens Inc. was represented by Webb Hubble (who later came into Clinton's justice department and was indicted during the Whitewater investigation) and the Rose law firm (to which Hillary Clinton belonged). Over the ensuing seven years, the WTI plant has burned nearly a half-million tons of toxic waste—5,000 truckloads of toxic material every year—spewing chemicals such as mercury, lead, and dioxin out of its stacks and onto the surrounding neighborhoods. The inevitable illnesses have followed.

* * *

Up in the Douglas fir forests of the Pacific Northwest, a similar saga of betrayal unfolded. In the late 1980s and 1990s, federal judge William Dwyer, a Reagan appointee, rocked the Bush Administration when he sided with environmentalists in a series of lawsuits involving the northern spotted owl. Dwyer ruled that the fierce pace of Forest Service logging in ancient forests was driving the spotted owl, and more than 180 other species that dwell in the deep forests west of the Cascade Mountains, to extinction. In 1991, Dwyer handed down an injunction halting all new timber sales in spotted owl habitat. He famously called the Bush Administration's forest plan "a remarkable series of violations of environmental laws."

Then along came Bill Clinton and Al Gore. At a rally in Portland, Oregon, on the eve of the 1992 election, Gore vowed to "end the standoff" over the fate of the Northwest forests once and for all. In fact, the standoff was serving the owl pretty well. By 1992, timber sales in the Northwest had declined from 20 million board feet a year in 1982 to 2 million board feet. What was to come would drive the owl even closer to extinction.

Within days of taking office, the Clinton-Gore team set its sights on getting Dwyer's injunction lifted and the big logs rolling back to the sawmills. The scheme was to become a template for the way Clinton and Gore would handle environmental disputes for the remainder of their term: convene a staged "town hall"-style meeting, put out a pre-fab plan, and induce your liberal friends to swallow their principles and sign off on it. This shadow play was the April 1993 Forest Summit, a display of consensus-mongering that saw some of the nation's leading environmentalists hunkering down with executives from Weyerhaeuser. The event, orchestrated by Gore and Katie McGinty, is best remembered for the administration's bid to censor the opening remarks of a local historian, who wanted to put the session in its proper context by describing the social effects from a hundred years of conscienceless logging by an industry that had treated its workers as ruthlessly as it had treated salmon streams.

Shortly after the Portland summit the political arm-twisting began. Gore's so-called "green relations team," led by McGinty, was sent to parley with environmentalists in the region. "They told us that during the campaign they'd made commitments to the timber lobby and the Northwest delegation that logging would be restarted before the end of 1993," Larry Tuttle later recalled. Tuttle, who formerly headed the Oregon Natural Resources Council (a lead plaintiff in the original spotted owl suit), now runs the Portland-based Center for Environment Equity. "McGinty made it clear that if greens wanted to get some of the provisions we wanted in the new forest plan, we had to offer up something in return." The Clinton emissaries wanted the plaintiffs in the spotted owl case to go to Judge Dwyer and ask him to release for logging some of the sales he had halted. Many of the big national groups, including the Wilderness Society, National Wildlife Federation, and the Sierra Club Legal Defense Fund, were ready to throw in the towel that very moment. Local groups still held out.

Then Clinton and Gore summoned Bruce Babbitt, secretary of the interior and former president of the League of Conservation Voters. Babbitt came carrying a big stick. The former Arizona governor knew exactly how to scare the hell out of his former colleagues—by threatening them with "sufficiency language," a legal device that would allow federal agencies, such as the Forest Service and the BLM, to violate laws like the Endangered Species Act with impunity. Unless they were willing to go along, Babbitt told the spotted owl plaintiffs, the Clinton Administration would be forced to ask Congress to enact a legislative rider that would overturn the injunctions and insulate the new plan from any future environmental lawsuits. The deal was struck over the dissent of grassroots groups.

Judge Dwyer had no choice. He had to let the injunction go, and he had to approve the new Clinton forest plan. There simply wasn't any opposition to it. However, the judge did issue a warning: if any one element of the plan was not implemented, its legal standing would crumble and an even more sweeping injunction could be in the offing.

For the greens who'd folded, the pay-off was scarcely worth it. The plan didn't stop the logging of ancient forests. In fact, more than 35 percent of the remaining spotted owl habitat was put into the free-fire zone called "the matrix," where logging could go forward. But even the remaining 65 percent of old-growth forest was not safe. Although the plan sequestered these lands in a category called Old Growth Reserves, such zones were not, in fact, off limits to logging. The plan's fine print allowed these lands to be, in Babbitt's unforgettable phrase, "cut for their own good." Ecological logging—considered a joke during the Bush era—came into its own with a vengeance during Clinton-Gore time.

Next came the salvage logging rider attached to an annual spending bill and signed by Clinton in 1995. Brent Blackwelder, president of Friends of the Earth, issued the dire judgment that "the salvage rider was arguably the worst single piece of public lands legislation ever signed into law." The bill consigned millions of acres of National Forest lands across the country to the chainsaw, and contained language exempting these sales from all environmental laws and from any judicial review. The consequences were especially dire in the Pacific Northwest. Gore later called this rider the administration's biggest mistake on the environment. But it was just one of many.

By 1998, the evidence was irrefutable. The Clinton-Gore plan was driving the owl to extinction much faster than the old, Dwyer-forbidden cutting plans of the Bush era.

In an April 1999 report, the Forest Service's own biologists found that, across its range, the spotted owl was declining at more than 8 percent per year since the Clinton plan had been put into effect. In California, the rate was even higher, more than 10 percent per year. But the most rapid decline was being seen on the Olympic peninsula, where the owls, isolated by geographical features such as the Puget Sound and surrounded by millions of acres of corporate land clearcut by Weyerhaeuser, Simpson, ITT-Rayonier, and John Hancock, were plummeting at the alarming rate of 12.3 percent per year. At that rate, the Olympic peninsula owl will be extinct in 2010 and maybe sooner. The spotted owl's population under the Clinton-Gore Administration declined more in five years than the plan's environmental impact statement predicted it would decline in a worst-case scenario of over forty years.

* * *

The fall of 1993 saw Gore broker a bizarre deal to trade missiles for dead whales. On September 23 of that year he entertained Norway's prime minister, Gro Brundtland, at the White House. Brundtland, a fellow Harvard grad and a longtime friend of the vice president, sought Gore's backing for Norway's effort to overturn the International Whaling Commission's ban on the hunting of minke whales in the northeast Atlantic Ocean. For years this had been Norway's aim, but they'd had little success with the Bush Administration.

Early in 1993, the Norwegian fleet flouted international law by killing nearly 300 whales, supposedly for "scientific" and "experimental" purposes, although a later investigation disclosed that Norwegian minke whale meat had ended up in the fish markets of Japan. American environmental groups lashed out at Norway and demanded that the US take action to punish the rogue whalers. Under a US law known as the Pelly Amendment, the Commerce Department can impose trade sanctions on nations that violate the whaling ban.

But Norway had so far escaped without even a mild rebuke. This was, in part, because Norway had softened up Congress and Clinton's Commerce Department through a $1.5 million influence-peddling campaign, led by the lobby firm Akin Gump, home of former DNC chairman Robert Strauss and that master of persuasion Vernon Jordan.

At the time of his meeting with Brundtland, Gore had several things on his mind. One was the situation in Bosnia. The Norwegians had one of the largest contingents of troops on the ground there, and Brundtland was under pressure to pull the peacekeepers out, a move that Gore, who was overseeing much of the Bosnian crisis for the administration, was desperate to avoid. Second, Gore was less than enthusiastic about an outright ban on whaling, feeling that it would impede his efforts to secure free trade pacts.

A White House transcript of the meeting, marked confidential by Gore's national security adviser, Leon Fuerth, records Brundtland denouncing environmental groups as "extremists" and liars. She tells the vice president that she doesn't want her nation's whaling fleet monitored "because that would allow Greenpeace to track them and disrupt our activities." Then Brundtland went on, "We do feel bullied, even by you simply evaluating the use of sanctions. Especially after several nations in the IWC have tried to change the organization from a whale monitoring mission to a forum to ban whaling outright."

Gore tried to placate the Norwegian prime minister, agreeing that the environmental groups had unfairly beat up on Norway. "As in arms control, there are those who attempt to exploit uncertainty for their own ends," Gore said. "This strengthens my argument for the need of a scheme that will allow resumption [of whaling], while removing the basis of suspicion that the RMS [i.e., new whaling rules] will be violated."

In the end, Gore agreed that the Clinton Administration would refrain from imposing sanctions on Norway and would work with Brundtland to weaken whale protection regulations at the IWC. To seal the agreement, Gore and Brundtland forged an arms deal involving the sale of $625 million worth of air-to-air missiles made by Raytheon to the Norwegian military.

* * *

Across the board, setbacks for the greens came at a dizzying pace during the Clinton Administration. A plan to raise grazing fees on Western ranchers was shelved after protests from two Western senators, one of whom, Max Baucus from Montana, later marveled at how quickly the administration caved. The EPA soon succumbed to pressure from the oil industry and automakers on its plans to press for tougher fuel efficiency standards, a move Katie McGinty defended by saying enviros were "tilting at windmills" on the issue. In the winter of 1994, the White House fired Jim Baca, the reform-minded director of the Bureau of Land Management, after his attempts to take on the ranching and mining industries riled Cecil Andrus, the governor of Idaho.

Tax breaks were doled out to oil companies drilling in the Gulf of Mexico. The Department of Agriculture okayed a plan to increase logging in Alaska's Tongass National Forest, the nation's largest temperate rainforest. The Interior Department, under orders from the White House, put the brakes on a proposal to outlaw the most grotesque form of strip mining, the aptly-named mountaintop-removal method. With Gore doing much of the lobbying, the administration pushed a bill through Congress that repealed the import-ban on tuna caught with nets that also killed dolphins. The collapse was rapid enough to distress so centrist an environmental leader as the National Wildlife Federation's Jay Hair, who likened the experience of dealing with the Clinton-Gore Administration to "date rape."

The White House quashed a task force investigating timber fraud on the National Forest, which had uncovered several hundred million dollars' worth of illegal timber cutting by big corporations, including Weyerhaeuser. The task force was disbanded, some of its investigators reassigned to, as one put it, "pull up pot plants in clearcuts."

As ugly as things got, the big green groups never abandoned Gore, swallowing his line that he was "after all, only the vice president." It is a hallmark of the Gore style that he knows how deftly to exploit public interest groups even as he betrays their constituents. Like the Christian right during the Bush era, the Beltway greens felt there was nowhere else to turn. They had never trusted Clinton, who as governor had turned a blind eye to fouling of the White River by Don Tyson's chicken abattoirs and shamelessly pandered after corporate cash during the primaries. Gore was the man on whom they had pinned their hopes.

Gore, they remembered, was the man who had held the first hearings on Love Canal and helped usher the Superfund law into being. Here was the man who popularized the term "global warming" and had warned of the dangers of the deterioration of the ozone layer. Here was the man who had led a contingent of Democratic senators to the 1992 Earth Summit in Rio, where he chastised George Bush's indifference to the health of the planet. Here was the man who had written *Earth in the Balance*, which called for the environment to be the "central organizing principle" of the new century and stressed strict environmental discipline for the Third World.

But, as Brent Blackwelder of Friends of the Earth pointed out, during all his years in Congress, Gore's record on environmental issues was far from sterling. In fact, he voted for the environment only 66 percent of the time, a rating that put him on the lower end of Senate Democrats. Moreover, Blackwelder says, Gore functioned rarely as a leader in Congress but more as a solo operator pursuing his own agenda.

That agenda, from the beginning, has been in line with his roots as a New Democrat. Gore has been a tireless promoter of incentive-based, or free-market, environmentalism, often remarking that "the invisible hand has a green thumb." Since the mid-1980s, Gore has argued that the bracing forces of market capitalism are potent curatives for the ecological entropy now bearing down upon the global environment. He has always been a passionate disciple of the gospel of efficiency, and a man suffused with an inchoate technophilia.

But Gore was also shrewd. He knew the environmental movement from the inside out, knew well that what the big green groups based in DC craved most was access. As vice president, he arranged to meet at least once a month with the Gang of Ten, the CEOs of the nation's biggest environmental outfits. It became a way for Gore to cool their tempers and deflect their gripes from him to the president, or more often, to Cabinet members such as Robert Rubin, Ron Brown, Mack McLarty, or Lloyd Bentsen. Moreover, Gore made sure to seed the administration with more than thirty executives and staff members from the ranks of the environmental movement itself, headlined by Babbitt, the former president of the movement's main PAC. Others came from the Wilderness Society, National Audubon Society, Environmental Defense Fund, and the Natural Resources Defense Council.

This experience was a new one for environmental lobbyists who had lived through the exile of the Reagan-Bush era. "It was good to have people in the White House call you by your first name," Brock Evans, once regarded as the most effective green lobbyist in DC, reflected at a gathering of environmental activists in Oregon in 1993. Evans' gratified cry summed it all up. Official greens got a bit of access, and that was about it.

The main conduit to the ear of power was Katie McGinty, formerly on Gore's Senate staff. Few people are closer to Gore than McGinty, one of only two staffers permitted to call the Veep "Al." (The other is Leon Fuerth.) McGinty grew up in Philadelphia, the daughter of an Irish-American cop in Frank Rizzo's police force. She got a degree in chemistry at St. Joseph's University and soon went to work for ARCO, the oil/chemical giant. A few years later McGinty pursued a law degree from Columbia in the Science, Law, and Technology program. Before joining Gore's Senate staff, she did a stint in DC as a lobbyist for the American Chemical Society, where she fine-tuned the techno-speak that Gore finds irresistible in a staffer. In answering a reporter's question about her favorite hobbies, McGinty once said, "Hiking and reading books on civic realization." It was a response only Gore could find exciting. McGinty became Gore's top environmental aide in 1990, helped him research *Earth in the Balance*, and accompanied him to the Earth Summit in Rio de Janeiro in 1992.

In 1993, McGinty, then only twenty-nine, was tapped to head the White House Office of Environmental Policy, a newly created panel that Gore pushed for to give him more of a presence inside the White House. The move didn't sit well with members of Congress or with some Clinton staffers, who felt Gore was grasping too much power. Ultimately, the office was merged with the Council on Environmental Quality, which oversees compliance with environmental laws by federal agencies. McGinty was named as its chair.

The years from 1993 to 2000 were bleak ones for environmentalists, as Clinton and Gore retreated from one campaign pledge after another. "Katie seemed out of the loop most of the time she was there," a seasoned environmental lobbyist told me at the time. "Or that's how she made you feel. Katie's great talent was to seduce you on the phone. She made you feel as if she was your best friend, a secret Earth First!er, who was shocked and pained when the inevitable betrayals came. Katie never delivered bad news herself, but she was always there to console us. She was very, very adroit at soothing irate enviros, calming them down so that they wouldn't attack the administration."

At the height of the budget negotiations in 1998, McGinty shocked many in DC when she abruptly announced that she was resigning from her post and was moving to India to take a job at the Tata Research Institute in New Delhi. TERI, as it's known, is an obscure sustainable development group that receives funding from the UN and works on energy, biotech, and forestry issues. McGinty's husband, Karl Hausker, an employee of the Center for Strategic and International Studies (an outpost of the national security establishment), had been assigned to India. Many thought McGinty would stay in DC, where her power in the administration would increase as the 2000 election approached. But apparently Tipper Gore convinced McGinty that she should follow her man.

Tipper had taken an unusual interest in McGinty's personal life. In 1995, she learned that McGinty had repeatedly postponed her marriage to Hausker, citing the "crushing workload" that kept her tied down at the White House. Evidently eager that McGinty cement her union and therefore leave Washington, Tipper intervened, handled the wedding arrangements and shipped the newlyweds off on a month-long honeymoon to Australia's Great Barrier Reef and the rainforests of Papua, New Guinea.

In 2000, McGinty returned to the United States from India. It didn't take her long to find a job—not with the Gore campaign but as the legislative affairs director of Troutman Sanders, a DC law firm with a reputation for defending the worst corporate polluters and using its lobbying might to carve up environmental legislation. In these unsavory surroundings, McGinty stayed true. "There would be no higher priority I would have," she had once said, "than to help or serve Al Gore." Opportunity did not dally. In the spring of 2000, McGinty co-founded a group called Environmentalists for Gore, designed to undercut the growing sentiment for greens to support Bill Bradley in the Democratic primary contests. Bradley was endorsed by Friends of the Earth in 1999, and this slap in the face had set off alarm bells in the Gore camp.

Among McGinty's labors for Gore in 2000 was her input in his energy plan, which promises $68 billion in subsidies and tax breaks for utilities. It so happens that among the biggest clients of McGinty's new firm, Troutman Sanders, are American Electric Power, the Southern Company and the Edison Electric Institute, one of the main opponents of stringent new air pollution standards. When confronted with this confluence of interest, McGinty answered irrefutably, "I provide advice and have provided advice to anyone who asks me. Does the vice president ask for my views? Absolutely. Do people in the business community ask me for my views. Absolutely. And is that anything new? Absolutely not."

* * *

Al Gore has always been fascinated with the CIA and the technology of snooping. In 1994, he ordered the agency to conduct an analysis of the causes behind the collapse of nation states. Gore was hoping to prove his thesis that environmental factors, such as deforestation, overpopulation, desertification, and poor sanitation, were the prime culprits. So the CIA spent the next six months entering more than 2 million pieces of information in its computers to come up with an answer. The result: the CIA's analysts reported that civilizations fall because of extreme poverty and high rates of infant mortality.

But Gore didn't give up on the spooks at Langley. In 1998, he convinced Clinton to issue an executive order expanding the agency's charter to include two new projects: the environment and free trade. The CIA quickly adapted to its new mission. In the summer of 1999, the *London Daily Telegraph* reported that the CIA had been spying on Michael Meacher, environment minister for the Blair government, presumably because Meacher—nearly alone among the Blairites—had been skeptical about Monsanto's plans to dump genetically engineered, or GE, crops on Europe.

The snooping came to light after the *Telegraph* made Freedom of Information Act requests to several US government agencies asking for any files on British ministers and elected officials. Most agencies replied that they had no files, while a few kept short biographical briefs, which they duly turned over. The exception was the Environmental Protection Agency, headed by Al Gore's former staffer, Carol Browner. The EPA replied that it had a file on Meacher but refused to turn it over, saying it "originated within the Central Intelligence Agency." The CIA also refused to release the file.

Meacher had drawn fire not only from Monsanto but from the US State and Commerce departments for his recalcitrance on GE crops. He had taken the position that such crops should not be commercially grown in Europe until they have been proved not to pose health problems or environmental risks. Meacher had also moved to reformulate a government panel on genetically engineered crops by reducing the number of industry representatives. The US maintained that any restrictions on Monsanto's ability to market its GE crops was an unfair restraint on trade. Gore, himself, made frequent calls to members of the Blair government to drive home the point.

Meacher expressed astonishment that the CIA had a file on him, and said he had no idea what the reason might be. Chris Prescott, head of Friends of the Earth's London office, offered one. "The immediate fear is that the CIA is working hand in glove with Monsanto to do anything they can to force this technology down our throats, whatever Democratic politicians have to say. What business is it of the CIA's to worry about any politician's views about biotechnology products?" Apparently, Prescott missed Clinton's new directive to the Agency made at Gore's instigation. Some wondered how thick the file might be on Prince Charles, Britain's most outspoken foe of genetically engineered crops.

Yes. The Prince of Wales. Now there's a real environmentalist.

PART FOUR

The Beautiful
and the Dammed

I don't blame you, I know
The place where you lie.
I admit everything. But look at me.
How can I live without you?
Come up to me, love,
Out of the river, or I will
Come down to you.

—From *Shall We Gather at the River?*
James Wright

A Premature Burial
The Remaking of Cataract Canyon

July, 2006.

A FEW YEARS AGO, DANIEL WOLFF AND I BEGAN A CASUAL EMAIL BANTER about floating one of the West's mighty rivers. We thought we might canoe the Missouri, rewinding Lewis and Clark's route, from Ft. Benton, Montana to the badlands of the Missouri Breaks. The summer passed and the Missouri rolled on without carrying us on its back.

The following year there was manly talk again, this time centering on Oregon's John Day River, which is born in the Elkhorn Mountains and cuts its way in a lazy arc through basalt canyons to the Columbia River. By most standards, the John Day is not a big river, but it now stands as one of the longest free-flowing streams in the American West. The dam builders have marred nearly everything else. But book tours and wars came in the way. So, another day for the John Day.

Still, desert rivers stalked my daydreams. One in particular: the one that begins on the south slopes of the Wind River Range in Wyoming and once emptied into the Gulf of California in Mexico, though not a drop of river water reaches that far today. That river is, of course, the Green-Colorado, the great river of the desert southwest.

Word had come from Moab that Lake Powell, that noxious sewage lagoon in the heart of Glen Canyon, was drying up and the river was regaining its flow, carving through canyons of sediment to reveal sections of Glen and Cataract Canyons that hadn't been seen since the floodgates closed at Glen Canyon Dam in 1963. I proposed to Wolff that a summer float down the river through Cataract Canyon, the most challenging stretch of whitewater on the river, might give us the rare glimpse of a river being reborn—a victory of nature over technology.

Wolff asked, "Why not?"

Why not, indeed.

Well, for starters, neither of us had the slightest experience with the kind of extreme rapids that would confront us in the throat of Cataract Canyon, especially in the harrowing triplet of cascades known as the Big Drops. And neither did our three companions in this flight from daily realities: Wolff's wife, the filmmaker and choreographer, Marta Renzi; their sixteen-year-old son, Lorenzo, a devotee of Edward Abbey and a stunningly gifted bass guitarist, coming soon to an arena near you; and my wife, Kimberly Willson, a librarian.

Lorenzo and Marta boast on their resume of several descents of the mighty Hoosick River in inner tubes. When she was eighteen, Kimberly paddled her surfboard from the south point of Ocean City across the channel to Assateague Island in the hope of glimpsing a stampede of wild ponies. And that's about it.

I have a few rivers in my past: the Little Beaver and Churchill in Canada; Michigan's Pine and Manistee; the French Broad in North Carolina; West Virginia's New and Gauley rivers; the Deschutes and Illinois in Oregon. But those descents were years, decades ago. Since 9/11 I haven't strayed away from my computer for more than three consecutive days. The Mac has extracted a terrible price from my body: hunched back, indiscreet waves of fat, tenderized hands and feet, and pixel-eroded eyes. A ruin.

These days Wolff gets out on the water much more often than I do. And even though he's a poet, and by all precedents of literary history should be confined to a consumptive sanitarium in the Poconos, Wolff's in better shape, too. He takes daily breaks from scribbling sonnets, or writing books about Sam Cooke or Springsteen's Ashbury Park or the Negro Baseball League, and escapes in his beautiful wooden sloop to sail up and down the Hudson, keeping an eye on the remorseless development biting into the Palisades and the grim cooling towers of Indian Point, America's most dangerous nuclear plant, a few miles upstream from the Renzi-Wolffs' mossy manse in Nyack.

Obviously, we needed help.

So I called up my old friend John Weisheit, one of the most acclaimed guides on the Colorado River. But there was a problem. After twenty-five years of guiding rafts down the Green and Colorado Rivers, from Dinosaur National Monument and Desolation Canyon through Labyrinth and Cataract to the Grand Canyon itself, Weisheit had become so disgusted by the state of the river ecosystem and the three big dams that were destroying it, that he hung up his oars and became a full-time environmental activist.

Weisheit and Owen Lammers, a battle-hardened veteran of global fights against hyrdodams from China's Three Gorges to the demented Animas-LaPlata scheme in Colorado, founded Living Rivers in Moab back in 2000. This two-person operation has done more for the preservation of rivers in American West in the past five years than Sierra Club with all its millions had accomplished in a decade. In his spare time, Weisheit and two of his colleagues, Robert Webb and Jane Belnap, wrote *the* book on Cataract Canyon. It's a meticulously detailed and passionate work, a model of environmental history writing that belongs on the same handy shelf with Donald Worster's *Rivers of Empire* and Mark Reisner's *Cadillac Desert*.

Weisheit is also the Colorado Riverkeeper. It's his job to keep an eye on the environmental changes in those canyons. Fortuitously for us, Weisheit was looking for an excuse to get back on the river and check out the latest revelations from the ongoing retreat of Lake Powell.

"Let's do it," Weisheit said. "Just one minor thing. Let's go Powell's route, down the Green River, rowing all the way. No motors."

The Powell in question was Maj. John Wesley Powell, the one-armed Civil War veteran who commanded two pioneering expeditions down the Green and Colorado Rivers in 1869 and 1871/72.

So we packed our bags (strike that. BAG: they only permit you one) and converged on Moab.

* * *

By the time we get the old International Harvester bus loaded with several thousand pounds of our gear outside the Tag-a-Long offices in Moab, the temperature has topped 90 degrees. It is 8 am.

Weisheit has already been working for hours, rigging the rafts. And, typically, it didn't take him long to provoke a confrontation with the owner of the company. Weisheit was wearing a Drain It! T-shirt, featuring an image of an giant sledgehammer smashing a hole in Glen Canyon Dam. The owner of Tag-a-Along and Weisheit's former boss was not amused. Outfitters don't want to offend anyone, even when their own livelihood is at stake. It's one of the big reasons Weisheit retired from guiding.

More and more, the outfitters are becoming apolitical and corporate, unwilling to defend the true source of their livelihood. The indigenous and family operations that sprang up in Moab during the 1960s are beginning to fade away and with them a personal connection to the canyons and the river. They are replaced by multi-national companies like Aramark that also manage Park Service visitor centers and peddle inedible food at schools and prisons.

The profiles of the river guides, once an outlaw culture of hippies and desert anarchists, are changing, too. More and more the guides are college students from LA or the east coast, game for summer kicks and big tips. They guide for a couple of years, then become lawyers and equity analysts. The intimate connection to the river and the forces—political and natural—that shape it is being lost. "The Colorado has been Wal-Marted," Weisheit sneers.

We drive north across the redrock, past Arches National Park, then turn west across cow-trampled BLM lands with expansive views of the glowing Book Cliffs to the north and the blue buckle of the Henry Mountains to the south, the last range to be explored by whites in the lower forty-eight states. All around us, blonde domes of Navajo sandstone breach through the surface of the earth like the rumps of humpback whales.

When we finally reach the rim of Labyrinth Canyon, the temperature has spiked to 100 degrees, on its way to 110 by late afternoon. From the red lip of the canyon, the road plunges downward 1,500 feet in a torturous swirl of extreme switchbacks that cling to the sheer cliffs of Wingate sandstone, laid down by the great sand dunes of the Jurassic period. The descent makes the crazy road on the island of Capri seem as leisurely as a drive down I-5.

We make our first snap decision: get off the damn bus! Much better to face the dust and the heat, now radiating off the vertical walls of sandstone, and walk to the bottom, leaving the groaning bus, loaded with rafts and gear, to its own uncertain fate. We smell the brakes sizzling all the way down.

At the fifth switchback, our cowardly decision is confirmed as we encounter the crumpled maroon hulk of a station wagon that had plunged off the road and smashed headlong into unforgiving boulders like Thelma and Louise, whose final ride into the blue negative spaces of the canyon were filmed nearby.

We watch from above as our bus attempts to negotiate the most perilous curve on this dangerous road. It takes Bob, our driver, a good five minutes to coax the rig the few hundred feet necessary to traverse the hairpin. But that was a manuever worthy of a Formula One driver compared to the fate of an oilrig that inched its way down the canyon a few days earlier. It took the giant drilling rig two and a half days to make that one curve. I can't help thinking the wrong vehicle crashed.

The oil companies have never given up their goal of extracting the last drop of oil from the shallow pools of crude lurking beneath Canyonlands. They can't drill directly into the National Park, so they take advantage of the BLM and state of Utah's open door policy and set their rigs on those lands and aim their drilling bores at an angle to pierce into the park from all sides. Slant drilling is one term for it. Backdoor larceny is a better one. Abetted by the government.

Halfway down the canyon, we spook a pair of desert bighorn sheep, ewe and lamb. The mother cuts down the canyon toward a copse of cottonwood trees, while the young lamb streaks straight up the nearly vertical face of the cliffs, as if gliding on air. You can see why the Anasazi and their contemporaries, the Fremont, carved more images of bighorns onto the rocks of the Colorado Plateau than any other animal. Both cultures also adorned their sandals with the dew claws of desert bighorns, no doubt as a kind of talisman for their own miraculous climbing feats to their secret granaries, cliff dwellings, watch towers, and astral observatories perched hundreds of feet above the canyon floor.

Finally we arrive at Mineral Bottom, our launch site. What mineral is that, you ask? Why uranium, of course. The ore that keeps on paying.

Back in the 1950s, little Moab was deemed the Uranium Capital of the World, thanks to H-Bomb Harry Truman. The bonanza created a handful of millionaires, like Charlie Steen, thousands of chronically sick miners, and many dead Indians, mainly Navajo, whose plight in the irradiated deserts of the Southwest is achingly portrayed in *If You Poison Us* by Peter Eichstaedt.

In the late 1950s, Disney did its part as a uranium booster. A special episode of the *Mickey Mouse Club* featured the Mouseketeers floating down the goosenecks of the San Juan River in search of uranium. Atoms for peace, naturally. This hour-long adventure rivals *Dr. Strangelove* for black comedy from that decade of group paranoia and imperial fantasias.

Still, the absurd episode offers some luscious footage of the San Juan before it was inundated beneath the waters of Lake Powell, which even now is soaking up the radioactive waste of the hundreds of uranium mines and tailings piles beneath its jewel-like waters.

As a memento of that iridescent era, courtesy of the Atlas Corporation, the town of Moab enjoys a large uranium dump on its outskirts, flush on the bank of the Grand River. On windy days—four or five afternoons on a good week—the air in Moab is peppered with uranium dust and its lethal sidekick Radon.

After decades of Zen-like contemplation, the Department of Energy has recently decided to solve Moab's little problem by excavating the contaminated soil, trucking it thirty miles up Highway 191, and burying it near the base of the Book Cliffs outside the old cowboy town of Thompson. In the True West, this is known as spreading the wealth.

* * *

With the river so tantalizingly close, it is hard to remain patient. But readiness is all. There is still much work to do, most of it by Weisheit and our swamper Brian McManus, an eighteen-year old psychology student at the University of Florida, who is one of Tag-a-Long's rising stars. They've sent Brian with us to crib some of Weisheit's unparalleled knowledge of the river, the canyon's hidden campsites, its geology, and natural and human history. Like the rest of us, Brian's mind seems fixated on the rapids of Cataract Canyon, especially the Big Drops, which he has never rowed. But those are distant challenges, days away.

We unload the bus and begin pumping air into two inflatable kayaks, known affectionately as "duckies." I soon espy Marta Renzi caressing the bow of the bright yellow single kayak, for which she has already developed an unnatural attraction.

The rigging and loading of the two large rafts takes nearly two hours, as a week's worth of gear and supplies is carefully piecemealed and clipped into the holds of the raft: eight 10-gallon canteens of water, each weighing fifty to sixty pounds; a dozen or so large metal ammo cans jammed with food and supplies; two tables; seven folding chairs; a portable toilet; sleeping bags, pads and tents; coolers stuffed with blocks of ice; a keg of sunscreen; allegedly waterproof bags for clothes, cameras, toenail polish; a stove and propane tanks; field glasses and field guides (i.e., Donald Baars' *The Geology of Canyonlands*, Sibley's *Western Birds*, Weisheit's *Cataract Canyon*, and natch, *The Monkey Wrench Gang*); Lorenzo's guitar; first aid kits and anti-venom; and the obligatory rocket launcher. If they'd permitted me to bring a suitcase, I could have scooped up some of the sand from Mineral Bottom and boarded the raft with my own dirty bomb. Next time, perhaps.

(Of course, in these days of government paranoia, you have to be careful allowing these quite natural thoughts to slip into your consciousness, never mind idly voicing them aloud. Consider the case of my old friend Jim Bensman, a seasoned enviro from southern Illinois. Yes, there are quite a few of "them" down there in the sticks. He recently testified at a public hearing that if the Army Corps of Engineers really wanted to facilitate fish migration on the Mississippi River it might consider blasting down some of the archaic fish-killing dams on the river. At light-speed this entirely rational observation was transmitted from the Corps of Engineers to the Federal Bureau of Investigation, which immediately launched a probe into the life and thoughts of Bensman. Never mind the fact that Bensman was only quoting from the Corps' own Environmental Impact Study, which put forth the idea of dam removal by dynamite as a legitimate means of saving the lives of fish. When thoughts are crimes, you know your government is on the run. A few months ago, the Reverend Pat Robertson predicted that the Almighty God would unleash from the heavens a torrent of dam-busting rains to drown the town of Dover, Pennsylvania for the heresy of teaching evolution in its schools. There's no word on whether the FBI opened an probe of the Supreme Deity and his bloodthirsty prophet.)

All of that and I forgot the Tanqueray! Dave Brower never left home for a river trip without a bottle or two of his favorite gin, but booze was impossible to buy in Utah on a Sunday afternoon. Just as well. Alcohol exacerbates dehydration and under these scorching skies we're in for a daily dose of desiccation.

At the first bend in the river, we flush a great blue heron hunting crawfish along a sandbar. The giant bird uncorks its angular body and flies awkwardly downstream, always downstream. I'd like to write that the herons escorted us down the river. But that wouldn't be true. The herons seemed agitated by our presence, barking angrily at us as they made their ungainly lift offs from beaches and the branches of cottonwoods. Compared to the scream of the jetboats, we are a fairly unobtrusive gang of interlopers, floating silently down the river, leaving no wake behind us. Still the herons scold us, as if we should know better.

As we laze down a corridor of crumbly Kayenta sandstone, Kimberly perches on the edge of the raft, shielded from the sun by a rainbow-colored umbrella, like a figure in a Seurat painting. She is reading *The Shadow of the Wind*, Carlos Ruiz Zafon's labyrinthine novel of secret libraries, coded texts, forbidden romances, and revolution during the fascist takeover of Spain. The book has startling resonances to America under Bush.

No time to brood on those matters. Look at those swallows overhead! They could teach the superstars of Cirque du Soleil a thing or two.

Ed Abbey longed to be reincarnated as turkey vulture. If I earn a right of return, I hope to come back as a cliff swallow, the most graceful and acrobatic of birds. Through Labyrinth and Stillwater Canyons, the darting, purple-winged birds with the cinnamon rump are a constant, though diminished, presence, feeding on mosquitoes and mayflies. Their dome-like mud nests with perfectly round entry holes are affixed in vast colonies to the faces of White Rim and Cedar Mesa sandstone. The adobe-like structures bear an eerie resemblance to the ancient granaries we will float by over the next week. I suspect the Anasazi learned much about architecture style from *Petrochelidon pyrrhonota*.

While we encounter hundreds of cliff swallows as we drift down the Green, we see few, if any, white-throated swifts, once a common resident of the canyon country. Apparently, the swift is in rapid decline, owing to the ever-diminishing populations of insects and an invasion of its nesting sites in the cracks of high cliffs by rock climbers, especially near Moab, where curtains of lycra-clad climbers festoon the red walls of Wingate sandstone.

Late in the afternoon, we make camp on a sand island fringed with tamarisk, wavy clumps of slough grass and sand willow, just inside the unmarked boundary of Canyonlands, the *real* Jurassic Park.

First things first.

Before the tents are erected, we must deploy the small metal box known affectionately as "the Groover." Like some desert reliquary, the Groover has its own tent. Instructions are given for its use. The shiny receptacle is for shit only. Urine gets heavy, Weisheit advises, so piss in the river. The Green can take it. Some among us are skeptical and hold out as long as they can. But, eventually, all must make the pilgrimage. One river, under a Groover.

Marta wanders off in search of a tent site. She soon scampers back to our riverside kitchen, where Weisheit is hunched over a tray of charcoal, grilling coho salmon seasoned with the pungent smell of dill snatched from his wife Susette's herb garden. Marta seems transformed, her body surrounded by a strange, hovering aura. An aura that buzzes. Then she whispers the fatal alarum we had all feared: "Mosquitoes!"

Believe it or not—and it does seem a stretch of logic under this evening's bombardment—the population of mosquitoes along the Green River has been in steady decline since 1964 when the floodgates closed on Flaming Gorge Dam, reducing the annual flows of the Green by 20 percent.

Mosquitoes require still water to breed, stagnant little ponds for sex pads and birthing rooms. But the yearly floods on the Green aren't as big or nearly as frequent as they used to be. There are fewer marshy places in the bottomlands and they dry up faster. Fewer mosquitoes means fewer swallows, swifts, and bats. Our little island has a small trench of stagnant water on the backside, near our tents, and tonight the orgy is on. But not like the good old days.

We varnish ourselves in non-toxic insect repellant, which, being non-toxic, proves to be no deterrent against the microscopic vampires. We slide into sweaters and long pants, gloves, bandanas, and sarongs. All to no avail. The mosquitoes penetrate every defensive shield mustered against them. We retreat to our tents, fleeing just as Weisheit is ready to serve us heaping mounds of strawberry shortcake topped with whipped cream. The horror, the horror.

Bottom line on day one: Nature bites back.

Day Two

We rise early to the crisp smell of bacon and coffee. Even the vegetarians follow the scent, uncorking their limbs after a long night inside mosquito bunkers. Those bunkers, naturally, were easily busted by the stealthy insects, who drained us as we slept.

Weisheit has been up for hours already. Over the course of the week we never once catch him nodding. He supposedly reposes on his raft, a bobbing waterbed, though this remains speculation. We greedily consume our food, too quickly to enjoy it, itching to cast off from Bloodsucker Beach.

We aren't in the water long. Our destination for the morning is Fort Bottom, less than a mile down river, where a prow of sandstone juts out into a bend of the Green River that is so contorted it would humble even the most accomplished yoga practitioner. The mesa is topped by a stone tower, the so-called Moki Fort, built a thousand years ago by the Fremont people.

It is fairly easy to find a spot to anchor the rafts; less so to break our way through the thicket of tamarisk to the trail leading us to the purple mesa.

The ground here shimmers in the morning sun. The pink sand beneath our feet is embedded with polished river stones and chunks of jasper. Call it desert pavement. The trail leads us through a parched landscape of tiny barrel cactus, Mormon tea, and shadscale, with its crunchy salty leaves, to a small, sun-blasted cabin built out of cottonwood and driftwood a century ago.

The tourist-oriented outfitters (those who bother to float the Green at all) regale their clients with stories about how the cabin was a hideout for Butch Cassidy. Perhaps it was. Cassidy was a cattle rustler who passed through the canyonlands many times and Fort Bottom was once nice pastureland, remote and hidden. But Weisheit tells a more compelling story. He believes the cabin is a relic of a kind of cowboy communism.

The pasture, he says, was a commons, open to all who didn't abuse it. Same with the lonely cabin. Any \one was welcome to stay in it, as long as they repaired the chinks in the walls, placed new sticks on the roof of the porch for shade, and maintained the dry-stacked chimney.

From the cabin we follow the twisty trail up the face of the mesa, scrambling over boulders, up slickrock, and, in a fancy display of technical climbing prowess, flop ourselves belly-first over the final wall of rubble to the rim, as gracefully as any sea lion.

At the tip of the mesa, with an unimpeded view of Labyrinth Canyon, sits the Moki Fort. This three-story tower of stacked and mortared stone was probably built sometime between 800 and 1000 AD. It is one of the several watchtowers on an archipelago of mesas stretching all the way to Moab.

By the time these towers were built, though, it does appear that the Fremont and the Anasazi to the south were in a state of cultural free-fall. Decades of drought and searing heat gripped the Colorado plateau. Springs and seeps dried up. The crops of beans and maze failed. Most of the wild game had long since been hunted to near extinction.

Most of the Anasazi's material wealth and manpower was sunk into the construction of defensive architecture: elaborate cliff palaces, remote granaries, and watchtowers. All made of stone, situated in extreme settings on the tops of buttes, in alcoves, clinging to the shear face of rock, accessible only by fragile ladders or Moki steps carved into the sandstone. There doesn't seem to be any evidence that the Anasazi were under attack from marauding tribes from the Great Plains. Instead, it appears they were fearful of raids from within their own tribes. All to no avail. The more human capital the Anasazi spent on defensive architecture and battlements, the more deeply the culture became consumed by desperation and paranoia. Sound familiar?

According to the evidence from middens and graves at Anasazi pueblos, many people were starving to death from lack of protein. The proof is in the state of their bones. The situation was so dire that toward the end they began eating mice, live mice. Other groups, according to the shocking work of anthropologist Christy Turner, resorted to cannibalism.

By the 13th century, the Anazasi and Fremont had largely vanished from the plateau. The Fremont, perhaps, fled to the Great Plains. The Anasazi to the Hopi and Zuni pueblos to the south. Within a few decades, the homeland of the Fremont and Anasazi was occupied by Paiutes, Utes, and Navajo.

Kimberly notes the presence of two circular depressions near the tower, edged in hand-hewn slabs of rock. The holes appear to be too shallow for kivas, but there's a distinct ceremonial feel to the excavations. We'll never know for sure. Most interpretive archaeology is informed guesswork, latter-day myth making.

* * *

Back on our boats, we soon glide by the Buttes of the Cross, not once, not twice, but four or five times, as if watching an instant replay with multiple reverse angles, as the river twists and turns through the impossibly tight meanders of Labyrinth Canyon. Christened by Powell, the atheist son of an itinerant Methodist preacher and abolitionist, the buttes—two highly eroded slabs of Wingate sandstone, one a tabletop mesa rising about 1,000 feet above the river and the other a soaring pinnacle perhaps 1,500 feet tall—are unlikely to inspire Christians into spasms of religious ecstasy. The cross in question seems, from this vantage, to have been stabbed upside down into the White Rim, like the one St. Peter was fatally affixed to by the pagans of Rome. In the distance, Cleopatra's Throne, a sculpted spire of Navajo sandstone, exerts its stately presence beyond the sacrilegious buttes. Perhaps, the austere Major Powell possessed a sense of humor after all.

The afternoon contracts and unwinds, slowly as the river itself. Lounging on the side of Weisheit's raft, Lorenzo breaks out his beater guitar, picking blues chords born on another river and singing his own hysterical parodies of George Jones songs. Later Kimberly recites poems by William Carlos Williams, Emily Dickinson, and Dorothy Parker, as the brutal sun lingers on the iridescent crest of the White Rim sandstone.

We can't coax any original poems out of Wolff, but he does let fly with snippets of two of our greatest poets: Smokey Robinson and Marvin Gaye. Meanwhile, Marta whispers unspeakable devotions to her ducky.

Out of the blue, Weisheit begins dissing ravens and their acolytes. Corvid bashing is one of his favorite past-times. Barry Lopez titled his book on the McKenzie River of Oregon, *Reflections in the Raven's Eye.* Ellen Meloy called her tremendous book on the Green River, *Raven's Exile.* Puffery, Weisheit hisses, mere PR to rehabilitate the reputation of the canyon's bad boys.

"Ravens get too much respect from literary nature writers," Weisheit mumbles. "They're nature's terrorists. Smart, sure, but nasty and obnoxious. They'll devise any kind of trickery to get our food. Consider, if you will, the etymology of 'ravenous.'"

Word seems to have spread through the Corvid community about Weisheit's prejudices. One morning as our captain prepares a thick pile of breakfast burritos, a raven flies over camp and drops a rock near the Groover. Later that afternoon, another raven circles Weisheit's boat flying upside down, emitting a maniacal laugh. That evening, still another raven struts back and forth on a small limestone alcove near camp, performing a mad parody of a super-model on a catwalk.

"If a group of crows is called a murder, how do we refer to a gathering of ravens?" Kimberly asks.

"A cell?" Marta says.

"A jihad," snaps Weisheit.

A few hours after Weisheit's vile imprecations, a raven astounds us all. Marta points to a large soaring raptor skimming the face of a cliff 500 feet above us. At first, the bird looks like an ordinary turkey vulture. Then we see a telltale flash of white near the tail, the signature of a juvenile golden eagle. Suddenly, a raven alights from the branch of a juniper tree on the rim of the canyon and dive-bombs the young eagle, screeching at him, nipping at his uneasy wings. The eagle tilts into a thermal and rises in an upward spiral; the raven, giving chase. Within a couple of minutes, the birds are 1,000, then 2,000 feet above us, and rising. The eagle hasn't flapped its wings once, gaining altitude and shifting directions with only the slightest adjustments to the angle of its wings and tail. Raven, though, must beat her wings furiously to keep up, but keep up she does, until both birds are mere specks against the afternoon clouds. Finally, perhaps at an altitude of 3,000 feet, the raven breaks off the pursuit, performs a sky dance, and streaks back to her perch on the rim, cackling forth a triumphant tale of homeland defense.

* * *

We make camp on a wide bend of the river near a rincon known as Anderson Bottom. Though Brian expresses a longing for something resembling a double-cheese-burger from Wendy's, Weisheit insists on preparing pasta shells stuffed with herbs and ricotta cheese. He is handing out plates of apple crisp, piping hot from his Dutch oven, when the sky begins to crackle.

Bulky storm clouds loom like bruises on the horizon, veined with lightning. Thunder convulses the canyon. We scramble to erect the ridiculous tents Tag-a-Long Tours has impishly supplied us with: tall, gangly domes with enough surplus headspace to accommodate even the crankiest Frenchman. All held together by fragile plastic poles that splinter when bent with the slightest touch of excessive force.

The wind lashes our tent, rips off the fly, uprooting the stakes, which hurtle toward the Wolff-Renzi encampment like glittery flying weapons in a kung fu movie. Fortunately, I discern no yelps of pain. Rain streams through every window, every seam, soaking our sleeping bags, our clothes, our books, our dessert.

I am ordered outside our trembling hovel to retrieve the fly and to do something, any damn thing, to stem the flow of water.

I take my bearings in the gale. Oddly, Weisheit seems to be doing the dishes, whistling "All Along the Watchtower" as he scrubs. The Hendrix version, naturally. He casually points toward the copse of trees at the edge of the beach. There I find our fly, snagged by the thorny branch of a desert olive tree. I race back toward our tent with my flapping trophy, but suddenly the storm abates. The wet air of the desert night blooms with the fresh scent of sagebrush, cottonwood, and cliffrose.

We slither into our drenched bags under the light of a fat yellow moon and listen to the mournful odes of the poorwills until we drift into sleep.

Day Three

In the morning, there is some anxiety concerning the fate of Lorenzo. His tent is a mangled ruin from the storm. The fabric has collapsed in a violent heap and the poles protrude at odd angles from the earth, like Sioux lances stuck into the corpses of the 7th Cavalry at Little Bighorn. Daniel gets on his knees, worms his way through the rubble and checks for signs of life. He detects deep snoring from within the rubble and flashes the okay sign.

At the other end of camp, Brian is heaving into the river. He attributes his illness to withdrawal from fast food. He craves Whoppers and Big Macs. But his intestinal distress is likely an early warning sign of heat exhaustion. Even the guides can get wasted by the fierce and undiscriminating desert sun.

It's not just our bodies that are taking a beating. The rafts and kayaks must be constantly ladled with water, especially when beached, to keep them from expanding in the heat. Ed Abbey's friend Ken Sleight, the model for Seldom Seen Smith in *The Monkey Wrench Gang*, once lost a raft that way, owing, as he puts it, to a "Sleight explosion."

As the sun peers over the crest of White Rim sandstone, it bathes the far wall of the canyon in a sultry, rose-colored light. There's no escaping the impression that these canyons are an eroticized landscape. In his narrative, the prudish Powell refers over and over again to the "naked" stones. Here's Powell writing about Stillwater Canyon, a few miles from our camp:

"We are now down among the buttes, and in a region the surface of which is naked, solid rock—a beautiful red sandstone, forming a smooth, undulating pavement."

And so it is. But the rock is not just naked, it also is eroded into fleshy colors and shapes, the whole Freudian montage of standing cocks (circumcised and not), breasts, slot canyons, nipples (Molly's, among others), and to use Powell's phrase, upended arses.

And then there's Upheaval Dome, a bizarre crater a few miles to the east of us where (although this remains the subject of vitriolic debate among geologists) apparently a meteor slammed into a bulging salt dome—an anhydrite diapir to be precise—blasting a giant hole in the bulge of sandstone. From the air, Upheaval Dome resembles an anatomically precise depiction of the female genitalia, clitoris included.

So the canyon throbs with Eros, not all of it sublimated. There's a lot of uninhibited screwing around going on down here. Though not at our campsite. Not yet, anyway.

Luminescent blue dragonflies join together in threesomes, foursomes, sextets, locked in fierce undulation on our paddles, on our toes, humping away indifferent to our presence. So are the grasshoppers and Mormon crickets. And the black-tailed jack rabbits—*Lepus Californicatus*—are fucking like, well, rabbits. Toads mount each other from the rear in fat quivering stacks. "Bufo bufu," quips one punster in our group, who shall remain anonymous for her own protection. I don't have the heart to tell her that her elaborate pun falters on a misidentification of the species. The humping amphibians in question are members of the well-known exhibitionist troupe, the Great Basin Spadefoots (*Spea intermontana*) and not the more dignified and modest Red-Spotted Toads (*Bufo punctatus*). Nice try, though.

* * *

We float backward into time, through an object lesson in stratigraphy, the laying down of rock and it's washing away. The making and the unmaking of the Colorado Plateau.

The strata, all laid out in horizontal lines, are an exhibition of the great geological story ever told. Rip up the Book of Genesis and start anew. Your founding myth stumbles here. But there are new mysteries to behold. Bow down and embrace them.

Most of the rock down here is a relic of the Mesozoic and Paleozoic ages. 250 million years ago, a shallow sea covered most of the Colorado Plateau, then a subtropical zone in the latitudes of the Yucatan on the ancient super-continent of Pangea. Those inland seas rose and fell, rose and fell, innumerable times over the course of the turbulent Permian epoch, creating sandstones, mudstones, shales, and fossil-encrusted limestones in, for the most part, sharply defined horizontal layers. The Moenkoepi Formation gives way to the gorgeous benches of the White Rim Sandstone, which sits astride the maroon cliffs of the Organ Rock Formation, which covers the tall, blond cliffs and amphitheaters of the Cedar Mesa Sandstone, which surrenders to the Halgaito Shale and the strange Honaker Trail Formation. Underneath all of this is the Paradox Formation, a bulging dome of salt, a kind of salt volcano, that is pushing upward and warping all of those layers of rock, creating grabens, anhydrite diapirs, and the large rotational slumps on the cliffs of Cataract Canyon.

When the continent began to shred apart, the plateau province turned hotter, drier, raked by violent winds. Climate change on an epochal scale. The ocean beds turned to seas of blowing sand, interwoven with small streams, shallow lakes. Buried and solidified. Buckled and titled by dozens of faults, upwarps, and mountain-building orogenies.

The massive buttresses of the Wingate and Navajo formations, great reefs of stone that are as distinctive as the orders of Greek architecture, are lithified sand dunes, a thousand feet thick—great waves of Earth. The Navajo and Wingate are separated by a crumbly bench of shale called the Kayenta Formation, while the thick bulk of the Wingate weighs down upon a thin layer called the Chinle Formation, highly prized by uranium miners. Collectively, these strata of rock, in some places more than 2,500 feet thick, are known as the Glen Canyon Group.

These days the best place to see the complete tapestry of the Glen Canyon Group is on the Green River, in Labyrinth Canyon, near where we put in at Mineral Bottom, 150 miles up river from Glen Canyon itself, where half of the geological story now lies unread beneath those solemn depths.

As the price of gas spikes ever upward, those shales woven in thin layers between the sandstones, and trapped by the great Meander Anticline, may soon be as valuable as gold. At $80 a barrel, some petro-geologists speculate (and speculation is ever the name of the energy game) that the oil shales will become profitable (with generous federal subsidies and exemptions from the petty constraints of environmental laws) to exploit—meaning blast, drill, strip mine, crush, slurry, dump, and then run, with your indemnification papers in your vest pocket.

Oil shale extraction, the fervent dream of James Watt during Reagantime, promises to be the most noxious assault to hit the West since the open air nuclear blasts in Nevada of the 1950s. It combines the worst aspects of oil extraction and strip mining. All under the guilt-free banner of national security, naturally.

The Colorado River and its three major tributaries, the Green, the Grand, and San Juan, began cutting into those thick layers of sedimentary rock about 10 million years ago, chiseling out the most dazzling sequence of canyons on earth: Lodore, Dinosaur, Desolation, Gray, Labyrinth, and Stillwater on the Green; Westwater and Meander on the Grand; Cataract, Narrow, Glen, Marble, Grand, Boulder, and Black canyons on the Colorado.

The amount of sediment hauled away every year by a river whose annual water yield is less than the tiny Delaware River is astounding: 195 million tons, as measured at the mouth of the Grand Canyon. In flood years, the number rises dramatically. In 1936, gauging stations recorded that the Green River alone flushed downstream 2.2 million tons of sediment in a single day.

Those rivers have already carted away nearly half of the original rock on the Colorado Plateau, from the Book Cliffs to the Kaibab and beyond. The Green and the Colorado are indiscriminate and voracious eaters, chewing through dinosaur bones, pools of oil, uranium beds, and coal seams. All going downstream. Until the dams went up. Now the sludge is piling up in the backwaters of the reservoirs, at the base of the dams, and in the mouths of the side canyons. Happy water skiing!

"Imagine the hubris of the dam builders," Marta says. She knows about hubris. Dance is the most ephemeral and riverine of arts. Or so they tell me. Compulsory attendance at Mrs. Gates' Ballroom Dancing Academy obliterated most of the joy of that art for me at age eight. But lately Marta has been choreographing her dances in communities and buildings that are under immediate threat of extinction, facing down the developer's wrecking ball. Dance becomes an act of resistance, an aesthetic assertion of the collective power of memory.

The bravado of the dam builders, the hydro-imperialists, will almost certainly come back to haunt them, their adherents, and their dupes. They have pawned off the self-glorifying illusion that their mighty plugs have arrested the geological processes that have excavated canyons, 5,000 feet deep and fifty miles wide. It is a con and a dangerous one, the same species of hubris that sank New Orleans.

Let it rain.

* * *

The squat butte looming in front of us was named Turk's Head by Powell, who thought it resembled a fez, though there's not the slightest evidence in the biographical record that the major had ever seen a fez, never mind encountered a Turk. From my vantage, it looks more like a Bundt cake, slightly charred.

This stretch of river offers the densest concentration of Fremont sites—granaries, signal towers, burials, middens, petroglyphs—that we'll encounter on the Green. But there are no dwellings, no cliff palaces. For some reason, the Fremont and Anasazi didn't like living near the big rivers. Perhaps they feared floods or rockfalls. Perhaps they felt too exposed to enemy attacks. In any event, they built their pueblos in the side canyons miles from the Green and Colorado, except in Glen Canyon, which was the heartland of the Anasazi. Thousands of Anasazi sites, dwellings, granaries, burials, and rock art, were lost in the drowning of Glen Canyon.

Our captain motions us to beach our boats at the gaping mouth of Deadhorse Canyon. Yellow-breasted chats chide us as we thread our way through the tangle of tamarisk and take our first step into the blast furnace called the Maze—the land of standing rocks, the technicolor epicenter of Abbey's world, scene of the rip-roaring chase and shoot out at Lizard Rock during the climax of *The Monkey Wrench Gang*.

Weisheit leads us to a house-sized chunk of rock coated in desert varnish and loaded with petroglyphs pecked into the sandstone by Fremont rock artists using the antler-points of elk and mule deer. Some of the images may date back 2,000 years or more. It is a crossroads site and almost every inch of rock has been etched upon over the centuries. Much of it is almost certainly ancient graffiti, bathroom humor. Some of the images seem to function as an early version of PowerPoint, depicting maps of rivers, mountain ranges, and trails; the locations of springs, corn, and melon fields and granaries; the migratory routes of bighorn sheep; weather patterns; the omnipotence of the shaman. Some of the art is as abstract as anything produced by Jackson Pollock or Franz Klein. There are spirals, shields, bison, and bighorn, power lines and rattle-snakes, and strange zoomorphic monsters from the dreamtime. Kokopelli is there, too, looking like Coltrane hunched over a soprano sax, sporting a prodigious erection. A love supreme, indeed.

The canvas of rock also displays the spooky floating anthropomorphs that obsessed the Fremont rock artists, large legless figures with elongated trapezoidal bodies, horned heads, and ornate necklaces adorned with what appear to be shrunken skulls. The largest of these figures seems to be carrying a human head in the hand of its frail, stick-like arm.

Did the Fremont hunt heads or did their gods? Were spine-tingling images merely illustrations to enhance Fremont ghost stories designed to scare the crap out the kids or were they warning signs to interlopers? To me, the floating figures resemble water creatures, spirits of the deep, vengeful ghosts of a drowned world.

The faint trail switchbacks up the parched slope to a bench of shattered jasper and chert at the base of a towering red cliff. On this field of worked stone are the remains of a Fremont factory, a lithic scatter site, spread across several acres, where Fremont weapons-makers manufactured their precision projectiles: arrow heads, lance points, axe blades.

In the glittering pile of red and white rubble I find a round black stone that Weisheit calls a Moki Marble. These sun-polished rocks are highly prized by Navajo shaman, who collect them as wards against skinwalkers. Perhaps, it will also repel the demons of nuclear Armageddon. Kimberly and I place the black stone on a small cairn overlook-ing the river as a memorial to our friend Wilson Howes ,who died a few days ago of cancer. His funeral is being held in Maryland at this very hour. Wilson may have been another victim of the atomic age. While in the Navy in 1948, he and his shipmates were forced to stand on deck of the USS Albemarle as observers of the Operation (yes) Sandstone nuclear test at Eniwetok Atoll in the Marshall Islands of the South Pacific.

The desert southwest was also ground zero for nuclear testing; the residents of southern Utah were unwitting witnesses and guinea pigs to the Pentagon's H-bomb pyrotechnics. Between 1950 and 1962, the Atomic Energy Commission and the Pentagon detonated 126 nuclear bombs above the desert at the Nevada Test Site east of Las Vegas. Each blast was aimed downwind. Destination Utah. Thousands fell ill from the radioactive fallout, lost their hair, lost their lungs, lost their breasts, gave birth to sick children with horribly deformed bodies, watched their sheep and cattle herds perish, died painfully from thyroid cancers and leukemias. No apologies were issued, no admissions of responsibility. Just collateral damage in Zion, the glowing land of the saints.

The radioactivity from those blasts persists in the sand and dust across the region, all around us here at Deadhorse Canyon, clinging to our clothes, our skin, embedding hot microscopic flakes into the tissues of our lungs.

Geologists probing the sediment mounds piling up behind Flaming Gorge, Glen Canyon, and Hoover dams carry Geiger counters and record the distinctive ping-ping-pings of Cesium-137 to date the layers of silt: 1951, 1954, 1959. Like a Bordeaux wine, each nuclear shot emits a unique signature, its very own radioactive vintage.

Even down here in the red basement of the continent, there's no secure refuge from the chronic hazards of everyday life in the post-nuclear age.

* * *

We ease down the river for another hour or so, working our way along the large meander around the Turk's Head, and then tie our rafts to a crack in the roof of an alcove in the flesh-toned Cedar Mesa Sandstone. It's a cool and shady spot for a floating lunch and yet another swim. Weisheit whips up tuna fish wraps, apple cobbler, and amazingly, watermelon that is ice-cold and delicious.

There's a small hanging garden lurking on the cliff-face above us. Glen Canyon was famous for them, but they are much rarer here than in Stillwater and Cataract. Hanging gardens are usually found under alcoves of porous rock, such as sandstone, where water seeps through the face of the cliff to create a lush microhabitat for maidenhair ferns, alcove columbine, and desert orchids.

Here, sprouting out of a nest of ferns is a close relative of poison ivy (to which I am pathologically allergic and more frightened of than rattlesnakes) called the Lemonade bush. But far from being toxic, this leafy shrub offers up pink flowers and sour berries that can stimulate saliva production for the parched desert nomad. I pop off a couple of tart berries in my mouth, swill them around until my mouth begins to erupt with foam. Hmm. Might make for nicely perverse treats for Halloween.

After lunch, Lorenzo dives into the deep pool. He breaks the surface of the reddish water, yelping. "Hey, something bit me!"

"Nothing to worry about," I say. "Probably just a minnow."

Yeah, a minnow alright. The Colorado Pikeminnow: once the most voracious predator in the Colorado River system. The Pikeminnow is far from a tiny fish. When Powell descended the canyons, his men caught Pikeminnows that were bigger than barracudas. One was six feet long and weighed around 100 pounds. When they gutted the mighty minnow, its large heart continued beating on the ground at a rate of twenty beats a minute for four minutes.

Then again that little nibble probably wasn't a kiss from a Pikeminnow, since those cruisers of the Green and Colorado have nearly been wiped out, along with all of the other native fish in these salty, silty, hot, and turbulent desert rivers.

What the dams didn't kill, the rotenone did. Fish managers considered the native minnows and suckers "trash fish" to be eradicated and replaced with catfish, striped bass, and cold water fish like rainbow trout, which now thrive in the clear and frigid waters in the reaches downstream from the spillways of Flaming Gorge and Glen Canyon dams.

As a consequence of the dams, eradication regimes, and competition with exotics, four of the eight species of native fish are now on the endangered species list: the Colorado Pikeminnow, razorback sucker, humpback chub, and bonytail chub. The other four species are also in freefall.

* * *

In the sizzling glare of the late afternoon sun, the water of the Green River appears flat, mellow. But once you're in it up to your neck, the pull of the current is strong and decisive. A weak swimmer could easily be swept downstream, tire, slip under, surrender to the river's covert power. It happens. Whiskey helps make it so. Most of the deaths in Cataract Canyon involve the consumption of spirits, of one kind or another.

One by one, we wade out to the channel and plunge in, breast-stroking across the silent surge of tepid water to get a closer look at a Fremont granary clinging to the canyon wall. Here the river is perhaps 200 yards across and yet it sweeps us a hundred yards downstream before we reach the far bank and once again fight our way through an unyielding hedge of tamarisk. If the only the French had planted the Maginot Line with a thicket of tamarisk, they might have been able to repel the onslaught of the Nazi Wehrmacht.

We contour around the base of the cliff, casually looking for the pot-shards Weisheit found here a few years ago. But the site has been picked clean by looters.

A decade or so ago, the looters were mainly Mormon ranchers busting across the desert on ATVs. They would dig up Anasazi and Fremont sites for pots, metates, sandals, jewelry, and skeletons and sell them to eastern collectors and museums. Now the threat largely comes from New Agers seeking a personal connection to Anasazi mysticism, a potshard to serve as a talisman to transport them to the spirit world. They are spiritual trespassers and there are legions of them, criss-crossing the plateau, festooned in coral and turquoise jewelry bought in the haute salons of Santa Fe and Sedona, spewing misty platitudes about the interconnectedness of the universe.

And they're not only after human antiquities. Several of the anthills we've come across have been looted as well, dug up in search of shark's teeth from the Triassic Epoch. Give them the slightest pretext and humans will mine almost anything. During World War II, there was an all-out blitz on rabbitbrush—a desert scrub that used to be a ubiquitous plant in the canyonlands that could thrive for 150 to 200 years—when the Pentagon offered contracts for uprooted plants for use in the manufacture of tires for jeeps and airplanes.

The maroon granary looms thirty feet above us, blending in with the dark reds of the Organ Rock Formation. The rectangular structure is about twelve feet tall and eight feet wide, with a small window framed in wood near the top. It is affixed to the sheer wall of the cliff, like a tick, with no visible means of access. Once, the structure was reached by a rickety ladder, which was tied together with strips of yucca and deer sinew. But there is no sign of that now. These are the kinds of seemingly inaccessible, floating buildings that led the Navajo to conclude that the Anasazi and Fremont practiced black magic; that somehow they had learned to fly.

The granary is a corn bin fortified as if it were a missile silo. The beautifully austere building must have been incredibly dangerous to build. At least a ton of sandstone rock would have been hauled up to the small alcove, where it would have been drystacked on the perilous cliff, probably with some kind of scaffolding, though there are no apparent holes in the rockface as signs of such an edifice. Then cottonwood branches would be used as window frames and as vegas and latillas for the roof. The whole structure was then coated in adobe.

In the fall, women, most likely, would carry woven baskets and pots stuffed with corncobs and beans up a series of ladders and ropes to the granary and dump the seeds through the tiny window. Then in the spring the grain would be retrieved for the planting season. Both ventures were very risky propositions. Surely many tumbled to their deaths on the sharp rocks below.

The Fremont and Anasazi were desert farmers, planting their corn, beans, and melons in these sun-scorched bottomlands, dependent on the summer monsoons and snow-melt floods. They picked spots where the water table was near the surface, so that their crops could be moistened from below. On the Hopi mesas, women still cart down water in clay pots to irrigate the crops during the driest weeks. The Fremont probably did the same.

It seems unlikely that these kinds of extreme precautions were taken merely to secure the grain from the elements or from ravens. Something much darker was haunting the Anasazi culture; their art and architecture display all the signs of a highly developed society slipping into a self-consuming paranoia.

This granary, I called it the Maroon House, was probably constructed around 1100 AD and perhaps used for less than a decade. There are at least a dozen similar structures within a few square miles. The capital and human investment in the construction and maintenance of these buildings must have been a huge drain on the resources of the community. By 1300, the Fremont, as known through their rock art, pottery, architecture, and burial figurines, had largely vanished as a culture across the Great Basin, where they had arrived so mysteriously a thousand years earlier.

If the anthropologists are right, and that's a very frail "if," the religious beliefs and customs of the Fremont and Anasazi still resonate in the rituals of the Hopi and other pueblo tribes living on the sun-blasted mesas of northern Arizona and New Mexico. That means the Fremont were end-timers, believers in the approach of a great, cleansing apocalypse that would sweep away the tormenters and redeem the believers. From Mount Sinai to the Trinity Site, most desert religions cleave to this chilling faith in a final cataclysm.

I imagine the Maroon House as the cell of a visionary, an entombed Wovoka, the Paiute shaman, eyes starring through that tiny window at the searing arc of the sun, day after day, year after year, until the final vision of how it would all come to an end burned into his soul, giving rise to the Ghost Dance movement that swept across Native America, promising that soon, very soon, the skin of the earth itself would rise up and consume the white invaders.

And, yes, we still have to get past Rockfall Canyon.

I look across the river. Brian is doing a little dance as he tries to drain a big boiling pot of pasta without the use of a strainer, which seems to have mysteriously vanished from the cargo hold. Raven, again? It's time for dinner: Chicken Alfredo. The intoxicating smell of Susette's herbs being put to efficient use lures us back.

Night falls suddenly in what Powell called "these solemn depths." Weisheit passes around a plate of brownies. No one asks if he has perhaps slipped a little hashish into the mix. No one needs any embellishment for what is unfolding above us. The planetarium sky is pulsating with stars, unbleached by even the faintest strains of light pollution. We begin to notice yellow streaks blazing down toward the earth then burning out in a fast orange fizz. One after another. A meteor shower, perhaps, though it's a month too early for the glorious annual migration of the Perseids.

"Probably not meteors," Weisheit advises. "Might be space junk. There's a hole in the sky up there, a window in the ionosphere, where the space shuttle and other debris from deep space slips through into the Earth's atmosphere. That's one reason Moab attracts a lot of sky watchers, alien hunters."

So here we sit, munching brownies, smack on the landing pad of God's trash chute. Perhaps that explains how Upheaval Dome came to be.

Day Four

The dawn is hot. Even the rocks seem to tremble at the appearance of the morning sun. The sky is cloudless. Again. Spotless, except for a single Swainson's hawk probing the bottomland for lizards and mice.

There's a new pulse to the camp this morning, an excitement, a tension. If all goes well, by noon today we will swing around the final bend of the Green River to its famous barbed confluence with the Grand River, where the true Colorado is born and makes its stunning debut in rough-and-tumble Cataract Canyon. Eighteen frenzied miles of freedom. And then…

The rafts must be re-rigged, all the gear lashed down tightly for the tumult of the rapids. Weisheit is pulling bags out of the catchall, the small hold in the center of his raft, when he suddenly jumps back, bouncing on his tiptoes on the side of the raft in a delicate balancing act worthy of Nadia Comaneci. He squats, peers down into the catchall and confronts the deadliest mammal in Canyonlands: the deer mouse. The big-eared, glassy-eyed, innocent-looking rodent is the leading vector of the deadly Hantavirus, a form of hemorrhagic fever like Ebola and Marburg, which the little critter disseminates through its urine. Over the next two days, Hanta the Mouse eludes capture, pissing in the hold of Weisheit's raft an average of six times an hour.

Here's what I know about Hantavirus. It begins with a subtle stiffness of the muscles, progresses within hours to an incapacitating fever, and ends with blood gushing out of your ears, eyes, and asshole. There are better ways to die.

And that's not all. Only last week, biologists discovered dead pack rats in a rock-shelter at Natural Bridges National Monument, fifty or so miles to the southeast of our campsite. The rodents died of black plague. Yet another defensive strike in nature's guerilla war.

We float leisurely on the Green, at one with the pace of the river, paddling only to loosen stiffening joints or to reverse our view of the canyon as it slips inexorably away from us.

We move slowly, but not slowly enough. Not for me. There are birds that escape identification, canyons that slide by unexplored, granaries on ledges that we just might be able to reach, dinosaur tracks frozen in sandstone, shady cottonwood groves and blooming gardens of claret-cup cactus, pictograph panels in the ancient Barrier Canyon style up slickrock gorges that end in hidden waterfalls, past sites marked for dams by the demented engineers at the Bureau of Reclamation, past sunken barges, badger dens and peregrine nests on lofty aeries in crevices of the White Rim Sandstone, now scrolling by 1,000 feet above us.

Lorenzo longs to come face-to-face with a cougar or, at the very least, catch a glimpse of her tail as she leaps from one ledge of Cedar Mesa to another. And surely she is out there. Waiting.

But we must press on. We have a plane to catch in Hite. Three days from now. It will not wait.

Even here, in the silent depths of Stillwater Canyon, the gravitational force of civilization grips us, tugs us down the river, pulls us toward our rendezvous with the chill waters of the Blue Death. And we relent.

* * *

Marta calls our attention to a gathering of odd, frenetic birds with plump bodies and tiny heads, strutting nervously on a pink plate of sand at the mouth of Jasper Canyon. Chukars. Another Asian import. These pheasant-like gamebirds from the steppes of China were set loose in the arid west a century ago by the followers of Teddy Roosevelt, who had evidently grown bored of blowing away sharp-tailed grouse, prairie chickens and wild turkeys. The chubby chukars have done pretty well for themselves, even though as a species they may well be, as my pal John Holt calls them, the goofiest birds in the West. Holt, one of the best outdoor writers in America, kills Chukars as often as he can across the plains and canyons of Montana and Wyoming.

Killing chukars is harder than it sounds. As a rule, chukars are dumb. Dumb, yes, but lucky too. When flushed, they don't simply face their danger, as novice kayakers are instructed, they fly right toward it, in short, erratic bursts. En masse. Holt swears you can blow your own head off hunting chukar, even when, inexplicably, you haven't been sipping Jack Daniels all afternoon. Mr. Cheney, this bird's for you.

Suddenly, the chukars freeze, as a scream pierces the sky, like fingernails scraping a blackboard. A peregrine falcon careens on a laser-line from the canyon rim toward the covey of chukars at nearly 200 miles per hour, the fastest living creature (and the most beautiful). As the sleek raptor nears its mark, the bird breaks off its assault and veers back up into the canyon air only a few feet from the cowering chukars, who seem immobilized by the falcon's mesmerizing cry.

"The falcon seems to be playing a game of Chinese Chukars," Kimberly quips.

The fact that the chukars are so common on the beaches of the Green River is slightly disorienting and yet another sign that something is amiss. The peregrines may be tired of eating Kung Pao Chukar, but coyotes aren't. Coyotes normally keep the chukar population of the canyon penned down much farther upslope. Then it occurs to me that in our six days on the river, I haven't seen nor heard the midnight yowling of a single coyote, once a ubiquitous presence across Canyonlands. The ranchers who ring the park have taken their toll on the coyote, stringing their skinned corpses from barbed wire fences, planting poisoned meat, dousing their dens with gasoline and then igniting the mothers and their pups, studding the desert with M-80 bomblets that explode when touched, mangling paws, shredding jaws, killing many outright, leaving others to wander mortally wounded across the desert. Coyote, the desert trickster, is a magnet for the most sadistic impulses of the western land barons.

* * *

The thin riparian curtain of tamarisk that parallels the river shivers with life: fly-catchers and phoebes, finches and phalaropes, painted ladies and calliope humming-birds.

I'm beginning to develop a grudging, guilty admiration for some of these invasive species, tamarisk and Chukars, catfish and Russian thistle (AKA tumbleweed) for their relentless hold on life, for their resilience under conditions of extreme environmental stress.

The tamarisk, also known as salt cedar, not only crowds out willows and other native trees and shrubs through prolific growth and deep rooting, it also engages in biological warfare, secreting a toxin that kills off competing vegetation.

Time is accelerating. The climate is in overdrive. Only the most adaptable have a good shot at survival in the long term. So let us praise the blasted tamarisk, willow-eating plant of the Colorado. There is a tenacity to the life force which suggests it will withstand anything we throw at it, from global warming to H-bombs. Consider the endoliths, organisms that burrow deep inside of rocks. Canyonlands is chock full of endoliths, who, one hopes, will come slouching out of their quartzite fissures as the final rebuttal to the Rapture, the ultimate death wish of the Christian hordes and the physicists of Armageddon, who count down the End Time to the last nanosecond. Sorry boys, life goes on.

* * *

We round yet one more bend in the Green—let there always be one more bend to this river—and are greeted by a thrilling cascade of notes. It's either Sonny Rollins or *Catherpus Mexicanus*, the canyon wren. A true troglodyte.

The tiny wren's undulating song floats on a current of cool air sliding out of Powell Canyon, an amphitheater-like gouge in the red wall near the confluence of the Green and the Grand. The one-armed Major stopped here for a day and hauled himself up the terraced walls of the canyon to the rim for a stunning view down the Meander Anticline to the Grand River and the spiny back of what is now called the Needles District.

My thoughts turn to Powell, a fellow Midwesterner drawn to this harsh and vulnerable landscape. Powell was born in 1834 at Mt. Morris, near Palmyra, New York, to an itinerant Methodist preacher. At an early age, Powell rejected his father's religious fervor and, instead, fell under the spell of a local naturalist named George Crookham, who encouraged Powell to go west. Under Crookham's advice, Powell left home at the age of sixteen, spent time in Wisconsin, and studied natural science at Oberlin College and later in Illinois, where he began teaching school, taking float trips down the Mississippi, studying geology, and collecting fossils. A passionate abolitionist, Powell enlisted in Lincoln's Army soon after the attack on Ft. Sumner, and quickly proved himself a favorite of Ulysses S. Grant, who valued Powell's engineering skills. Powell commanded one of the artillery batteries at the battle of Shiloh, where he lost his right arm. He was nursed to health by his wife, Emma Dean, and then threw himself back into the war, especially at the bloody battle of Vicksburg.

After the war, Powell returned to Illinois, where he taught natural sciences at several small Illinois colleges, founded the Illinois Natural History Society, and began making summer explorations in the Colorado Rockies. In 1869, five years after losing his arm, Powell launched his first venture down the Green and Colorado Rivers. This wasn't an Army expedition. It didn't enjoy the backing of the federal government. Powell wasn't the hired errand boy of an eastern industrialist turned philanthropist. He wasn't searching for gold or oil. He was merely a largely self-educated teacher at a small college in rural Illinois with a consuming interest in geology. Locals admired his shell collection. His expedition to the Colorado Plateau was financed by the Illinois Natural History Society, of which he was the president. Powell was the oddball on the roster of explorers of the American outback. He didn't have the educational pedigree of Clarence Dutton, nor the imperial ambitions of John Fremont. His trip was as close to pure science as the continent had yet seen.

Powell's first voyage began at the small town of Green River, Wyoming with four small boats and a crew of nine other men, hunters, drifters, friends, and shell-shocked Civil War vets, including his paranoid and unstable brother Walter. The trip would take them through some of the world's deepest and most beautiful canyons: Lodore, Whirlpool, Desolation, Labyrinth, Cataract, Glen, Marble, and the Grand, over vicious rapids and through sizzling uncharted deserts and Indian country to Colorado's confluence with the Virgin River at Grand Wash in southeastern Utah, 1,000 miles downstream.

Two years later Powell returned to the Colorado Plateau, flush with $12,000 of federal government cash for the mapping of the Colorado Plateau. The second expedition, this one crewed by geologists, photographers, and painters, was closely followed by the booster press and congress. Powell's self-glorifying account of his excursions, *Exploration of the Colorado River and Its Canyons*, was published in 1875 by the

Smithsonian. Although the book conflates the two journeys into a single narrative and elides almost all mention of the work of his colleagues, it stands as one of the most thrilling adventure stories ever written. The book became a bestseller and helped Powell win his position as the head of the Bureau of Ethnology. Like many misguided progressives of his time, Powell believed that Native Americans should be compensated for their lands and then forcibly assimilated into white society. Even so, Powell was a sensitive and humane ethnographer, a model of sorts for the later work of Franz Boas and Robert Marshall.

Three years later, Powell published his influential *Report on the Lands of the Arid Region of the United States*, which called for a reorganization of the settlement and development of the west under the auspices of a new government agency, which he, of course, wanted to head. Powell was rewarded with the leadership of the US Geological Survey. But the fate of the West ended up in the hands of the Bureau of Reclamation and the Bureau of Land Management.

Powell was a man of science, yes, but also of technology. Powell was one of the first apostles of scarcity. The age of exploration would give way to the age of managed exploitation of nature. He dreamed of harnessing the river, capturing its power, putting it into utilitarian service. Powell didn't share Thoreau's belief in the redemptive power of wilderness and wild, untamed rivers. At various turns Powell could be called a progressive, a realist, a technocrat—ready to re-engineer nature and western society through the distribution of water, an advocate of centralized planning on a vast scale.

Powell remained a Jeffersonian, an agrarian, even though the Major would reject Jefferson's gridded township system for a political cartography contoured to watersheds, hydrographic basins. He embraced the progressive ideal that the arid wasteland could be redeemed by the judicious application of irrigation principles—the atheist could not escape the framework of his father's Methodism.

Like Jefferson, Powell believed that democratic values flourished from small farms and ranches. An irrigated West, Powell believed, would keep the interior reaches of the country from falling into the hands of the monopolists and robber barons.

Powell was willing to impound nearly every drop of the Colorado River's water behind dams—built not in the depths of the canyons, but higher in the mountains in order to minimize evaporation. The major was quite explicit about his intentions, writing: "All the waters of all the arid lands will eventually be taken from their natural channels." Note the double "alls."

Even so, Powell estimated that all of that water—taken from the Green, the Colorado, the Gila, the Missouri, and the Rio Grande—would only succeed in making 2 to 3 percent of the land in the arid west yield viable crops or grazing lands. Like Gifford Pinchot and other progressive conservationists, Powell sought to rationalize and control the development of these irrigation lands by reserving them in the public estate, making most of the west a kind of federal commons interspersed with home-steads and small communities.

"I early recognized that ultimately these natural features would present conditions which would control the institutional or legal problems," Powell wrote in the *Report on the Arid Lands*. He believed the landscape would shape the political geography, form a natural safeguard to over-population and economic exploitation.

He was wrong, of course, and soon began to realize just how completely the power elite had captured the government and used its clout to redesign the plumbing of the West's rivers, training the spigots to their own enterprises, irrigating the vast plan-tations of the Imperial, San Joaquin, and Sacramento valleys, worked by the West's equivalent of slave labor. Irrigation led to servitude, not liberation, cartels not small-scale democracies. The centralized water bureaucracy became a servant of the hydro-imperialists, not an honest broker of the public interest.

Powell began to see the shape of the future, the perversion of his vision and began to object. He engaged in fierce congressional combat with Senator William Stewart of Nevada, the Ted Stevens of his time. Powell was one of the first whistleblowers and he met the fate reserved for most of his kind: he was chased out of office, running from trumped up charges of corruption and financial malfeasance.

The Colorado River system is crying out for a new generation of whistleblowers, government biologists, hydrologists, and geologists, who are willing to risk their own careers to save a river ecosystem on the brink of collapse. They will, naturally, be vili-fied, ridiculed, investigated, and threatened by the cabal of interests profiteering on the demise of the Colorado and their political hacks in Washington. Now comes word that the Bush administration, in collusion with its wholly owned Supreme Court, is axing the last frail protections federal whistleblowers enjoy against government purges. So these scientists, should they ever step into the public spotlight, will need cover. But will they get it from the big DC enviro groups, like the Sierra Club and the Wilderness Society—the very environmental groups that gave you Glen Canyon Dam (and so many more)? Fat chance.

Here's a snapshot of what some of the scientists have told me privately. They paint a bleak portrait of a river in terminal decline. And not just any river, either, but the Colorado, the great river of the West. The annual floods of the Green, Grand, and Colorado rivers have been neutered, as upstream dams straight-jacket the flow of the rivers, turning the volume on and off at will, according to the whims of the power grid. The channel of the river is narrowing. The seasonal wetlands and marshes are van-ishing. Springs and seeps are drying up. Beaches are disappearing. The water table is dropping. The cottonwood groves are dying off, and so are the sand and coyote willows, squeezed out by tamarisk. The river is losing its organic nutrients, as driftwood and other debris is entombed behind the dams. Endemic species of fish, like the humpback chub, which evolved only in the Colorado Basin, are sliding toward oblivion, replaced by catfish and carp. The water behind the dams is evaporating, turning saline, loading up with pesticides, petrochemicals, and fecal matter. The reservoirs are silting up, losing storage capacity and electrical generating capability. The dams themselves are vulnerable to catastrophic breaches and terrorist attacks—and they're not referring here to terminally ill river-rats with access to a houseboat and seventeen beer coolers packed with C-4 explosives.

* * *

You don't see the Grand River coming. It sneaks in from the northeast, down a vaulted corridor of rock. You feel its muscular pulse first, sucker-punching you with a new surge to the current. The river runs a vibrant reddish-brown, the color of native America.

Here at the marriage of the Grand and the Green is where the real Colorado River is born. It flows freely for eighteen miles then dies beneath the chill waters of Lake Powell. These eighteen miles are the only free-flowing stretch of the Colorado River from here to the Sea of Cortez: turbulent, tepid, freighted with silt.

The river that runs through Grand Canyon is not free. It bears no resemblance to the natural Colorado. Its flow is minutely fine-tuned by the hydro-engineers that operate Glen Canyon Dam. The water emerges from the spillways at 47 degrees, 50 degrees cooler than the Colorado on an average summer day. Cold enough for rainbow trout. Frigid and blue. Cataract Canyon is all that remains of the river Powell encountered. And half of it has been drowned.

Weisheit motions us over to a beach on river right where several other rafts are anchored. This is the famous Spanish Bottom. One of the guides is leading a group of jolly Germans, who look almost as Aryan as the suburban saints of Provo. He gestures at our rafts and kayaks and tells his clients with a smirk and a theatrical shake of his head, "Those are self-bailing boats."

Then the rival guide pushes his raft (a non-bailing bucket boat) off the beach and heads down Cataract Canyon. On the bucket boat's stern, the icon of authenticity wears a propeller. I guess that's how you run Fast Food Rapids. Get 'em in, get 'em out. The whitewater quickie. But who is bailing the hydrocarbons?

The river clientele are becoming increasingly international, as younger Americans opt for extreme sports, such as base jumping, or root themselves in front of online gaming monitors and swell to such obese proportions that they can no longer squeeze through security screens at airports, never mind stuff themselves into a kayak.

Moab is a favored destination for Germans obsessed with John Wayne. They urge their guides to haul them off to places where they can get their photos snapped in front of locations from John Ford films.

Australians come to the river to tempt death, badgering their guides to take the most dangerous course through the biggest rapids. One Aussie offered Weisheit $1,000 to intentionally flip his raft in the cauldron of Big Drop One. "I'm not going to do that," Weisheit told him. "But will you still pay me $1,000 if the river flips us anyway?"

The English, as a group, tend to be prissy. They refuse to swim naked, make odd, animal-like noises in the Groover, wear dress shoes in the raft, and according to the late river-runner and writer Ellen Meloy, insist on referring to river eddies as, yes, *Edwards*.

It will surprise no one that the French come to dispute. They complain about the lack of standing room in their tents, the omnipresence of bugs, the paucity of rapids prior to Cataract, the soaking from the rapids themselves. Most vociferously, they bitch about the quality of riverside meals, prepared by the river guides following a hard day rowing in sweltering heat. After being offered a plate with Indiana-grown corn-on-the-cob lathered in garlic butter, a French tourist shoved the fare back at his guide and exclaimed, "Why do you serve me this pig food?" These are the clients you send out for firewood near the scorpion's nest and the faded midget rattlesnake's den.

But the consensus of the guides is clear. The crudest, cheapest, and most demeaning patrons are Russian men, led by their President Vladimir Putin.

A few years ago, as those who guided him vividly recall, Vladimir Putin journeyed to the American Southwest to take his illegitimate son on an initiation ritual. The boy's mother is now an American citizen. First stop was a big game ranch in Texas, where Putin and Jr blasted zebras, antelopes, and bison. Apparently, Putin, reenacting a scene out of Mailer's *Why Are We In Vietnam*, marked his son's forehead in the blood of one of these hapless creatures.

Then it was on to Moab, Utah, for a raft trip down Cataract Canyon on the Colorado River. The Moab river guide community is still shaking its head from its close encounter with the Russian president and former KGB man. "We get a lot of whacked-out people coming down the river, but Putin really is a dangerous guy, a real mobster," a guide told me.

"His packs were loaded with guns, vodka, and tens of thousands of dollars in cash," the guide said. "He seemed to be a little on edge. He was a real bully. He was drunk much of the time and bossed people around as if they were his personal slaves. They refused to use the Groover. They pissed and defecated wherever they wanted. They fired off their guns. They caught channel catfish and bashed their heads in with rocks."

Putin and his son were soon bored by the red rock canyons and Class five rapids. "By the third day, Putin demanded that the guides call in a helicopter to have his party picked up and flown out. Then he got drunk and began to threaten the guides. He started bragging about how many people he had personally killed. More than forty, he said."

The rafts finally exited Cataract and motored across thirty miles of Lake Powell's flat water to the marina complex at Hite. The next stop on the Vlad and son's tour was supposed to be a four-wheeler excursion tearing up the desert in the bizarre Needles District of Canyonlands. But Putin opted for a more traditional form of initiation for his son, straight out of Dostoevsky's *Notes from the Underground*. From the Hite marina, he placed a call to Las Vegas.

"Get us some whores," Putin shouted into his cell phone. "Price is no object."

* * *

As Weisheit and Brian deal with some administrative matters and check the rigging of the rafts for the first rapids, I take a short walk through the meadows of Spanish Bottom, following a trail that winds up into the Maze and a group of strange multi-colored rock spires called the Doll House, which could pass for Utah's version of Antonio Gaudi's Sagrada Familia Cathedral.

Cairns mark the way, even though the way is obvious. Everyone wants to leave their testimonial to treading the wilderness. I leave my own by toppling the cairns as I pass them, scattering the stones among the yellow beeplants and Indian ricegrass.

I stumble across a lithified mound of cowshit. Cows haven't grazed here in at least forty-five years, since Canyonlands became a national park and all the bovine marauders were finally evicted. Even the most mundane scars take decades to heal in this desert. Putin's shit is out there too, slowly turning to stone.

* * *

I return to the beach a few minutes late, a victim of prior appropriation. The kayaks have already been claimed by the Wolff-Renzi clan in a ruthless application of western water law: first in time, first in right. Kimberly is sitting on Weisheit's raft, already gripping the straps so tightly her hands are turning the color of a blind cavefish. I look at Brian. It's 115 degrees, the sun is bouncing microwaves off the cliffs, and he's not wearing a shirt. Is that smart? He hasn't rowed this river before. He's written crib notes about the routes through the rapids on his arm like a rookie quarterback thrown into a playoff game. He's only eighteen. He's even more excited than I am. What the hell, I think, as I step onto his raft, it could be fun.

Now everyone must strap on lifejackets, our orange carapaces. We've entered a region of laws and regulations. Our names must be entered in a register beneath a gaudy sign that warns: DANGER! EXTREME RAPIDS AHEAD. We must inform the government where we will camp. How long we will stay. We must promise not to piss in a claret cup, shit on a prickly pear, feed the cougars, swim naked, have sex in public, or stomp on the blue-black cryptogamic crust that stitches the desert topsoil in place.

The consumption of the Colorado's water is scarcely regulated at all. It ends up in the drip-dry lawns and lagoon-sized pools of Phoenix; the stubby alfalfa-bearded hills of northern New Mexico; the emerald fairways of Scottsdale, the dark slurry pipes that flush coal, strip-mined from the gaping maw of Black Mesa to the power plants that smudge the skies of the Four Corners; the crusty, salinated plantations of the Imperial Valley; the neon nihilism of Las Vegas.

But travel on the Colorado's waters is as restricted as a border crossing from Mexico. Visitation through Cataract is ordered, directed, controlled by plans concocted in Washington and enforced by river cops and park rangers in mirror shades who pack pepper spray and automatic weapons. Precisely 7,954 rafters will be permitted passage through Cataract in a given year and not a person more: unless they happen to be a federal judge, a Russian dictator, an engineer. There's much for a desert anarchist to resist, but few places to hide down here anymore. Butch Cassidy wouldn't find sanctuary in the new Canyonlands. Neither would Alonzo Turner, friend of Joe Hill, Wobbly and sometime resident of the canyons, who carved his name followed by "Socialism 1912" on the now submerged walls of lower Cataract.

Despite the thrills that await us downstream, I already long for the anonymous freedom of our indolent days on the Green River.

* * *

The walls of Cataract begin to squeeze together, edging out even the tenacious tamarisk. There is only rock and river, which is beginning the most extreme descent since its fall from the Rockies and the Wind Rivers. Over the next eighteen miles, the Colorado drops at the rate of 17.3 feet per mile, more than twice the slope of descent in Grand Canyon. As Roderick Nash wrote, "For years men have marveled at the Grand and feared Cataract." There's no turning back now.

We hear the rapids twenty minutes before we round that last bend. We glide past the point where Bureau of Reclamation zealot Eugene LaRue wanted to build the Junction Dam to inundate the Green, Grand, and Colorado with one concrete plug, past the mouth of Red Lake Canyon, and the ghostly, charred remains of a cottonwood grove torched by hikers in 1989, and finally meet them face to face. A low, steadily mounting rumble carries up the canyon, like the rolling bassline in a Temptations song played by the great James Jamerson.

Weisheit stands in his raft; scans the river; finds the silky tongue of the rapid, known as Brown Betty after a boat that broke free of its line here in 1889; and slides over the three foot waves. We follow taking a line slightly to Weisheit's right. The crest of the first big wave pops the raft up and then the bow dips into the hole, spraying us with warm water, then we're up again and into a rollercoaster of v-shaped tailwaves.

I look back and catch a glimpse of Lorenzo's head, poking out of a frothy wave, nearly get whacked by Brian's long oar. Zo either followed us too closely or shot much faster through the rapids in his yellow kayak. Brian issues a stern warning. Lorenzo executes a pirouette on the crest of wave and raises his paddle in a gesture that is open to more than one interpretation.

We reach the eddy, catch our breath, and almost immediately plunge into Rapid Two, which, for some peculiar reason, Weisheit seems to be running backwards, oars raised to the heavens like the outstretched wings of an anhinga.

Brian and I take a more conservative approach—after all, we're carrying the Groover. But once again Brian hits the waves slightly to the right of the Master's line. The first swell jolts our raft, twisting it slightly so that we enter the hole at a precarious angle, spray drenching the raft as it tilts into the torrent and toward a shiny stiletto of rock, before settling back down into the safe tumble of tailwaves. And there goes Lorenzo flashing out of the mist on our left, this time, scooting past us in his Buddy Holly glasses and Hank Williams straw hat. Brian's scatological exclamation drowns in the feedback of the rapids. Where are that child's parents?

Well, it so happens that at this very moment the nose of Daniel and Marta's blue tandem kayak is penetrating the back of a standing wave like the beak of a pileated woodpecker piercing a rotten aspen branch. Their heavy rubberized behemoth, difficult to maneuver in the calmness of the eddies, exhibits all the nautical grace of a Civil War submarine in whitewater. It doesn't slide over rapids so much as bust through them. The Sledgehammer.

And so it goes. Rapids, pool. Rapids, pool. Rapids, pool. Until Weisheit stands again, striking his best Sacajawea pose, and points to a beach of shattered rock on a large pool at the ragged lip of Rapid 5, which hisses and growls at our approach.

After we tie the boats to the sand anchor, Weisheit begins preparing lunch. Out of his catchall he plucks a bag of lobster meat, a jar of olives, a red onion, two celery stalks, sea salt and black pepper, tortillas, French mustard, sprigs of fresh cilantro and thyme, two bags of chips, eight brownies, five apples, a melon and a jug of powdered lemonade. Like a sommelier of French wines, he sniffs each item for the faintest trace of deer mouse urine. I don't enquire as to how he came to familiarize himself with the distinctive scent of mouse piss.

I take a look around. We have entered a new geological architecture and none of us even noticed, our attention has been so firmly riveted for the last hour on the river's rapids and rocks. We are now in the lower level of the Permian, a transition zone where the geology gets weird. The dominant rock here is called the Elephant Canyon Formation, a clastic mélange of stones, a mixing of shales, limestone, and sandstones into a bulky mass formed during one of the most cataclysmic ages in the history of the Earth. The Elephant Canyon rocks wear the scars of that time of titanic geological combat.

The early Permian period also bore witness to a great explosion of life forms, when 90 percent of the animal phyla on Earth originated. These stones spit out fossils as compulsively as Daniel Wolff expectorates the shells of sunflower seeds. The ground is littered with crinoids and brachiopods, fusulinds and trilobites—both of which disappeared after the great Permian extinction. All frozen in stone. Here the past keeps reasserting itself in deep cycles of burial, petrifaction, and resurrection, exposing paleontological inscriptions that undermine the revealed Word, real-time geological apostasies.

Glen Canyon Dam itself may end as a fossil: its abutments buried in silt, its gray death-arc sealed in sediment. Even in its shackled state, the Colorado is a river of dissolved stone, a river of mud, sand, and rock. It carries a more robust sediment load than any river in the country, all piling up in the riverbed, up the lateral canyons, behind the dam. One of the reasons put forth for building Glen Canyon Dam was to serve as a sediment trap to save Lake Mead from becoming a mudflat. By 1955, only thirty years after the floodgates closed at Hoover Dam, more than 10 percent of Lake Mead's storage capacity was clotted with sediment. Since then, the death of Lake Mead has slowed—but only marginally—and the death of Lake Powell has begun.

More than 44 million tons of sediment are dumped into Lake Powell every year. That works out to eighty-five tons every minute. The dam's outlet tubes are already silting up. The Bureau of Reclamation itself estimates they will be filled with muck within a 100 years, probably less. More than 100 miles of the reservoir are now clogged with silt. The silt-laden side canyons are eerie badlands of sediment. The recent drought has exposed the relentless march of mud. But even under the most extreme global warming scenarios, there will still be wet years, El Niño winters, seasons of heavy snows and tumultuous floods. In a big flood year, all of that accumulated sediment will be flushed down the canyon in one traumatic event, pushing it all to the base of the dam itself, turning the once blue waters of Lake Powell blood red. In a mere 700 years, a geological nanosecond, the silt will have topped the dam, sealing it up as a fabricated intrusion, a temporary diversion for the restless river, an encased relic of human folly.

* * *

Rapid Five (the USGS simply numbered the rapids of Cataract, instead of naming them, because they assumed the entire canyon would eventually be inundated under dam-clogged water) is the first truly dangerous falls in Cataract Canyon. Powell capsized in a dory here. Punctuated by spiky rocks, two vicious holes, and a tricky turn, it's one of the rapids that can be most dangerous during the lower flows of July. We walk downstream about 200 yards to a ledge above the river for a heron's-eye view of the cascade.

Weisheit charts our intended course in the sand, noting the danger points, the shards of rock, the lateral waves, and sucker holes.

As we are studying the rapid, a man in a pricey toe-nail-polish-red fiberglass kayak shoots past the rocks, hits the hole head-on, flips, submerges under the wave. One, two, three, four, five seconds pass. He pops back up thirty feet downstream, gripping his paddle and chasing his kayak. Score one for Rapid Five.

Some of us are properly chastened. Others in the group openly calculate the cost-benefit ratio of scrambling around the rapids across a rubble pile of rock that looks as if it might possibly be the Cancun of the *Crotalus viridis* set.

"Don't fear the river," Weisheit counsels. "I've been down Cataract more than 300 times, sometimes encountering thirty-foot waves, sometimes scraping bottom. It's always different, but the river will always take you through. Follow where it leads you." May the flow be with you.

After digesting this Aquarian koan from our normally hyper-rational leader, we begin to refer to Weisheit behind his back as "Sensei." Later he will quote Yoda, confirming our impression of a river mystic waiting to break free. His white wide-brimmed hat, like the one John Wayne wears in the last act of *The Searchers*, enhances the karmic aura of the Riverkeeper.

Before our Sensei allows us back in our boats, he makes us practice the procedures for self-rescue in the vortex of a killer rapid. Never lose your paddle. If the raft is listing or stuck on a rock, go to the high side. Cling to the boat even if it ejects you. Flip an overturned kayak as soon as you can, hurl yourself into it and resume paddling before you are punched by another wave or stabbed by a thorn of rock. Failing that, float downstream feet-first. Avoid the boulders. Hold your breath. Find the eddy. Don't expect much help. And always keep this in mind: drowning is a relatively pleasant way to check out. Very poetic, in fact. See: P. Shelley or H. Crane.

We line up our boats behind the Riverkeeper. Lorenzo is firmly admonished once more to stop cutting in line. He responds by singing, "Yeah, yeah, yeah," in a falsetto that would humble Little Willie John. Overhead, a dark raptor circles. Eagle or vulture?

Weisheit and Kimberly pause at the edge of the rapid, their raft hovers like a marsh hawk, then plunge into the foam, disappearing from view.

Brian and I hold back for a few seconds then make our own cautious approach. An incisor of sandstone protrudes on our right; a fat boulder lurks to the left. The river compresses between the two stone guardians in a slick, almost glassy current, until all hell breaks loose a few yards downstream at a deep trough backed by a curling wave. Again we slide right, scraping the nasty rock. The minor collision bounces us back left, correcting our line just as we hit the hole. Water pours over my head as we slice through the grinning wave, then pivot past a hidden shard of rock and ferry furiously across the tailwaves toward the recirculating waters of the eddy on river right, where Kimberly and Weisheit are shaking their heads at Lorenzo, who, staying more than the obligatory oar's length away from our raft, charts his own route down the dangerous waters surging to the right of the gleaming rock. The punk easily beats us to the eddy, wagging the yellow blade of his paddle at me like a severed head on the outstretched arm of a Fremont water demon.

"Wanna try?"

＊ ＊ ＊

The view of the river from the kayak is different. In fact, down here there is no view of the river. There is only the smirking mouth of the wave. Then a prong of rock. Then a whirlpool. Then a pourover. Then an even bigger wave. Then a boulder the size of Rhode Island—and less forgiving. Then a hole that sounds like a garbage disposal crushing coffee beans or raw bones.

Of course, that's when you can see at all. Once you hit the first wave, a blinding spray splinters into your face and you can forget all about the nuances of reading the river or following the complex sequence of steps in Weisheit's elegant choreography for dancing through the run of rapids.

Pummeled from all directions, including an impertinent jab at my ass by something as sharp and unyielding as a prison shank, I try to recall the basics. Slip down the tongue. Watch the air bubbles. (But watch them do what, exactly?) Paddle through the big waves. Lean into the rocks. Face your danger. Hold your breath. Squeeze the paddle so tightly your knuckles turn white. Yes, it's white-knuckle time at Rapid Six, familiarly known as, gulp, Disaster Falls.

But in the end, it all comes down to touch, balance, and dumb luck. So I close my eyes against the boiling froth, let the river seize my kayak and careen blindly through the rapids, tilting and twisting, diving and listing, like a startled Chukar taking off in a duststorm. It's so easy when you're stupid.

The next stretch of river is known as the North Sea. In big water, Rapid Five washes out, its waves, holes and rocks submerge under the brawny, unobstructed current. But at 70,000 cubic feet per second, the North Sea rears up, its waves swelling to titanic proportions. In early June, the North Sea regularly produces waves that are thirty feet tall. And not just one wave, but a train of them: ten to twelve raft-swamping waves in a row, each feeding off the other. The entire run is boxed in by vicious lateral waves that foreclose easy retreats.

Weisheit has descended those rapids several times under the most harrowing conditions, battling not only waves taller than any building in Moab, but also cottonwood trees and railroad ties shooting through the rapids like battering rams. So did his friend, Big Linda Wittkopf—by herself, in an eighteen-foot bucket boat, on a day when the waves grew to forty-five-feet tall. Imagine that. But that is not our river, not today anyway.

Weisheit tells me that Big Linda has just been diagnosed with cancer. She has rejected the useless blasts of chemo and is fighting for her life with alternative therapies. Here we confront some of the cruel facts of life for river guides. They perform back-wrenching work in extremely dangerous conditions, expose themselves day-after-day to melanoma-inducing sunshine, killer rapids, rattlesnakes, scorpions, black (and occasionally horny) widows, earn meager pay without pensions, regularly get stiffed on tips from chintzy European clients, and almost always lack even the most basic level of health insurance. It's a great life, at a stiff price.

Weisheit's wife, Susette, was a top river guide for twenty years, easily John's equal. A native of Colorado, Susette spent part of her youth riding broncos on the rodeo circuit. She also raced motorcycles across the desert. But river-guiding took its toll on her back. She stopped rowing and took up deep-tissue massage. Many of her clients are guides. Now Susette is making a film with director Chris Simon about the life of one of the first river guides on the Colorado, Kent Frost, a native Utahan from the uranium boom-bust town of Monticello. Frost, who wrote a beautiful memoir of his life titled *My Canyonlands*, just turned ninety. Susette safely portaged to a new life. Other guides aren't so lucky. Alcohol, drugs, and depression take their toll.

"Why don't the guides organize into a union?" Wolff asks.

"It's not in their character," Weisheit says. "They're loners and tribalist, suspicious of organizations. The family-owned operations, like Tag-a-Long, treated the guides more humanely. Gave them places to stay. Fed them. Encouraged them to learn about the cultural and natural history of the area. But conditions are changing as the bigger corporations take over. The guides are increasingly treated as interchangeable parts in the machine."

* * *

As the sun eases below the crimson rim, the big obstacles downstream are sharp rocks, a few seething holes, two shadowy boulders that would, if given the chance, pin you down for eternity, and naturally, my own incompetence with a paddle. But I pinball my way through this diminished North Sea, exhausted and exhilarated, and zigzag over to the most beautiful beach in Cat Canyon: Tilted Park.

Weisheit is already on the riverbank, but curiously he shows no signs of preparing the evening's culinary fare. What gives?

"Playtime!" Weisheit yells.

Here is what passes for fun and games among the elite river guides of the Colorado. Pile as many people as you can into inflatable kayaks. Hand the paddles to the two most credulous members of the crew (that would be me and Wolff) and point them downstream toward a Class 4 rapid, snickering with evil confidence that the two morons with the paddles will find some damn way to flip the boats.

Wolff goes first, his yellow, single person kayak over-loaded with Marta and Brian. Rapid 10 is a series of three large waves of mounting ferocity. We watch as the yellow kayak vaults over the first wave, shudders across the second, rises and then cartwheels backwards on the third, dumping all three into the torrent.

Oh, shit.

I ease the blue barge into the current as Wolff desperately tries to catch his kayak before it is swept into Lake Powell ten miles downstream. Weisheit begins bellowing commands. "Left, I said, left damnit." At the same moment, Kimberly screams, "Right, right!" Okay, so who would you obey?

As it happens, the kayak is about as maneuverable as the Exxon Valdez after shredding its hull on Bligh Reef. So we limp into the rapids, at one with the river. At last, satori! ·

The blue nose of the kayak tunnels through the first wave, submarines through the next, and, even though I catch a glimpse of our Sensei deviously trying to scuttle the boat, we bust through the lethal third wave and lumber into the eddy.

"AGAIN!" Weisheit screams, maniacally slapping the sides of the kayak.

This time Kimberly and I transfer to Wolff's wounded duck of a kayak, leaving Weisheit to his own kamikaze mission in Big Blue.

Apparently, Cappy Wolff's pride is bruised after his capsize. He insists on paddling again. Once more into the breach we go. This time I sit in the bow, my feet dangling over the edge of the small boat, gripping a carabiner clipped to the bowring. The first wave jolts me five inches off my seat. Then we dive into the hole, Wolff and Kimberly sliding forward toward the gaping trough, nearly nudging me out of the kayak, until we are punched up and over the crest of the second wave, where we are suspended for a moment, eye to eye with the Last Wave, performing its best imitation of the Earth-cleansing tsunami of aboriginal eschatology. Then it hits us with the force of a Mike Tyson body shot. The kayak shivers and stalls. We are pounded again and yet again, when I make a fatal error. Instead of leaning into the rapid, absorbing the blows of the hydraulic and pushing us forward, I instinctively lunge backwards, pulling the bow of the kayak with me. For a moment, we assume the position of a Tlingit totem pole: Wolff as beaver, Kimberly as bear, me as raven. Then, over we go, back flipping into the river.

The hole is deep, the water warm as fresh urine. Mine? The current contorts my body into angles it was never meant to bend—Rolfing by rapids. After a few seconds of this odd, violently erotic sensation, the hole expels me. I surface twenty feet downstream and scan the river. Kimberly has safely made it to the eddy. Wolff is pursuing his runaway paddle, and the over-turned kayak is hurtling downstream, aimed directly at my head.

I snatch the bowring and lug the kayak in a cross-chest carry toward the eddy. My progress is interrupted by a rock protruding from the river like the Colossus of Maroussi. Our initial encounter is a glancing blow to my shin in the middle of a finely executed scissor kick, then the current pens me against the sandstone obelisk, the kayak pressing on my face like a waffle-iron. Out of the corner of one eye, I see Weisheit on the bank. Is he actually skipping? Hard to say. But the Sensei is definitely shouting, "Again, again! This time, no boats!"

Kimberly demurs.

Marta says, "No thanks, boys."

And it looks like the teenagers won't be joining us either. Brian is curled up asleep under an arching cottonwood, dreaming of a Double Whopper with Cheese and Lorenzo has already hustled back to camp, where we find him reading two books at once, Jack London's *The Iron Heel* in his right hand, *Walden* in the left. He prefers the London. "Thoreau," he says, "can't stick to one idea and work it all the way through. *Walden*'s a hodgepodge of unfinished thoughts." .

"If only Ralph Waldo had slipped some Ritalin into Henry's porridge, perhaps he wouldn't have been so easily distracted," I say.

"Thoreau just needed to get laid for once in his life," concludes Marta.

After this definitive diagnosis, what can a poor boy do, but slide into the Colorado one last time, wearing only a life vest for flotation? After all, are we not men? Wolff, Weisheit, and I lean back into the current, wave our farewells and surrender to the flow like three plump Ophelias, singing Hey, nonny, nonny, as the rapids grip our feet and pull us down.

Day Five

I rise early to a golden halo of light flaring off the rim of the canyon, the radiant glow of a painting by Masaccio. The edges of this trenched world are sharp, chiseled, distinct. The ragged landscape is defined by negative spaces, by absence, by what has been carved away, by what has been lost. Here are the sun-polished bones of an ancient world.

This is Tilted Park. Beneath us looms a giant salt dome, a kind of saline volcano, bulging up through the sedimentary weight of time, warping the walls of the canyon into shapes that defy geometry. This is where the past bursts through the surface of the Earth in a compound fracture of rock, contorting great reefs of stone into outlandish angles, paradoxical jumbles, and unconformities, geological hauntings.

I am jolted out of this Keatsian coma by a mechanical roar rumbling through the canyon from above, jarring the rockwalls with violent echoes. I look up to catch the tail of a fighter jet stitching a pallid contrail across the turquoise slit of sky.

And it all comes flooding back, the waking nightmares of my daily life. The war in Iraq. The invasion of Lebanon. The secret prisons and torture chambers. The chemical haze over Salt Lake City. The aerial machine-gunning of wolves in Alaska. The shredding of the Constitution. The tedious monoculture of suburban Portland. The dead zone off the Oregon coast. The radioactive ooze slipping off the Hanford Nuclear Reservation and into the Columbia River. The naked profits and the dead.

Why are they here? This is a national park. Sure, its boundaries are a silly political delineation of bureaucratic turf, meaningless to a cougar or a netleaf hackberry. But the designation must stand for something. Canyonlands should enjoy a grant of immunity from such incursions. If only because there ought be some places off-limits to the military's demand for full-spectrum dominance. If not here, where?

But don't tell it to the Pentagon. After the first Gulf War, the Air Force announced its intentions to fly fighter jets, drones and Stealth bombers over Canyonlands at low altitude, improbably arguing that the terrain resembled Iraq and Iran. Wildlife biologists, among others, objected, stating that roars from the jet engines would so startle bighorn sheep that many would fall to deaths from their tenuous trails on steep cliffs. The Air Force dismissed such arguments and claimed in an Environmental Impact Statement that they were actually doing the bighorns a favor by "culling" the herds of weaker stock, thus preventing a dreaded population explosion.

Of course, desert bighorns, rare throughout the West, aren't particularly vulnerable to population spikes. Crashes are their problem. In 1987, just such a crash devastated the bighorn herds in the Needles district of Canyonlands, when a disease transmitted from nearby cattle herds wiped out nearly 90 percent of the native bighorns. Twenty years later, the population still hasn't recovered.

While the rest of our party snoozes, Weisheit walks over with two mugs of coffee. We sit on the siltbank, gaze at the mighty Toreva Block at the mouth of Y Canyon, and tell sad stories of the deaths of rivers: the Green, the Dolores, the Umcompaghre, the Dirty Devil, the Escalante, Gunnison, the San Juan, the Colorado. Gone, but not forgotten.

The most brutal battles over the Colorado River haven't been between environmentalists and dam builders, but between the Western states over the last drop of Colorado water. Call it a basin war. Upper versus Lower, and everyone against California.

The execution papers for the Colorado River were signed in 1922 with the Colorado River Compact, negotiated by Commerce Secretary Herbert Hoover. As a reward for his services, Hoover got his name affixed to the dam that inundated Black Canyon and formed Lake Mead. The compact split the Colorado into two basins, upper and lower, and allocated an equal percentage of water to both—even though nearly all of water originated in the sparsely populated Upper Basin states of Colorado, Wyoming, New Mexico, and Utah.

The dividing line was drawn at Lee's Ferry, Arizona—the hideout of the Mormon assassin John D. Lee, a notorious member of Brigham Young's death squad called the Destroying Angels or the Danites. Lee, it should also be noted, was the great-grandfather of Congressman Mo Udall and his brother, Stuart, Secretary of the Interior under JFK and LBJ and the man who closed the floodgates on Glen Canyon Dam. Lee's Ferry marks the end of Glen Canyon and the beginning of Marble Canyon.

The compact was sedulously pushed by two of the twentieth century's greatest thieves, William Randolph Hearst and William Mulholland. Having stolen the water from the Owens Valley for Los Angeles, Hearst and Mulholland set to work on a scheme to grab the Colorado's water for the plantations of the Imperial Valley and the creeping suburban sprawl into the coastal deserts of southern California.

Under the terms of the deal, both basins would be allocated 7.5 million acre feet of water each year, with another 1.5 million acre feet awarded to Mexico. Not a drop was left to the river itself. The compact set the total flow of the Colorado at 16.5 million acre feet a year. But the river had rarely ever yielded this much water, even in flood years. A National Academy of Sciences study found that, over the last 100 years, the average annual flow of the Colorado has been 14 million acre feet, with many years falling far short of that mark. A recent tree-ring data study looking back 400 years suggests that the true average flow of the Colorado is closer to 13.5 million acre feet, and current climate change models predict that the river's flow will sink by another 18 percent in the next fifty years. In other words, the Colorado's water was over-allocated in the 1920s, before the rise of Phoenix, Denver, and Las Vegas—not to mention the trifling needs of the humpback chub and razorback sucker.

At the time of the compact, the Reclamation Service (soon to become the Bureau of Reclamation) was headed by Arthur Powell Davis, the can-do nephew of John Wesley Powell. A craftier politician than his uncle, Davis immediately sniffed the opportunity to begin building his own bureaucratic fiefdom through the construction of Colorado River dams and vast irrigation projects. Davis dispatched engineers to the river basin to scout out potential dam sites on the mainstem of the Colorado, the Green, the Grand, the Yampa, and the San Juan—from Needles, California to the foothills of the Wind River Range in Wyoming.

Many of those sites are marked by the initials of the engineers chiseled into the walls of canyons, signposts for an age of technology gone amok.

In the end, the Bureau of Reclamation set their sights on four big dams: Bridge Canyon at the lower end of Grand Canyon, Glen Canyon, Echo Park in Dinosaur National Monument, and Flaming Gorge on the Green River, near the Utah-Wyoming border. The grand scheme was spelled out in a creepy document titled "The Colorado River: From Natural Menace Becomes a Natural Resource," which laid out the Bureau's blueprints for more than 150 impoundment and diversion projects that would have turned the Green, Colorado, and San Juan rivers in a stagnant staircase of holding tanks.

Entranced by the public relations appeal of hydropower, the Bureau intended to make the big dams electricity generators, so-called "cash-register" dams that would generate money to, yes, build more dams. The income derived from power sales was meant to fund smaller dams, irrigation projects, and water diversions.

Bridge Canyon dam was the first to fall, undone largely by internal dissent from within the Department of Interior over flooding the lower reaches of the Grand Canyon. Of course, the Bureau never actually killed a dam project. The agency just moved Bridge Canyon to the back of the line. They would return to Grand Canyon with even more malign schemes in the 1960s.

What the hydro-engineers, then riding high as the most powerful bureaucratic enclave in the West, didn't anticipate was that their scheme to flood 100 miles of canyons in the remote and little known Dinosaur National Monument would prompt a popular rebellion that scuttled the Echo Park Dam and humiliated the once omnipotent agency.

The story of the Echo Park dam is well known. Distressed at the prospect of another national park property being drowned by a big dam (half of Yosemite had already been lost to the Hetch Hetchy Dam), the young environmental movement, led by the scrappy executive director of the Sierra Club, David Brower, launched a sophisticated national campaign to save Dinosaur from the hydro-engineers.

Fixated on keeping the dam out of Dinosaur, the conservationists offered their support for an even bigger dam near the mouth of Glen Canyon. The Bureau chafed, but the western politicians snapped at the deal, realizing that it almost certainly could have been worse for them: the environmentalists in league with the California water interests could have defeated the entire Colorado Storage Project.

For Brower and his cohorts, it was a tough call, but the wrong one. Here we arrive at the lethal logic of the environmental trade-off. You give us our dam and we won't build one in your precious park. Plus, we'll offer you a new national park (Canyonlands) as a bonus. What remains unsaid, though all parties are conscious of it, is that the dam will kill both parks and infect the environmental movement itself with a terminal rot.

To his credit, Brower almost immediately regretted the deal and wanted to fight the Colorado River Storage Project. But his board pulled the plug. "Never trade a place you know for one you don't," Brower admonished a new generation of greens. "That's how we lost Glen Canyon." And half of Cataract, too.

"Hey, where's the coffee?"

It's Marta. She has risen from her yellow neoprene sarcophagus. Weisheit puts on another pot of water and I begin to fret about the rapids that will confront us this morning, some of the biggest and most lethal in North America.

* * *

This morning I steal the ducky from Lorenzo, who is erect but not yet awake. He slides on Weisheit's raft with Kimberly. Marta and Daniel settle themselves into the blue kayak. The roar of the rapids drowns out our voices as we push off into the frothing current.

Almost immediately the big rafts smash into the standing waves that flipped us so viciously last night. But I cheat the river, slip to the far right of the channel, catching only a minor jolt from the fierce hydraulics of Rapid Ten. Even the tailwaters of the rapid prove a challenge for my novice whitewater skills. I bounce off a hidden rock and am slugged by a brutal lateral wave that hurls the kayak on its side, where it wobbles for a moment before settling back into the cradle of the river.

The next mile of river is relatively calm, alternating between point bars and cobble banks. Gradually, the canyon narrows, squeezing out the light. The crumbling cliffs of ancient shale and limestone rise a thousand feet above us, revealing for a moment the famous Crum Domes of the Paradox Formation, the giant bulge of gypsum and salt laid down by a shallow sea 300 million years ago. The curious geomorphology of Cataract results from two conflicting forces: the erosion of the river and the uplift by the Paradox Formation that contorts upper layers of rock into such strange and fractured angles.

I ride through the next rapid with little trouble, skimming across the wave train, and am jerked into Rapid 12, a short run that ends abruptly in a violent three-foot drop.

Weisheit calls this stretch of river the Ice Cream Drops, after an ill-fated resupply mission. In June 1985, a group descending Cataract stopped at the lovely apron of beach by the deep pool below Rapid 12. They had arranged for friends in Moab to supply them with ice cream here as a special treat. On that June afternoon, a single-engine plane circled the pool, forty feet above the water. As one of the men in the plane lowered tubs of ice-cream wrapped in life-jackets out the cockpit window, the engine stalled and the aircraft plunged into the water, sinking to the bottom of the forty-foot deep pool, where it remains today, serving as rearing habitat for the Humpback Chub.

So much for the tune up. The big rapids are calling. We can hear them rumbling up the canyon: Hell to Pay, Mile Long Rapids, the Big Drops. We pull over to scout the scene at the mouth of Range Canyon, a sharp gouge in the western wall of Cataract that spews out the largest debris fan on the river. These debris flows of boulders, slabs, and cobble energize the rapids, hence the tumult below.

The beach here is muddy and desolate. Kimberly quickly locates a fallen slab of sandstone and claims it, waving us on. The rest of us head downstream over a cobbly trail, framed by cactus and poison ivy. Weisheit admonishes us to watch for rattle-snakes. He didn't have to warn us. There's a sinister vibe to the place. We scramble up a broken pile of rock to a view of the rapids, eight major cascades in fast succession punctuated by sharp rocks and grim boulders that flip dozens of boats each year. On a rock near our perch is a famous inscription from the ill-fated Best Expedition of 1891: "Camp #7, Hell to Pay, No. 1, Sunk & Drown."

Now things are getting serious.

As we work our way down from the inscribed rock, I notice a blur on a boulder in front of us—the frantic movements of a whiptailed lizard, the cheetah of the reptile world. Unlike the beautiful collared lizards that wait stealthily for their prey to stumble upon them, the whiptails are in nearly constant motion, sucking up toads, insects, and smaller lizards. They are also all females, nature's clones. Whiptails reproduce by parthenogenesis. But that doesn't mean the lizards don't like having sex. Indeed, whiptails engage in frequent pseudo-copulations, often with the same partner. Some girls just want to have fun.

Back at the beach, we wait for Kimberly to finish her Salutation to the Sun, tighten the rigging on the raft, and chart out a route through the rapids. Lorenzo reclaims the yellow kayak. His mother hands him a funky blue helmet that resembles the space gear worn in that classic Sci-Fi movie *Mars Needs Women*. Daniel and I bicker for a moment over who will sit in the stern of the tandem kayak. He prevails.

Kimberly offers to ride with Brian. As she pushes the swamper's raft off the beach, her leg is seized by the mud, and she begins to sink—ankles, calves, knees. Brian chuckles. Wrong move. Kimberly cauterizes him with a single glance. Bottom suction can be a terribly dangerous affair. Weisheit issues a series of complex instructions that resemble Tai C'hi moves that magically end up freeing her feet—though not her shoes, which are tithed to the river gods.

Daniel and I hold back, suspended in the cloudy pool of water at the lip of the rapids, as first the two rafts and, then Lorenzo, dive into the foaming chute. As we wait, our raft is encircled by a cloud of red dragonflies, reminding us both of the butterflies that follow the lovelorn electrician, Mauricio Babilonia, through the pages of *One Hundred Years of Solitude.*

Finally, we must enter. The river snatches the kayak and thrusts us into the first wave train. Almost immediately, our finely detailed plan for zigzagging through the torrent is rendered obsolete. The roar of the rapids is deafening, washing away all attempts to communicate. We are riding so low in the water that our view of the river is limited to merely the snarling crest of the next standing wave. At the top of the wave, we are granted a brief glimpse of the obstacles downstream before being slapped down into the trough and drenched by frenzied brown water.

And so we ride our way down, each wave taller than the next, each hole deeper, until we spot the spines of red rock that signal the entrance to Hell to Pay. Our Sensei instructed us to visualize this rapid as a baseball diamond, with our kayak as a runner on second base trying to score on a single. Such visualization techniques are yet more evidence of Weisheit mystical trickery, "Inner River Running." Wolff and I played baseball for much of our youth, but neither of us can make the slightest sense of this metaphorical schematic.

The river makes the call for us, slamming us into a stubby rock at the head of the rapid. The kayak bounces off the rock and we hit the next big wave at an awkward angle. Water pours over the left side of the craft as we struggle over the hydraulic and down the backside where we are confronted with the implacable wall of Capsize Rock. I stick my paddle straight down into the maw and pull back, against the current. The force of the water almost flings me from the kayak as we sideswipe the boulder and hurtle into the rough concatenation of waves below, known as the Davis Rapids—after Bill and Fern Davis, who flipped their raft here and were sucked underwater until finally being released 300 feet downstream.

We stutter across the waves of Davis Rapids, gradually acquiring a new confidence in our skills as boatmen on a wild river. After all, we have stayed upright where so many others have wrecked, flipped, and perished. High on the cliffs to our right, I notice a small knob of rock that resembles the red-button on the nuclear black box that shadows Dick Cheney wherever he goes.

As I point out the rock to Wolff, we collide into a curling wave that could have been drawn by Hokusai. The wave stops our progress downstream. Slowly and inexorably, the bow of the kayak lifts out of the water, twists, and deposits us into a roiling vortex of water. In river-guide-speak, the term is dump-trucked. I tumble in the agitated water for a few long seconds, trying to remember if there's any special technique for freeing yourself from the rinse cycle of a deep hole, and then, finally, the river spits me out. I break the surface gasping for breath and still clutching my paddle. A moment later, Wolff's head emerges near the upturned kayak. Still the hole sucks at our legs, trying to pull us back down.

"We've got to flip the damn boat before we get swept into the next rapids," Wolff yells, over the maniacal cackling of the river.

As lateral waves hammer us from both sides, we heave the heavy kayak right-side-up, place our paddles in the boat, push down on the rubber sides of craft, and hoist ourselves up and over. In tandem, as in water ballet. From downstream come sounds of laughter and mock applause. Tough crowd.

We paddle up to Weisheit's raft.

"Hey, what do they call that killer rapids?" Wolff inquires of our Sensei.

"The Button Hole," Weisheit snickers.

Dump-trucked by the Button Hole? That hardly seems descriptive of our ordeal. There may have to be some judicious editing before we publicly tell our tale of terror and triumph. Surely, a more fitting name would be the Devil's Arsehole, Shock Corridor, the Grim Reaper. Wolff's the poet. He'll come up with something worthy of our feat.

* * *

Teapot Canyon on river right marks the spot. Here is the entrance to the Big Drops, three concussive waterfalls that constitute the most thrilling and dangerous run of water on the Colorado. The river plummets thirty-two feet in less than a mile.

We beach our boats on a gray beach and thread our way through boulders and hackberries to a ledge above the first falls, a kind of foreplay in the terrors of rushing water. Weisheit says something about the debris fan on river right, a keeper hole on river left, and the dangerous tailwaves that will grip a swimmer and drag them directly into the jaws of the even more dangerous Big Drop 2. But most of what he says is drowned out by the growls of the rapids.

A sandy trail leads through fallen rock for another quarter of a mile to a prow-shaped wedge of sandstone that overhangs Big Drop 2. Our Sensei calls this Poop Rock, as in Poop Deck, since it offers a clear view for scouting a route through the thrashing waves of the second falls. For me, the scatological definition also resonates, as in Shit Your Pants Rapids.

Big Drop 2 is the most lethal rapid in Cataract. Most of the damage is inflicted by a fiendishly placed boulder, called Little Niagara Rock, and the sucker hole below it, which is capable of crushing and sinking an eighteen-foot raft. Boats that flip here sustain serious damage. Rafters pulled into the hole often drown. Little Niagara, Weisheit warns, is to be avoided at all costs.

But that's not the only danger. There's also the Marker Rock, the Ledge Wave, the Fang Rocks, and the Red Wall. None of which are disposed to give quarter.

Onward to Satan's Gut, the macerating trench of Big Drop 3. If possible, the river is even louder here. Weisheit flashes us hand signals none of us understand. But we all get the drift. The notion of going over this cataclysm in little neoprene rafts is ridiculous, verging on the thanatic. Yes, Freud observed that the purpose of life is death. But that's no reason to rush the inevitable.

Guarding the left side of the river is a morbidly obese green boulder called Big Mossy. Hit that rock wrong and your boat will flip into Satan's Gut, a hole of such power that it is capable of crushing the metal frames of rafts—not to mention human bones. Slide too far right of Big Mossy and you'll get stuck on Table Rock, which tends to either keep you perpetually pinned to it or, again, flip you back into Satan's Gut. On the far right of the river is an exuberant lateral wave called Brahma that has capsized motorboats. As Barry Goldwater discovered during his trip down the Colorado in 1940, the middle of the river here is a dizzying maze spiked with rock shards that simply chew you up alive and sometimes, though not always, spit you out the other end.

I creep back up the wild canyon. My legs are unsteady. My stomach churning from exhilaration and anxiety. I turn to Wolff.

"You game for taking the blue kayak over that?"

"Nope."

"Good."

We deflate the blue beast and roll up the husk into the shape of the fat joints once favored by Bob Marley and strap it on Brian's raft.

This is Brian's first time to row down the Big Drops. Usually, the rookie Swamper rows alone. He is nearly as anxious as I am. I volunteer to ride with him.

As we begin to rig our boats for the rapid, two ivory white speedboats scream past us. These are expensive Park Service patrol boats that skim across the water like hovercraft in the Everglades.

Suddenly, the two jet boats spin around in a kind of river *pas de deux* and come back toward us. They've spotted our Sensei beneath his signature hat and Drain It! T-shirt.

Weisheit turns to me as the patrol boats idle in front of us, purring out a haze of hydrocarbons in the heart of the national park. "Here we go again," he says.

The two of us seem to attract cops. A few years ago, we decided to have a little tour of Lake Powell in a speedboat we rented in Plague, Arizona (AKA Page). We revved the boat up to max speed and took out straight for Glen Canyon Dam with Weisheit trailing behind on water-skis, holding a banner reading "Drain It!"

Apparently, this unsolicited public service announcement aggravated the dam-tourists, who called the cops. Soon a park ranger and rangerette chased us down in their own stylish jetboat, lights blazing and siren blaring. They detained us for an hour and forbade us from any more shenanigans near the dam. National security, you know. The story spread through the Park Service police force. Weisheit and I were marked men.

"Hey, John," one of the river cops brays, his teeth gleaming as white as the enamel on his boat. "You're not going to let anyone go down the rapids in those kayaks, are you?"

"Yep."

There are six cops and they all look alike. Beefy arms, '70s porn moustaches, fat heads bulging out of their caps. All the hallmarks of steroid abuse, though from here it's impossible to determine if their testicles are shrunken to the size of the sunflower seeds Daniel Wolff keeps nibbling on and spitting out.

Most of the cops are familiar to Weisheit. They are former river guides who've gone over to the dark side. They've become gun-toting cops in a place that should be off-limits to the enervating grip of the police state.

"You know if we arrested you today," another cop taunts, "you could be processed in five different legal jurisdictions. Heh, heh, heh."

This patrol isn't about law enforcement; it's high-end imperial tourism. This is a VIP trip. The gang of cops is escorting a group of federal judges down the river, at thirty-five miles per hour. Godspeed, gentlemen. Over to you, Big Mossy.

* * *

As the scream of the jetboats fizzles out, Lorenzo announces that he will be taking the yellow ducky down the Big Drops. "I've come all this way," Lorenzo argues. "If I don't do it, I'd regret the rest of my life." Which may be about thirty minutes.

Marta remains quiet, head down, choreographing with her foot the transit of a pebble across the sand. Daniel pretends to be consumed by watching a pair of Say's phoebes chase each other through the willows—a reverse psychology of some sort. Zo doesn't fall for it.

"What are my chances of making it through without flipping?" Lorenzo asks the Master.

"Less than 15 percent," Weisheit predicts, grimly, then charts a complicated course around rocks, over pillows of soft water, skirting holes and crusher waves to the calm recirculating flow of the pools below.

Lorenzo absorbs half of Weisheit's befuddling maze of instructions and lets the rest flow by him. He'll precisely mimic those mandatory opening strokes to set his path into the rough portal of the rapids, then, like a jazz musician, improvise his way through the riotous whitewater. His approach is more Weisheitian than Weisheit. Let the river lead the way.

As it turns out, Lorenzo the Magnificat navigates each of the Big Drops on his own line, grinning and unscathed. Call him the Big Dropper.

My descent into the maelstrom is not nearly so smooth. At the entrance to Big Drop 1, our raft drifts too far to the right, the rushing current swings the boat, and we hit the falls at an unfortunate angle, water pouring over our heads. Brian makes a correction and we race down the tailwaves toward Little Niagara, where, again, we enter the chute too far to the right. The raft buckles, then tickles the face of the big standing wave and stalls. The bow of the raft bends, giving us a front-row look at watery perdition. Finally we are thrashed free and propelled directly into a triangular rock. We careen to the left into a vicious lateral wave that tips the raft on its side and we glide downstream like the trembling blade of an ice skate.

As we teeter on the lip of Big Drop 3, Brian shouts above the cacophony of the rapids, "We need a song, so that we will always remember this descent when we hear it played."

"How about this," I reply as we dip into the tongue of the cascade. "I can't get no, sat io fac-tion, 'til I get some wave re-action … "

Suddenly, the current jerks the raft, pulls us into the rapids and toward the right, too far right again. The boat spins, uncontrollably. The rear of the raft is thrust on to the Table Rock that Weisheit had repeatedly instructed us to avoid at all costs. Across the foaming chute looms the implacable face of Big Mossy. Water streams into the boat, which convulses in the current. The port side sinks under the weight of the water. One of Brian's oars goes flying past my head and into the current, then the other.

I look into the gnashing hole of Satan's Gut. Satan looks back, licking his chops. "High side!," I scream.

Brian and I clamber on the elevated side of the raft and begin to bounce up and down in a frantic effort to jolt the boat free from the grip of Table Rock. This is our moment of crisis.

Oarless, we surrender. Call it an act of enlightened river-consciousness or simply dumb-ass luck, but free from our attempt at control, the raft begins to dance on its own, letting the river take the lead.

For a split second, the raft levitates then dips downward and we descend into the violent whirlpool.

Look, we have come through. Still trembling with the thrill of having escaped the crushing jaws of Big Drop 3, another song runs through my head, "Get up, stand up, stand on the high side; get up, stand up, stand up for your life."

Still, we must retrieve our oars, which are standing erect in the water, pounding up-and-down like furious pistons. I dive off Brian's raft, swim across the large pool below Satan's Gut, and snatch the large, now scarred oars.

As I tread water, Lorenzo waves his victorious paddle at me. "Your turn." He executes an otter slide off the ducky, crawls onto Brian's raft, curls up in the bow, and appears to fall asleep. Ah, youth.

To my surprise, some of the largest waves on the river are just downstream at Powell's Pocket Watch and Rerun Rapids. I track the line taken by Weisheit's raft, which takes me into the roughest water. The faces of the waves are steep and peaked and I hit them head on. The little kayak rockets across the swift wavetrain, delightfully free of keeper holes and killer rocks.

At the pool below Rerun Rapids, Weisheit summons us to his raft. As I tie my kayak to the rigging on his boat, Weisheit rummages through his pack for a bottle of Dr. Bonner's soap, then he cannonballs into the deep eddy and lathers up. The elevation here is precisely 3,700 feet—the maximum pool level of Lake Powell. We all dive into the red water and wash ourselves—all except for Lorenzo who seems to be snoozing beneath his straw hat. This is a purification ritual, a lustration before entering the waters of the dead.

Back on the river, we descend the long, bumpy rollercoaster of Rapid 26, race past the deep gorge of Imperial Canyon and begin to see the first gray silt banks emerge on both sides of the river, the spooky evidence of a shrinking lake.

A few years ago, the river ended here at Imperial Canyon. But now the reservoir is in retreat, humbled by drought, climate change, seepage into stone, evaporation, and the steady accretion of silt.

Today the flat pool is ninety feet below the intended level of the lake and it is dropping year-by-year, excavating small canyons of accumulated mud and exposing once drowned stretches of whitewater, such as the rugged Imperial and Waterhole Rapids.

Below Waterhole Canyon, Weisheit rises from his seat and gives a loud shout as his raft is summoned into a big, newly-revealed rapid that has emerged in the last two weeks. It is a thrilling and wet ride. We name the newborn run Resurrection Rapids. Glen Canyon dam drowned thirty-three rapids in Cataract Canyon between Imperial Canyon and Narrow Canyon. Ten have now reappeared on their own. Twenty-three to go.

Here, at Gypsum Canyon, the river settles into the cold embrace of the lake. The canyon is quiet, the air curdled from the stench of the siltbeds. This place has the feel of a sensory deprivation tank. No matter how hard I listen I can't detect even the faintest sound of the last rapid, the pulse of the living river. We have truly entered the dead zone.

A kingfisher, considered a soothsayer by many tribes on the Colorado Plateau, skims the muddy surface of the reservoir, tracking back upstream toward the river.

There are no true beaches between here and our takeout at Hite. Our camping choice is between sleeping on the rafts and finding a stable siltbank. The sun fades below the rim of the canyon and a somber mood descends on our little group.

South of Clearwater Canyon, we locate a terraced siltbank that might make a suitable camp. We lash the rafts to the leafless limbs of a dead cottonwood tree protruding from the silt. We keep most of the gear on the rafts, including the camp stove. These siltbanks are unstable. Last summer one collapsed into the reservoir, taking an entire kitchen with it.

Weisheit and Brian make our last supper in a makeshift kitchen on the rafts: some kind of spicy Mexican stew. The food is fine, but our minds are elsewhere. It is difficult to enjoy eating in this creepy place, now drenched in crepuscular orange light.

As Kimberly meditates on a flat slab of Halgaito Shale, Zo plucks a few melancholy bars of an old blues—a blues with a lineage dating back to Charley Patton and the big flood of 1927 that terrorized the people of Mississippi Delta.

"Someone tell a story," Marta pleads.

I offer a coyote tale, passed down from Johnny Whiz, an old dipnet fisherman of the Yakima Tribe. Whiz told me the story years ago on a foggy morning as we motored in his skiff up the choppy Columbia toward Memaloose Island, the ancient burial ground of the river tribes. It goes like this.

Coyote is walking on the beach contemplating a curious thing: the mighty Chinook River has run dry, its big delta now a stinky mudflat. Coyote sits down on a driftwood log, scratches his ear.

After a while, Coyote hears a whistle from the ocean. It's Old Man Salmon, poking up from the surf. His face is flaking off.

"Hey, Coyote, come here."

Coyote is wary. He's never seen Old Man Salmon looking quite this bad. You can see his bones. He skulks closer to the fish, but keeps a safe distance.

"What's the matter with your face, Salmon?"

"That's I what I need to talk to you about, Coyote. You need to help us. The Frog People have built a dam across the river. No water flows. It is past time for us to spawn. That is why my skin is falling off. If we don't get up the river soon, the Salmon People will die without children."

Coyote ponders the situation. Typically, his mind is muddled. So he takes a dump.

"Hey, Coyote, what's the problem?" It's his turd talking.

"The Frog People have done a bad thing, Coyote Turd. They have built a dam across the river. They are hoarding all the water and keeping the Salmon People out."

The Turd summons Coyote to bend down. Coyote lowers his furry ear next to the Turd.

"So, here's what you do, Coyote ... "

Coyote digs in the sand and uncovers some old bones of a sea lion. He takes one of the rib bones, chews it awhile and spit polishes it so that the shard resembles a dentalia shell, highly prized by the Frog People.

Coyote takes the bone and runs, his tail flat out, across the Coast Range, through the mossy rainforest, to a large dam made of earth and downed trees. Through the fog, Coyote sees a green lake behind it.

Coyote is panting when he meets the Frog People. He holds out his homemade gift.

"Hello, I'm very thirsty. I'll give you this shiny shell, if you let me drink." Old Man Frog takes the object from Coyote and holds it before his face like a mirror. Coyote doesn't wait for an answer. He dives into the lake and begins lapping up the water in giant gulps.

"Don't worry about me, this might take awhile. I'm parched."

Coyote drinks and drinks and drinks and the lake begins to lower. Soon he has consumed half the water.

"Hey Coyote," yells Old Man Frog. "If you keep drinking like that, you'll owe us another shell!"

Then Coyote submerges beneath the water. Coyote is down there for a long time, digging furiously at the base of the dam until finally it breaches and the water cascades down the canyon.

"The river is for all the people, Old Man Frog. It needs to run free."

Coyote is so full of water he looks like an engorged tick. He races to a hole in the ground near the top of a mountain, lifts his leg and pisses a mighty stream of water that soon fills the hole.

"Frog People, this is your pond. It is not a big pond, but it is yours."

Then Coyote hops on a cedar log floating down the river and rides it all the way to the ocean. That night the Salmon People treat Coyote to a great feast. He eats and eats until he falls asleep with his ass plugging the entrance to Badger's den. Badger gets irate at the intrusion and steals Coyote's anus in revenge. Now Coyote will never again be able to seek advice from his turd and his mind will forever be muddled with too many conflicting ideas.

One way or another, Coyote always fucks up.

"What the hell was that all about?" Lorenzo interrupts. "Don't you know anything, well, scarier?"

"I know a ghost story," offers Weisheit. "A true one. It goes like this."

In the winter of 1983, big snows piled up in the Rockies for the second straight year. As the snow melted, the waters rushed into Lake Powell and the reservoir began to rise. By May, the water surpassed the 3,700-foot mark that was deemed the maximum pool level for the reservoir. And still the waters rose. Then it began to rain. Hard. The waters threatened to pour over the lip of the dam. Bureau of Reclamation engineers bolted flashboards to the dam and ordered the spillways to be opened in a last ditch effort to save the structure.

The cartoon-blue water galloped through the spillways and gushed out of the tunnels a maroon color. The cavitating torrent of water gouged deep holes in the concrete spillway and gnashed into the mushy, saturated Navajo sandstone below, excavating forty-foot deep craters in the bedrock and spewing out rebar, concrete, and chunks of stone the size of Dodge trucks. The dam shuddered under the strain. Two guide wires strung between the dam and walls of Glen Canyon snapped. The abutment of the dam moved forward six inches or more.

Up to this point we're grounded in fact. Now we enter the realm of informed speculation, probability.

Slowly the dam begins to unmoor itself from the rotten walls of Navajo sandstone and suddenly it swings open like a great gate, before tumbling into the deluge, forming Powell Rapids. A wall of water 600 feet tall roars down the narrow canyon demolishing Lee's Ferry and wiping out Navajo Bridge. The frenzied train of water rumbles through Marble Canyon, down Grand Canyon itself, crushing Phantom Ranch, swamping houseboats and porn shoots on Lake Havasu until finally it hits Lake Mead. The water of the reservoir is momentarily pulled back and then rockets forward with the force of a tsunami. The water cascades over Hoover Dam in a waterfall that is seventy-feet thick and 730-feet tall. Hoover, too, begins to shiver. Finally, the dam that was supposed to stand for a thousand years buckles and collapses under a wall of liberated water, an archetypal flood.

"Awesome!" Lorenzo yells, strumming his beater guitar with a powerchord worthy of Black Sabbath's Tommy Iommi.

Day Six

I awaken sometime after midnight with an urgent need to commune with the Groover, perched perilously on the crumbling edge of the silt bank a few hundred feet from where we threw down our sleeping bags in the midst of the dust storm that hit us last night.

Somehow I find my tiny flashlight and begin walking toward the ripening metal box. Almost immediately I stop in my tracks. There's something strange happening near my bare feet. The ground is writhing with squiggly, glowing traces of light, like the power lines of Anasazi rock art set into motion. I wipe sand from my eyes and bend down for a closer inspection.

Powerlines, hell. They're scorpions, the big blue see-through ones with the orange legs called, I believe, *Hadrurus arizonesis,* familiarly known as The Big Hairy Motherfucker from Arizona. A dozen of them, dancing across the crusty earth with raised tails, tipped with that oh-so-sharp toxic probe. Not fatal, so they say, but exquisitely painfully.

The creatures look alien, but it turns out that scorpions are some of the most adaptable and energy efficient creatures on earth, a species capable of surviving almost any holocaust we throw at them.

Perhaps the scorpions, which (advisory to houseboaters!) have proliferated into booming colonies up and down the shorelines of Lake Powell, are engaging in their bizarre act of fornication by proxy, in which the male deposits his sperm deep in moist sand inside a kind of pocket, where it is picked up some days or even weeks later by Mrs. Hadrurus, who carries the satchel of sperm around for up to six months before finally deciding to impregnate herself—nature's answer to sperm donation.

I look at the sleepers lined up on the bank, islands in florescent waves of scorpions, and retreat back to my bag, give it a vigorous shake and zip myself inside. The Groover can wait. I decide not to tell Kimberly about this night vision, discretion being the better part of matrimony.

* * *

We rise at four in the morning, sand embedded in our hair, our ears, our teeth. It is dark. The sky swirls with vesper bats chasing the last remains of yesterday's mayfly hatch.

At this predawn hour, the only person I can readily identify is Lorenzo, whose lower half appears to be glowing. He is sporting cherry-red hip-hugger bell bottoms that would make Ike Turner squeal with envy.

Everyone seems grim. It is our last day together in the canyon. The rapids, petroglyphs and desert bighorns are behind us. We have twenty-two miles to paddle across the dead outer reaches of Lake Powell.

The first few meanders of the canyon go by silently, except for the occasional splash of a siltbank calving into the river like a melting glacier. The air is cool, the canyon bathed in the soft pinks of morning light.

After a few sullen hours of paddling, we approach the mouth of Dark Canyon, a deep and branching chasm on our left that stretches back through nearly eighty miles of wild country. The big debris flows from Dark Canyon created a set of sharply dropping rapids with lethal boulder fields and holes that rivaled the Big Drops at certain flows. Those rapids are long gone, but Dark Canyon itself is reviving.

We anchor our boats at the mudflat at the mouth of the canyon and begin hiking, trying to avoid the quicksand and mudpits.

The ground quivers and groans beneath our feet. We have to keep moving or the mud will suck off our sandals. What is now sludge was once the bottom of the reservoir, which has retreated from the canyon entirely. Dark Canyon creek now empties into the Colorado.

Weisheit used to row his raft a mile up the canyon to a campsite on a sandstone ledge overlooking a run of waterfalls tumbling through the slickrock.

Now we have to hump our way through the mudflats, sticking as much as we can to the newly liberated streambed. All of this is good news for Dark Canyon, but a more ominous portent for the dam-operators and water-users downstream. Sediment is piling up and water is disappearing. A bad combination.

One day a few years ago Weisheit was walking up Dark Canyon and stumbled on an old man dressed in the olive-colored uniform of the US Geological Survey, taking notes and making measurements. The hunched figure in green was none other than Luna Leopold, son of Aldo Leopold, and one of the world's leading hydrologists.

"Luna, what are you doing here?" Weisheit queried.

"I'm making some calculations about sediment," Leopold responded, jotting down a complicated equation in his notebook. "I'm trying to determine how much sediment we're standing on top of."

"Any rough ideas, yet?"

"It appears to be precisely 167 feet thick," Leopold concluded. Or roughly the height of Niagara Falls.

The mud terraces of Dark Canyon are merely a microcosm of what is piling up in Flaming Gorge and Glen Canyon and, perhaps, more importantly, what is being denied to Grand Canyon: sediment for beaches, driftwood for organic debris, floods to revitalize the closed system.

* * *

The whitewater of the past two days is replaced by whitecaps, the steady four mile per hour current transformed into a nasty backwash. The color of the water has turned from reddish-green to the lifeless tones of sun-charred meat.

The unforgiving winds pick up around noon, raging in our face. Always in our faces. The herons and ravens have gone AWOL. Even the conquering tamarisk seems timid about venturing up Lake Powell's cruel shores.

The rafters take the brunt of these hostile changes. Our kayaks sit in the evaporation zone, giving our bodies a little moisture and a few degrees of respite from the heat. The rafters ride higher in the choppy waters, braised by the sun and the wind. Moisture is sucked from the flesh. Simply drinking water, bottle after bottle, isn't enough to keep you hydrated. The body needs salt, too. If you consume water but no salt, your body begins to toxify and it's a long way to an IV out here.

I paddle back to Kimberly and Brian's raft. They've fallen about a half-mile behind us, struggling with the wind and the physical dissipations of heat exhaustion. Both are nauseous. Both are slightly dizzy. It doesn't take long for the body to revolt against these conditions and simply begin shutting down.

I refill my water from the cask on the raft. It is tepid and sour. The chunks of ice that had cooled our food and water for the week have finally melted. Entropy grips us. Everything is giving out.

Kimberly implores me to abandon the kayak and join them on the raft.

I refuse. "I need to defeat this fucking reservoir," I exclaim, madly spinning the kayak back into the cruel wind. "I need to arrive in triumph at Hite."

"You're delirious!" Kimberly shouts from the bow of her raft.

She's right, natch—a desert dementia has set in. That's on top of my chronic case.

But her pleas are lost to the winds.

I pass Weisheit's raft. He is wrapped up like Omar Sharif in *Lawrence of Arabia*. The old river runner seems to be in better shape than the rest of us. These days he spends as much time chained to a computer as I do, but he shows no outward signs of slowing down. Yesterday, as we encountered the first morbid stretches of the reservoir a gloomy pall fell over Weisheit. But now he seems almost giddy.

"Hey, lookit this," Weisheit jests, showing me his palms. "After 100 miles of rowing, not a single discoloration. I guess calluses are forever."

The bastard.

My own hands are swollen and throbbing with a pain so deep I am nearly unable to grip the paddle. I examine them closely. Both palms resemble those of an Italian saint in the full flow of a stigmata: bruised, blistered, bleeding. I feel my lips cracking and peeling away. My chest is sautéed to the color of a boiled Maine lobster.

I suffer from the delusion that I am pitting myself against the forces of the reservoir, the dam, the ghost of Floyd Dominy. And I row for those who never stopped fighting the dam: Katie Lee, Kent Frost, Ken Sleight.

With each trembling stroke, I feel as if I am performing a kind of penance for past sins—for Dave Brower's gravest mistake, for Abbey not strapping himself with dynamite and hurling his dying body against the dam in one final glorious explosion, for the bankrupt carcass of environmentalism when the planet came calling for help.

A screaming comes across the reservoir, ripping me out of my reveries. Jetboats! Two of the monsters zip past us, trailing US flags, giant wakes, and blue streams of exhaust.

"Cheaters! Cowards!! Collaborators!!!" I scream above the roar, shaking an Earth First!-fist at them as they zoom off toward a distant arm of the lake.

A sun-bronzed blonde in a bikini, sprawled on the side of the craft, responds to my impotent gesture with a faint, Princess Di flick of her wrist. Then they disappear in a puff of smoke—though the canyon walls reverberate with machine growls long after their passing.

We finally slog our way under the surreal steel span of the Hite bridge. The trip ends as it began: at a uranium site. Before the dam, Hite was home to one of the largest uranium mills in the Southwest, a joint operation between the Department of Energy and the Vanadium Corporation. The mill's huge pile of toxic tailings was simply left in situ to be covered by Lake Powell's encroaching waters. No one ever told the submerged mill that the Cold War ended, so for the past forty years it has been steadily irradiating carp, catfish, heron, bald eagles, water-skiers.

Evidence of the Hite marina is hard to detect amid the mounting walls of muck. The vaunted boat launch now looms more than 100 feet above the draining pool of water. Sorry, boys, the stairway to houseboat heaven is defunct, but cheer up: Lake Powell has manufactured its first ghost town of the new century. True West.

Yes, one way or another, a change is gonna come.

Going Down on the Rocks in Dinosaur

September, 2007.

THESE DAYS THERE ISN'T A VACANT HOTEL ROOM TO BE FOUND IN VERNAL, Utah. Or Craig, Colorado. Or Pinedale, Wyoming for that matter. The rooms are all booked up with oil workers, pipe-layers, explosive technicians and tax accountants versed in the intricacies of the depreciation allowance.

The "No Vacancy" signs at upscale Best Westerns and dusty Mom and Pop trailer parks out here, in the Interior West, have been flashing for a year and half. From the Pinedale Anticline to the San Rafael Swell, the Green River basin is taking the brunt of the new oil boom, brought to you by the Iraq war, Alan Greenspan, and the Bush Interior Department, where the latest spasm of fossil-fuel looting was orchestrated by the convicted felon, Stephen J. Griles. No need to shed a tear for Mr. Griles, as he marks down his five months in Club Fed. Upon his release, the oil lobbyist turned Assistant Secretary of Interior will be lavishly rewarded for his sacrifice. While environmentalists rot in jail for a decade for the supposed crime of burning down a heinous horse-slaughtering factory, Mr. Griles, who illegally gave away billions of dollars worth of public resources to his cronies in Big Oil and Big Coal, will spend a few months in a cushy federal facility waiting for the right moment to cash in his stock options. Just another object lesson in the ways of the True West.

The current bonanza will last two or three years then fizzle out into another twenty-year long bust. It's the oldest and dumbest cycle in the post-conquest West. With each iteration, the booms become less frenzied, the depressions more entrenched. Vernal, its city limits demarcated by a pink brontosaurus, will survive, thanks to the National Monument. But Craig and Pinedale may well decay into post-modern ghost towns. Few will shed tears for their passing. But as a preventative measure, the last ones out alive should consider torching the remains. Pinedale *delenda est*.

We come here not to drill the Green, but to float the river as it carves through Dinosaur National Monument. The burning question isn't whether there will be places to sleep, but whether there will be enough water to carry our three rafts, loaded with a week's worth of gear, water, food, shitter, and beer, through sixty miles of rock-studded canyons. You see, the ever considerate hydro-barons at the Bureau of Reclamation have squeezed closed the gates on their misbegotten plug in Flaming Gorge, thirty miles upstream from our put-in, permitting only an ice cold dribble of water to escape into the ancient channel of the Green River.

We're on a pilgrimage, of sorts. The river's twisting course through the heart of Dinosaur should be designated a National Battlefield site, after the first great victory of environmentalists over the forces of industrial pillage. This is our Little Big Horn, where David Brower and his cohorts, Wallace Stegner, Howard Zahniser, and Ulysses Grant III, routed the hydro-imperialists, saving one of the most stunningly beautiful landscapes in the world from inundation by two ill-conceived dams: one at Split Mountain and the other in Whirlpool Canyon near the glorious sandstone amphitheaters of Echo Park. But as with the Sioux's great victory over Custer, the battle of Dinosaur proved to have its own pyrrhic consequences. The fatal price of saving Dinosaur from being flooded was the nearly uncontested construction of equally monstrous dams at Flaming Gorge, Fontenelle, and most infamously, in Glen Canyon.

But these stories of triumph and tragedy must come later. Now there is unloading and raft-rigging to do, the hours of grunting, groaning, and eruptions of profanity that are the opening act of any true river expedition.

We assemble in Brown's Park, a secluded hole in the mountains that was once the redoubt of the suave black cattle rustler Isom Dart, hunted down by the grim mercenary Tom Horn, who, if truth be told, looked nothing like Steve McQueen.

There are seven of us, led by the two Weisheits—John and Susette. Both are acclaimed river guides. Both are militant defenders of the rivers of the Colorado Plateau—rivers anywhere, for that matter. Both are gifted naturalists and fine campfire cooks. But only Susette is a master of the delicate art of deep tissue massage. It's a crucial distinction—especially at our age.

Up from Moab come Judy Powers—a former river guide and a gifted actor, specializing in musical comedies—and Jennifer Speers—owner of a critter-friendly ranch at the confluence of the Colorado and the Dolores Rivers and a raconteur of deliciously rude jokes.

Down from Salt Lake City—the sprawling Mormon metropolis wedged between the Wasatch and the Great Salt Lake that is rapidly outstripping Los Angeles as the Smog Inversion capital of the country—arrive documentary film-maker Chris Simon, a vital (and grossly unheralded) contributor to Les Blank's best films, and Craig Miller, a folklorist and geographer who is putting the finishing touches on a fascinating social history of Highway 12, which runs through the ranch lands of central Utah from Panguitch to Torrey—an old road of a disappearing culture.

I'm the outsider in the group, a mossy-toed lowlander from Oregon who begins huffing and puffing while merely hauling modest-sized water canteens in the thinnish air of Dinosaur's mile-high altitude. But we share much in common. Namely we are all supplicants to the mesmerizing power of the Green River, the canyon-cutting umbilicus of the Interior West.

At last, the truck is emptied, the gear lashed onto the inflatable rafts powered by wooden oars on the only river in the Colorado basin devoted to non-motorized boats. The sun slips behind the peaks of the Uintas, the evening sky a surreal collage of purple and orange thanks to the big fires up in Idaho. The night winds whistle through the canyon, as Chris and Craig prepare a fabulous dinner of garlic bread and homegrown eggplant with pasta on the propane stove in the bed of Judy's red truck. Susette has miraculously conjured up a round of Mojitos. Judy belts out a Broadway show tune, the first of many. The coyotes chime in. Up in the hills a bull elk broadcasts the news that he is ready for sex. His come-and-get-it call reminds me of the darkly erotic growl of the great soul singer Clarence Carter. The temperature drops and the Milky Way spreads across the abbreviated sky. I slide into a supreme sleep and dream of a one-armed geologist in a small wooden boat dissolving into the jaws of a cleaved mountain.

* * *

I awake well before dawn. Only the bats are active, cruising through their final circuits of the night.

The air is cold, frosty. It occurs to me that I haven't prepared very well for this trip. I packed for a week on a desert river. But we aren't in the desert. These are mountains, big ones, with autumn bearing down.

I wiggle out of my sleeping bag, put on my headlamp, and go for a walk to get the blood flowing and the body temperature up.

A cobbly trail switchbacks up a cliff above our campsite to an outcrop with a view into the Gates of Lodore. I scuffle past sagebrush and juniper, stunted barrel cacti and rabbitbrush top-heavy with fat yellow blooms. After an hour or so the sun peers over the distant Rockies in the east, and the western walls of Lodore alight in dazzling crimson.

As I snap a photo of the canyon's glowing ramparts, a desert bighorn bounds in front of me and disappears below, dancing down the terraced face of the cliff toward a marsh by the river. Instinctively, I follow the young ram. I have notoriously bad instincts. Suicidally, bad. I take two steps and fall, hurtling down the rocky slope until finally I arrest my descent by clutching the only stable thing around. My salvation, such as it is, happens to be that most unforgiving of plants on the Colorado Plateau, the blackbrush. Its spiky branches dig aggressively into my hands, but I hold on and, eventually, scramble back up the cliff, lucky not to have bitten it right at the gate—so to speak.

My left leg is chewed up from my ankle to my hip. I vow to conceal this ungainly mishap from the group, not wanting to alarm them with the fact that they are about to embark on a challenging week down a dangerous river with someone who has the common sense and directional acumen of Lindsay Lohan after a night of tooting and toking in a West Hollywood hot spot.

Even from these heights, I can smell coffee percolating and bacon sizzling back at the campsite. Chris and Craig are at it again. Amen. I hobble down the trail, presenting my relatively unscathed side to the group.

"Oooh, nasty cut."

Damn. It's Judy, who emerges from the feathery curtain of tamarisk behind me.

"Would you like some tree oil for that?"

Tree oil? As in sap?

"Uhhh"

She waves the bottle at me. Was she expecting this? Had Weisheit already informed everyone I was a terminal klutz prone to self-mutilation?

"Don't worry. Natural antibiotic. Seal it right up."

No, not like sap, apparently. More like varnish. Shellac.

"Well"

Judy takes this as informed consent. She smears the concoction over the most ragged part of the wound. Now it is sealed. Now it is shiny. Now it is preserved as a warning for all: Stand back; don't follow.

We finish breakfast, visit the last latrine on the river until Echo Park, strap the final bags onto the rafts. And then we wait. We wait for Park Rangers to come down the forty-mile road from Maybell, Colorado to inspect our permits and bureaucratically release us from our concrete mooring.

The rangers don't come. Instead, a group of two canoeists and a kayaker pull up at the put-in site. One of the paddlers is a former ornithologist at Grand Canyon National Park, who conducted an acclaimed study documenting the tenuous status of passerines in the canyon country. He knows Weisheit. Most people around here do. After all, John is the Colorado Riverkeeper. They are a friendly and intelligent group of accomplished river runners who express concern about whether we will be able to navigate our rafts safely down the diminished river. They are good company and, incredibly, they are the only other people we will encounter in the next three days.

Another hour goes by and still the rangers don't come. Distilling the consensus of the group, Susette sez: "Fuck it, time to go!" We untie the rafts and push off. It is 11:30 in the morning. Finally, we are on the river. Legally or not.

Through the Gates of Lodore

The Gates of Lodore confront us from the river like a misty portal in a Romantic ode. That must be why John Wesley Powell lifted the name from Robert Southey's clunky poem, "The Cataract of Lodore." Jack Sumner, the most seasoned outdoorsman on the Colorado River Exploring Expedition of 1867, protested. He derided Southey's poem as "musty trash." Sumner was right.

A radical turncoat, the David Horowitz of his time, Robert Southey is one of the more odious figures in the canon of English literature. As a young man, Southey dreamed of establishing a utopian community in the United States. His partner in this endeavor was Samuel Taylor Coleridge. They were going to call their commune of virtue on the banks of the Susquehanna: Pantisocracy. It never got beyond the lines on a map and an airy poem by Coleridge. Instead, unnerved by the French Revolution, Southey the utopian turned government snitch, informing to the British secret police on the subversive activities of a radical circle of English writers, including Hazlitt, Byron, Cobbett, Godwin, and even his old friend Coleridge. Southey was rewarded for his treachery with the title of Poet Laureate.

There is the infamous Lake District incident, when a police snoop was dispatched to Wordsworth's cottage at Grasmere, perhaps on information passed along from Southey. As the officer crouched beneath an open window, he eavesdropped on a raging debate between Wordsworth and Coleridge over the merits of Spinoza's thoughts on government. The officer wrote excitedly back to the Home Office with the news that sedition was indeed afoot in the English countryside and that the poets were in covert contact with an agent of the French menace known as "the Spy Nozi."

Yes, we live in a new age of government paranoia, of snitches, spies, and informants. But must we commemorate them in our national parks?

In any event, even the best English Romantic poetry (Keats' "Ode to Autumn," say, or Coleridge's "Frost at Midnight") doesn't hint at the mysteries to be found in the canyons of the Green River, which over the eons have been the haunts of some of the strangest creatures on the planet: the Allosaurus, the sabre-toothed herbivore (Why the long teeth? Think: rough sex), the ringtail cat, and the Bureau of Reclamation engineer.

Lodore is a deep and narrow fissure in the High Uintas, that odd east/west range that strides across northern Utah. It is a canyon of echoes and shadows. Cool and dark. Spooky. Here the rocks show their age.

And old they are. Very old. The red quartzite of the Lodore Formation dates back nearly a billion years to the Cambrian period. Back to a time—an unimaginably extended epoch of time—when the future direction of life on Earth would take was being decided, a drama which the great evolutionary biologist Stephen Jay Gould eloquently narrates in his fascinating and controversial book, *Wonderful Life: The Burgess Shale and the Nature of History*. Would the chordata prevail over the spineless soft-tissued oddities, setting the stage for the rise of the vertebrates? For Democrats (and some environmentalists), it remains an open question.

In addition to the Gould and my river maps, I've brought along three other volumes, which, for handy access, I've wedged under a strap in the bow of Weisheit's raft: David Allen Sibley's *Field Guide to the Birds of Western North America*, John Wesley Powell's *The Exploration of the Colorado River and Its Canyons*, and G.E. Untermann's *Guide to the Geology of Dinosaur National Monument*. Putting the books in the bow of the raft will prove to be a fatal mistake—fatal for the books, anyway. (And, perhaps, for me too, given that I cohabit with a librarian who puts the rough treatment of texts on the same unpardonable level of moral degeneracy as the abuse of animals.)

The Untermann volume is a heretical choice, which Weisheit immediately notices and passes condemnatory judgment upon. Let this be known: the Riverkeeper doesn't forget and he doesn't forgive.

Like many progressives of his time, Untermann was a cheerleader for the Echo Park Dam back in the 1950s, even though the concrete monstrosity would have flooded most of the geological, archaeological, and paleontological sites that the geologist writes about with such zest and awe in his little monograph.

There was a time when the American left, of which Untermann was a member, viewed hydro-power as the democratizing salvation for the industrial economy, promising a future of cheap power, high-paying jobs and freedom from the shackles of big oil. (Go read John Gunther's *Inside USA* for a taste of just how deeply these hydrodelusions were cherished by liberals and leftists of mid-century America.) Inexplicably, many progressives, including some self-advertised environmentalists, persist in promoting these long discredited myths in the name of saving the planet from global warming.

Consider the case of liberal icon Woody Guthrie, the Okie troubadour. In the 1940s, Guthrie prostituted himself for the Department of the Interior, which paid him to write propaganda songs to promote the big salmon-killing dams on the Columbia River. While penning "Roll On Columbia" and similar doggerel, the folksinger watched silently from his rented house in Portland as the river tribes were forcibly evicted from their villages and salmon fishing sites to make way for the dams. The Red Okie remained mute in the face of cultural genocide. As for the electrical power, it sure wasn't disseminated to Guthrie's rural poor, never mind the dispossessed tribes of Celilo and Wishram. Most of it crackled down giant power lines to the H-bomb making factories at the Hanford Nuclear Reservation. Guthrie never apologized for being the Leni Riefenstahl of the Columbia and Untermann, as far as I can tell, never retracted his support for the proposed dams that would have turned Dinosaur National Monument into a holding tank for dead water and toxic silt.

Still, I admire the way the man writes. The prose in most geology books is as arid as the floor of Death Valley. But Untermann writes about fractures and faults, upthrusts and grabens, as if telling the story of a mighty battle, a thrilling dialectical struggle between the competing forces on the crust of the Earth.

Untermann knew something about dialectics. As I waited to rendezvous with Craig and Chris in Vernal, I took a stroll through the town's top attraction: the Utah Field House Museum of Natural History. I've toured many natural history museums, from New York to Paris. The sprawling Field Museum in Chicago is my favorite haunt, but Vernal's more compact and concentrated offering is a close second. The building unfolds like a strand of DNA, spiraling up through the ages of the earth, from trilobite fossils of the pre-Cambrian to a stunning mural of petrified maple leaves and fossilized bird feathers from the Green River shales of the Eocene, which are currently being cannibalized in the Bush oil rush.

Thanks to the rich trove of fossil-bearing loads from the Morrison Formation in Dinosaur National Monument, the little museum in Vernal offers some of the most complete dinosaur skeletons in the world, including a stegosaurus, a rare Haplocanthosaurus, and one of the most ferocious predators of the Jurassic Period, the allosaurus—a sleeker, faster, and more colorful version of T-Rex. T-Rex with feathers.

The tour concludes in a room of vibrantly colored oil paintings featuring fearsome battles between dinosaurs. I am a sucker for dioramas and these scenes of terror and tragedy in the Triassic age are incredibly exciting. They were all painted by Untermann's father, Ernest.

Untermann, Sr. was one of the founders of the Field House Museum. He was also one of the founders of the American Socialist Party and an early translator of the works of Karl Marx into English. Apparently a committed Trotskyist, in 1935 Ernest wrote a book-length attack on the Stalin titled, *Lenin's Maggot*. Born in Brandenberg, Germany in 1864, Untermann came to Vernal, Utah in 1919 looking to strike it rich in the gold fields. But the gold rush was long over and Untermann was soon distracted by excavations of fossils in Dinosaur National Monument by paleontologist Earl Douglass, who had been hired by Andrew Carnegie to bring back to Philadelphia a dinosaur "as big as a barn."

After a few years, Untermann left Utah for Milwaukee, where he ran the city zoo, and Chicago, where he studied painting at the Art Institute. By 1940, Ernest was back in Vernal where, over the next fifteen years, he executed more than 100 paintings of life in the Uinta region during the thrilling Mesozoic period. Like many socialists of his era, he lived a long and adventuresome life, dying in 1956 at the age of ninety-two.

Busloads of Utah school children are shipped off to Vernal every year for an obligatory visit to the museum. It must be a mind-blowing experience for them. Although Mormon doctrine embraces the existence of dinosaurs (the Terrible Lizards are good for the economy and, given the heavy tithing obligations imposed on the Saints, for church coffers as well), it also teaches that the Earth is only 7,000 years old—a chronology that the museum exhibits dispute with what Gould called "geology's most frightening facts." But complex geological timelines depicting the fossil record are easily forgotten by the minds of young Mormons (or adult Gentiles, for that matter). Less so are the subversive messages encoded in the dinosaur dialectics, painted by the Marxist of the Uintas.

As I scan the maroon cliffs of Lodore, trying to make sense of the geological processes Untermann describes, I am distracted by a growling sound coming from the river itself. We round a sharp bend in the canyon and are rudely jerked into our first rapids: a short, violent run of water. The tumult is over almost before it began. A case of premature excitation. Not to worry. There are thirty more where that one came from. Bigger, wetter, nastier.

* * *

We break for lunch at a place called Winnie's Grotto, a dark slot canyon draped with maidenhair ferns and fuzzy mosses—a moist exemplar of the marvels of microclimate. A pair of ravens scrutinize our meal, but noisily dismiss the fare of smoked oysters with Pringles chips, and wheel off in search of more robust offerings.

Chris hands me a frosty Tecate. I remove my jacket and recline on a warm slab of stone that only months ago was submerged under four-feet of calamitous water.

"Pssst."

It's Judy again. This time she seems to have sprung from behind a stand of rippling willow trees—one of the few such groves left in the canyon thanks to the dam, the dropping water table, the invasion of the tamarisks. These stage actresses sure know how to maximize the effect of their entrances.

"Can I ask you a favor?"

"Sure." Thinking she needs me to perform a manly task, like setting up the shitter or standing between her and a marauding tarantula. In post-feminist America, it feels good to finally be needed.

"Can you take your shirt off?"

This is one request I wasn't expecting. But...

"Or at least turn it inside out. It's disturbing me."

I look down at one of my favorite shirts. I've worn it once a week for six years. The cotton is pliant and soft, pleasantly frayed, familiarly stained. Nearing perfection. The offensive image on the front was designed by my pal Steve Kelly, the environmentalist and artist in Bozeman, Montana. It reproduces one of Kelly's best paintings, a field of slain bison, their blood staining the snowy plains. The caption above the startling image reads: "Grown in Yellowstone, Slaughtered in Montana."

The painting, which Kelly placed on billboards along I-90, protests the ongoing killing of Yellowstone's wild bison on the bogus pretext of protecting cattle from being infected with brucellosis. I've nearly come to blows over this shirt before: in a bar in Salmon, Idaho (one of America's meanest towns) and at a rusty diner in the cattleburg of Burns, Oregon.

But here, in the depths of Lodore, in the blood red basement of the Uintas? This is the last place in the world I'd expect to be censored. But Judy is an animal lover. She works closely with the Humane Society in Moab. The shirt clearly upsets her. Still, I'm usually a cantankerous asshole at precisely these critical moments and I surprise myself by relenting without even a nasty quip. Kelly's painting has done its work. I reverse the shirt, but secretly vow to flash its brutal truth if we ever encounter one of them damn park rangers.

Jennifer snaps the tension by popping another Tecate and retelling a joke that the Riverkeeper still doesn't get: "A termite walks into a saloon and asks: Is the bartender here?"

At Disaster Falls

Now we enter the very marrow of Lodore. Fractured and fused cliffs of metamorphosed stone soar 3,500 feet above the Green River. Up in the narrow wedge of sky, a golden eagle sails a thermal in a tightening spiral like those etched on the canyon walls by the Fremont a thousand years ago, before dissolving into fierce sunlight.

The roar of an unseen rapids booms up the canyon. Disaster Falls. Yes, we are floating in the deepest corridor of Lodore and it is impossible not to turn your mind to thoughts of Powell and his men. This strange and shadowy chasm was, in many ways, the real beginning of their historic expedition, and Disaster Falls nearly proved its traumatic undoing.

Powell the man and his expedition have been relentlessly romanticized by western writers of the 1950s and 1960s, in particular. And the worst offenders happen to be, coincidentally, two of my favorite essayists: Wallace Stegner and Edward Abbey. Stegner's Powell, as presented in *Beyond the Hundredth Meridian*, is a scientific messiah for the enlightened stewardship of the fragile resources of the arid West. Abbey's Powell is, typically, a figure who looks and smells a lot like Abbey's vision of himself: a gritty desert rat, a fearless river-runner, a rural anarchist.

It wasn't until 2001 with the publication of Donald Worster's sprawling biography, *A River Running West*, that we finally got a full and unvarnished portrait of the man. Far from being an anarchist, for much of his life Powell was an office-bound Washington bureaucrat, engaged in mundane and soul-sapping struggles on Capitol Hill over budgetary line items, the editing of government reports and petty feuds with rival agency heads and members of congress, such as his fateful dust-up with the behemoth of Nevada, Senator William Stewart.

Still, Powell is a decisive figure in the modern history of the Interior West. His only real rival is Gifford Pinchot, intimate advisor to Teddy Roosevelt and first chief of the US Forest Service. Pinchot and Powell not only helped to define the public estate and draft the regulatory prescriptions for its use, but more critically, they also shaped the bureaucratic agencies charged with managing the federal lands and rivers of the West: Forest Service, BLM, Geological Survey, Bureau of Reclamation, and Bureau of Indian Affairs.

Preservation of wilderness and wild rivers wasn't on the agenda of either Powell or Pinchot, who went head-to-head against John Muir in support of the Hetch-Hetchy Dam in the heart of Yosemite. Both men were utilitarians. They were political progressives who evangelized, in the phrase of historian Samuel P. Hays, the Gospel of Efficiency. They viewed oil, timber, grasslands, gold, coal, and water as public resources awaiting managed exploitation—managed by federal bureaucrats, exploited for the public good.

Even though Powell cautioned about the intrinsic limits of the Interior West for agriculture and the development of large cities, Worster makes clear, where Stegner and Abbey do not, the unsettling fact that the one-armed major envisioned a system of small-scale, upper basin dams and water diversions that would have "drained every drop" of the Colorado River system.

The really bruising battles back then were over how those public resources would be distributed: to the land barons, railroads, and corporations or, following the old Jeffersonian vision, to the small farmers, homesteaders, and rural communities of the West. Guess which prevailed? Both Powell and Pinchot lost their jobs in the fight, early causalities in the power plays of the Western Imperialists.

Even so, it's not hard for me to prefer Powell, with all of his faults, to Pinchot. As a fellow son of the prairies, I empathize with the Major, understand his midwestern eccentricities, and lament the way the war that took his arm at Shiloh cast such a long-range shadow over his psyche.

Pinchot is another beast entirely: an east coast Brahmin, educated at Yale, parlor guest of the Vanderbilts and Roosevelts. Where Powell scraped up his own meager resources and those of the tiny Illinois Natural History Society to finance his first expedition down the Green and Colorado rivers, Pinchot lived off of trust funds and grants from the oldest money on the continent and learned the art of tree-killing on a silvicultural sabbatical in Germany's Black Forest directly from the old meisters, soaking up their peculiar ideas about order and genetics.

Powell recognized that the land had limits and sought to devise a system for putting the waters of the West to use without inflicting permanent damage on the productive capacity of the landscape. Pinchot rejected such dusty realism for what historian Paul Hirt aptly calls "a Conspiracy of Optimism." The forester loftily asserted that by imposing his system of scientific management on western woodlands, the national forests could be transformed into eternally productive tree farms. Pinchot was wrong. Fatally wrong. But then so was Powell, only less arrogantly.

* * *

Mystique aside, the Powell expedition was not the first group of white men to venture down the Green River through the canyons of Dinosaur. Far from it. In 1825, William Ashley, the impresario of the Rocky Mountain fur trade, floated the Green from Wyoming through Flaming Gorge, Red Canyon, Brown's Park, Lodore, Whirlpool, and Split Mountain canyons, all the way to the Uintah River south of Vernal. Ashley was searching for a speedy, Indian-free route to transport beaver and otter furs to market. The master of the skin trade rapidly concluded Lodore Canyon wasn't the easy way and instructed his brigades of mountain men to cart their bloody cargo by horse to the notorious annual rendezvous on the Green up at the Henry's Fork in Wyoming.

Ashley made two fortunes, first as a defense contractor in the War of 1812, and later amassing enormous wealth from the beaver pelt trade, which, in the grim year of 1826 alone, topped 325,000 skins. He bought himself the title of General and a seat in congress from St. Louis. Little known today, Ashley was an almost mythical figure, who ventured down more than fifty crushing rapids on the Green River in a bull-boat, a floating saucer made of stretched bison hides.

Then there is the strange case of Denis Julien, the Kilroy of the Green River, who carved his initials on rock walls from Lodore to Cataract Canyon. (Later we will examine one of Julien's faint inscriptions in a shady cove in Whirlpool Canyon, near the planned site of the Echo Park dam. Beneath the fur-trapper's initials, river otters have come to defecate, as if to render a final judgment on the merits of his enterprise.)

Julien was a Frenchman from New Orleans, and later St. Louis, who trapped along the Green in the 1830s. If one of his carvings is to be believed, Julien traversed the tumultuous river in a poleboat similar to those used on the lazy lower stretches of the Missouri.

Twenty-five years after Ashley first navigated the Green, William Manly and a group of bullwhackers from Missouri, desperate to stake their claim in the California Gold Rush, set off down the Green in a ludicrously unstable ferry boat. After a series of close calls, they encountered Disaster Falls, where the miners came across a mangled boat with a note attached advising, "Walk to California." They portaged. Portaged again and again and again. And finally abandoned their brittle boat for an arduous overland route across the mountains.

Despite extensive research at the US Archives, Powell, it appears, knew none of this history. Oddly, he had never even heard of Ashley, despite the fur trader's fame as the leader of the Mountain Men and blazer of what would later become the Oregon Trail. In fact, when Powell discovered an inscription by Ashley near Flaming Gorge he misread the date as 1855, not 1825. Ashley's hair-raising journal entries might have prepared the Major for the challenges to come inside Lodore.

For starters, Powell might have opted for a better design for his boats. The geologist drew up the plans himself, and the boats were crafted from sturdy oak by the Chicago boat-builder Thomas Bagley. They were big, heavy, rode deeply in the water and resembled the ferry-tenders plying the Chicago River and Lake Michigan—scarcely a trim suited for descending a river that falls 9,000 feet in a mere 730 miles. In Powell's design, the oarsman rowed the boat facing upstream, his back to the rapids—a technique now known by many river-runners as "Powelling," as in "Powelling right into that fucking rock."

Powell himself, of course, was not a boatman. For most of the journey, the Major found himself strapped into a chair on the deck of the Emma Dean, like Odysseus tied to the mast during the frightening passage through the Straits of Messina.

At the big rapids, Powell and his top scout, Jack Sumner, would scan the obstacles and decide whether or not to risk a descent. By the time the group entered Lodore, Powell had devised a tedious method of lining the boats down rock-strewn passages and over cataracts. It was time-consuming and difficult and the men generally preferred the excitement of running the rapids.

A few hundred yards upstream from Disaster Falls, Powell pulled over and scrambled up on a ledge to get a better view of the falls. He instructed the young William Dunn to flag the other three boats over to the river bank. From his perch Powell watched as the Maid of the Canyon and Kitty Clyde's Sister tied up near the Emma Dean, but the No-Name hurtled right by the other boats and got sucked into the tongue of the rapids. The No-Name survived the first big drop, but the second falls, of a reported fifteen to twenty feet, punched the two Howland boys and Frank Goodman from the boat and into the roiling whitewater. Swept into the lower run of rapids, the No-Name smashed into a sharp boulder, shattering its oak planks and breaking the boat in half.

Miraculously, the Howlands and Goodman survived, thanks largely to the quick actions of Sumner. But the No-Name and its cargo were lost, including clothing, rifles, maps, journals from the first month of the trip, field instruments, and most critically, three months worth of food. The morale of the expedition sank as well, and never fully recovered.

The Howlands may have missed Powell's signal because they were drunk. The Major had banned alcohol from the voyage. But on an island downstream from Disaster Falls some of the wreckage of the No-Name washed up. Among the debris were Powell's precious barometers and a 10-gallon keg of whiskey, which had been secretly cached in the bow of the boat. The Major was so ecstatic at having recovered his instruments of atmospheric measurement that he uncharacteristically overlooked the contraband and encouraged all the men to have a round of drinks.

* * *

The rapids we face this afternoon don't much resemble the ferocious falls that sundered the No-Name and nearly destroyed the Powell expedition on that June day in 1869. According to Weisheit, nearly omniscient in these matters, the Green was likely running at 24,000 cubic feet per second when Howland "Powelled" his boat into Disaster Falls. Today, the river spurts along at a mere 650 cubic feet per second, thanks to the water wardens at Flaming Gorge dam.

Yet, this miserly flow presents its own challenges and unique dangers. The river has been turned into something resembling a pinball machine, a machine with teeth of stone. Under natural flows, most of these rocks would be safely submerged under several feet of rushing water. Now they are all hazards, each one waiting to trap a foot, rip a raft, smash a skull.

We scout the run for about an hour, charting and discussing every possible route. At Disaster Falls proper, the river is squeezed between two large rocks, pours over a four-foot ledge and into a snarling standing wave. Below the falls, the rapids continue for another quarter of a mile through a glistening maze of prong-like rocks.

Weisheit turns to me and asks, "What do you think?"

I play it cool, shrug my shoulders, kick a stone, quote Peter Tosh: "Bad, mon. Plenty bad."

"Let's do this thing," Susette exhorts, over the thunder of Disaster Falls. I love Susette. Susette gets my vote as the best river guide on the Green and Colorado Rivers. She's ridden long-distance motorcycle races and is a champion barrel racer of horses. She is a gifted desert gardener and a genuine Reiki master. She is lovely, smart, and strong. But...Susette also thinks Niagara Falls is a Class Five rapid! The exalted Class Six designation, according to Susette, is reserved only for rapids that are always fatal. Emphasis on the always. And, of course, the fatal.

"Now, go get 'em, boys," she says, kicking our raft into the maw of the current with the Vibram sole of her Chaco sandal. As the river asserts its claim on us, my last image is of Susette's toenails, shimmering with purple polish.

With an unnerving directness of intent, we approach the two boulders that guard the falls, boulders the size of Wooly Mammoths. Weisheit thrusts the bow of the raft into the mossy rock on river right, the boat rotates and we slide backwards over the cataract, just like Howlands and Co.

Water pours into the raft as the stern dips into the curling wave, then we pop up, slam into a hidden rock. The raft swings in the swirling water and rights itself. We rattle and scrape through Lower Disaster, a dicey run of swift water punctuated by thorny rocks. Finally we reach an eddy and turn to watch Susette delicately pivot her raft between the twin rocks and down the falls. It's a gorgeous run. Susette evades every hazard with the easy precision and grace of a gifted slalom skier.

I only have two questions: How did she do that? And where the hell is Judy's raft?

* * *

The circulating waters of the eddy hold our raft in place as we scan the river for the yellow nose of Judy's boat. Four bighorns look down on us from a ridiculously narrow ledge of rotten rock, casual and free from fear. With still no sign of our missing cohorts, we tie our raft to a rock, grab two rescue bags, and stumble up the stony shore.

Susette, as usual, is ahead of us. She points to a small tangle of driftwood. "I saw a snake slip into that pile. Couldn't tell if it was a rattler."

Weisheit hops over the den of sticks. I give it a wide berth. I'm wearing sandals and have an aversion to rattlesnakes that is either Jungian or Freudian—I'm much too jittery to undergo analysis for a definitive answer. Only images of dentists with drills strike me with more psychic terror.

Driftwood piles are becoming more and more rare along the Green River, especially in this part of Dinosaur. The big piles are all more than fifty years old and loom far up on the banks. Flaming Gorge Dam not only traps water behind its bland concrete arc, but also all of the woody and organic debris that play such a crucial role in recharging the rich ecology of riparian areas: providing nutrients for the river, nesting and feeding habitat for fish in floodtime, and shelter for bugs, mice, scorpions, and yes, snakes.

We wade across a stagnant pool, the surface of which is etched by the trails of waterstriders, and onto a sandbar, desolate except for the stalking prints of a great blue heron.

On the far side of the river, the yellow raft is wedged between two rocks. Judy strains at the oars, while Craig, hip-deep in the river, pushes at the stern of the boat. Prudently, Jennifer adheres to the Apocalypse Now! Rule of River Safety: Stay in the boat. Whatever happens, stay in the fucking boat.

Craig has long legs, but still he must be careful. Foot entrapment here is a real danger. It's easy to get your foot wedged between two sunken rocks, especially when you're working to dislodge a snagged raft. Then the force of the river, even at these reduced flows, pushes you down and grips you there, parallel to the river bottom, where, as they said in the *Alien* movies, no one can hear you scream.

There's not much we can do from this side of the river but watch. They are too far away for us to toss them a rescue line. Then, with Jennifer giving a forceful tug on the rigging, the rocks release the raft. Craig scrambles onto the boat just as it smacks another boulder and bumps and grinds its way down to the sanctuary of the eddy.

We trudge back through a wavy thicket of wild cane. Weisheit tells me to look high on canyon walls downstream at the white planking of rock near the rim, the first appearance of the Madison limestone formation. As I take out my binoculars and scan the distant rim of the canyon, which looks like icing on a cherry layer cake, I am interrupted by a hollow buzzing, an emphatic buzzing, coming from beneath my left foot, which at this precise moment is rapidly descending toward the very driftwood pile that Susette had, only moments before, warned us to avoid.

I freeze. I look down. The snake is coiled into a ball not much bigger than my fist. Its tail is erect and is making a declarative statement. You know the one. Not a large snake. And from the stern and unflinching posture of its flat, triangular head with the distinctive loreal pits, not a happy snake, either. And, oh yes, Susette, it's most definitely a rattler. Most likely the relatively passive, yet potently toxic, Midget Faded Rattlesnake—though I defer from looking for the distinguishing characteristics that would definitely mark this agitated little creature as *Crotalus viridis concolor*.

Weisheit crunched across the driftwood pile without even pausing. The Riverkeeper leads a charmed life, and long may it be so. The man has spent thirty years in the canyon country, scaling slickrock and tackling the worst rapids in Cataract and Grand Canyon, and has never required more than a Band-Aid. So he says. I, however, retreat, scramble down to the river and slop my way through the knee-deep mud to the raft.

* * *

Back on the Green, the lovely Green.

We exit the eddy and promptly hit a rock. Hard. Our red raft swings violently to the right, slamming into another concealed shard of stone with such force that one of the Riverkeeper's oars jolts free from his hand and rips my head. The raft tilts to the left and down, down into the river. Currents of silver water flood into the raft, creating our own little reservoir and drowning my books, one by one.

"High side," Weisheit instructs, calmly. I clamber up to the elevated side of the raft and gaze down at the churning water and spiky rocks below, which resemble a scene from the illustrated torture manual at Abu Ghraib. (Think Water boarding meets the Bed of Nails.)

I look back at Weisheit. Our acute encounter with the rocks has knocked the huge-brimmed white hat off his head. It hangs down his back like Kokopelli's bag of seeds. "Now!" he shouts, above the orgasmic roar of the river. We bounce on the side of the raft, again and again, in a kind of unison. Eventually, one rock relinquishes its grip and the stern of the raft wheels, pointing downstream.

"Need a kickstart?"

It's Judy's boat, returning the favor. Craig extends his leg from the side of the raft, long as advertised. All it takes is a vigorous little stomp and we are free. Wet and free. The way all river-runners (and rivers) should be.

* * *

We anchor our rafts for the night on a small beach, lushly framed in cottonwoods, at the mouth of a broad technicolor valley we call Cascade Canyon and the Park Service labels Pot Creek. Why Pot Creek? Who knows? This bench of Indian ricegrass, red boulders, and fire-scarred Ponderosa pines is too arid for marijuana plantations and for that we have no regrets. Some in our crowd prefer mushrooms instead, though no one seems to have had the foresight to secrete any dried Liberty Caps (known to Latin-speaking pranksters around the globe as *psilocybe semilanceata*) into the food cache, even though the fungal treats would have made a highly patriotic addition to our larder.

First things first. The rafts must be unloaded, the kitchen erected, and yes, the shitter must be deployed.

This curious device is not the shiny aluminum Groover found on commercial river trips, the Airstream trailer of Honey Pots. No. Ours is a humble US Army ammo can, about twenty inches long, six inches wide, and twelve inches deep. The vintage is hard to discern. It may be a relic from our glorious triumph at Grenada—or perhaps the charge up San Juan Hill.

Thankfully, Weisheit has fashioned a crude but ass-cradling seat so that it doesn't exactly feel like shitting in a can, though proper posture and a delicate balance must be maintained at all costs. Naturally, defecating is done in public. Strike a pose.

It is our night to cook. Weisheit builds a small fire with twigs and coals in the firebox laid on top of a rug made of glass fibers to keep from scarring the beach, while I get pots boiling and pans sizzling on the propane camp stove. Tonight's menu: smoked trout, pepper jack cheese, salad with red onions and green peppers, filet of sole with couscous and broccoli, and brownies baked in a Dutch oven. There will be no leftovers for the ringtails and ravens.

Jennifer mixes drinks. She hands me a gin and tonic and inquires, "What do you call a Mormon gynecologist?"

"Overworked?" I ask.

"No. A Box Elder." Touché.

Night descends early in this narrow, somber region of the canyon and I fade into sleep to the frantic incantations of coyotes.

A Half Mile of Hell

Dawn in the canyon.

The early morning light is liquid and orange, amniotic. Everyone is sleeping. Jennifer is zipped up tight under a spreading box elder. Craig and Chris have opted for a shimmering white tent from which you might envision the gap-toothed Omar Sharif emerging with wrinkle-free clothes and perfect hair. While Judy threw her bag down on a white stretch of beach and was lulled to sleep by the steady hiss of the river, John and Susette, old hands at desert camping, are serenely mummified in a pharaonic mound of quilts, pads, and sleeping bags. Should I inform them that our beach seems to have been previously reserved for a convention of scorpions? No. Better to let sleeping innocents lie.

I fill the pots with water, light the burners and brew a riverside version of Turkish coffee. I grab a gray plastic mug with "Drain It!" stamped on the side, top it off with the grounds-flecked coffee and head up a trail in Cascade Canyon to watch the sun ease over the high parapets of Lodore.

On a ledge above our camp I am struck by an overwhelming odor of cat. More precisely, cat shit.

It doesn't take long to find the source: a fresh mound of cougar feces, still warm to the touch, recently deposited near the plated trunk of a fat Ponderosa pine. I poke around in the steaming pile with a stick. The big cat appears to have recently sampled three of the four basic food groups: ground squirrel, jackrabbit, mule deer. No evidence of the remains of a Forest Service timber sale planner, though. Still, there are many hours left in the day for our *felix concolor* to fulfill her dietary regimen. After all, the Ashley National Forest, currently being blitzed by clearcuts, is only a few miles away. Up the canyon and take a right. Just follow the survey stakes.

I've spent many weeks in remote western wilderness areas and this is the closest I've come to a mountain lion—though I'm sure they've spied on me many times. Perhaps you know the sensation? Those eerie moments, alone in the outback, when you feel a cold prickling ripple across your skin, the hairs on your neck stiffen, the air electrifies, and the world goes silent. Being scanned by a cougar is like walking in the presence of a ghost—your own.

As the suburbs continue to sprawl mercilessly into the mountains and deserts of the West, a new frenzy of mountain lion panic has broken out with calls to revive the old bounty campaigns to wipe out the big cats, once and for all. The cover of a recent book on mountain lion attacks depicts a cougar looming menacingly over the city of Boulder, Colorado, as if to suggest that a lion had snatched Jon Benet.

But the lions of the West are survivors. Only wolves and coyotes have suffered more grotesquely at the hands of the hired killers in the government's war on predators. This grim history is recounted in harrowing detail by my friend, Michael Robinson, in his painfully researched book, *Predatory Bureaucracy: The Extermination of Wolves and the Transformation of the West*.

For the past 100 years, mountain lions have been trapped, poisoned, skinned alive, blown up by M-44 cyanide bomblets planted in bait, hunted with dogs, gunned down from helicopters, and had their decapitated heads stacked into a grisly pyramid as a photo-op for western newspapers. Someday, someday soon, there will be a mighty reckoning. Even big empires can go defunct, have their equilibrium punctuated almost overnight—geologically speaking. Thank Bush for that. He didn't open the fissures in the American behemoth, but his presidency has revealed how quickly the foundations of power can erode away when arrogance is genetically encoded with stupidity.

Still the big cats endure. And with the decimation of the grizzly, mountain lions are becoming the supreme predators of the American West. But perhaps they always were.

While the griz asserts its dominance through direct confrontation, which inevitably results, sooner or later, in the death of the bear (and nearly every other bear in the neighborhood), the lion settles on a different stratagem: stealth, speed, adaptation. It is the ninja of the quadrupeds: a cat that is capable of flying thirty feet across slot canyons, scaling vertical walls, killing in silence, and savoring a secret revenge.

We see something of ourselves in wolves and bears. Perhaps that familiarity explains our cruelty toward those species and our small measure of guilt for the torments we've inflected upon them. But the cougar seems to be an alien presence, inscrutable and unknowable. Consider the Fremont people. Their rock art represents an amazingly complete catalog of the flora and fauna of the Green River basin, from bison and bears to scorpions and rattlers. But you'll search the sandstone walls in vain for an image of a cougar, even though the cats must have taken many Fremont lives. Some beings are too powerful to make engraven images of. And perhaps that fact, to this point at least, has made all the difference.

I amble back to camp, now alive with activity. The first face of the morning I see is Susette's. It's a pleasant face: bright, confident, inviting. She waves and smiles. Oddly, her smile turns to a frown, the frown to a paralyzing glare. She's staring at my coffee mug. The one with Drain It! stamped on one side and SUSETTE on the other. Uh oh. The hairs on my neck stiffen. A prickling sensation runs up my back. Busted.

Susette has handed down the two laws of the river. Don't tangle the bowline and don't—don't ever—pour coffee into her mug. Like a good anarchist, I have violated both strictures on the second morning and am promptly placed on probation. One more transgression and she'll boot me back to Pinedale with a note pinned to my shirt: "This is one of them Earth First!ers. He wants to raze your town and sow it with salt. Dispose of him in the customary manner."

I pledge to behave—though I never get the knack of tying those insanely complicated knots. I take comfort only in the fact that Craig's rope-knotting skills are even more chaotic than mine. In fact, I admire him for it.

* * *

As a folklorist, Craig spends his time unknotting more complex matters, such as the exquisite dances of Mormon farming communities (endemic variations on the old quadrilles), interpreting the techniques and symbolism in Ute weaving and pottery, tracing the lineage of cowboy songs and tall tales. It's a race against time to get it all down before it dissipates into the white noise of sprawl culture, its remorseless homogeneity, the cold logic of the clone.

Utah remains a cultural refugium for traditional Mormons, Utes and Paiutes, and desert loners of all kinds. As in Appalachia in the 1930s and 1940s, the old ways still persist here—for a while. Vast stretches of Utah remain cable free and serve as dead zones for cell phones. But even Utah is changing and the oil bonanza is exacerbating the worst manifestations of American techno-culture, as cell phone towers sprout along the red-rock ridges above the new oil fields.

Fresh out of Florida State, Craig came to the west back in the 1970s to work as a geographer and cartographer for the BLM and the Forest Service, working mainly out of Rangely, Colorado. One of his last assignments was to perform a survey in the Piceance Valley, where in one of the most unnerving and least known episodes in the modern history of the American outback, the federal government nuked western Colorado.

The idea sprang from the diseased brain of Edward Teller, architect of the hydrogen bomb. At the prodding of David Lilienthal, head of the Atomic Energy Commission (AEC), Teller developed a series of schemes designed to display the utilitarian side of nuclear weapons. At first, Teller called his initiative Atoms for Peace. It later became known as Project Plowshares. First on Teller's agenda was plan to explode three nuclear weapons off the coast of Alaska to excavate an instant harbor. At a public meeting in Point Hope, Alaska, where he was confronted by angry Inuits, Teller said, infamously, "Don't worry about your fish. Most of that radiation dissipates in a matter of seconds. If your mountain is in the wrong place, just drop us a card."

That was in 1960. And Teller suffered a humiliating defeat at the hands of the Inuit and a nascent environmental movement. But the project lived on in new and more devious incarnations. In reality, Project Plowshares was a way for the H-bomb boys to continue nuclear testing under the guise of domestic works projects.

In all there were three big nuclear explosions in the Colorado Basin: Project Gas Buggy, Project Rio Blanco (in the Piceance where Craig did his survey work) and Project Rulison. Rulison was the last major episode in the Atoms for Peace program. The peace in question wasn't a cooling of the tensions between the US and the Soviet Union, but between two even more entrenched rivals: the nuclear industry and the oil companies, then locked in fierce combat over which sector would control America's energy future. The AEC wanted to prove that a few well-placed nuclear bombs could strategically rearrange the geology of the Earth's crust in such a way as to release deeply buried, and once untappable, reservoirs of oil and gas.

At the Rulison site on Doghead Mountain, near Rifle, Colorado, there is a layer of gas trapped by a barrier of sandstone called the Williams Fork Formation. In the spring of 1969, the AEC's nuclear team showed up, drilled an 8,500-foot bore hole into the ground, lowered a forty-kiloton nuclear bomb down the chute and blew it up. Teller pushed the button himself. The blast knocked several unsuspecting local residents to the ground, and at least one rancher was blown off of his horse.

Gas began to percolate up. Not much, but some. There was a problem, though. An intractable one. The gas was dangerously radioactive.

The AEC and Department of Interior plugged the bore holes with cement and left. After all, this flank of Doghead Mountain wasn't their land. It was a private ranch. In the grand tradition of western mining law, the nuclear excavators only owned the subsurface rights.

The radioactive waste remains. Lots of it, eternally mixed with shattered rock, ground water and natural gas. No one knows how to remove the radiation. Most people out here hope they never try.

Think again. They are trying to remove it. The gas that is. A Texas company called Presco, Inc. is intent on drilling sixty-five new gas wells in the blast zone, squeezing it out through an experimental process known as hydrofracturing. In other words, Presco wants to pulverize those subterranean sandstone reefs with blasts of pressurized water. Where will the water come from? Lake Powell? Will the water become radioactive when it hits the nuclear blast zone? Will the gas? Who knows?

Stiff-arming fears from local residents that the drilling will release those long-buried radioactive fumes, the BLM and the State of Colorado have already given Presco the greenlight.

Yes, it looks a lot like war out here on the Western front, where thousands of volunteers are enlisting as mercenaries for the oil industry, which seems intent on putting the boom back into bonanza.

* * *

The rocks of Dinosaur don't need to be shattered. This is already a fractured landscape.

In the Grand Canyon, the stratigraphy of rock layers is laid down chronologically, with an inexorable precision that demolishes the creed of the Creationists. But the landscape of Dinosaur is different. As in a different planet. Here the canyons and mountains present themselves in contorted galleries of geological cubism. Here strata of rock stand on their head, bend over backwards, break off into space and then resume miles away. This is Jumbleland. Chaos theory in stone.

Here some of the oldest rocks in the West sit on top of much younger deposits, younger by a half billion years. And some strata of rock have gone missing altogether, giant gaps of time elided from the geologic record—and that's before the coal companies started strip mining.

But perhaps no mystery is more opaque to the untutored mind than why the Green River, not a mighty stream by most measures, decided to drive south smack into the eastern flank of a nearly impregnable massif with 13,000-foot peaks, otherwise known as the Uinta Mountains, and, having made this fateful turn, how such a modest little river could have cleaved so savage a wound through this formidable range of billion-year old rocks, rising from the depths of the Pre-Cambrian zone.

The explanations for this phenomenon have changed over the decades. John Wesley Powell opted for the antecedent theory. He postulated that an early incarnation of the Green River flowed through this region before the Uinta Mountains began their amazing uplift from the basement of the planet, during what is known to geologists as the Laramide Orogeny and the rest of us as "The Making of the Rocky Mountains." Under Powell's scenario, which is laid out in his intriguing monograph *The Geology of the Eastern Portion of the Uinta Mountains*, he contends that the Green River functioned as a saw, cutting through the quartzite of the Uintas as they began their dramatic uplift in the late Tertiary period, a mere five million years ago.

Having witnessed the vast void of the Grand Canyon, Powell believed in the omnipotence of erosive forces. He was right to concede such power to erosion. Consider the fact that the Uinta Mountains have risen nearly 45,000 feet, but have probably never been taller than they are today. In other words, aside from that first great thrust upward, erosion has essentially leveled the Uinta uplift, inch for inch. (By the way, the mountains remain in an aggressively tumescent phase.)

Still, Powell was almost certainly wrong, and the first to contradict him was his brilliant student Grove K. Gilbert, who postulated what is now known as the superimposition theory. Under this scenario, the Uinta Mountains rose nearly five million years ago, then were flooded under a vast inland sea, which deposited layer upon layer of sediments. As the sea drained, the Green River formed on the eastern fringe of the range and began its steady excavations through the rock.

Gilbert's theory held sway for many decades. Then, in the 1960s, an even stranger explanation was put forth by Wallace Hansen, a top research geologist at US Geological Survey. In his monograph, *The Geologic Story of the Uinta Mountains*, Hansen merges Powell and Gilbert. He demonstrates, fairly persuasively to blank slate minds like my own, that there was indeed an ur-Green River in the general vicinity of Dinosaur before the rise of the Uintas. But he also argues that the current course of the river was superimposed over the newly revealed mountains.

Then he throws a bomb. Hansen argues that the Upper Basin of the Green River used to flow not southwesterly to the confluence with the Grand River and to the Sea of Cortez, but easterly toward the North Platte to the Missouri and, ultimately, the Gulf of Mexico. In other words, sometime in the last four million years, the Green River jumped the Continental Divide. Hansen calls this event "stream capture," a kind of geomorphologic imperialism where, through a complex gymnastics of faulting and uplift, one drainage steals the water of another.

These geologic arcana take on a more tangible meaning here on the floor of Cascade Canyon, which less than a million years ago formed the main channel of the Green River. The old, abandoned riverbed can be found in a hanging valley, some 500 feet above where we made our camp. This is an object lesson about flux and dynamic change.

The Earth hasn't stopped shaping itself. Not by a long shot.

The ground continues to shift. The restless river eats relentlessly into the rocks. Cliffs collapse. Valleys sink. Ridges buckle. Even human structures aren't immune to Powell's omnipotent forces. Last summer, only a few days after my son Nat and I spent an enjoyable afternoon inspecting the ancient bones lying in situ, the foundation of the great museum at the Dinosaur Quarry cracked, its footings detaching from the fossil-bearing slopes of the Morrison Formation. The building is now closed.

Flaming Gorge Dam take heed.

* * *

We glide onto the river late this morning. The sky is pallid and sickly, stained by smoke from distant fires.

It will be a short day of big rapids and sharp rocks, in unbroken succession: Harp Falls, Triplet, and the monster of them all, Hell's Half Mile.

Time seems to move, if not in circles, at least deeply entrenched meanders. Dawn, breakfast, loading, rapids, Tecate, lunch, rapids, unloading, dinner, gin, coyotes, sleep. And it's not just time that is moving this way, but the river, too, as it loops, twists, and circles back on itself, presenting different angles on the same mountain peaks, passing through layers of geological strata and then witnessing the same formations of rock unfold in reverse order.

Sky, stone, river. Our stable trinity. All we really need.

At the entrance to Harp Falls, we are joined by five Mergansers. The birds will accompany us on and off for the next two days. The flashy red crests of the Mergansers are exquisitely coiffed in the style of the early Little Richard. The ducks sluice over the falls and ride the wave train in a fluid line of crimson. They wheel into the eddy below the rapids and wait patiently for us to complete the run.

In higher water, the overhanging cliff at Harp Falls could easily become Decapitation Rock, as the main current of the river drives into the sharply angled stone. This after-noon in such low water Harp Falls is simply a thrilling short chute that pulls us within a few inches of the imposing rock and then spits us downstream into the rough-and-tumble descent of Triplet Falls. The next ten minutes are a miasma of cold spray and jarring collisions with river-smoothed boulders. All in all, this is the most enjoyable stretch of rapids in Lodore.

We pause in an eddy below the last cascade and a debate breaks out over whether *Mergus serrator* is a dabbling duck or a diving duck. I reach for my Sibley's Guide. But after our trauma at Lower Disaster, the soggy pages of the book have blurred into a gooey and unintelligible mess, like Bush's sentences when the teleprompter blinks out.

It doesn't matter. Subverting such rigid categorizations, the Mergansers settle the dispute for us with an empirical demonstration that they go both ways. They are both dabblers and divers and so much more. Try watching closely instead believing every-thing you read, they seem to say.

We tie the rafts to a cube of rock, freshly spalled from the cliff-face, and walk ten-derly over sharp shards of chert to a view of Hell's Half Mile, a boulder strewn reach of river that has earned a fearsome reputation for flipping rafts and mangling kayaks. The rapids are powered by two debris flows of spiny rocks spewed from large canyons on each side of the Green and by the Disaster Fault, which strikes across the ramparts of Lodore near the beginning of the run.

From our perch above the falls, the rapids resemble the thrashing tail of a stego-saurus.

Weisheit leans toward me and whispers that he feels more anxious about this rapid than any he has run in the last decade. This confession comes from a man who has descended the raging torrents of Cataract Canyon more than 400 times, in all kinds of conditions.

Since no one brought along crash helmets, I size up the corridor of stone along the river. Not that hard of a walk, really. A small cliff to scramble up, some rubble, poison ivy, probably a snake or two. Piece of cake, once I change my shoes.

Then I notice the look in the eyes of the Riverkeeper. No sign of fear or trepidation. He's actually grinning. It's a look of glee and calculation. The thrill of the new, I guess. Oh, what the hell. If danger be fun, play on.

As it turns out, Weisheit executes a perfect run over the falls and through the dizzying maze of rocks. More or less perfect, anyway. We do go down backwards. And we knock and scrape rather rudely against a few rocks. But he alleges that those were premeditated collisions, demonstrating his refined technique of using boulders to make minute course corrections in mid-stream. Who am I to dispute him?

Judy comes next and, despite seeming to be slightly off line at the lip of the falls, makes a smooth descent, weaving gracefully through the prongs of stone. All eyes fix on Susette as her raft comes hard over the craggy drop, smacks the standing wave, buckles and snags on a spindle of rock, where the neoprene craft spins like an old vinyl record and hangs in the air, suspended at a gut-squeezing angle above the gnashing water. Then with a deft flick of an oar, the raft pivots and leaps off the rock into the spastic rhythms of the wave train. All ends well here in Hell's Half Mile.

In the tailwaters of the next small rapids, we strain hard across the pulse of the current and haul out on a secluded white beach at the foot of Wild Mountain.

* * *

It's birthday night at Wild Mountain. Craig and Jennifer are both looking hale and fit on the bright side of fifty. Steaks sizzle on the small grill. Someone mixes a cask of margaritas. A porcupine shuffles through the sagebrush near my sleeping bag. Did I zip up?

The night is cold, but our campsite is warmed by the walls of the canyon, which absorbed the heat of the day and now releases it slowly back.

Susette reaches into a neon river bag and begins hauling out an assortment of psychedelic clothes of such outrageous designs that even George Clinton and Bootsie Collins would be embarrassed to wear them on stage.

I seem to have been awarded a snugly fitting jacket and pant suit adorned with glowing cheetah spots and made of the cheapest velour. Velour with ruffles. I hold them before me like dead carp and shake my head.

"Put them on, Jeffrey," Susette commands. "And lose that T-shirt." These Moabites seem to have a particular fetish about my attire. I slide into the costume, which feels like it is made from the latest in skin-devouring lichens. Even Elvis never sank this low. Did he?

Someone has brought an iPod and battery-powered speakers, which have been strategically placed inside two aluminum pots to maximize the reverb. John, dressed discreetly in a leather top hat with purple polka dots, stokes the fire with branches of sweet-smelling juniper. The music begins. Christ, is that Donna Summer? Yes. Followed quickly by the BeeGees. Then Kool and the Gang. On and on in rapid succession (but not rapid enough). You get the drift. The coyotes sure did. They seem to have fled for another scene—perhaps the ornithologists camped up river are performing "Bye Bye, Birdie?"

People once familiar to me, some of them wearing illuminated devil's horns (or are they the headdresses of Fremont anthropomorphs?), initiate a kind of dancing around the leaping flames of the fire. Chris, an unrepentant Bay-Area hippy, calls for the Dead. Susette begs for the Talking Heads. I yell: What about that Bill Monroe! Merle Haggard!! The Drive-By Truckers!!! Our requests go unheeded. Disco rules. The night descends into a blur of Bacchanalian rites. And, like Iago in his final scene, from this moment forth I shall speak no more about it.

Greetings from Echo Park

Below Hell's Half-Mile, the Green River relaxes into a series of undulating bends. The red rocks of Lodore slip away, replaced by the calming brown tones of the Weber sandstone. You might be in Glen Canyon. But, of course, you're not. On river left looms Jenny Lind Rock, named after the Swedish Nightingale, who captured the hearts of antebellum America during her 1846 tour with Gen. Tom Thumb under the direction of P.T. Barnum. In front of us, a peninsula of sandstone rises 760 sheer feet above the river. Someone lets loose a wolf howl. It bounces back, over and over again. We all join in, an oscillating chorus. Euphonies of stone.

We have entered one of the world's great amphitheaters: Echo Park. The acoustics are clear, crisp, resonant. Even the softest sounds reverberate five or six times down the chambers of rock. Please don't tell Paul Winter. There's no need for him to unbundle his New Age band here to record another CD *au naturale*. Leave the music to the canyon wrens and coyotes.

Powell called the sinuous wall of sandstone Echo Rock. He was right to resist his natural inclination to dip into the classical name bag for some obscure minor deity out of the Greek Myths or the Bhagavad-Gita. Echo Rock is concise, descriptive, and right.

Of course, the Park Service inexplicably chooses to call this entrenched meander Steamboat Rock. What do steamboats have to do with it? Perhaps Park Service recreation planners were envisioning the day when they could offer steamboat tours of Narcissus Lake in the new improved Echo Aquatic Park, after their pals at the Bureau of Reclamation had flooded the canyon under 550 feet of dead water, turning the big rock into a small island illuminated by Klieg lights with a faux adobe hotel perched on the edge accessorized in Anasazi chic, with shuffleboard courts, Kiva-shaped hot tubs, and fishing platforms. You chuckle. But they've done worse. Been to Yosemite lately? Bought gas at Grant Village in Yellowstone? Seen the big stumps at Olympic National Park?

As we glide around Echo Rock, our raft is buffeted by a rush of current coming from the East. I turn and gaze into a gaping canyon of streaked stone. This is the mouth of the Yampa River, concluding its wild course down from the Colorado Rockies.

The Yampa is one of the last free-flowing, undammed rivers in the West. Undammed, except for about 100 small, trout-killing irrigation impediments on the river's high country tributaries. Yeah, except for them. But novelist Jim Harrison has scripted a solution for those obnoxious little plugs. Go read *A Good Day to Die*, if you are so inclined. It's out of print, so check it out from a library. Don't worry. The librarians won't turn you in. Most of them.

(Advisory Note to Homeland Security. *A Good Day to Die* is fiction. That is, fantasy. Please do not dispatch your goons to Livingstone, Montana for the rendition of Jim Harrison to Uzbekistan. Mr. Harrison is now a portly, Cabernet-swilling, sushi-eating, bone-fishing millionaire who has long since denounced the juvenile escapades detailed in his novel.)

We beach our rafts downstream from the confluence and prepare lunch under the lacy shade of two box elder trees. We are down to our last six-pack of Tecate, but they are still icy cold. I unwrap a special treat for the crew: smoked wild chinook salmon from Oregon, caught in dip-nets at Shearer's Falls on the Deschutes River by young men of Warms Springs Nation. The thick filets are lightly salted and embedded with garlic. One gets hungry, lazing on the river. The salmon disappears. Same old story.

We drain our last beers, grab a fistful of brownies and trudge up into the golden meadows of Echo Park, once the home of the desert hermit Patrick Lynch, and long before him, the Fremont people, who inscribed on these walls some of the most fascinating and exquisite art to be found anywhere on the continent, including the National Gallery and the Guggenheim. All of which would have been destroyed by the Echo Park Dam. It would have been an act of desecration as extreme as Napoleon's troops gouging out the eyes of the disciples on DaVinci's *Last Supper* in the dining hall of Santa Maria delle Grazie, which the French had turned into an armory.

The Fremont people (named after the Fremont River in central Utah) are often lumped in with the Anasazi, who occupied the Four Corners region during approximately the same period. But these were strikingly distinct cultures. The Anasazi, for example, were almost exclusively agrarian, growing maze and melons, squash and beans. They were sedentary and built large multi-room structures out of stone and adobe. Later, they constructed vast defensive palaces on inaccessible cliffs. About a thousand years ago, Anasazi culture seems to have decayed into inter-tribal wars, paranoia, a priestly dictatorship, perhaps even cannibalism. (See the controversial, but well-documented study, "Man Corn" by Arizona State University anthropologist, Christy Turner.) The famous roads radiating from the religious compound at Chaco Canyon may have been military highways for Anasazi militia and the secret police of Chaco's high priests. At least, that's the heterodoxical view of anthropologist David Wilcox. I tend to agree. There's something creepy and oppressive about the later Anasazi sites. Many Navajo feel the same kind of trepidation near the haunted castles of Betatakin and Keet Seel.

By contrast, the Fremont, who occupied a territory spanning from central Utah to the Snake River plains of Idaho, and from the Great Basin in Nevada to the Yampa Canyons of Colorado, were a more versatile and nomadic culture, less centralized and not nearly so death-obsessed. They practiced both agriculture and hunting and gathering; often farming one year and gathering the next. They lived in pit houses and small settlements at the mouths of canyons, usually near mountains, such as the Wasatch or Uintas. Close to bighorns and elk, alpine herbs and berries, trout.

In rock-shelters across the region the Fremont left black trapezoidal figurines with deeply lidded eyes that are adorned with ornate necklaces, belts, and earrings. The enlarged ghosts of those figures are painted, carved, and pecked into the walls of Echo Park.

So what happened to the Fremont? No one really knows. Through radiocarbon testing of cornhusks and other debris from the middens at Fremont sites, it seems that their culture began to fade away in Utah around 1250 AD, before petering out altogether around 1500. Some anthropologists contend that climatic changes in the thirteenth century wiped out Fremont crops. While this may hold for the religious slave-farmer society of the Anasazi, it doesn't fit the Fremont, who never gave up their hunting and gathering lifestyle.

Others argue that the Fremont were gradually assimilated with the new arrivals in the region, the Numic-speakers from down south in the doomed Owens Valley: the Utes, Paiutes, Comanche, and Shoshone.

But there is another, more unsettling explanation for the demise of the Fremont that is convincingly sketched out in David B. Madsen's excellent little monograph, *Exploring the Fremont*. Under this scenario, the Numic-speakers, relatives of the Aztec, weren't interested in making a pact with the Fremont, but instead waged a war of imperial aggression against them, seizing their land, annihilating their culture. The best evidence behind this theory is that the last known Fremont sites, near Pocatello, Idaho and in the Yampa Canyons, are all on the remote northern and northeastern fringes of the Fremont territory, the last stretches of land to be occupied by the Numic invaders. So the concealed meadows and rock shelters here at Echo Park may well have been a last hold-out of Fremont culture, a people under siege. I don't have to tell you how it all ends.

Our walk ends before an overhang of sandstone that displays an astonishing panel of rock art, which for no good reason is known as the Poole Creek petroglyphs. The images soar above us, 30–35 feet above the creek bed.

I envision a Fremont artist clinging to a frail ladder of cottonwood branches held together by elk sinews as he pecks out his masterpiece, like Michelangelo painting *The Judgment of Christ*.

But Weisheit says no. This little canyon has been entrenched by a phenomenon known as arroyo cutting. Well, phenomenon may not be the right word since it almost certainly involved cows. Overgraze the meadow, trample the microbiotic crust, compact the soil to the texture of concrete and when a big rain comes along it plows the pleasant grassy little canyon into something resembling the badlands of South Dakota. Over night. Grazing in a national park, you say? Happens all the time. We even have a national park devoted to cattle grazing. It's called Great Basin, pride of Nevada and Sierra Club-approved.

In Dinosaur National Monument, local ranchers were permitted to graze their cows and sheep in the park through the 1980s. The land shows the strain. Most of the hills and small buttes in Echo Park, Browns Park, Jones Hole and Island Park have been trampled under hoof into terraced ziggurat-like mounds. Bovine pyramids that will last for a thousand years or more.

The strange images scroll across about 500 feet of rock. Technically, they are called petroglyphs, meaning that the figures have been etched into the rock, rather than paint-ed—although many petroglyphs also show signs of weathered paint. But not these. These images of flying headdresses, sun disks, shields, floating spirits, sheep, and spirals have been drilled into the rock in intricate dot patterns. Using drills on rock, there is no margin for error and here at Echo Park there is no evidence of error. Pointillism on stone. This is the work of a master of technique and composition. Often, rock art on the Colorado Plateau has the feel of a graffiti-tagging war, a collage of images inscribed by different artists across the centuries. But some sites, such as the Grand Gallery in Canyonlands National Park, vividly described in Doug Peacock's book *Walking It Off*, are clearly the work of a single artist, perhaps working on commission. So, too, with the Echo Park panel. It tells a story as surely as *Guernica* does. And, perhaps, a similar one.

I'm sure there's deeply religious and probably astronomical significance to these surreal images. But even the best interpreters, such as Polly Schaafsma, author of the indispensable *Rock Art of Utah*, agree that their readings of the petroglyphs are little more than informed guesswork. Ultimately, the images defy critical deconstruction-and are all the more powerful because of it. I'm struck by the fact that these flying necklaces and strange beasts scrolling across the sandstone are fundamentally differ-ent than most Fremont rock art: scarier, weirder, and funnier, too. Perhaps the images functioned as a kind of drive-in movie screen to entertain Fremont kids, illuminated for night-time viewing by campfires along the creek bank.

A dust-devil scuffles down the dirt road into Echo Park that, in the 1940s, was secretly punched into Dinosaur by the Bureau of Reclamation. From the dust cloud, a hybrid SUV with Colorado plates emerges. The door opens. A man in yellow golf pants slides out, wielding a camera with a giant lens, a lens the size of the Hubble telescope—though still not powerful enough to locate the weapons of mass destruction.

In the passenger seat, a woman with meticulously maintained blond hair examines her nails as if they were retractable claws. She adopts a look of supreme indifference. She doesn't once glance at the rock art. The man clicks three tightly zoomed photos of the cliff-face, re-enters his $50,000 climate-neutral truck, slams the door, turns the cumbersome machine around, and hurtles up the road.

It's thirty miles of dirt and gravel back to the gate and Highway 40. They were here for two minutes max. I flash to Anna Karina's nine-minute race through the halls of the Louvre in Jean-Luc Godard's film *Band of Outsiders*. But Karina and her cohorts were having fun, breaking the rules, subverting convention, tweaking the art cops. This couple expresses the heavy dullness at the core of Bush's America, a cancerous imperial ennui. Still, their snap-and-click moment counts as two more visitor days in the Park Service's bureaucratic accounting system and they didn't even harass the bighorns. If only Yellowstone was so lucky.

* * *

As the river unfurls around Echo Rock, the winds pick up and, suddenly, rowing the rafts becomes real work. On most rivers, the commercial guides would simply fire up the outboard engine and roar across the wind-whipped flatwater.

But not here. The canyons of Dinosaur are the only stretch of river in the entire Colorado system free of motorized boats. Even in the Grand Canyon, outfitters slued the holy silence of the chasm with the metallic shriek of motors. Dinosaur is unique and long may it be so. If only the river itself wasn't motorized, controlled by engineers, valves, turbines, and computers—the industrial waterworks of the big hydro-dams that trade the wild for the automaton.

The narrow slot of Whirlpool Canyon resurrects the red Cambrian rocks of the Uinta Mountain Group. Gothic spires of rock stab at the sky above us. The fissured walls of the canyon are the remnants of ancient sea stacks and reefs, interlaced with petrified dunes. A great blue heron is spooked by the approach of our raft, barks her annoyance, and takes flight on giant wings.

As we pass the dark mouth of Wild Canyon, our raft is swept into a brief but energetic rapids. On river left, a chuck of iron pipe protrudes from the wall of the canyon, like a stake driven into the heart of a zombie—and let no man or woman remove it. Here lies the site of Echo Park Dam, the wet dream of the Bureau of Reclamation that perished on July 8, 1955.

I want to stop and sketch the walls of the canyon, pock-marked with the dam-builders' bore holes to a height of 550 feet, but the river pulls us relentlessly on, through the footings of a dam that isn't there, downstream another two miles, out of Colorado into Utah and our shady camp at Jones Hole.

* * *

I sit on my on bedroll and try to salvage pages from the ruined Sibley guide. I'm looking for paintings of my favorite birds: Vermillion Flycatcher, Swainson's Hawk, Cerulean Warbler, Northern Spotted Owl, American Coot, and of course, the Red-Necked Stint. It's a useless endeavor. The entries have blended into an abstraction resembling a Helen Frankenthaler lithograph, a swirling delta of greens, yellows, and reds.

A cry from Weisheit interrupts my melancholy funk.

"Bighorn!"

Then, a pause.

"Wait a minute. Otter. River otter!"

I shake my head, despondently. All of a sudden this trip is going to hell. The Riverkeeper has snapped. The most rational man I know has finally lost his faculties of reason. John Freakin' Weisheit can no longer distinguish a cliff-walking bovid from a riverine weasel with a bright innocent-looking face that bears an uncanny resemblance to the young Meg Ryan.

Perhaps someone brought along a few of those Liberty Caps, after all. Perhaps that same someone slipped a magic mushroom into the trail mix. Weisheit has been as straight as the All-American Canal for twenty years. He hasn't even sipped a Tecate since before James Watt was indicted for perjury. This little prank has obviously hit him harder than the Big Drops at full throttle.

How will we ever explain the indiscretion to Bobby Kennedy, Jr.? Such a default in decorum might prompt the Green Czar to strip the Riverkeeper logo from Weisheit's red raft. Then Kimberly would never meet Leonardo DiCaprio. No. We simply must keep it under wraps, bury it like Bush's "pretzel" episode.

I amble through a bank of purple desert asters toward the river, thinking of how Burson-Marsteller would spin the incident.

It's worse than I feared.

Caught in a moment of urinary tract overload, Weisheit is standing in the river with his pants bunched around his knees pointing urgently, like Sacajawea when the Corps of Discovery neared Beaverhead Rock. Across the river, a single bighorn ram nuzzles at grasses, indifferent to the man's wild gesticulations.

Did anyone pack a taser?

Just as I am poised to pat the Riverkeeper on the back and gently usher him to camp, I spot a dark hump breaching the glassy surface of the water near the far bank, like one of those grainy stills of Nessie. Then another and another. A head pops up, radiant and glistening, stares our way, grunts, submerges. Two more repeat the same curious inspection, scanning us like living periscopes.

One otter bolts out of the river, scrambles across the bank and slides onto a boulder, where it smashes something on the rock, eats it, urinates, dives into a pool, resurfaces, chomping on a fish. The others follow, acting out the same frenetic routine, sleekly working their way down river, pool by pool, feasting on fish, diving for crustaceans, dining on the rocks, spraying their foul musk to ward us off.

What looks like play or clowning is actually hard work. River otters, perhaps the most active of all mammals, must eat upwards of 12 percent of their total body weight each day just to refuel.

In total, we spot five river otters, all adults. A rare sighting, indeed. River otter generally travel in pairs and, except during mating season, adult males are loners. Perhaps they have been drawn to this spot because of the clear, spring-nourished waters of Jones Hole Creek, just a few hundred yards upstream from our camp.

Otters are piscavores, mainly, tracking down the movements of young trout and carp with their motion-detecting whiskers, before catching and crushing the fish in their powerful, unforgiving jaws. Far from being cuddly, otters are the premier predator of the river, as aggressive and grouchy as the badger, to which they are closely related. Their grunting and barking indicates a fierce resentment at our intrusion into their territory.

This stretch of the Green River used to be prime otter habitat. But the fish-eaters were nearly extirpated from the basin by the 1920s, largely at the hands of one of Weisheit's heroes, the early river guide Nathaniel Galloway, who floated the Green River all the way down to the confluence with the Colorado and through Cataract Canyon six times. Galloway is revered by river runners because he invented a new style of whitewater rowing, which allowed the oarsman to face downstream, ferrying his boat at an angle toward the rocks and rapids.

Galloway, who lived in a cabin outside of Vernal around the turn of the last century, made his money, such as it was, selling furs. Each month he set out his traplines along the Green, the Yampa, and the Colorado rivers, killing beaver, muskrat, otter, lynx, coyote, kit fox, long-tailed weasel, raccoon, ringtail cat. A Park Service brochure on Dinosaur flaunts a photo of Galloway proudly gripping six dead otters by their tails, each snared in his merciless traps. On a single trip in 1912, Galloway boasted of trapping ninety-five beavers. This, at a time when beavers were themselves heading beyond the zero of extinction in Utah.

As the apex predator on the Green River, the otter population was never very robust. One estimate by the biologists at the US Fish and Wildlife Service suggests that at its maximum density, the Green River probably supported one breeding pair of otter for every ten river-miles. So, in that single trapping blitz, Nathaniel Galloway may have wiped out a third of the adult otters in what is now Dinosaur National Monument. But, then again, he did perfect the proper angle for the downstream ferry!

Our otters are almost certainly recent transplants from southeast Alaska, which may be another reason they have opted to forage in a pack: protection in numbers. Over the past decade, more than forty river otters have been released on the Green in or near Dinosaur National Monument, most of them kidnapped in Alaska, flown to Salt Lake, trucked to Vernal, and unceremoniously dumped in Browns Park, Little Hole, and Sand Wash.

No one really knows how well river otters raised in a temperate rainforest will thrive in a murky desert river, which offers a fare of carp and catfish instead of salmon and steelhead. Indeed, the Alaskan otter (*Lontra c. pacifica*) is an entirely separate subspecies from the one that originally ruled the Green River (*Lontra c. nexa*). Are there still Nexa otters in Dinosaur? Will they breed with the Alaskans? If so, will they lose their genetic identity? Or will the newcomers simply drive them out altogether, finishing the job Galloway started? None of these questions were answered before the reintroduction program began. Likely, they weren't even asked.

But these northern otters certainly are smart and crafty. They've already zeroed in on the easiest pickings in the neighborhood: the Jones Hole Fish Hatchery, where otters have been making nightly raids on the genetic mutants in the rearing tanks for the past five years. If the environmentalists can't shut down the disease-spreading hatchery with a lawsuit, perhaps the otters in a concentrated attack can wipe it out by other means.

Why is the state of Utah engaged in a river otter recolonization program, anyway? Is this a rare act of predator altruism from a state that once, not that long ago, rewarded ranchers who gassed coyote pups as they slept in their dens? No. The ultimate goal of the program is to artificially propagate the otter population to a level where the state can begin selling licenses for so-called annual otter "harvests," as if the "liquaceous creatures," in Edward Abbey's poetic phrase, were organic vegetables. Grown in Alaska, Harvested in Utah.

Yes. Otter fur is back in demand, at least according to the fashionistas at *Vogue* magazine, which has repeatedly featured the emaciated bodies of supermodels draped in otter pelts. Is the wearing of a scalped otter an erotic or necrotic fetish? A recent fur trade publication takes note of the upswing in the dead otter market, propelled in part by the rise of the Chinese middle class: "May auction sales established record levels for Otter, with a $104.00 average and a top of $195.00 per pelt. These new price levels show that promotional efforts in China and elsewhere in the world, continue to pay huge dividends. There should be excellent demand for Otter again next season, with the paler types bringing the most money."

Swim for your lives, swift Lontras of the Green! And be sure to muck up your coats along the way!

* * *

After otter hour, Susette orchestrates a meal of startling complexity, headlined by perch in south Indian curry sauce with eggplant, red peppers, and rice. As we devour the meal, the sky blackens prematurely, the winds stiffen, and shards of lightning splinter the sky. The bats retreat and even the coyotes scatter as power-chords of thunder crash down the canyons.

With the storm bearing down on us, I reluctantly set up my tent for the first time. I dislike sleeping in tents. They are claustrophobic, steamy structures that occlude the night sky. Yet, sometimes the elements compel your submission.

In an interior pocket of the little nylon shelter, I find a chapbook of poems that I'd accidentally left behind from my last outing, a weekend in the wind-sculpted Sweetgrass Hills of northwestern Montana. The verses are by Wang Wei, a Taoist painter, naturalist, and political prisoner during the T'ang Dynasty in eighth-century China, who wrote his best poems during his long exile on the Wheel-Rim River deep in the Whole South Mountains.

As the tent shivers in the wind, I recite Wang's poem "Golden-Rain Rapids" over and over, a mantra for dreams.

> Wind buffets and blows autumn rain,
> Water cascading thin across rocks,
> Waves lash at each other. An egret
> Startles up, white, then settles back.

The Dam That Isn't There

A raven wakes me at dawn with the scratchy-throated call of a two-pack a day smoker. I dredge myself out of the sleeping bag, which is saturated with dew. The air is sharp, autumnal.

I lumber to the river, strip and dive in. I haven't bathed in four days. I'm beginning to smell like roadkill. As I submerge in the dark current, my testicles leap toward my throat from the cold shock. The water is still chilled from its black impoundment in the guts of Flaming Gorge reservoir, where it emerges at a flat and frigid 54 degrees—almost precisely the temperature of a grave.

The raven chuckles and flies down the canyon, a perpetual agent of mischief.

I dry off, slip on a ratty pair of jeans and a thick fleece and head up Jones Hole through a tall thicket of cane grass. After a mile or so, I strike off to the south and into a deep side canyon chiseled by a small stream called Ely Creek.

A few hundred yards up the white-walled ravine, Ely Creek plunges in a thin blue ribbon over a twelve-foot ledge of the skin-toned Weber sandstone. The shallow pool at the base of the falls reflects the early-morning sky. It is filled with glittering cobble. A multi-colored stone draws my attention. I reach into the pool and pick it up. The fist-sized stone swirls with red, white, and black streaks. The curious rock is smooth and exquisitely polished.

Perhaps the stone is a gastrolith, a stomach rock. But whose stomach? A giant sauropod, maybe. The big plant eaters loaded their stomachs with grinding stones to masticate the tons of foliage passing through their cavernous bodies every week. Some of the dinosaur skeletons in western Utah and Colorado have yielded as many as forty gastroliths.

There's a peculiar mystery to the gastroliths of Dinosaur National Monument. Most of the stones examined here by paleontologists are composed of rocks not found in Utah. In fact, many of them derive from Nevada and California. Apparently, the huge sauropods had impressive home ranges, thundering across hundreds of miles through swamps and savannahs like thirty-ton bison, only faster and more agile. Or perhaps they simply marched off to Nevada in search of replacement gastroliths, the way we visit the dentist.

As I roll the strange stone in my hand, I think about alternate histories. What if, for example, that asteroid hadn't smashed into the Yucatan, gouging a giant crater in the crust of the earth and coating the planet in an irradiated cloud of dust that blocked the sun for a thousand years? Contrary to popular belief, the dinosaurs didn't fail to adapt to changing climatic conditions. Indeed, they were incredibly adaptable creatures: intelligent, social, and perhaps, the most successful beings to inhabit the planet—aside from the scorpions. It has always been, after all, an arthropod world. Instead, the dinosaurs of the Cretaceous age were annihilated by something like a full-scale thermo-nuclear war. The Terrible Lizards were whacked by the untamed geology and astrophysics of the heavens.

This rocky bench at Jones Hole has its own alternate history. If the Bureau of Reclamation had been permitted to fulfill its schemes, the mouth of Jones Hole Canyon would have been submerged under twenty feet of water and silt, held back by a 118-foot tall dam the engineers wanted to build at the entrance to Split Mountain Canyon. The dam would have flooded Island Park, Rainbow Park, and every inch of Whirlpool

Canyon all the way up to the footings of the Echo Park Dam. The canyons of Dinosaur would have become two giant holding tanks. That's where David Brower steps in to change the course of history.

These days the Bureau of Reclamation is a broken and dysfunctional agency, a mere outlier in the vast labyrinth of the Department of the Interior. But back in its heyday of the 1940s and 1950s, the Bureau was a titanic force, perhaps the most powerful government agency in the Western States. It was the epicenter of the dam-industrial complex: promising cheap hydropower, irrigation, drinking water for expanding cities, water playgrounds, and industrial jobs. Exploiting Cold War anxieties, the Bureau presented itself as internal bulwark against the Communist Peril—even though most American Communists, such as Woody Guthrie, applauded its plan to dam nearly every Western river. In fact, the Bureau of Reclamation is the most Stalinist of federal agencies, cleaving closely to the masterplan of Old Joe who dictated to Soviet dam-builders: "No river should ever reach the sea."

The Bureau's leaders, men like Mike Strauss and the infamous Floyd Dominy, were as arrogant as defense contractors in the early days of the Iraq war. Everything was going their way. They steamrolled internal opposition, like that offered by Park Service chief Newton Drury, vilified conservationists as starry-eyed patsies, and intimidated members of Congress who had the temerity to question any of the outrageously priced line items in their budget requests.

The Bureau drilled a tunnel through Rocky Mountain National Park for the Big Thompson water diversion. They built a dam across the Snake River in Jackson Hole National Monument at Grand Teton. They had no qualms about proposing dams in Yellowstone and Grand Canyon. They didn't have the slightest clue that they were about to be cold cocked over their plans for two dams in a remote national monument that almost no one, including the leadership of the Sierra Club, had ever heard of, never mind visited.

The year 1946 was a fateful one for the rivers and canyons of the Colorado Plateau. FDR was dead. His Secretary of the Interior, Harold Ickes, wanted to designate most of Utah's canyon country as a huge national park larger than Yellowstone, but was rudely dismissed from office by Harry Truman. The world war was over, the Cold War heating up.

Enter Mike Strauss, the new head of the Bureau of Reclamation. Unlike the previous commissioners, Strauss was a deal-making politician, not an engineer. Under Strauss' direction, the Bureau published its document of doom, a study titled *The Colorado River: A Natural Menace Becomes a Natural Resource*. The book was nothing less than a death warrant for the Green, Colorado, and San Juan rivers. It targeted 136 potential dam sites and envisioned a dam project or water diversion scheme in nearly every canyon and tributary on the Colorado Plateau. Central to the plan were four big main-stem dams: Flaming Gorge, Glen Canyon, Bridge Canyon on the western flank of Grand Canyon National Park, and at Echo Park, where the Yampa River meets the Green in the heart of Dinosaur National Monument.

The Colorado River Compact of 1922 had divided the river's water between upper basin states and lower basin states. The line of demarcation was drawn at Lee's Ferry in Arizona, near the mouth of Glen Canyon. In an act of political wish-fulfillment, the Bureau ordained that the annual flow of the Colorado was 17.5 million acre feet of water and allocated 7.5 million acre feet to each basin. In theory, another 1.5 million acre feet was supposed to flow to Mexico. Of course, the Colorado River no longer flows to Mexico. But the Mexicans did inherit a toxic delta of pesticide-laden sludge.

In reality, the annual flow of the Colorado over the course of the last hundred years has averaged 13 million acre feet, a flow that continues to fall as a result of persistent (some might say permanent) drought and global warming. Naturally, the allocation of water between the basins has never been amended to reflect hydrological reality.

The Californians struck first with the construction of Hoover Dam in Black Canyon in 1936, quickly followed by Parker Dam and the All-American Canal, which diverted most of the flow of the Colorado into the fields of the Imperial Valley.

Panic broke out among the upper basin states of Utah, Wyoming, and Colorado, who feared that California was raiding more than its share of water. Prodded by the Bureau of Reclamation, the upper basin states demanded dams of their own in order to hoard their water rights. But these states were also at war with each other over how much each state could claim. This testy debate was finally settled in 1948 with the passage of the Upper Colorado Basin Compact, an exercise in computational fantasy that never once paused to examine how much water was actually flowing down the rivers.

These were big, but sparsely populated states that were intensely motivated by those twin engines of American politics: jealousy and greed. Each state wanted its own big dam and large water impoundment, even if they couldn't use the water and had no foreseeable need for the hydropower. They would rather see the waters of the Green, San Juan, and Colorado evaporate into desert skies than flow into the hands of the Californians.

With the compact signed, the Bureau of Reclamation was primed to roll. It swiftly unveiled plans for three large upper basin dams: Glen Canyon, Echo Park, and Flaming Gorge, followed by smaller dams on the Gunnison River, the San Juan, and at Split Mountain in Dinosaur.

Deviously, the Bureau had anticipated that the centerpiece of their scheme, the Echo Park Dam, might generate a modest amount of public outcry because it would flood more than 100 miles of canyon inside a national monument. They had an ace up their sleeve that almost no one knew about it. In 1943, the Bureau of Reclamation had signed a secret agreement with Park Service Director Newton Drury called a "reclamation withdrawal." Essentially, the Park Service had already ceded the dam site to the Bureau of Reclamation. The deal was so covert that the park manager at Dinosaur, Dan Beard, knew nothing about it and when he protested to his superiors about unauthorized incursions into the monument by Bureau of Reclamation engineers in 1948, he was ordered to stand aside. "We see no advantage to be gained now in questioning the legality of the withdrawal," wrote Arthur Demaray, assistant director of the Park Service. "To do so would be extremely embarrassing to the Department."

By now Park Service boss Newton Drury knew he had made a tragic mistake by signing the agreement with the Bureau of Reclamation. Drury began to leak his opposition to the dam to his allies on the advisory board for the national parks, people like Rosalie Edge, Alfred Knopf, and the crusty Utahan Bernard DeVoto. In 1950, Truman's Interior Secretary, Oscar Chapman, forced Drury to resign. With him gone, it was going to be up to an outside force to save Dinosaur—if, indeed, it could be saved.

The first blow was struck in 1950 by the historian and polemicist, Bernard DeVoto, in *Reader's Digest*, at the time the most influential and widely read publication in America. DeVoto was one of the original dam-busters, a rare western critic of the politically-driven exploitation of western lands. DeVoto was an irritant, as prickly as Edward Abbey. Reportedly, DeVoto's feisty introduction to *Beyond the Hundredth Meridian* cost Wallace Stegner a Pulitzer Prize—not that Stegner ever griped about the loss.

DeVoto's onslaught on the Bureau of Reclamation was titled "Shall We Let Them Ruin Our National Parks?" DeVoto's acidly written article was most people's introduction to the remote Dinosaur National Monument. And they didn't like what they read. One of those outraged by the DeVoto essay was Howard Zahniser, the crusading leader of the Wilderness Society. Zahniser had never heard of Dinosaur before, but he riled at the idea of a National Monument being flooded by a big dam.

Over at the Sierra Club fortuitous changes were afoot. The young Dave Brower had just been hired as the Club's executive director and first paid staffer. Brower didn't know much about Dinosaur either. But unlike most Sierra Clubbers of his era, Brower did not hold any particular prejudice against the Interior West. He had spent time in the Rocky Mountains and on the Colorado Plateau. During World War II, Brower trained at Camp Hale in central Colorado with the famous 10th Mountain Division of the US Army. And, in 1939, he had made the first staggeringly difficult ascent of Shiprock, the ghostly volcanic plug on the Navajo Reservation in northern Arizona.

In the summer of 1953, Brower made his first float trip through Dinosaur, guided by the early river-runner Bus Hatch, who operated out of Vernal. Brower made two more trips that summer—one with the writer, Wallace Stegner, and the other with Dr. Harold Bradley, the former dean of the medical school at the University of Wisconsin.

During those trips, the strategic outlines of a battle plan were drawn up. Time was short. Congress was scheduled to move forward with the Colorado River Storage Act in the winter of 1954. Brower devoted himself to the study of western water law and the region's peculiar political pressure points. He leaned heavily upon the scientific acumen of Bradley and the legal advice of a brilliant lawyer named Northcutt Ely, who, ironically, represented the California water users.

Meanwhile, Stegner went to work on a book that would become a classic text in the history of environmental politics. Published by Alfred Knopf, a staunch opponent of the dam, *This is Dinosaur: The Echo Park Country and Its Magic Rivers* contained eight essays, all keenly edited by Stegner, and a gallery of evocative photos of the monument. The book was hand delivered to every member of congress and nearly every newspaper editor in the country.

This is Dinosaur may have been the most potent American political pamphlet since Tom Paine's *Common Sense*. Wayne Aspinall, the flinty congressman from western Colorado who served as a political overlord for the Bureau of Reclamation, said he knew his dream of a dam at Echo Park was shattered the moment the book hit his desk.

Still Brower had much to overcome, notably the eccentricities of some of his colleagues, particularly the ridiculous Zahniser, who wasted his precious minutes before the Senate Interior Committee by reciting Southey's ridiculous poem, "Cascades of Lodore." After Zahniser's strange performance, Utah Senator Arthur Watkins grunted to a fellow member of the committee, "What did I tell you? Abominable nature lovers."

Fortunately, Brower, even though he had never testified before congress, came armed with facts. He humiliated the engineers at the Bureau of Reclamation by proving that they had made grievous mathematical errors in their calculations of evaporation rates in the planned reservoirs. Unfortunately, in exposing the Bureau's fraudulent science, Brower doomed Glen Canyon and Flaming Gorge.

It was a premeditated decision. Instead of opposing the entire Colorado River Storage Project, the environmentalists decided to focus on saving Dinosaur National Monument by recommending that the Bureau of Reclamation raise the height of the Glen Canyon Dam. Brower demonstrated during his testimony that a high Glen Canyon dam would store 700,000 acre feet more water than a lower dam at Glen Canyon and Echo Park. Though they squealed about it publicly, this was a deal even the water barons couldn't pass up. On July 8, 1955, Aspinall deleted the Echo Park dam from the bill.

Dinosaur was saved. The neophyte environmental movement had beaten the mighty Bureau of Reclamation and its political backers with better science, more savvy public relations, and shockingly, bigger political clout. But the victory came at a very high price: Flaming Gorge, Glen Canyon, and half of Cataract Canyon would be inundated.

Looking back, the problem isn't just that Brower and his cohorts made a political deal to save Dinosaur and, as they saw it, the integrity of the national park system, by consenting to the larger scheme of the Colorado Storage Project, which meant big dams at Glen Canyon and Flaming Gorge and smaller, but equally damaging impoundments, on the San Juan, Dolores, and Gunnison Rivers. No, the problem was in fixating on institutional names, bureaucratic boundaries, regulatory classifications, and legal designations and not on the river itself and the green current of life that flowed with it.

Yes, they were men (and nearly all of them were men) of their era. Yes, they had fought hard for the national park system, for the idea of wilderness. For many, the wounds from the Hetch Hetchy battle were still tender. No more dams in national parks. The conservationist contingent didn't have recourse to legal weapons such as the Endangered Species Act or the National Environmental Policy Act. They fought an intense political battle with what they had, an Emersonian ideal of primitive wilderness as represented in the park system—a vision, as illusory as it was, they correctly believed would appeal to a new generation of mobile post-war Americans seeking respite from the oppressive monotony of their suburban existence.

Still, some knew better. Stegner advised strenuously against the deal Brower struck. So did the photographer Eliot Porter, river guide Ken Sleight, folksinger Katie Lee—even Georgia O'Keefe, who executed a beautiful but little known series of paintings in Glen Canyon during the 1950s.

Olaus Murie, the naturalist with the Wilderness Society, should have raised the ecological issues more forcefully. Even Brower himself realized the disastrous consequences shortly after the passage of the Colorado River Storage Act, dooming Flaming Gorge and Glen Canyon. But at the time his organization of Bay Area elites remained mired in an ice-and-rocks mindset that might be diagnosed as Sierracentrism. In many ways, it still is.

As astounding as their triumph over the Bureau of Reclamation was, it is now clear that the conservationists didn't save the wildness of Dinosaur by preventing it from being flooded by two big dams, for a simple reason: the dam that they consented to at Flaming Gorge continues to inflict terrible ecological damage downstream, robbing the canyons of some essential chords of life. Even today, Dinosaur is being starved of sandbars, starved of organic debris, starved of driftwood piles and spring floods, starved of willows and cottonwoods, razorback suckers and bony chubs. Starved of its unpredictability, its temporality, in a word its naturalness. Through most of its course in these glorious canyons, the Green is a mechanized river, cold as a machine.

The fallout from the operations of Glen Canyon Dam have proven even worse. Not only did the giant cenotaph drown the most magnificent canyon on the continent, but it mauled the ecology of the Grand Canyon, as well. The hard lesson is that dams kill in both directions.

Still Brower's accomplishment here can't be discounted. He stopped a dam and built a powerful new movement, a movement that beat back dams in Grand Canyon National Park in the 1960s and enacted the signature environmental laws of our time: the Endangered Species Act, the Wilderness Act, and the Wild and Scenic Rivers Act.

Even crusty Wayne Aspinall realized that the battle of Echo Park had shifted the dynamics of political power in the West. "If we let them knock out Echo Park," Aspinall warned, "we give them a tool they'll use for the next 100 years." By the congressman's math, that means we've got fifty more years to bust a couple big dams. You know the ones. Time to get to work.

I toss the gastrolith back in the streambed in case some creature needs it for efficient digestion in an alternate future. Who knows when the Earth will once again be ruled by titanic vegans? Perhaps that's the secret karma of global warming.

* * *

We lounge around camp until noon, writing in our journals, watching golden eagles twist in the sun, listening to Judy and Craig belt out Broadway show tunes. This is a comfortable campsite and we are loathe to leave it. But evacuate we must. The Park Service permits no layovers.

Whirlpool Canyon is another misnomer. For most of its run through this dark slot, the Green River is calm and meditative, as if brooding over its narrow escape from engineered extinction.

A few hundred yards below our camp, the river splits around a green island of tamarisk and old cottonwoods, where herons have nested. As the threads of river rejoin, we encounter a boisterous group of boaters harassing a bighorn ram and his harem. The men have crowded their rafts and kayaks to within a few feet of the sheep and are clicking away with their cameras, snickering obscenely, tossing beers from raft to raft. The ewes are skittish, poised for flight. But the ram doesn't move. Like an old Mormon patriarch, he stares defiantly at the fat interlopers, poised for confrontation. Almost willing one. Finally, the drunken boaters depart and, under darkening skies, we slide silently past the bighorns, noticing that their ears are free of tags and that their throats are unencumbered by radio collars. Long may it be so.

As we float by the flanks of Hardscrabble Mountain, the familiar red rocks of the Lodore Formation give way to the blocky white ramparts of the Madison limestone, tiger-striped with black desert varnish. The angular walls of the canyon are cluttered with the adobe summer homes of cliff swallows. The birds, among the fastest and most beautiful on earth, have already migrated south to the Yucatan, Guatemala, and Honduras, leaving behind their odd, gourd-like mud houses, surely the architectural inspiration for the granaries of the Anasazi.

Most of the summer birds have followed the swallows south, but every now and then we spot one of my favorite bird species jittering on a rock at the river's edge: the water ouzel. Look up "ouzel" in your field guides. You won't find it, even though it was immortalized by the best passages John Muir ever wrote. That's because the nomenclature Nazis at the American Ornithological Union arbitrarily determined that the water ouzel should be exclusively known as the American Dipper.

I refuse to submit to this tyranny. Dipper describes only a small part of the wren-like bird's behavior. Ouzel evokes its essence. Back home in Oregon, I've spent hours mesmerized by the acrobatics of ouzels flying around, in, and—yes—up waterfalls in the Columbia Gorge. Here in Whirlpool, the chunky black ouzel dives into the dark current of the Green, pops out of the river a dozen feet upstream, lands back on the flat rock, shakes the water off its stubby tail, and chastises us as we pass by with a bug-like song: Dzeet, dzeet, dzeet.

* * *

Around the next twist of the river, we once again encounter the flotilla of boaters. They have stopped for lunch. Their spread gives the appearance of a tailgate party before a college football game. Beer (well, Coors, anyway) is being guzzled from hydration packs. Whiskey bottles have been set up like bowling pins on a shelf of rock. Two ravens, hunched on a low-hanging cottonwood branch, have already taken notice of the main course: an Army helmet stuffed with orange Cheetos.

The seven men range from pudgy to corpulent. Their rafts must groan under the load. To a man, they are smoking fat cigars. The smell sours the canyon air. One demands another Coors as he urinates on a thatch of sage. An aluminum can is promptly launched his direction, like a frozen monkfish flung through the air at Seattle's Pike Place Market. He flubs the catch, pisses on his leg. Someone has constructed a crude sand sculpture that vaguely resembles a prone Monica Lewinsky. The giveaway is the cigar protruding from the crotch. They are from Colorado, naturally, on a frat boy reunion of some sort. This beach is being subjected to an depraved hazing ritual.

Calling all cougars.

* * *

Whirlpool Canyon ends abruptly at a contorted upthrust of rock called Island Park Fault. At the mouth of the gorge, the red walls of the canyon descend sharply back into the earth, and the landscape smoothes into rolling hills of cheatgrass, another tenacious exotic. These fuzzy mounds are the rounded tops of ancient dunes, now solidified into Navajo sandstone.

This is Island Park, where, according to the map, the Green River braids through a series of islands, shaded by groves of cottonwoods. The Park Service has assigned us a campground for the evening on the southern flank of Big Island. There's just one problem. The islands seem to have disappeared—and so have most of the cottonwoods. The shrunken river is restricted to the main channel. The old course of the Green is clotted now with horsetail, cane grass, and the ubiquitous tamarisk.

We pull our boats out on a rocky beach at the foot of the Island Park Fault. Chris and I slip off the Riverkeeper's raft and walk downstream toward the alleged campsite. We slop through the sucking mud of the old riverbed and spook two young mule deer that had bedded down in the cane. They jolt to their feet, but don't scamper too far away from this cool and moist spot. They stare at us balefully. They have alert, Yoda-like ears.

Finally, we bushwhack our way to a signpost designating Big Island Camp, nearly concealed behind a veil of willows. The little beach is landlocked, at least a hundred yards from the river. A dead end.

What gives? Why did the Park Service consign us to a campground on a dried out channel? Did they finger us as anti-dam fanatics? Is this some kind of bureaucratic set up? Is that why they demanded our social security numbers?

Back at the rafts, Susette has already made the call. We're spending the night here at Red Wash, near the broken end of Whirlpool Canyon. We unload the boats, set up the kitchen, search for sandy sleeping spots among the spines of rock.

Susette plants the shitter on a spit of sand near the river and gives it a test drive. As she finishes her business, the inebriated armada of Coloradoans emerges noisily from the canyon. Two of the men take out cameras with zoom lenses and snap dozens of photographs of her and then the rest of us. Invaders, gluttons, and voyeurs. One of them yells: "Lookee! Tree huggers! Envirofeminazis!!"

These guys aren't merely aging fratboys, after all. Almost certainly, they are also Bush-appointees at the Department of the Interior. They sure have the pedigree.

* * *

Weisheit is meant to be cooking dinner, but he's standing near the firebox instead, pointing dreamily to the curving Island Park Fault that looms above us. "Someday we must climb that," he muses.

"No time like the present, Johnny," says Jennifer. "Chris and I can handle dinner. Besides, we like to watch. This might be damned amusing."

The fault is a buckled reef of layered rock that resembles the dorsal fin of an attacking Orca—if it had been painted by Peter Max. From here the anticline seems to offer a relatively modest climb of maybe 500 vertical feet. From here.

On closer inspection, this flying fault soars nearly 2,000 vertical feet above the floor of the canyon, all of it nearly straight up. The ascent will prove to be more like 3,000 feet for us, since for every two steps we climb, we slide back one. The surface of the upwarp of limestone is flaked with scree, a slippery coating of shattered chert and jasper.

No one has brought a rope, climbing shoes, or a stretcher. The only handholds are prickly pear cactus, thorny blackbrush, and trick branches of juniper that snap off when you need them most. Pick your poison.

A sweaty hour of grunting, stumbling and profanity brings us to the top, where the arc of stone abruptly terminates in a concave drop of 2,000 feet to the lazy river below. I enjoy climbing, but am unnerved, justifiably I tell myself, by extreme exposure in high places. I cower on a flat ledge of limestone and look down river across the meadows of Island Park to the fissured flank of Split Mountain. The Riverkeeper shows no such inhibitions. Weisheit perches like a gargoyle on the edge of the precipice, an unstable cornice of fractured rock through which fat rays of light seem to be seeping. Is he wearing flip-flops?

Craig ventures down first, glissading on stones, kicking up a trail of dust behind him. A splendid strategy—for a solo descent. But Susette is next out of the starting gate. She slips, slides, and stumbles a few hundred feet down the broken spine of rock, and kicks loose a boulder the size of a peccary, which begins careening down the slope.

"Head's up!" Judy yells. "No, down. Get your head down, Craig."

The tumbling rock seems to harbor a magnetic attraction for Craig. He moves left; it tracks left. He dodges right, the boulder follows suit. Finally Craig ducks and covers as the maniacal stone skims over his head and into a juniper tree, which disintegrates in a puff of debris like an atom in one of Edward Teller's cyclotrons.

My own descent is less than glorious, something between a crawl and an uncontrolled skid. I shed vital layers of epidermis all the way down.

Back at camp, Chris and Jennifer have bemused themselves by watching the tragicomedy unfold at a comfortable distance. They also seem to have dipped rather deeply into the tequila while preparing tonight's feast, a fiery quesadilla, stuffed with cheese, black beans, and habanero peppers. The biomass of the meal is heavily weighted toward the habanero. As our mouths blister, there's a good deal of obscene snickering from the chefs.

A line forms in front of Susette, who is slouched in her river chair with a drink in her hand and a hunk of ice on her ribs. Requests are made: backrub, neck massage,

Chakra realignment. She waves us away, one by one, with an imperious flick of her hand. The Reiki master is on vacation and she's taking no new patients. We limp back to our seats, lick our wounds, and try to find an angle of repose that doesn't ache. Then Jennifer comes along, bearing Mojitos. "Two guys walk into a bar," she quips, turning to Craig. "The third one ducks."

This is our last evening in open air and there's a melancholy mood to the camp. After dinner we each shuffle off to our own sleeping spaces. On this night, only Judy resorts to a tent.

The quark-quick western pipistrelles dart through the cool darkness. A lone coyote, sitting on a hidden rib of sandstone, does a keening imitation of an Ornette Coleman riff, phase-shifting between dissonant shrieks and sweet melodies.

The moonless sky is nearly black, lit only by a lustrous stream of stars.

Splitsville

I am awakened abruptly in the pitch dark. There's something tip-toeing across my chest. Something much heavier than a canyon mouse. Christ, surely it's not a porcupine?

I wiggle back and forth in my bag gently encouraging the animal to continue its explorations elsewhere. The invitation is refused. Instead, it feels as if the creature has taken up residence on my sternum. A bouncing kind of residence.

I slide my hand out of the sleeping bag, grapple for my headlamp, and flash on the light. I am confronted by eyes the size of billiard balls, glassy and neurotic. A ringtail cat, the nocturnal clown of the desert, caught in the act. Gripping in its right paw what appears to be a tortilla chip left behind from last night's feast, the ringtail bounces one more time, then levitates into the night. Gone. Just like that.

Ringtails aren't cats. No one seems to be precisely sure what they are. The creatures are a quirk of mammalian evolution, apparently related to the raccoon, with whom they share a passion for thievery and mischief. The naturalists call them *Bassariscus astutus*. The accent here is on *astutus*. Ravens with fur.

I don't know if we are communing with nature, but nature seems to be communing with us. Last night, Weisheit found a scorpion in his bedroll. This morning Jennifer awoke to find that a beaver had homed in on her sleeping bag and had deposited an oily and pungent pile of beaver stool a few inches from her head. Only otter shit exudes a more disagreeable odor. Perhaps, the animal kingdom is sending us an eviction notice: Time to go.

* * *

The mood is solemn as we dismantle our last camp, rig the rafts, sweep away the traces of our stay. Call it a pre-partum depression. It happens on the final day of nearly every river trip.

Naturally, we all vow to remain friends and to run this river together again. Soon. We talk about tackling others: the frenzied Bruneau, the croc-laden Zambezi, the mysterious Tsang-Po, and of course, Glen Canyon Dam Falls.

But who can predict the future? We only know this is our final day on this manifestation of the Green River, a river that has consecrated us as a group, bound us together, a river that will flow through our dreams.

Jennifer tries to snap us out of our gloomy reverie. "How do you get down off an elephant?" she asks. "You don't! You get down off a duck." Her jokes are getting progressively worse and our response to them more demented. Perhaps it's time to wrap this excursion up after all.

A few hundred yards downstream from Red Wash, the Green River loops through the small, white cliffs of Island Park. On river left, Weisheit points out the image of a bison etched onto the canyon wall. The carving is large, perhaps eight feet wide and four feet tall, and it has narrowly escaped destruction after a huge chunk of the rock wall next to the petroglyph exfoliated into a mound of rubble and dust.

The bison carving was made by an Ute shaman, probably in the eighteenth century, after the arrival of the horse in the Rockies. The image refutes the notion, perpetrated by many environmentalists and government bureaucrats, that the canyons of Dinosaur had been essentially vacant of human habitation from the demise of the Fremont to the arrival of white fur-trappers.

It's the same old story floated about most lands whites wanted to grab from Native people. In Yosemite, the Mewuk were prodded out of the Merced Valley, first by infectious disease, then by gold miners, followed by the notorious butchers in the Mariposa Battalion, and finally by the Park Service, which tried to wipe them out of history. Until recently, Park Service literature on Yosemite postulated that the Mewuk had abandoned the Yosemite Valley in the late 1700s, claiming the tribe considered it the valley of "black death." And that was before Hetch Hetchy dam went up. Of course, they could have simply asked Chief Tenana his opinion.

In Yellowstone, the Sheepeater Shoshone were discounted as mere transients and were disparaged by early Park Service historians as a "lazy" and "primitive" people who were not worthy of the landscape. The mountain men knew better. In his journals, the fur-trapper Osbourne Russell described the Sheepeater Shoshone tribe living in the Lamar Valley as "neatly clothed in dressed deer and sheepskins of the best quality, well-armed with bows and arrows pointed with obsidian and seemed to be perfectly happy."

These are the myths that sanctify our brittle and self-serving concept of the wild, as a landscape devoid of any trace of previous human occupation. It is a perverted fantasy, indeed, that finds a way to sanction Grant Village and Ahwahnee Lodge into national parks, but excludes the presence of native people who co-existed with grizzlies and bison for 10,000 years.

The canyons of Dinosaur are scattered with historical evidence of recent Ute occupation: campsites, fire pits, middens, the remains of wickiups, and petroglyphs of horses and bison. Yet, in most of the literature about Dinosaur National Monument, the Utes are inexplicably elided from history in favor of extended passages about the long-vanished Fremont. Of course, the Fremont come guilt-free. They disappeared long ago, before the white conquest. No mention is made of the fact that the Green and Yampa basins were once, very recently, Ute land, from which hundreds of families were forcibly evicted and confined to small reservations under treaties that were later declared to be manifestly unjust. Steal their land, then claim they were never there.

* * *

As we struggle against the stiff winds of Island Park, Weisheit, and I talk about our late friend and mentor Dave Brower, the man who saved both Dinosaur and Grand Canyon National Park from being inundated behind big dams.

Like Dinosaur, Brower had his own faults. But he had the rare talent of turning them to his advantage. That's how he got Weisheit to forsake his river-guiding career and devote himself to becoming the Colorado/Green River's most forceful advocate. Weisheit confronted Brower at a meeting over the old man's role in the political-deal-making that led to the construction of Glen Canyon Dam (and Flaming Gorge, too, which often escapes mention). Brower didn't flinch under the assault. He was used to it by now. Hell, Katie Lee had been carping at him for nearly forty years about the dam—and her criticism was not always good-natured in tone. "Yes, I've made mistakes," Brower confessed to the river guide. "Now, what are you going do to fix them?"

Weisheit was stumped. But not for long. He soon joined forces with Owen Lammers, the brilliant anti-dam campaigner from the Bay Area, and my old pal David Orr, the most militant environmentalist ever incubated in the swamps of Arkansas, to establish Living Rivers, a group dedicated to draining Lake Powell and restoring ecological rhythms of the Colorado/Green River system. In tandem with their allies at the Center for Biological Diversity in Tucson, they have grown into one of the most powerful and innovative force in American environmentalism. Living Rivers is a testament to how much you can accomplish with a little bit of money, a lot of smarts, and a bright-line mission that defies political compromise.

I had a similar encounter with Brower twenty years earlier than Weisheit. Fresh out of college and 200 pages into a sprawling and inchoate novel about a doomed expedition in the snowy wilderness of Manitoba, I ran into Brower at a rally in Baltimore against the nuclear power industry, which had nearly burned a hole through the earth at Three Mile Island a few dozen miles up the Susquehanna. We both spoke at the protest (I got the mic for thirty seconds, Brower for thirty minutes) and went out for drinks afterwards. Drinks with Brower meant martinis—often just Tanqueray gin, straight up. One after another.

I was inebriated after four rounds. Brower showed not the slightest tic of impairment. We drained two more martinis and then he asked me to explain what I was doing with my time now that Kimberly had given birth to our daughter, Zen.

"Changing diapers and writing a novel," I said. "Changing diapers, mostly."

He laughed. Then swooped in for the kill.

"There's plenty of time for novels in your dotage, Jeffrey," Brower said, zeroing in with his impish eyes. "Not so much time left for those Chesapeake blue crabs out there in the Bay or the grizzlies that you love and that frighten me. Why don't you write about them?"

So I mulched the novel and went to work for Brower at Friends of the Earth for a few months. It wasn't always a smooth relationship. He often felt I was too critical of the big environmental groups and lacked an ultimate faith in the political system to deal with acute environmental problems. Of course, on any given day of the week, Brower adopted both of these opinions as articles of faith. He was a complex and contradictory man. Some might call it character.

We hadn't spoken in about five years when I ran into Dave at the Environmental Law Conference in Eugene, where we were both featured speakers. Jim Ridgeway and I had just written a vicious little book called *A Guide to Environmental Bad Guys*, which we had dedicated to the fall of Glen Canyon Dam. I handed a copy to Brower. He flipped through the pages absently, tossed it to his wife, Ann, and resumed a conversation with his latest recruit to the Sierra Club, Adam Werbach, now hustling as a frontman for Wal-Mart.

If Dave and I endured a fractious relationship, Ann and I had always shared fundamental values and a warm and unwavering friendship. Through many fraught hours, Ann Brower served as Dave's spine and his conscience—not to mention editing his sometimes tangled prose into clear and potent sentences. As I turned to walk away, miffed at Brower's snub, Ann grabbed my wrist. "I'll make sure he reads it." She winked. And so she did. I received beautiful notes from both of them a few weeks later.

I last saw Brower at Glen Canyon Dam, during the protest that served as the coming out party for Living Rivers. He was in a wheelchair, fiercely battling the illness that would soon claim his life. As the speeches rambled on, I rolled Dave across the parking lot to the Glen Canyon Bridge with a view down into the last seventeen undammed miles of the canyon.

"Right the wrong," he demanded.

Seven years after his death, the only real commemoration of the life of America's greatest environmentalist is on a building in Berkeley, now under green construction, that will house Earth Island Institute and other environmental and social justice organizations. Supposedly Dave gave his enthusiastic assent to the project in the waning weeks of his life. But I think Dave was probably just happy that Earth Island, his last organizational progeny, would have a permanent base of operations from which to cause global trouble in the name of sea turtles and killer whales.

Dave Brower wasn't about buildings, even earth-friendly ones. His legacy resides in what Howie Wolke calls the Big Outside. Brower deserves to have his name immortalized on a Sierran peak, an ancient forest grove in Oregon, a wild run of rapids in Grand Canyon, and a living canyon in Dinosaur... Lodore, perhaps?

* * *

Dozens of trout rise before us, puckering the smooth surface of the river as it squeezes through the brooding walls of Split Mountain Canyon. A fat rainbow finally makes a twisting leap out of the water, snatching an unwary damselfly.

These rainbows aren't native to the Green River, whose warm and silty waters never produced many trout, and then only the brightly marked and sleek Colorado Cutthroat, now endangered, largely as a consequence of the government's stocking the river basin with non-native competitors, such as the ubiquitous rainbow.

Most of these fish found their way into the Green River from the Jones Hole Hatchery a few miles upstream, which is why the facility must be closed immediately. All hatcheries should be shuttered eventually, but this one deserves to be first in line. It is polluting the Green River with alien beings, android trout, generated in cloning tanks that sacrifice identity for the identical. The phony fish are eating away at Dinosaur's aquatic ecosystem, still more ecological blowback from Flaming Gorge Dam. Among other serious problems, the hatchery is a vector for infection, especially a fatal disorder called whirling disease, known to ichthyophiles as "trout AIDS."

The Jones Hole Hatchery was constructed a few yards outside the Dinosaur National Monument boundary by the Fish and Wildlife Service with money provided by the Bureau of Reclamation. The hatchery was meant to mitigate the damage done by Flaming Gorge dam. Mitigation can be succinctly defined as making amends for one bad act by doing something worse.

Here the federal government deliberately eradicated the native species (which the Bureau men dubbed "trash" fish) of the Green River above and below the dam by saturating the waters with poison, an act that gives new meaning to liquidation. Then the waters of the reservoir and the stretch of river below the dam through Browns Park and into Dinosaur were seeded with non-native lake trout, brown trout and rainbows. The Bureau of Reclamation now touts Flaming Gorge and Browns Park as "a world class trout fishery." Yet, you'll cast in vain for a Colorado Cutthroat, considered by many to be the most beautiful trout in the world. That's a strange kind of progress.

This begs another question. Should sport-fishing even be permitted in national parks? There's an easy and emphatic answer for that. No. No more than digging for fossils, gathering potsherds, gunning down bison, recreational operation of bulldozers, torturing grizzlies or building big resorts. Leave the fishing in the parks to eagles, osprey, bears and otters. Where else are they going to eat?

Yellowstone shut down its hatcheries in 1960. Why is the FrankenFish factory at Dinosaur National Monument still pumping out drones forty-seven years later? Because the hydro-potentates at the Bureau of Reclamation desperately need to maintain a recreational constituency to defend their dam—and the houseboaters keep killing themselves off. To Congress, a trout-fishing lobby sounds authentic—even when the trout are not.

The rainbows, brown trout, and channel cats are also edging out the native desert fish—the Colorado pikeminnow and humpback chub, in particular. These fish are now endangered. None of these species were considered commercial fish, so, naturally, they were boxed in by the dams—the Hoover, Glen Canyon, and Flaming Gorge—before biologists even knew much about their life histories.

This much we now know: They like warm, murky water, and the turbulent pools below mighty rapids. Though not anadromous, these big predators are migratory, sometimes moving dozens of miles between spawning grounds, rearing spots, and feeding zones. They breed in the submerged limbs of cottonwoods and willows during the spring floods. They eat other fish, including their own young.

But in the post-dam system, the water runs clear and cold, released from the icy belly of the reservoir at 54 degrees in the heat of August. The rapids are diminished or inundated entirely. The spring floods are regulated. The prey species, including most critically (and ironically) their own young, are disappearing, year-by-year. The endemic fishes of the Green/Colorado River are now mere flashing shadows in a closed system. As the humpback chub goes, so goes the river ecosystem. And once they are gone, they can't come back. They exist nowhere else in the world.

So let us resolve to unplug that hatchery, dry it out and leave behind the empty buildings, vats, and tanks as another memorial of science gone wrong. Call it the Dachau of the Cutthroats.

* * *

And so the afternoon passes, down the halls of red rock on the dark river. There's much to say, but no reason to speak. Not now. No reason at all to violate the wild silence.

It's only early afternoon, but already the sun has melted on the high rim, igniting the walls in slanted light, canyon glow.

The gorge narrows, the river accelerates, the current grips the raft, flexes its hidden strength. Rapids aren't the only testimonial to its power.

But rapids are coming. Vicious ones that will shoot us through the center of Split Mountain in a five-mile long conspiracy of rocks and water: Moonshine, Schoolboy, SOB. We rocket over them one after another, cutting through standing waves, twirling on mossy table rocks, bouncing off boulders that do not yield. We are attuned to the rhythms of the river now. For a moment, at least, we are at one with the current of the water. A Zen thing.

So it flows.

We break for lunch one last time on a thin crescent of beach at the mouth of SOB rapids. I unwrap four smoked brook trout, caught on dry flies in the Warm Springs River on the eastern flank of Mt. Hood—our last treat. The beer is gone; so is the Tequila. We settle for water, cool and delicious.

Suddenly, the wind picks up. Powered by the tightening walls of the canyon, the wind scalps the surface of the river, lifting up peels of water and driving the spray upstream against the rapids. The sky darkens, thunder pounds the mountains, lightning stabs the rim of the canyon. Close, very close. This is no mere light show. The hair rises on my arms, prickling with electricity.

Rain pelts us, lightly at first, then in a furious torrent that soaks our clothes and food. There's nowhere to hide. We huddle together as the rain morphs into hail, pecking at us like buckshot. Newly formed waterfalls erupt from the rim, pouring in wispy tails over the face of the canyon. The water runs red.

The storm rages for thirty minutes, then dissipates, leaving behind a disc of lemon sun and a fat rainbow arching across the canyon in an unmarred sky.

Back on the rafts, we float the final mile through the belly of Split Mountain in silence, down an eerie corridor of violently eroded limestone to the stark gate of the canyon and the slab of bland concrete at the takeout point.

As we empty the rafts and heave them onto the boat trailer, a Park Ranger pulls up in a grumbling SUV. He slides out and slams the door, leaving the monster truck idling, a blue smudge of hydrocarbons belching from the tailpipe. He saunters toward us, walking with that calculated limp made iconic in Sergio Leone movies and crudely adopted as the war-strut of George W. Bush. The ranger is a little man with a big gun strapped to his thigh, which he fingers obsessively. The shadow of a Kevlar vest sprouts from beneath his starched Park Service uniform. From his military-style belt dangle plasti-cuffs, a taser, and pepper-spray—all the toys of a post-modern cop.

With his eyes shaded behind the obligatory Ray-Bans, the tiny ranger begins to question Susette about our trip. In his puff-adder voice, he demands to see our permits and interrogates her about where we camped last night. He says he is "in receipt of information" that we didn't stay at Big Island. Apparently, the frat boys have filed their snitch report.

Susette handles the tedious interview as coolly as she navigates rapids. She explains that thanks to the incompetence of Park Service recreation staffers, who had assigned us a landlocked campsite, and the engineers at Flaming Gorge Dam who had shrunk the river, we had no choice but to beach our boats at Red Wash.

I don't have Susette's capacity for patient explanation. Or her subtle sense of irony. But I suddenly realize that I am wearing my verboten t-shirt. Inside-out, natch. I flip the park cop the Curse of the Slain Bison, turn my back to him, and watch the flowing and living river one last time before heading back to Oregon and eight months of moss, fog, and rain.

The storm has flushed a juniper stump into the current, bobbing its way down stream to lodge like a bone in the throat of Glen Canyon Dam.

Roll on, little juniper, roll on.

A Bibliography of the American West

I LIKE BOOKS WITH BIBLIOGRAPHIES. EVEN NOVELS SHOULD HAVE BIBLIO-graphies—especially novels. In that spirit, here is a list of books that have helped me understand what the American West was, what the region became, and what, against all the odds laid down in Vegas, it yet might become.

Abbey, Edward. *Desert Solitaire: a Season in the Wilderness*. New York: McGraw-Hill, 1968.

———. *Down the River*. New York: Penguin. 1982.

———. *One Life at a Time, Please*. New York: Owl. 1988.

———. *Postcards from Ed: Dispatches and Salvos from an American Iconoclast*. St. Paul: Milkweed. 2007.

———. *The Journey Home: Some Words in Defense of the American West*. New York: Penguin. 1984.

Abbott, Carl. *The Metropolitan Frontier: Cities in the Modern American West*. Tucson: University of Arizona Press. 1993.

Ackland, Len. *Making a Real Killing: Rocky Flats and the Nuclear West*. Albuquerque: University of New Mexico Press. 2002.

Aguilar, George W. *When the Rivers Ran Wild: Indian Traditions on the Mid-Columbia and the Warm Springs Reservation*. Seattle: University of Washington Press. 2007.

Allen, Durwood. *Our Wildlife Legacy*. New York: Funk and Wagnalls. 1962.

Allen, John L. *Lewis and Clark and the Image of the American Northwest*. New York: Dover. 1991.

Allin, Craig. *The Politics of Wilderness Preservation*. Westport, Conn.: Greenwood Press. 1982.

Archer, Sellers and Bunch, Clarence. *The American Grass Book*. Norman: University of Oklahoma Press. 1953.

Arrington, Leonard. *Brigham Young*. New York: Knopf. 1985.

———. *Great Basin Kingdom*. Lincoln: University of Nebraska Press. 1966.

Athearn, Frederick. *An Isolated Empire: a History of Northwestern Colorado*. Denver: BLM. 1982.

Athearn, Robert. *The Mythic West in Twentieth Century America*. Lawrence: University of Kansas Press. 1986.

Atherton, Lewis. *The Cattle Kings*. Lincoln: University of Nebraska Press. 1972.

Audubon, John Woodhouse. *Audubon's Western Journal*. Tucson: University of Arizona Press. 1984.

Austin, Mary. *Land of Little Rain*. Albuquerque: University of New Mexico Press. 1974.

Baars, Donald. *The Geology of the Colorado Plateau*. Albuquerque: University of New Mexico Press. 1983.

Ball, Howard. *Justice Downwind: America's Atomic Testing Program in the 1950s*. New York: Oxford University Press. 1988.

Barber, Kathrine. *The Death of Celilo Falls*. Seattle: University of Washington Press. 2005.

Barclay, Harold. *The Role of the Horse in Man's Culture*. London: Allen Press. 1980.

Bardacke, Frank. *Good Liberals and Great Blue Herons: Land, Labor and Politics in the Parajo Valley*. Watsonville: Center for Political Ecology. 1994.

Bari, Judi. *Timber Wars*. Monroe, ME: Common Courage Press. 1994.

Barker, Rocky. *Saving All the Parts: Reconciling Economics and the Endangered Species Act*. Washington, DC: 1993.

———. *Scorched Earth: How the Yellowstone Fires Changed America*. Washington, DC: Island Press. 2007.

Barlow, Thomas, et al. *Giving Away the National Forests*. New York: NRDC. 1980.

Barney, Daniel R. *The Last Stand: Ralph Nader's Study Group Report on the National Forests*. New York: Grossman Publishers. 1974.

Bass, Rick. *The Lost Grizzlies: a Search for Survivors in the Colorado Wilderness*. New York: Mariner Books. 1997.

———. *The New Wolves: the Return of the Wolf to the Southwest*. New York: Lyons Press. 1998.

———. *The Ninemile Wolves*. New York: Mariner. 2003.

Beal, Merrill D. *The Story of Man in Yellowstone*. Yellowstone National Park: Yellowstone Library and Museum Association. 1960.

Beck, M. G. *Shamans and Kushtakas: North Coast Tales of the Supernatural*. Anchorage: Alaska Northwest Books. 1991.

Beck, Warren and Hasse, Ynez. *Historical Atlas of the American West*. Norman: University of Oklahoma Press. 1989.

Behan, Richard W. *Plundered Promise: Capitalism, Politics and the Fate of Public Lands*. Washington, DC: Island Press. 2001.

Benedek, Emily. *The Wind Won't Know Me: a History of the Navajo-Hopi Land Dispute*. Norman: University of Oklahoma Press. 1999.

Berger, Samuel. *Dollar Harvest: the Story of the Farm Bureau*. Lexington, Mass.: Heath. 1971.

Bergman, Ray. *Trout*. New York: Knopf. 1938.

Berkman, Richard L. *Damming the West: the Ralph Nader Study Group Report on the Bureau of Reclamation*. New York: Viking. 1973.

Berthrong, Donald. *The Southern Cheyennes*. Norman: University of Oklahoma Press. 1963.

Black, Jack. *You Can't Win*. Oakland: AK Press. 1997.

Blew, Mary Clearman. *Bone Deep in Landscape*. Norman: University of Oklahoma Press. 2006.

Bordevich, Fergus. *Killing the White Man's Indian: Reinventing Native Americans at the End of the Nineteenth Century*. New York: Doubleday. 1996.

Botkin, Daniel. *Discordant Harmonies: a New Ecology for the Twenty-first Century*. New York: Oxford University Press. 1990.

———. *Our Natural History: the Lessons of the Lewis and Clark Expedition*. New York: Berkeley. 1996.

Bowden, Charles. *Blood Orchid: an Unnatural History of America*. San Francisco: North Point Press. 2002.

———. *Blue Desert*. Tucson: University of Arizona Press. 1988.

————. *Desierto: Memories of the Future.* New York: Norton. 1983.

————. *Killing the Hidden Waters.* Austin: University of Texas Press. 2003.

Boxberger, D.L. *To Fish in Common: the Ethnohistory of Lummi Indian Salmon Fishing.* Lincoln: University of Nebraska Press. 1986.

Boyd, Robert. *The People of the Dalles.* Lincoln: University of Nebraska Press. 1996.

Bramwell, Anna. *Ecology in the Twentieth Century.* New Haven: Yale University Press. 1989.

Brechin, Gray. *Imperial San Francisco: Urban Power, Earthly Ruin.* Berkeley: University of California Press. 1996.

Brooks, Juanita. *John Doyle Lee.* Salt Lake City: Howe Press. 1984.

————. *The Mountain Meadow Massacre.* Norman: University of Oklahoma Press. 1964.

Brower, David R. *David R. Brower: Environmental Activist, Publicist and Prophet.* Berkeley: Bancroft Library Oral History Program, University of California, 1980.

————. *For the Earth's Sake.* Salt Lake City: Gibbs Smith. 1990.

————. *Let the Mountains Talk, Let the Rivers Run.* New York: HarperCollins. 2000.

Brown, Bruce. *Mountain in the Clouds: a Search for the Wild Salmon.* New York: Simon and Schuster. 1982.

Brown, David. *The Grizzly in the Southwest.* Tucson: University of Arizon Press. 1985.

————. *The Wolf in the Southwest: the Making of an Endangered Species.* Tucson: University of Arizona Press. 1992.

Brown, Dee. *Bury My Heart at Wounded Knee.* New York: Holt, Rinehart and Winston. 1970.

Brown, Lauren. *Grasslands.* New York: Knopf. 1985.

Brown, Tom. *Oil on Ice: Alaskan Wilderness at the Crossroads.* San Francisco: Sierra Club Books. 1971.

Buechner, H. K. *The Bighorn Sheep in the United States: Its Past, Present and Future.* Washington, D. C.: The Wildlife Society. 1960.

Bunte, Pamela and Franklin, Robert. *From the Sands to the Mountain: Change and Persistence in a Southern Paiute Community.* Lincoln: University of Nebraska Press. 1987.

Bunting, Robert. *The Pacific Raincoast: Environment and Culture in an American Eden, 1778-1900.* Lawrence: University of Kansas Press. 1997.

Bureau of Reclamation. *The Colorado River: a Comprehensive Report on the Development of Water Resources.* Washington, D.C.: U.S. Department of the Interior, 1947.

Caldwell, Lynton K. *Citizens and the Environment.* Bloomington: Indiana University Press. 1960.

Cantor, George. *North American Indian Landmarks: a Traveler's Guide.* Detroit: Visible Ink Press. 1993.

Carey, C. H. *A General History of Oregon.* Portland: Binford and Mort. 1971.

Carranco, Lynwood and Beard, Estle. *Genocide and Vendetta: the Round Valley Wars of Northern California.* Norman, University of Oklahoma Press, 1981.

Carrels, Peter. *Uphill Against Water: the Great Dakota Water War.* Lincoln: University of Nebraska Press. 1999.

Carson, Rachel. *Silent Spring.* Greenwich, Conn.: Fawcett Crest. 1962.

Carter, Vernon Gill and Dale, Tom. *Topsoil and Civilization.* Norman: University of Oklahoma Press. 1974.

Cassady, Neal. *The First Third: the Real Life Adventures of Jack Kerouac's Hero.* San Francisco: City Lights. 1971.

Catton, William R. *Overshoot: The Ecological Roots of Revolutionary Change.* Urbana: University of Illinois Press. 1980.

Chaney, Ed, et al. *Livestock Grazing on Western Riparian Areas.* Washington, DC: EPA. 1990.

Chapin, Frederick. *Land of the Cliff Dwellers.* Tucson: University of Arizona Press. 1988.

Chapple, Steve. *Kayaking the Full Moon: a Journey Down the Yellowstone River to the Soul of Montana.* New York: Harper Perennial. 1994.

Chase, Alston. *Playing God in Yellowstone.* Boston: Atlantic Monthly Press. 1986.

Christenson, Andrew. *The Last of the Great Expeditions: the Rainbow Bridge Expedition, 1933-38.* Flagstaff: Northern Arizona University Press. 1987.

Churchill, Ward. *Indians Are Us? Culture and Genocide in Native North America.* Monroe, ME: Common Courage Press. 1994.

Clark, Ella E. *Indian Legends of the Pacific Northwest.* Berkeley: University of California Press. 1953.

Clark, Robert. *River of the West: a History of the Columbia.* New York: Picador. 1995.

Clary, David. *Timber and the Forest Service.* Lawrence: University of Kansas Press. 1986.

Clawson, Marion. *Forests for Whom and for What?* Baltimore: Johns Hopkins Press. 1975.

———. *The Bureau of Land Management.* New York: Praeger. 1971.

Clifford, Hal. *Downhill Slide: Why the Corporate Sky Industry is Bad for Skiing, Ski Towns and the Environment.* San Francisco: Sierra Club Books. 2003.

Cockburn, Alexander and St. Clair, Jeffrey. *Five Days That Shook the World: Seattle and Beyond.* London: Verso. 2000.

Cockburn, Alexander. *The Golden Age is in Us.* London: Verso. 1995.

Coe, Sue, with Alexander Cockburn. *Dead Meat.* New York: Four Walls, Eight Windows, 1995.

Cohen, Michael P. *The History of the Sierra Club: 1892-1970.* San Francisco: Sierra Club Books. 1988.

Cole, D. and Caikan, I. *An Iron Hand Upon the People: the Law Against Potlatch in the Northwest Coast.* Seattle University of Washington Press. 1990.

Cole, Douglas. *Captured Heritage. The Scramble for Northwest Coast Artifacts.* Seattle: University of Washington Press, 1985.

Cole, Sally J. *Legacy on Stone: Rock Art of the Colorado Plateau and Four Corners Region.* Boulder: Johnson Books. 1990.

Collier, Michael, et al. *Dams and Rivers: a Primer on the Downstream Effects of Dams.* Denver: US Geological Survey. 2000.

Commoner, Barry. *Science and Survival.* New York: Viking Press. 1963.

———. *The Closing Circle.* New York: Knopf. 1971.

Cone, Joseph. *The Northwest Salmon Crisis: a Documentary History.* Corvallis: Oregon State University Press. 1996.

Cooper, Michael. *Remembering Manzanar: Life in a Japanese Relocation Camp.* New York: Clarion. 2002.

Cornell, Stephen. *The Return of the Native: American Indian Political Resurgence.* New York: Oxford University Press. 1988.

Craighead, Frank. *A Naturalist's Guide to Grand Teton and Yellowstone National Parks.* Helena: Falcon Press. 2006.

———. *Track of the Grizzly.* San Francisco: Sierra Club Books. 1977.

Crampton, Gregory. *Ghosts of Glen Canyon.* St. George, Publisher's Place. 1986.

———. *Land of Living Rock.* New York: Knopf. 1972.

———. *Standing Up Country.* New York: Knopf. 1964.

Cremony, John C. *Life Among the Apaches.* Glorieta, NM.: Rio Grande. 1969.

Cronon, William. *Nature's Metropolis: Chicago and the Great West.* New York: W.W.Norton, 1991.

Crosby, Alfred. *Ecological Imperialism: the Biological Expansion of Europe, 900-1900.* New York: Cambridge University Press. 1993.

Crow Dog, Mary, with Richard Erodes. *Lakota Woman.* New York: HarperPerennial. 1991.

Crutchfield, J. and Pontecorvo, G. *The Pacific Salmon Fisheries: a Study in Irrational Management.* Baltimore: Johns Hopkins Press. 1969.

Dana, Samuel T. and Fairfax, Sally K. *Forest and Range Policy: Its Development in the United States.* New York: McGraw-Hill. 1980.

Dary, David. *The Buffalo Book.* Chicago: Swallow Press. 1974.

Davis, Mike. *City of Quartz: Excavating the Future in Los Angeles.* London: Verso. 2006.

———. *Ecology of Fear: Los Angeles and the Imagination of Disaster.* New York: Vintage. 1999.

Davis, Susan. *Spectacular Nature: Corporate Culture and the Sea World Experience.* Berkeley: University of California Press. 1997.

Debo, Angie. *A History of the Indians of the United States.* Norman: University of Oklahoma Press. 1970.

———. *Geronimo.* Norman: University of Oklahoma Press. 1976.

DeBuys, William. *Enchantment and Exploitation: the Life and Hard Times of a New Mexico Mountain Range.* Albuquerque: University of New Mexico Press. 1986.

Dellenbaugh, Frederick. *A Canyon Voyage.* Tucson: University of Arizona Press. 1984.

Deloria, Vine, Jr. *Custer Died for Your Sins: an Indian Manifesto.* New York: MacMillan. 1969.

———, ed. *American Indian Policy in the Twentieth Century.* Norman: University of Oklahoma Press. 1985.

Denhardt, Robert. *The Horse of the Americas.* Norman: University of Oklahoma Press. 1975.

Denton, Sally and Morris, Roger. *The Money and the Power: the Making of Las Vegas.* New York: Vintage. 2002.

Despain, Don. *Yellowstone Vegetation: the Consequences of History and Environment in a Natural Setting.* Boulder: Roberts Rinehart. 1990.

Devall, Bill and Sessions, George. *Deep Ecology.* Salt Lake City: Gibbs Smith. 1985.

DeVoto, Bernard. *The Easy Chair.* Boston: Houghton Mifflin. 1955.

———. *The Journals of Lewis and Clark.* Boston: Houghton Mifflin. 1953.

———. *The Year of Decision, 1846.* Boston: Houghton Mifflin. 1943.

Dietrich, William. *The Final Forest: the Battle for the Last Great Trees of the Pacific Northwest.* New York: Simon and Schuster. 1992.

———. *Northwest Passage: the Great Columbia River.* New York: Simon and Schuster. 1995.

Dillon, Richard. *Burnt Out Fires.* Englewood Cliffs, NJ: Prentice-Hall. 1973.

———. *Fool's Gold: the Decline and Fall of Captain John Sutter of California.* New York: Coward-McCann. 1967.

Dobie, J. Frank. *The Longhorns.* New York: Bramhall House. 1941.

———. *The Mustangs.* Austin: University of Texas Press. 1984.

Dobyns, Henry E. *Their Numbers Became Thinned: Native American Population Dynamics in Eastern North America.* Knoxville: University of Tennessee Press. 1983.

Dodds, G. *The Salmon King of Oregon: R.D. Hume and the Pacific Fisheries.* Chapel Hill: University of North Carolina Press. 1959.

Dorado Romo, David. *Ringside Seat to a Revolution: An underground history of El Paso and Juarez: 1893-1923.* El Paso: Cinco Puntos Press. 2005.

Doughty, Robin. *Feather Fashions and Bird Preservation: a Study in Nature Protection.* Berkeley: University of California Press. 1975.

Douglas, David. *The Oregon Journals of David Douglas During the Years 1825-1827.* Ed. David Lavender. Ashland: Oregon Book Society.. 1972.

Drago, Henry S. *The Great Range Wars.* Lincoln: University of Nebraska Press. 1970.

Dunbar-Ortiz, Roxanne. *Red Dirt: Growing Up Okie.* Norman: University of Oklahoma Press. 2006.

———. *Roots of Resistance: Land Tenure in New Mexico.* Norman: University of Oklahoma. 2007.

Dunlap, Thomas. *Saving America's Wildlife: Ecology and the American Mind.* Princeton: Princeton University Press. 1988.

Durbin, Kathie. *The Tongass: Pulp Politics and the Fight for the Alaska Rain Forest.* Corvallis: Oregon State University Press. 2005.

———. *Tree Huggers.* Seattle: Mountaineers. 1998.

Durham, Philip and Jones, Everett. *The Negro Cowboys.* Lincoln: University of Nebraska Press. 1965.

Eaton, Allen. *Beauty Behind Bars: the Arts of the Japanese in Our War Relocation Camps.* New York: Harper. 1952.

Edmonds, Carol. *Wayne Aspinall: Mr. Chairman.* Lakewood: Crown Point, 1980.

Egan, Timothy. *A Good Rain: Across Time and Terrain in the Pacific Northwest.* New York: Knopf. 1990.

Ehrenfeld, David. *The Arrogance of Humanism.* New York: Oxford University Press. 1978.

Eichstaedt, Peter. *If You Poison Us: Uranium and Native Americans.* Santa Fe: Red Crane Books. 1994.

Engler, Robert. *The Brotherhood of Oil: Energy, Politics and the Public Interest.* Chicago: University of Chicago Press. 1977.

———. *The Politics of Oil: a Study of Private Power and Democratic Directions.* New York: Macmillan. 1961.

Errington, Paul. *Of Predation and Life.* Ames: Iowa State University Press. 1967.

Evans, Howard. *The Natural History of the Long Expedition to the Rocky Mountains, 1819-1820.* New York: Oxford University Press. 1997.

Ewing, Sherm. *The Range.* Missoula: Mountain Press. 1990.

Fagan, Brian. *The Great Journey: the Peopling of Ancient America.* London: Thames and Hudson. 1987.

Faris, James C. *Navajo and Photography: a Critical History of an American People.* Albuquerque: University of New Mexico Press. 1996.

Faunce, Hilda. *Desert Wife.* Lincoln: University of Nebraska Press. 1981.

Ferguson, Denzel and Ferguson, Nancy. *Sacred Cows at the Public Trough.* Bend, Ore.: Maverick Publishers. 1983.

Ferguson, Gary. *Hawk's Rest: a Season in the Remote Heart of Yellowstone.* Washington, DC: National Geographic Press. 2003.

Findlay, John. M. *Magic Lands: Western Cityscapes and American Culture After 1940.* Berkeley: University of California Press. 1992.

Fixico, Donald. *Termination and Relocation: Federal Indian Policy, 1945-1960.* Albuquerque: University of New Mexico Press. 1986.

Flader, Susan. *Thinking Like a Mountain: Aldo Leopold and the Evolution of an Ecological Attitude Toward Deer, Wolves and Forests.* Columbia: University of Missouri Press. 1974.

Fleherty, Eugene. *Wild Animals and Settlers on the Great Plains.* Norman: University of Oklahoma Press. 1995.

Fletcher, Colin. *The Man Who Walked Through Time.* New York: Vantage. 1989.

Flippen, J. Brooks. *Nixon and the Environment.* Albuquerque: University of New Mexico Press. 2000.

Flores, Dan. *Horizontal Yellow: Nature and History in the Near Southwest.* Albuquerque: University of New Mexico Press. 1999.

———. *The Natural West: Environmental History in the Great Plains and Rocky Mountains.* Norman: University of Oklahoma Press. 2001.

Foreman, Dave and Wolke, Howie. *The Big Outside: an Inventory of the Big Wilderness Areas of the U.S.* Tucson: Ned Ludd Books. 1989.

Foreman, Dave. *Confessions of an Eco-Warrior.* Tucson: Three Rivers Press. 1993.

Foss, Philip. *Politics and Grass.* Seattle: University of Washington Press. 1960.

Fowler, Loretta. *Shared Symbols, Contested Meanings: Gros Ventre History and Culture, 1778 to 1984.* Ithaca: Cornell University Press. 1987.

Fox, Stephen R. *John Muir and His Legacy: The American Conservation Movement.* Boston: Little Brown, 1981.

Fradkin, Philip. *A River No More: The Colorado River and the West.* New York: Knopf, 1981.

———. *Fallout: an American Nuclear Tragedy.* Boulder: Johnson Books. 2004.

Frank, Robert and Kerouac, Jack. *The Americans.* New York: Scalo. 1998.

Frazier, Ian. *Great Plains.* New York: Farrar, Straus and Giroux. 1989.

———. *On the Rez.* New York: Picador. 2000.

Frazier, Kendrick. *People of Chaco: a Canyon and Its People.* New York: Norton. 1999.

Frey, Rodney. *The World of the Crow Indians.* Norman: University of Oklahoma Press. 1987.

Frison, George. *Prehistoric Hunters of the High Plains.* New York: Academic Press. 1978.

Frome, Michael. *Battle for Wilderness.* New York: Praeger. 1984.

———. *The Forest Service.* Boulder: Westview Press. 1984.

Frost, Kent. *My Canyonlands.* London: Abelard-Schuman. 1971.

Gallagher, Carole. *American Ground Zero: the Secret Nuclear War.* New York: Random House. 1994.

Garavaglia, Louis and Worman, Charles. *Firearms of the American West*. Albuquerque: University of New Mexico Press. 1984.

Garcia, Mario. *Mexican-Americans*. New Haven: Yale University Press. 1990.

Geist, Valerius. *Buffalo Nation: History and Legend of the North American Bison*. Stillwater, Minn.: Voyageur Press. 1996.

Gerber, Michele. *On the Home Front: the Cold War Legacy of the Hanford Nuclear Site*. Lincoln: University of Nebraska Press. 2002.

Gibson, J. R. *Farming the Frontier: the Agricultural Opening of the Oregon Country, 1786-1846*. Seattle: University of Washington Press. 1985.

Gillenkirk, Jeff and Motlow, James. *Bitter Melon: Stories from the Last Rural Chinese Town in America*. Seattle: University of Washington Press. 1987.

Gilmore, Melvin R. *Uses of Plants by the Indians of the Missouri River Region*. Lincoln: University of Nebraska Press. 1977.

Glass, Matthew. *Citizens Against the MX: Public Languages in the Nuclear Age*. Urbana: University of Illinois Press. 1993.

Glick, Daniel. *Powder Burn: Arson, Money and Mystery on Vail Mountain*. New York: Public Affairs. 2003.

Glover, James. *A Wilderness Original: the Life of Bob Marshall*. Seattle: Mountaineer Books. 1996.

Goetzman, William H. *Exploration and Empire: The Explorer and the Scientist*. New York: Knopf. 1966.

Goldwater, Barry. *Delightful Journey Down the Green and Colorado Rivers*. Phoenix: Arizona Historical Foundation. 1970.

Gomes-Quinnones, Juan. *Chicano Politics*. Albuquerque: University of New Mexico Press. 1990.

Gould, Stephen Jay. *Bully for Brontosaurus*. New York: Norton. 1991.

——. *Wonderful Life: the Burgess Shale and the Nature of History*. New York: Norton. 1990.

Gribbin, John and Mary. *Children of the Ice*. London: Blackwell. 1990.

Gumerman, George. *A View from Black Mesa: the Changing Face of Archaeology*. Tucson: University of Arizona Press. 1984.

Haeger, John D. *John Jacob Astor: Business and Finance in the Early Republic*. Detroit: Wayne State University Press. 1991.

Haines, Aubrey, ed. *Osborne Russell's Journal of a Trapper, 1876-77*. Lincoln: University of Nebraska Press. 1965.

——. *The Yellowstone Story*. Boulder: Yellowstone Library and Museum Association. 1977.

Halfpenny, James and Ozanne, Roy D. *Winter: an Ecological Handbook*. Boulder: Johnson Books. 1984.

Hall, Edward T. *West of the Thirties: Discoveries Among the Navajo and Hopi*. New York: Anchor. 1995.

Hardin, Blaine. *A River Lost: the Life and Death of the Columbia River*. New York: Norton. 1996.

Hardoff, Richard. *Lakota Recollections of the Custer Fight*. Spokane: Clark Press. 1991.

Harmon, David. *The Antiquities Act: a Century of American Archaeology, Historic Preservation and Nature Preservation*. Tucson: University of Arizona Press. 2006.

Harvey, Mark W. T. *A Symbol of Wilderness: Echo Park and the American Conservation Movement*. Albuquerque: University of New Mexico Press. 1994.

Haycox, Stephen. *Frigid Embrace: Politics, Economics and the Environment in Alaska.* Corvallis: Oregon State University Press. 2002.

Hays, Samuel T. *Beauty, Health and Permanence.* Cambridge, Mass.: Harvard University Press. 1987.

———. *Conservation and the Gospel of Efficiency: the Progressive Conservation Movement, 1890-1920.* Cambridge, Mass.: Harvard University Press. 1959.

Heat Moon, William Least. *PrairyErth.* Boston: Houghton, Mifflin. 1991.

Heinrich, Bernd. *Ravens in Winter.* New York: Summit. 1989.

Helvarg, David. *The War Against the Greens.* San Francisco: Sierra Club Books. 1997.

Hendricks, Steve. *The Unquiet Grave: the FBI and the Struggle for the Soul of Indian Country.* New York: Thunder's Mouth. 2006.

Herndon, Grace T. *Cut and Run: Saying Goodbye to the Last Great Forests in the West.* Telluride: Western Eye Press. 1991.

Herrero, Stephen. *Bear Attacks: Their Causes and Avoidance.* New York: Lyons Press. 2002.

Hess, Karl. *Visions Upon the Land: Man and Nature on the Western Range.* Washington, DC: Island Press. 1992.

Hevly, Bruce and Findlay, John. *The Atomic West.* Seattle: University of Washingotn Press. 1998.

Hildebrand, John. *Reading the River: a Voyage Down the Yukon.* Madison: University of Wisconsin Press. 1997.

Hogrefe, Jeffrey. *O'Keefe: the Life of an American Legend.* New York: Bantam. 1992.

Holder, Preston. *The Hoe and the Horse on the Plains: a Study of Cultural Development Among North American Indians.* Lincoln: University of Nebraska Press. 1970.

Holt, John. *Coyote Nowhere: In Search of America's Last Frontier.* New York: Lyon's Press. 2004.

Horgan, Paul. *Great River: the Rio Grande.* Austin: Texas Monthly Press. 1984.

Houle, Marcy. *The Prairie Keepers: Secrets of the Zumwalt.* Corvallis: Oregon State University Press. 2007.

Houston, Douglas. *Northern Yellowstone Elk: Ecology and Management.* New York: Macmillan. 1982.

Houston, Jeanne Wakasuki. *Farewell to Manzanar: a True Story of a Japanese American in a World War II Internment Camp.* New York: Bantam. 1973.

Hoxie, Frederick. *The Crow.* New York: Chelsea House Publishers. 1989.

Hundley, Norris. *The Great Thirst: Californians and Water, 1770-1990s.* Berkeley: University of California Press. 1992.

Huntington. Sidney. *Koyukuk: an Alaska Native's Life Along the River.* Anchorage: Alaska Northwest Books. 1993.

Hurt, R. Douglas. *Indian Agriculture in America: Prehistory to the Present.* Lawrence: University of Kansas Press. 1987.

Hurtado, Albert. *Indian Survival on the California Frontier.* New Haven: Yale University Press. 1988.

Huth, Hans. *Nature and the American: Three Centuries of Changing Attitudes.* Berkeley: University of California Press. 1957.

Hyde, Philip. *A Glen Canyon Portfolio.* Flagstaff: Northland Press. 1979.

Hymes, Dell. *"In Vain I Tried to Tell You:" Essays in Native American Ethnopoetics.* Lincoln: University of Nebraska Press. 2004.

Ickes, Harold. *The Secret Diaries of Harold Ickes*. New York: Simon and Schuster. 1955.

Isenberg, Andrew. *The Destruction of the American Bison: an Environmental History, 1750-1920*. New York: Cambridge University Press. 2001.

Iverson, Peter. *When Indians Became Cowboys: Native Peoples and Cattle Ranching in the American West*. Norman: University of Oklahoma. 1994.

Jackson, Donald. *Thomas Jefferson and the Stoney Mountains: Exploring the West from Monticello*. Chicago: University of Illinois Press. 1981.

Jackson, Wes. *Altars of Unhewn Stone*. San Francisco: North Point Press. 1987.

Jacobs, Lynn. *Wasting the West: Public Lands Ranching*. Tucson: Jacobs Press. 1991.

Janetski, Joel. *The Indians of Yellowstone National Park*. Salt Lake City: University of Utah Press. 1987.

Jansen, Joan and Miller, Darlis. *New Mexico Women*. Albuquerque: University of New Mexico Press. 1986.

Jeffrey, John M. *Adobe and Iron*. La Jolla: Prospect Press. 1969.

Jennings, Jesse D. *Glen Canyon: a Summary*. Salt Lake City: University of Utah Press. 1966.

Jensen, Derrick and Draffan, George. *Strangely Like War: the Global Assault on Forests*. White River, VT: Chelsea Green. 2003.

Jensen, Derrick, et al. *Railroads and Clearcuts: The Legacy of Congress's 1864 Northern Pacific Railroad Land Grant*. Spokane: Keokee Press. 1995.

Johnson, N. K., et al. *Alternatives for Management of Late-Successional Forests of the Pacific Northwest* (aka, Gang of Four Report). Wash. DC: GPO. 1991.

Jones, Stephen. *The Last Prairie: a Sandhills Journal*. Camden, ME: Ragged Mountain Press. 2000.

Jordan, Terry. *North American Cattle-Ranching Frontiers*. Albuquerque: University of New Mexico Press. 1993.

Josephy, Alvin, Jr. *Now That the Buffalo's Gone: a Study of Today's American Indians*. New York: Knopf. 1982.

———. *The Nez Perce Indians and the Opening of the Northwest*. New Haven: Yale University Press. 1971.

———. *The Patriot Chiefs: a Chronicle of American Indian Resistance*. New York: Viking. 1969.

Kahrl, William. *Water and Power: the Conflict Over Los Angeles' Water Supply in the Owens Valley*. Berkeley: University of California Press. 1983.

Katz, William Loren. *The Black West*. Seattle: Open Hand. 1987.

Kaufman, Herbert. *The Forest Ranger: a Study in Administrative Behavior*. Baltimore: Johns Hopkins Press. 1960.

Kerouac, Jack. *On the Road: the Original Scroll*. New York: Viking. 2007.

Kesey, Ken and Babbs, Ken. *The Last Round Up: a Real Western*. New York: Penguin. 1995.

Kesey, Ken. *Demon Box*. New York: Penguin. 1987.

Kessler, Lauren. *Stubborn Twig: Three Generations in the Life of a Japanese American Family*. Portland: Oregon Historical Society Press. 2006.

Kirk, Ruth and Franklin, Jerry. *The Olympic Rainforest: an Ecological Web*. Seattle: University of Washington Press. 1992.

Kittredge, William. *Hole in the Sky: a Memoir*. New York: Vintage. 1993.

———. *Owning It All*. Missoula: Graywolf Press. 2002.

———. *Who Owns the West?* New York: Mercury House. 1996.

Knight, Dennis. *Mountains and Plains: the Ecology of Wyoming Landscapes.* New Haven: Yale University Press. 1994.

Krakauer, Jon. *Into the Wild.* New York: Anchor. 2007.

———. *Under the Banner of Heaven: a Story of Violent Faith.* New York: Anchor. 2004.

Krakel, Dean. *Downriver: a Yellowstone Journey.* San Francicso: Sierra Club Books. 1987.

Kramer, Dale. *The Truth About the Farm Bureau.* Denver: Golden Bell. 1964.

Kruckeberg, A.R. *The Natural History of the Puget Sound Country.* Seattle: University of Washington Press. 1991.

Krutch, Joseph Wood. *More Lives Than One.* New York: Sloane. 1962.

Kurten, Bjorn and Anderson, Elaine. *Pleistocene Mammals of North America.* New York: Columbia University Press. 1980.

La Barre, Weston. *The Ghost Dance.* New York: Delta. 1970.

Lannoo, Michael. *Okoboji Wetlands: a Lesson in Natural History.* Iowa City: University of Iowa Press. 1996.

Lavender, David. *River Runners of the Colorado.* Grand Canyon: Grand Canyon Naitonal History Association, 1985.

Lawson, Michael. *Damned Indians: the Pick-Sloan Plan and the Missouri River Sioux, 1944-1980.* Norman: University of Oklahoma Press. 1994.

Lazarus, Edward. *Black Hills, White Justice: the Sioux Nation Versus the United States, 1775 to the Present.* New York: HarperCollins. 1991.

Lee, Katie. *All My Rivers Are Gone: a Journey of Discovery Through Glen Canyon.* Boulder: Johnson Books. 1998.

———. *Sandstone Seduction: Rivers and Lovers, Canyons and Friends.* Boulder: Johnson Books. 2004.

———. *Ten Thousand Goddamn Cattle: the History of the American Cowboy in Song, Story and Verse.* Albuquerque: University of New Mexico Press. 2001.

Leed, Eric. *The Mind of the Traveler: From Gilgamesh to Global Tourism.* New York: Basic Books. 1991.

Leopold, Aldo. *Sand County Almanac.* Oxford: Oxford University Press. 1949.

Leydet, François. *Grand Canyon: Time and the River Flowing.* San Francisco: Sierra Club Books, 1964.

Lichatowich, Jim. *Salmon Without Rivers: a History of the Pacific Salmon Crisis.* Washington, DC: Island Press. 1999.

Lien, Carsten. *Olympic Battleground: the Power Politics of Timber Preservation.* San Francisco: Sierra Club Books. 1991.

Limerick, Patricia Nelson. *Desert Passage: Encounters with the American Desert.* Albuquerque: University of New Mexico Press. 1985.

———. *Something in the Soil: Legacies and Reckonings in the New West.* New York: Norton. 2000.

———. *The Legacy of Conquest: the Unbroken Past of the American West.* New York: W.W. Norton. 1987.

Linderman, Frank B. *Pretty-Shield: Medicine Woman of the Crows.* Lincoln: University of Nebraska Press. 1974.

Lingelfelter, Richard. *Death Valley and the Amargosa*. Berkeley: University of California Press. 1986.

Loeffler, Jack. *Adventures with Ed: a Portrait of Abbey*. Albuquerque: University of New Mexico Press. 2003.

Lopez, Barry. *Giving Birth to Thunder, Sleeping with His Daughter: Coyote Builds North America*. New York: Avon. 1977.

———. *Of Wolves and Men*. New York: Scribner's. 1978.

Lowitt, Richard. *The New Deal and the West*. Norman: University of Oklahoma Press. 1993.

Luckert, Karl W. *Navajo Mountain and Rainbow Bridge Religion*. Flagstaff: Museum of Northern Arizona. 1977.

Luhan, Mabel Dodge. *Movers and Shakers*. Albuquerque: University of New Mexico Press. 1985.

Lukas, J. Anthony. *Big Trouble: a Murder in a Small Western Town Sets Off a Struggle for the Soul of America*. New York: Simon and Schuster. 1997.

Lumholtz, Carl. *Unknown Mexico: Explorations in the Sierra Madre and Other Regions, 1890-1898*. New York: Dover. 1987.

Lummis, Charles. *The Land of Poco Tiempo*. Albuquerque: University of New Mexico Press. 1925.

Luoma, Jon. *The Hidden Forest: Biography of an Ecosystem*. Corvallis: Oregon State University Press. 2006.

Madsen, John. *Where the Sky Began: The Land of the Tallgrass Prairie*. San Francisco: Sierra Club Books. 1982.

Mailer, Norman. *The Executioner's Song*. New York: Little Brown. 1979

Malin, James. *The Grassland of North America: Prolegomena to Its History*. Lawrence: University of Kansas Press. 1948.

Malone, Michael. *The Battle for Butte: Mining and Politics on the Northern Frontier*. Helena: Montana Historical Society Press. 1995.

Manes, Christopher. *Green Rage: Radical Environmentalism and the Unmaking of Civilization*. San Francisco: Back Bay Books. 1991.

Manning, Richard. *Grassland: the History, Biology, Politics and Promise of the American Prairie*. New York: Viking. 1995.

———. *Last Stand: Logging, Journalism and the Case for Humility*. Salt Lake City: Peregrine Smith Books. 1991.

Marshall, Robert. *Alaska Wilderness: Exploring the Central Brooks Range*. Berkeley: University of California Press. 1956.

Martin, Calvin. *Keepers of the Game: Indian-Animal Relationships in the Fur Trade*. Berkeley: University of California Press. 1978.

Martin, Paul, ed. *Quarternary Extinctions: a Prehistoric Revolution*. Tucson: University of Arizona. 1984.

Martin, Russell. *A Story That Stands Like a Dam: Glen Canyon and the Struggle for the Soul of the West*. Salt Lake City: University of Utah Press. 1989.

Martinez, Oscar J. *Troublesome Borders*. Tucson: University of Arizona Press. 1986.

Maser, Chris, et al. *From the Forest to the Sea: a Story of Fallen Trees*. Portland: USDA. 1988.

Maser, Chris. *Forest Primeval: a Natural History of an Ancient Forest*. New York: Random House. 1989.

————. *The Redesigned Forest.* San Pedro: R. and E. Miles. 1988.

Matson, R.G. and Coupland, G. *The Prehistory of the Northwest Coast.* New York: Academic Press. 1995.

Matthews, Anne. *Where the Buffalo Roam* New York: Weidenfeld. 1992.

Matthiessen, Peter. *In the Spirit of Crazy Horse.* New York: Viking. 1992.

————. *Indian Country.* New York: Penguin. 1992.

McCarthy, G. Michael. *Hour of Trial: the Conservation Conflict in Colorado and the West, 1891-1907.* Norman: University of Oklahoma Press. 1977.

McConnell, Grant. *Private Power and American Democracy.* New York: Knopf. 1966.

McDonnell, Janet. *The Campo Indian Landfill War: the Fight for Gold in California's Garbage.* Norman: University of Oklahoma Press. 1995.

McEvoy, A.F. *The Fisherman's Problem: Ecology and Law in the California Fisheries, 1850-1980.* New York: Cambridge University Press. 1986.

McGregor, A. *Counting Sheep: From Open Range to Agribusiness on the Columbia Plateau.* Seattle: University of Washington Press. 1982.

McHugh, Tom. *The Time of the Buffalo.* New York: Knopf. 1972.

McKee, B. *Cascadia: the Geologic Evolution of the Pacific Northwest.* New York: McGraw Hill. 1972.

McMillion, Scott. *Mark of the Grizzly: True Stories of Recent Bear Attacks and the Hard Lessons Learned.* Bozeman: Falcon Press. 1998.

McNamee, Gregory. *Gila: the Life and Death of an American River.* Albuquerque: University of New Mexico Press. 1994.

McNitt, Frank. *The Indian Traders.* Norman: University of Oklahoma Press. 1962.

McNulty, Faith. *Must They Die? The Strange Case of the Prairie Dog and the Black-Footed Ferret.* New York: Doubleday. 1971.

McPhee, John. *Encounters with the Archdruid.* New York: Farrar, Straus and Giroux. 1971.

McPherson, Robert. *Sacred Land, Sacred View: Navajo Perceptions of the Four Corners Region.* Provo: Signature Books. 1992.

McWilliams, Carey. *Southern California: an Island Upon the Land.* Salt Lake City: Peregrine Smith. 1973.

Meager, Mary. *The Bison of Yellowstone National Park.* Washington, D.C.: U.S. Government Printing Office. 1973.

Means, Russell, with Marvin Wolf. *Where White Men Fear to Tread: the Autobiography of Russell Means.* New York: St. Martin's Press. 1995.

Mech, L. David. *The Wolf: the Ecology and Behavior of an Endangered Species.* New York: Natural History Press. 1970.

Meinig, Donald. *The Great Columbia Plain: a Historical Geography, 1805-1910.* Seattle: University of Washington Press. 1995.

Meloy, Ellen. *Eating Stone: Imagination and the Loss of the Wild.* New York: Vintage. 1997.

————. *Raven's Exile: a Season on the Green.* Tucson: University of Arizona Press. 2003.

————. *The Last Cheater's Waltz: Beauty and Violence in the Southwest.* New York: Henry Holt. 1999.

Melville, Elinor. *A Plague of Sheep: the Environmental Consequences of the Conquest of Mexico.* New York: Cambridge University Press. 1994.

Meyer, Michael. *Water in the Hispanic Southwest.* Tucson: University of Arizona Press. 1984.

Mighetto, Lisa. *Wild Animals and American Environmental Ethics.* Tucson: University of Arizona Press. 1991.

Mills, Stephanie. *Whatever Happened to Ecology?* San Francisco: Sierra Club Books. 1989.

Minge, Ward Alan. *Acoma: Pueblo in the Sky.* Albuquerque: University of New Mexico Press. 1991.

Momaday, N. Scott. *The Way to Rainy Mountain.* Albuquerque: University of New Mexico Press. 1969.

Morgan, Dale. *Jedediah Smith and the Opening of the West.* Lincoln: University of Nebraska Press, 1953.

Morrison, Peter. *Old Growth in the Pacific Northwest: a Status Report.* Washington, D. C. Wilderness Society. 1988.

Muir, John. *My First Summer in the Sierra.* New York: Penguin. 1987.

Munford, J.K. *John Ledyard's Journal of Captain Cook's Last Voyage.* Corvallis: Oregon State University Press. 1963.

Murie, Adolph. *Ecology of the Coyote in Yellowstone.* Washington, D.C.: U.S. Government Printing Office. 1940.

Murray, Keith. *The Modocs and Their War.* Norman: University of Oklahoma Press. 1959.

Nabhan, Gary Paul. *The Desert Smells Like Rain.* Tucson: University of Arizona Press. 1985.

Nabokov, Peter, ed. *Native American Testimony: a Chronicle of Indian-White Relations from Prophecy to the Present, 1492-1992.* New York: Penguin. 1992.

Nasatir, A. P. *Before Lewis and Clark: Documents Illustrating the History of the Missouri River, 1785-1804.* St. Louis: Historical Documents Foundation. 1952.

Nash, Gerald D. *World War II and the West: Reshaping the Economy.* Lincoln: University of Nebraska Press. 1990.

Nash, Roderick. *The Rights of Nature: a History of Environmental Ethics.* Madison: University of Wisconsin Press. 1989.

——. *Wilderness and the American Mind.* New Haven: Yale University Press. 1982.

Natapoff, Sasha. *Stormy Weather: the Promise of the U.S. Environmental Movement.* Washington, DC: IPS Books. 1989.

Neihardt, John. *Black Elk Speaks: Being the Life Story of a Holy Man of the Oglala Sioux.* New York: Pocket Books. 1972.

——. *The River and I.* Lincoln: University of Nebraska Press. 1968.

Nichols, John. *On the Mesa.* Salt Lake City: Peregrine Smith. 1986.

Nisbet, J. *Sources of the River: Tracking David Thompson Across Western North America.* Seattle: Sasquatch Books. 1994.

Norris, Kathleen. *Dakota: a Spiritual Geography.* New York: Ticknor and Fields. 1993.

Norse, Elliot. *Ancient Forests of the Pacific Northwest.* Washington, D.C.: Island Press. 1990.

O'Donnell, Terence. *An Arrow in the Earth.* Portland: Oregon Historical Society Press. 1991.

O'Neill, Dan. *The Firecracker Boys: H-Bombs, Eskimo and the Birth of the Environmental Movement.* New York: Basic. 2007.

O'Toole, Randal. *Reforming the Forest Service.* Washington, D.C.: Island Press. 1988.

Oelschlaeger, Max. *The Idea of Wilderness from Prehistory to the Age of Ecology.* New Haven: Yale University Press. 1991.

Olsen, Jack. *Slaughter the Animals, Poison the Earth.* New York: Simon and Schuster. 1971.

Ontko, G. *Thunder Over the Ochoco.* Bend: Maverick Press. 1993.

Ortiz, Alfonso. *The Tewa World: Space, Time, Being and Becoming in a Pueblo Society.* Chicago: University of Chicago Press. 1969.

Outwater, Alice. *Water: a Natural History.* New York: Basic Books. 1996.

Paehlke, Robert. *Environmentalism and the Future of Progressive Politics.* New Haven: Yale University Press. 1989.

Palmer, Tim. *Endangered Rivers and the Conservation Movement.* Berkeley: University of California Press. 1982.

Parman, Donald. *Indians and the American West in the Twentieth-Century.* Bloomington: Indiana University Press. 1994.

Peacock, Andrea. *Libby, Montana: Asbestos & the Deadly Silence of an American Corporation.* Boulder: Johnson Books. 2003.

Peacock, Doug and Peacock, Andrea. *The Essential Grizzly.* New York: Lyons Press. 2007.

Peacock, Doug. *Grizzly Years: In Search of the American Wilderness.* New York: Henry Holt. 1990.

———. *Walking It Off: a Veteran's Chronicle of War and Wilderness.* Cheney, Wa.: Eastern Washington University Press. 2005.

Peattie, Donald C. *A Natural History of Western Trees.* New York: Houghton Mifflin. 1991.

Perry, Richard. *Apache Reservation: Indigenous Peoples and the American State.* Austin: University of Texas Press. 1993.

Peterson, David. *Ghost Grizzlies.* New York: Henry Holt. 1995.

Peterson, Keith. *River of Life, Channel of Death: Fish and Dams on the Lower Snake River.* Corvallis: Oregon State University Press. 2001.

Pielou, E. C. *After the Ice Age.* Chicago: University of Chicago Press. 1991.

Pinchot, Gifford. *Breaking New Ground.* New York: Harcourt Brace. 1947.

Pomeroy, Earl. *In Search of the Golden West: the Tourist in Western America.* New York: Knopf. 1957.

Porter, Eliot. *The Place No One Knew: Glen Canyon and the Colorado River.* San Francisco: Sierra Club Books. 1963.

Powell, John Wesley. *The Exploration of the Colorado River and Its Canyons.* Mineola: Dover. 1961.

Power, Thomas M. *Lost Landscapes and Failed Economics: the Search for a Value of Place.* Washington, DC: Island Press. 1996.

Puter, Stephen A. *Looters of the Public Domain.* Portland, Ore.: Ayer Co. 1971.

Pyne, Stephen. *Fire in America: a Cultural History of Wildland and Rural Fire.* Princeton: Princeton University Press. 1982.

———. *How the Canyon Became Grand: a Short History.* New York: Penguin. 1999.

———. *Karl Grove Gilbert: a Great Engine of Research.* Iowa City: University of Iowa Press. 2007.

Raban, Jonathan. *Bad Land: an American Romance.* New York: Pantheon. 1996.

Ramenofsky, Ann. *Vectors of Death: the Archaeology of European Contact.* Albuquerque: University of New Mexico Press. 1993.

Raphael, Ray. *Tree Talk: The People and the Politics of Timber.* Covelo, Cal.: Island Press. 1981.

Rapp, Valerie. *What the Water Reveals: Understanding and Restoring Healthy Watersheds.* Seattle: Moutaineers Press. 1997.

Rea, Amadeo. *Once a River.* Tucson: University of Arizona Press. 1983.

Reed, Ishmael. *Blues City: a Walk Through Oakland.* New York: Crown. 2003.

Rees, H. *Shaniko: From Wool Capital to Ghost Town.* Portland: Binford and Mort. 1982.

Reiger, John. *American Sportsmen and the Origins of Conservation.* New York: Winchester Press. 1975.

Reisner, Marc. *Cadillac Desert: The American West and Its Disappearing Water.* New York: Viking. 1986.

Richardson, Elmo. *Dams, Parks and Politics: Resource Development and Preservation in the Truman-Eisenhower Era.* Lexington: University of Kentucky Press. 1973.

Ridgeway, James and St. Clair, Jeffrey. *A Guide to Environmental Bad Guys.* New York: Thunder's Mouth. 1999.

Rifkin, Jeremy. *Beyond Beef: the Rise and Fall of Cattle Culture.* New York: Dutton. 1992.

Ringholz, Ray. *Uranium Frenzy.* Provo: Utah State University Press. 2002.

Rittenhouse, Jack. *A Guide to Highway 66.* Albuquerque: University of New Mexico Press. 1946.

Robbins, William. *American Forestry: a History of National, State and Private Cooperation.* Lincoln: University of Nebraska Press. 1985.

———. *Hard Times in Paradise: Coos Bay, Oregon, 1850-1986.* Seattle: University of Washington Press. 1988.

———. *Lumberjacks and Legislators: Political Economy of the U.S. Lumber Industry, 1890-1941.* College Station, Tex.: Texas A&M Press. 1982.

Roberts, David. *In Search of the Old Ones: Exploring the Anasazi World of the Southwest.* New York: Simon and Schuster. 1996.

———. *Once They Moved Like the Wind: Cochise, Geronimo and the Apache Wars.* New York: Simon and Schuster. 1993.

Robinson, Charles. *A Good Year to Die: the Story of the Great Sioux War.* New York: Random House. 1995.

Robinson, Gordon. *The Forest and the Trees: a Guide to Excellent Forestry.* Washington, D.C.: Island Press. 1988.

Robinson, Michael C. *Water for the West: the Bureau of Reclamation, 1902-1977.* Chicago: Public Works Historical Society. 1979.

Robinson, Michael J. *Predatory Bureaucracy: The Extermination of Wolves and the Transformation of the West.* Boulder: University of Colorado Press. 2005.

Roe, Frank G. *The Indian and the Horse.* Norman: University of Oklahoma Press. 1955.

Rohlf, Daniel. *The Endangered Species Act: a Guide to Its Protections and Implementation.* Stanford: Stanford Environmental Law Society. 1989.

Ronda, James. *Lewis and Clark Among the Indians.* Lincoln: University of Nebraska. 1984.

Rothman, Hal. *Devil's Bargains: Tourism in Twentieth Century America.* Lawrence: University of Kansas Press. 1998.

———. *Preserving Different Pasts: the American National Monuments.* Urbana: University of Illinois Press. 1989.

Rowley, W. D. *Reclaiming the Arid West: the Career of Francis G. Newlands.* Bloomington: Indiana University Press. 1996.

Rowley, William. *U.S. Forest Service Grazing and Rangelands: a History.* College Station, Tex.: Texas A&M Press. 1985.

Rubin, Rick. *Naked Against the Rain: the People of the Lower Columbia River.* Portland: Far Shore Press. 1999.

Ruby, Robert and Brown, John. *The Chinook Indians: Traders of the Lower Columbia.* Norman: University of Oklahoma Press. 1976.

Runte, Alfred. *National Parks: the American Experience.* Lincoln: University of Nebraska Press. 1979.

———. *Public Lands, Public Heritage: the National Forest Idea.* Niwot, Col.: Roberts Rinehart. 1991.

Rusho, W. L. *Everett Reuss: a Vagabond for Beauty.* Salt Lake City: Gibbs M. Smith, 1983.

Sale, Kirkpatrick. *Dwellers in the Land: The Bioregional Vision.* San Francisco: Sierra Club Books. 1985.

———. *The Green Revolution: the American Environmental Movement, 1962-1992.* New York: Hill and Wang. 1993.

Sanders, Ed. *The Family* (Rev. Edition). New York: Thunder's Mouth. 2002

Sanger, S. L. *Working on the Bomb: an Oral History of WW II Hanford.* New York: CEP. 1995.

Santee, Ross. *Horses and Men.* Lincoln: University of Nebraska Press. 1977.

Sapir, Edward. *Wishram Texts and Ethnography.* Berlin: Mouton de Gruyter. 1990.

Schaefer, Standard. *Water & Power.* New York: Agincourt Press. 2005.

Schlieser, Karl, ed. *Plains Indians, A.D. 200-1500.* Norman: University of Oklahoma Press. 1994.

Schneider, Bill. *Route 66 Across New Mexico.* Albuquerque: University of New Mexico Press. 1991.

Schneiders, Robert Kelley. *Big Sky Rivers: the Yellowstone and Upper Missouri.* Lawrence: University of Kansas Press. 2003.

Schueler, Donald. *Incident at Eagle Ranch: Man and Predator in the American West.* San Francisco: Sierra Club. 1980.

Schullery, Paul. *Mountain Time: a Yellowstone Memoir.* Boulder: Roberts Rinehart. 1984.

———. *Searching for Yellowstone: Ecology and Wonder in the Last Wilderness.* Helena: Montana Historical Society Press. 2004.

———. *The Bears of Yellowstone.* Worland, Wyoming: High Plains Publishing. 1992.

Schwartz, E.A. *The Rogue Indian War and Its Aftermath, 1850-1980.* Norman: University of Oklahoma Press. 1997.

Sears, John. *Sacred Places: American Tourist Attractions in the Nineteenth Century.* New York: Oxford University Press. 1989.

Sears, Paul B. *Deserts on the March.* Norman: University of Oklahoma Press. 1959.

Sellars, Richard. *Preserving Nature in the National Parks: a History.* New Haven: Yale University Press. 1997.

Shelton, Richard. *Going Back to Bisbee.* Tucson: University of Arizona Press. 1992.

Shepard, Paul. *The Others: How Animals Made Us Human.* Washington, D.C.: Island Press. 1996.

Sheperd, Jack. *The Forest Killers.* New York: Weybright. 1975.

Sherrill, Robert. *The Oil Follies: How the Petroleum Industry Stole the Show.* New York: Doubleday. 1983.

Short, C. Brant. *Ronald Reagan and the Public Lands*. College Stations: Texas A&M University Press. 1989.

Slotkin, Richard. *Gunfighter Nation: The Myth of the Frontier in Twentieth Century America*. New York: Harper/Collins. 1992.

———. *The Fatal Environment*. New York: Atheneum. 1985.

Smalley, Eugene. *History of the Northern Pacific Railroad*. New York: Putnam. 1883.

Smith, Annick. *In This We Are Native*. New York: Lyons Press. 2004.

Smith, C. L. *Salmon Fishers of the Columbia*. Corvallis: Oregon State University Press. 1979.

Smith, Douglas and Ferguson, Gary. *Decade of the Wolf: Returning the Wild to Yellowstone*. Guilford, Conn.: The Lyons Press. 2005.

Snyder, Gary. *The Practice of the Wild*. San Francisco: North Point Press. 1990.

Spicer, Edward. *Cycles of Conquest: the Impact of Spain, Mexico and the United States on the Indians of the Southwest, 1533-1960*. Tucson: University of Arizona Press. 1963.

St. Clair, Jeffrey. *Been Brown So Long It Looked Like Green to Me: the Politics of Nature*. Monroe, ME: Common Courage Press. 2003.

St. Pierre, Mark. *Madonna Swan: a Lakota Woman's Story*. Norman: University of Oklahoma Press. 1991.

Steen, Harold. *The U. S. Forest Service: a History*. Seattle: University of Washington Press, 1976.

Stegner, Wallace, ed. *This is Dinosaur: Echo Park Country and Its Magic Rivers*. New York: Knopf, 1955.

———. *Beyond the Hundredth Meridian: John Wesley Powell and the Second Opening of the American West*. Boston: Houghton Mifflin. 1954.

———. *The American West as Living Space*. Ann Arbor: University of Michigan Press. 1987.

———. *The Sound of Mountain Water*. New York: Dutton. 1980.

———. *Wolf Willow*. New York: Viking. 1955.

Steinberg, Ted. *Down to Earth: Nature's Role in American History*. New York: Oxford University Press. 2002.

Sterling, Keir B. *The Last of the Naturalists: the Career of C. Hart Merriam*. New York: Arno. 1977.

Stevens, Joseph E. *Hoover Dam: an American Adventure*. Norman: University of Oklahoma Press. 1988.

Stewart, H. *Indian Fishing: Early Methods on the Northwest Coast*. Seattle: University of Washington Press. 1977.

Sudworth, George. *Forest Trees of the Pacific Slope*. Washington, US Government Printing Office, 1908.

Sunder, John. *The Fur Trade of the Upper Missouri, 1840-1865*. Norman: University of Oklahoma Press. 1965.

Szasz, Ferenc. *The Day the Sun Rose Twice: the Story of the Trinity Site Nuclear Explosion*. Albuquerque: University of New Mexico Press. 1984.

Takaki, Ronald. *Strangers from a Different Shore: a History of Asian-Americans*. New York: Little, Brown. 1989.

Tatum, Stephen. *Inventing Billy the Kid*. Albuquerque: University of New Mexico Press. 1982.

Taylor, Ronald J. *Sagebrush Country: a Wildflower Sanctuary*. Missoula: Mountain Press. 1992.

Thomas, Jack Ward, et al. *A Conservation Strategy for the Northern Spotted Owl* (aka Thomas Report). Portland: USDA. 1990.

Thomas, Jack Ward and Steen, Harold. *The Journals of a Forest Service Chief.* Seattle: University of Washington Press. 2004.

Thomas, Keith. *Man and the Natural World: a History of Modern Sensibility.* New York: Pantheon. 1983.

Thompson, Gerald. *The Army and the Navajo.* Tucson: University of Arizona Press. 1976.

Thompson, Hunter S. *Fear and Loathing in Las Vegas.* New York: Vintage. 1998.

———. *Hell's Angels: a Strange and Terrible Saga.* New York: Ballantine. 1996.

Tobin, Richard. *Expendable Frontier: U.S. Politics and the Protection of Biological Diversity.* Durham: Duke University Press. 1990.

Tokar, Brian. *Earth for Sale: Reclaiming Ecology in the Age of Corporate Greenwash.* New York: South End Press. 1997.

Toole, K. Ross. *The Rape of the Great Plains: Northwestern America, Cattle and Coal.* New York: Little Brown. 1976.

———. *Twentieth Century Montana: a State of Extremes.* Norman: University of Oklahoma Press. 1972.

Turner, Jack. *Teewinot: Climbing and Contemplating the Teton Range.* New York: St. Martin's. 2000.

———. *The Abstract Wild.* Tucson: University of Arizona Press. 1996.

Uchida, Yoshiko. *Desert Exile: the Uprooting of a Japanese-American Family.* Seattle: University of Washington Press. 1984.

Udall, Morris. *Too Funny to be President.* New York: Henry Holt. 1988.

Udall, Stewart. *The Quiet Crisis.* New York: Holt, Reinhart & Winston. 1963.

Urrea, Luis Alberto. *Across the Wire: Life and Hard Times on the Mexican Border.* New York: Doubleday. 1993.

Utley, Robert M. *The Indian Frontier of the American West: 1846-1890.* Albuquerque: University of New Mexico Press. 1984.

———. *The Lance and the Shield: the Life and Times of Sitting Bull.* New York: Henry Holt. 1993.

Van West, Carroll. *Capitalism on the Frontier: Billings and the Yellowstone Valley in the Nineteenth Century.* Lincoln: University of Nebraska Press. 1993.

Varley, John and Schullery, Paul. *Freshwater Wilderness.* Yellowstone: Yellowstone Library and Museum Association. 1983.

Vileisis, Ann. *Discovering the Unknown Landscape: a History of America's Wetlands.* Washington, DC: Island Press. 1997.

Viola, Herman. *Diplomats in Buckskins: a History of Indian Delegations in Washington City.* Bluffton, SD: Rivolo Books. 1995.

Vogel, Virgil. *This Country Was Ours: a Documentary History of the American Indian.* New York: Harper & Row. 1972.

Wagner, Frederick. *Wildlife Policies in the National Parks.* Washington: Island Press. 1995.

Waits, Chris and Shors, Dave. *Unabomber: the Secret Life of Ted Kaczynski.* Missoula: Far Country Press. 1999.

Walker, Mildred. *Winter Wheat.* New York: Harcourt, Brace. 1944.

Walton, John. *Western Times and Water Wars: State, Culture and Rebellion in California.* Berkeley: University of California Press. 1992.

Warne, William. *The Bureau of Reclamation.* New York: Praeger. 1973.

Watkins, T. H. *Righteous Pilgrim: the Life and Times of Harold L. Ickes.* New York: Henry Holt. 1990.

Webb, Robert H., et al. *Cataract Canyon: a Human and Environmental History of the Rivers in Canyonlands.* Salt Lake City: University of Utah Press. 2004.

Weber, David. *The Spanish Frontier in North America.* New Haven: Yale University Press. 1992.

Welch, James. *Killing Custer: the Battle of Little Big Horn and the Fate of the Plains Indians.* New York: Penguin. 1995.

Wellock, Thomas. *Critical Masses: Opposition to Nuclear Power in California, 1958-1978.* New York: Critical Press. 1998.

Welsome, Eileen. *The Plutonium Files: America's Secret Medical Experiments in the Cold War.* New York: Delta. 2000.

White, Richard. *"It's Your Misfortune and None of My Own:" a New History of the American West.* Norman: University of Oklahoma Press. 1991.

——. *The Organic Machine: the Remaking of the Columbia River.* New York: Hill and Wang. 1996.

——. *The Roots of Dependency: Subsistence, Environment and Social Change Among the Choctaws, Pawnees and Navajos.* Lincoln: University of Nebraska Press. 1988.

Wiley, Peter and Gottlieb, Robert. *Empires in the Sun: the Rise of the New American West.* New York: Putnam, 1982.

Wilkinson, Charles. *Crossing the Next Meridian: Land, Water and the Future of the West.* Washington, D. C.: Island Press. 1992.

Wilkinson, Todd. *Science Under Siege: the Politcians' War on Nature and Truth.* Boulder: Johnson Books. 1998.

Williams, Chuck. *Bridge of the Gods, Mountains of Fire: a Return to the Columbia Gorge.* San Francisco: Friends of the Earth Books. 1980.

Williams, Michael. *Americans and Their Forests: a Historical Geography.* Cambridge: Cambridge University Press. 1989.

Williams, Terry Tempest. *An Unspoken Hunger: Stories from the Field.* New York: Vintage. 1995.

——. *Red: Passion and Patience in the Desert.* New York: Pantheon. 2001.

——. *Refuge: an Unnatural History of Family and Place.* New York: Pantheon. 2000.

Wilson, Gilbert. *Buffalo Bird Woman's Garden.* St. Paul: Minnesota Historical Society Press. 1987.

Wirth, Conrad. *Parks, Politics and the People.* Norman: University of Oklahoma Press. 1980.

Wishart, David. *An Unspeakable Sadness: the Dispossession of the Nebraska Indians.* Lincoln: University of Nebraska Press. 1994.

——. *The Fur Trade of the American West: a Geographical Synthesis.* Lincoln: University of Nebraska Press. 1979.

Wolf, Tom. *Colorado's Sangre de Cristo Mountains.* Boulder: University of Colorado Press. 1998.

Wolke, Howie. *Wilderness on the Rocks.* Tucson: Ned Ludd Books. 1991.

Worster, Donald. *Rivers of Empire: Water, Aridity and the American West.* New York: Pantheon. 1985.

————. *Dust Bowl: the Southern Plains in the 1930s.* New York: Oxford University Press. 1979.

————. *Nature's Economy: a History of Ecological Ideas.* New York: Cambridge University Press. 1977.

————. *Under Western Skies: Nature and History in the American West.* New York: Oxford University Press. 1992.

————. *The Wealth of Nature.* New York: Oxford University Press. 1993.

————. *An Unsettled Country. Changing Landscapes of the American West.* Albuquerque: University of New Mexico Press. 1994.

Wright, William. *The Grizzly Bear.* Lincoln: University of Nebraska Press. 1977.

Wuerthner, George and Matteson, Mollie. *Welfare Ranching: the Subsidized Destruction of the American West.* San Francisco: Foundation for Deep Ecology Press. 2002.

Yaffee, Steve Lewis. *The Wisdom of the Spotted Owl.* Washington, DC: Island Press. 1994.

Young, Robert W. *A Political History of the Navajo Tribe.* Tsaile, Arizona: Navajo Community College Press. 1978.

Zakin, Susan. *Coyotes and Town Dogs: Earth First! and the Environmental Movement.* Tucson: University of Arizona Press. 2002.

Zamora, Emilio. *The World of the Mexican Worker in Texas.* College Station, TX: Texas A&M University Press. 1993.

Zaslowsky, Dyan. *These American Lands.* New York: Henry Holt. 1986.

Zerzan, John. *Future Primitive.* Eugene: Autonomedia. 1994.

Acknowledgments

SOME OF THESE ESSAYS GO BACK TO THE DARK AGES. YES, I'M TALKING about Clintontime. A few people have been along for the ride from the beginning, most notably, of course, my senior partner at CounterPunch, Alexander Cockburn. Despite good-natured exchanges over the genesis of global warming and the virtues of Texas barbecue, it has been an exhilarating and enlightening journey and I trust there are many adventures yet to come. I don't know how she manages it under such crazy conditions, but Becky Grant holds CounterPunch together with brilliance, grace, and humor under fire—and we adore you (and Deva) for it. Tiffany Wardle skillfully designed *Born Under a Bad Sky* with care, talent, and a sharp eye for detail—you are a master of the craft. Zach and Lorna at AK Press incubated this book with patience and encouragement for many months as it slid ridiculously over numerous deadlines. AK Press is the best independent publisher in America (and Scotland) and I'm proud to be associated with them. Robin Silver may be America's greatest wildlife photographer. He took the astounding photo of an all too rare Mexican wolf that graces the cover of this book. Robin spends his nights saving lives as an emergency room physician and his days saving endangered species at the Center for Biological Diversity, one of the world's best green groups. John and Susette Weisheit shared the Green River with us and we will always cherish you, and Living Rivers, for that gift. May the Green one day soon flow freely from the Wind Rivers to Lee's Ferry. Thanks to Josh Frank for permitting me to include stories that we collaborated on and to Kelly Harris and Vingh Houng for their impeccable transcription. Much of this book was written in Jennifer St. Clair and Del Wilson's enchanting house in the rainforest along the Wind River. Thanks for sharing the view (and the puppies). My parents, Doreen and Hager, have been an unshakeable foundation of love and support for us through often turbulent times—now let the *good* times roll. Zen and Nat, you continue to astound us with your radiant lives. As always, this book is devoted to Kimberly, who inspired it, endured it and, on that blazing last day in Narrow Canyon, nearly perished because of it. In my defense, I can only say that I was following the prescription of that homeopathic healer D.H. Lawrence, who advised: "Take her out, into the Sun." *Born Under a Bad Sky* was written under the influence of Clifton Chenier, Sonny Rollins, Albert King, and Merle Haggard. Play on.

Index

AK Press
Ordering Information

AK Press
674-A 23rd Street
Oakland, CA 94612-1163
U.S.A
(510) 208-1700
www.akpress.org
akpress@akpress.org

AK Press
PO Box 12766
Edinburgh, EH8 9YE
Scotland
(0131) 555-5165
www.akuk.com
ak@akedin.demon.uk

The addresses above would be delighted to provide you with the latest complete AK catalog, featuring several thousand books, pamphlets, zines, audio products, video products, and stylish apparel published & distributed by AK Press. Alternatively, check out our websites for the complete catalog, latest news and updates, events, and secure ordering.

Also Available from AK Press

The first audio collection from Alexander Cockburn on compact disc.

Beating the Devil
Alexander Cockburn, ISBN 13: 9781902593494 • CD • $14.98

In this collection of recent talks, maverick commentator Alexander Cockburn defiles subjects ranging from Colombia to the American presidency to the Missile Defense System. Whether he's skewering the fallacies of the war on drugs or illuminating the dark crevices of secret government, his erudite and extemporaneous style warms the hearts of even the stodgiest cynics of the left.

Available from CounterPunch/AK Press

Call 1-800-840-3683 or order online from
www.counterpunch.org or www.akpress.org

The Case Against Israel
by Michael Neumann

Wielding a buzzsaw of logic, Professor Neumann dismantles plank-by-plank the Zionist rationale for Israel as religious state entitled to trample upon the basic human rights of non-Jews. Along the way, Neumann also offers a passionate amicus brief for the plight of the Palestinian people.

Other Lands Have Dreams: From Baghdad to Pekin Prison
by Kathy Kelly

At a moment when so many despairing peace activists have thrown in the towel, Kathy Kelly, a witness to some of history's worst crimes, never relinquishes hope. Other Lands Have Dreams is literary testimony of the highest order, vividly recording the secret casualties of our era, from the hundreds of thousands of Iraqi children inhumanely denied basic medical care, clean water and food by the US overlords to young mothers sealed inside the sterile dungeons of American prisons in the name of the merciless war on drugs.

Dime's Worth of Difference: Beyond the Lesser of Two Evils
Edited by Alexander Cockburn and Jeffrey St. Clair

Everything you wanted to know about one-party rule in America.

Whiteout: the CIA, Drugs and the Press
by Alexander Cockburn and Jeffrey St. Clair, Verso.

The involvement of the CIA with drug traffickers is a story that has slouched into the limelight every decade or so since the creation of the Agency. In Whiteout, here at last is the full saga.

Been Brown So Long It Looked Like Green to Me: The Politics of Nature
by Jeffrey St. Clair, Common Courage Press.

Covering everything from toxics to electric power plays, St. Clair draws a savage profile of how money and power determine the state of our environment, gives a vivid account of where the environment stands today and what to do about it.

Imperial Crusades: Iraq, Afghanistan and Yugoslavia
by Alexander Cockburn and Jeffrey St. Clair, Verso.

A chronicle of the lies that are now returning each and every day to haunt the deceivers in Washington and London, the secret agendas and the underreported carnage of these wars. We were right and they were wrong, and this book proves the case. Never leave home without it.

Why We Publish CounterPunch

By Alexander Cockburn and Jeffrey St. Clair

TEN YEARS AGO WE FELT UNHAPPY ABOUT THE STATE OF RADICAL JOURN-alism. It didn't have much edge. It didn't have many facts. It was politi-cally timid. It was dull. CounterPunch was founded. We wanted it to be the best muckraking newsletter in the country. We wanted it to take aim at the consensus of received wisdom about what can and cannot be reported. We wanted to give our readers a political roadmap they could trust.

A decade later we stand firm on these same beliefs and hopes. We think we've restored honor to muckraking journalism in the tradition of our favorite radical pamphleteers: Edward Abbey, Peter Maurin and Ammon Hennacy, Appeal to Reason, Jacques René Hébert, Tom Paine and John Lilburne.

Every two weeks CounterPunch gives you jaw-dropping exposés on: Congress and lobbyists; the environment; labor; the National Security State.

"CounterPunch kicks through the floorboards of lies and gets to the founda-tion of what is really going on in this country", says Michael Ratner, attorney at the Center for Constitutional Rights. "At our house, we fight over who gets to read CounterPunch first. Each issue is like spring after a cold, dark winter."

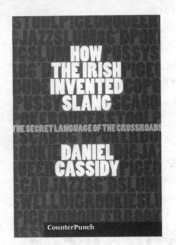

A Short History of Fear

By Alexander Cockburn

The idea that things are always getting worse, that Armageddon-in one form or another-is just around the corner, has been a common refrain since the very beginnings of Western culture. And, more often than not, the forces allegedlysending us to hell in a proverbial hand basket are shadowy conspiracies whose features are as murky as their nefarious power is supposedly Enter renegade journalist Alexander Cockburn to illuminate the darkest corners of our collective cultural unconscious. In his usual, take-no-prisoners-style, he battles an impressive collection of fear-mongers and the irrationalities they espouse. Likening the soul-saving indulgences sold by the medieval Catholic Church to today's carbon credits, Cockburn traces his subject through the ages, showing how fear is used to distract us from real problems and real solutions. Skewering doomsters on both the Left and Right, A Short History of Fear tackles: 9/11 conspiracy theorics; the twentieth-century witch craze of "satanic abuse"; eugenics; the Kennedy assassination, Pearl Harbor, and other "inside jobs"; terrorism; the "Great Fear" of the eighteenth century; today's eleventh-hour predictions of planetary decline; and much more. Scathing, often hilarious, and always insightful, this is Cockburn at the top of his controversial game.